TEN MASTERS

of the modern essay

Forster   Lawrence   Huxley   Graves
White   Orwell   Auden   McCarthy
Baldwin   Gold

TEN MASTERS

of the modern essay

EDITED BY

Robert Gorham Davis

Columbia University

Harcourt, Brace & World, Inc.

New York / Chicago / Burlingame

© 1966 by Harcourt, Brace & World, Inc.

Library of Congress Catalog Card Number: 66-15609

Printed in the United States of America

To H. H. D.

Muse and maker

CONTENTS

INTRODUCTION

MOST LITERARY forms developed slowly. Often their origin, like that of Greek tragedy, is lost in the shadows of prehistory. But we know exactly when the essay began and who began it. In an understandable burst of enthusiasm, Virginia Woolf declared that "talking of oneself, following one's own vagaries, giving the whole map, weight, colour and circumference of the soul in its confusion, its variety, its imperfection—this art belongs to one man only: to Montaigne."

She was not exaggerating so far as the personal or "familiar" essay is concerned, though in a broad sense the spirit of the essay did exist in earlier periods. We find it nearly a century before Montaigne in the *Adagia* and *Colloquia* of the brilliant humanist Erasmus. And some of Montaigne's essays, following earlier modes, were little more than collections of *belles pensées* ("fine thoughts") dealing rather loosely with some single theme. An example in this volume is "Of Death" by Francis Bacon, an English contemporary and imitator of Montaigne. But among the ninety-three short essays which Montaigne published in 1580 were many that struck an entirely new note in literature, with their frank self-portraiture, their grounding in immediate experience, their humor, their skepticism and lightness of touch. Montaigne, an unusual combination of savant, recluse, and high government official, not only invented the form, he gave it its name, spelled in French *essai*. The name helps to define what he was doing. To essay (in French, *essayer*) is to put to a test, to try out. "Essay" and "assay" come, through French, from the Latin *exagium*, a weighing. Ore from a new mine is assayed to see what proportion of valuable metal it contains. The word "test," in turn, comes originally from the Latin noun *testum*, a pot or vial in which chemical tests, or assays, were performed. In English, the word "try" can mean either "test" or "attempt." We say, "Try this to see how you like it," or "I shall try to arrive there tomorrow."

The essayist is trying something in both senses of the word. As in E. M. Forster's essay "What I Believe," he subjects idea and institutions to the test of his own experience, his own values, his own likes and dislikes. But this approach is tentative, not dogmatic or final. "What do I know? *Que sais-je?*" the essay's originator, Montaigne, was always asking. The essayist is experimenting. He is letting his thoughts take him where they will, to see what conclusions he may arrive at, not so much through logic as through discovering how general ideas and particular experiences, especially his own, throw new light upon each other.

The essayist often does his thinking in our presence; in fact, our imagined presence stimulates him to examine his thoughts and feelings with fresh objectivity. He is delighted to have the "dear" or "common" reader with him as companion when he ranges through the world of ideas and inner experience. He treats this reader as a friend or equal, not someone to be lectured at or denounced or refuted. But if we travel with him, we must be ready to explore any lane or uncharted river. We must not expect a railroad journey with a fixed schedule and tracks laid in advance. Though many essays incorporate facts and theories that everyone should know, we must be prepared also for much that is heterodox, whimsical, and intimately personal.

But does not this personal approach raise questions about the value of the essay? We are all theoretically in search of truth, of knowledge; for many this is a genuine passion. Why, then, should we be satisfied with the tentative? Why should we occupy ourselves with what is peculiar to one individual, often in an apparently trivial way, when there is so much accepted knowledge to be mastered in the physical and social sciences, in history and the practical arts?

Of course many essays do expound ideas or teach facts in a thoroughly logical, coherent, and objective way. This is true of a substantial proportion of those chosen for this book, for example W. H. Auden's "The Guilty Vicarage" or George Orwell's "Politics and the English Language." Within a hundred years after Montaigne wrote, his term "essay" was very broadly applied, especially in England. It was used not only for personal or familiar essays of a brief, light, tentative kind, but also for long, systematic disquisitions in science and philosophy. John Locke's principal treatise on psychology, published in 1690, was called *An Essay concerning Human Understanding*. Alternative terms would have been "inquiry," "discourse," and "dissertation." The philosopher David Hume, toward the middle of the eighteenth century, published *Essays Moral and Political* in two volumes. The twentieth-century philosopher Ernst Cassirer brought together all his brilliant theories about myth, government, language, science, and religion in a single work entitled *An Essay on Man*.

But many essays, among them some of the most delightful, continue to fit precisely Virginia Woolf's description of what Montaigne was doing. Their great value can be explained in both philosophical and artistic terms.

The philosophical explanation—to give it perhaps too fashionable a name—is existentialist. The writer of familiar essays is reminding us of a fundamental truth, that all human experience is ultimately a matter of individual consciousness, shaped by a unique private history. Whether we are poets or soldiers, scientists or politicians, facts and ideas always enter our lives at particular times under particular circumstances for particular reasons. They are inextricably bound up with our emotions, sensations, imaginations, and purposes. When creators of governmental or intellectual systems forget these facts, they are likely to do damage both to truth and to the possibility of human happiness. Through the essay the unique individual consciousness may assert its claims, not merely as an object of study, but speaking in its own right, autonomously and often defiantly.

Second, the essay at its best is an art form. Like other art forms, it mingles instruction and delight. Ever since the eighteenth century, the essay has provided the principal contents of the steadily more numerous popular magazines. No one is required to read such essays. They are read because they please. Sometimes the pleasure is primarily in being instructed, as with Aldous Huxley's "The Double Crisis," or Robert Graves' "Was Benedict Arnold a Traitor?" The author is deeply engaged by his subject. Our pleasure depends on his success in engaging us equally through the importance of his material and the persuasiveness of his argument.

Sometimes, as in the essays by Robert Benchley, Frank Sullivan, and Dr. Johnson, the writer appears content simply to amuse, to entertain. We seem to be offered delight free of instruction. But this is an illusion. If we examine more closely what he is doing, we see that he is always saying something significant. This "something" grows out of observation, often satiric observation, of the way people think, act, talk, and write. A witty remark is commonly called "pointed." To be so it has to have a point, an idea, a perception. No one can be funny about nothing. Wit consists of the brevity, specificity, verbal freshness, and discrimination with which a perception is expressed. The apparently trifling and artful personal essays, if they are good, always have substance. Even a sponge cake is made out of eggs. Examine some of the lighter pieces, sentence by sentence, paragraph by paragraph, to see how much they actually contain in the way of dialogue, description, narration, allusion, and a logic either fanciful or true.

In its freedom, its variety, its humor, its personality, the essay at its most characteristic resembles good conversation. We can appreciate it best, perhaps, by considering freshly the way human beings talk, and what they mostly talk about.

An amazing proportion of our lives is spent in conversation, or remembering conversation, or preparing to say something when the time is ripe. From morning until night, or even in some cases through the night, the words pour out—on trains, in offices and shops and factories and classrooms, at committee meetings and in after-dinner speeches, at cocktail parties and receptions, over bridge tables, at family meals and during social evenings in the home, on "open-end" television programs. A certain amount of this talk is technical or functional, consisting of commands, instructions, explanation, persuasion. But a surprising proportion of it, even during what are nominally business hours or at business luncheons, consists of talk simply for the joy of talking, talking about everything under the sun. The chief purpose of most entertaining in private homes is to let people indulge in undirected conversation about any topics that appeal to them. The food and drink are subordinate. When guests, leaving a party, say enthusiastically that they have had a good time, they are referring primarily to the liveliness and mutuality of the conversation.

What do people most like to talk about? First and foremost themselves, their likes and dislikes, their health, their opinions, their daydreams and night dreams, their children, their pets, their parties and dates, their automobiles, their travels, their taste in food, drink, and moving pictures, their financial, domestic, and professional problems, the real or fancied injustices which they have suffered from employers, employees, parents, teachers, governmental agencies, and business firms.

But if each person wants to talk about himself, how can he be made to listen to others? For some temperaments, this is difficult. When a group of young boys tries to organize a game of baseball, there is usually more arguing than playing, and there are moments when literally every boy is talking and none listening. Some adults are obsessive talkers, with a strong need to say everything that comes into their heads, to return repeatedly to certain themes, or to try to impose their opinions on everyone else. Often in excited arguments the impulse to speak, to interrupt, becomes almost uncontrollable, and the one who has the floor at the moment has to fend off the interruptions, if he can, with "Wait! Just let me finish."

On the whole, though, adults recognize that conversation is a social act with necessary ground rules, that there must be good listeners as well as good talkers. And fortunately, when the topics are right and the presentation is vivid, people are genuinely interested in what others have to say. They gobble up fresh news of famous people or mutual friends, especially when it is of a gossipy nature. Such talk need not be unfriendly, even when it emphasizes bizarre or ludicrous behavior. "Trooper Silas Tomkyn Comberbacke" by E. M. Forster and "Poe's Helen" by Virginia Woolf are examples of this kind of reminiscence.

Friends in common make subjects for lively conversation; so do shared activities and affections. Ideally, at least, those who cultivate children, pets, or gardens are interested in other people's problems or successes with children, pets, and gardens. So with learning languages, baking casseroles, sailing boats, reading Shakespeare, and curing sacroiliacs. When men get together they traditionally talk about business, politics, and automobiles. With nostalgic wit, E. B. White in "Farewell, My Lovely!" recaptures the fascinating exchanges that took place between owners of Model T Fords.

Human beings are egotistical, but in a social way. They want to be liked, to please, to win approval. Much conversation—and here we come back to the definition of the essay—is a testing out of one's opinions, tastes, and characteristic experiences by seeing how others respond to them or how they might look to other eyes.

With tastes in food or travel, such comparisons are fairly un-demanding or uncontroversial. When the subjects are books, plays, modern art, the education of children, or social life in cities, arguments are likely to develop. Specific theses will be put forward and vigorously defended. So long as a good temper is maintained, friendly argument adds to the interest. Religion, sex, politics, and the personal conduct of persons present are still more dangerous areas, but a skillful and sensitive conversationalist can usually avoid offense. He may hold his opinions with deep conviction, but he does not regard every disagreement as a blow to his ego or as the assault of an enemy who must be defeated at all costs. Rather he is challenged to see whether he can bring the other closer to his views and still keep the conversation friendly and entertaining. If others do not accept his views, perhaps he is not presenting them properly, or perhaps they need modification. And he regards this as a valuable test of his views. A democratic essayist, knowing how quirky some of his opinions may be, offers them for what they are worth, but he is ready to grant equal worth to the not yet fully ex-amined opinions of others.

If we want our views to prevail in social conversation or in writ-ing which others will read only if it pleases them, we must depend on persuasion, not force. Persuasion employs imagination, wit, and a sympathetic appreciation of how others may feel. The persuasive speaker or writer is not dogmatically relentless. He adapts himself to the listener's responses, shifts ground as the occasion requires, searches his own heart from time to time, remembering Montaigne's *"Que sais-je?"* If he uses *ad hominem* arguments, or other tactics not strictly acceptable in formal debate, he does so frankly in a spirit of fun, as part of a game played for the sport and training it gives, and not primarily to win.

The talented, intelligent, and intuitive talker develops conversa-tion into conscious art. He lets egotism satisfy itself in the social form of giving pleasure to others as an artist. Under these circum-stances, he does not hesitate to make amusing stories of his mis-adventures, to make fun of himself as Beerbohm does in "A Relic" or Benchley in "Take the Witness!"

When you hear good conversation, try analyzing it as carefully as you would the tactics of a football play or the structure of a sonata. See what themes are being developed and how; what facts or experi-ences are being called upon; how one topic suggests the next; what resources of imagination and language the speaker employs in order to amuse, amaze, or convince. The same kind of analysis can then be applied to essays in this volume, particularly to a group of three by the same writer.

Two significant differences between conversation and the essay have to be kept in mind, but these differences are not so great as may at first appear.

Conversation is not ordinarily planned in advance. It develops out of the unforeseeable give and take within a group. In an essay, on the other hand, only one person is writing, with nobody to interrupt him or challenge him. What he sets forth can be carefully planned and organized in advance. The results are evident in the more formal essays in this volume, like Huxley's "The Double Crisis" or Graves' "Was Benedict Arnold a Traitor?"

Ordinarily, however, familiar essayists favor a freedom, diversity, and unpredictability in structure very like that of conversation. If it is planned in advance, they prefer that this be not too evident. Art is used to conceal art.

In "The United States," E. M. Forster deals with two subjects not directly related, the friendliness of Americans and the landscape of New England. Both had impressed him on a recent trip to the United States and he brought them into his essay, as a man would into his conversation when he was talking to his friends about such a trip. Similarly, in Aldous Huxley's "Copan" we have a series of suggestive generalizations about travel and our sense of distance, about nationalism, death, early South American art, and a number of other themes, any one of which would make a sufficient essay in itself if organized and expanded in the usual way. The topics come together here entirely because of what happened to Huxley when he tried to sight-see in a hired plane. In "A Slight Sound at Evening," E. B. White shifts unexpectedly but agreeably from the physical circumstances in which Thoreau wrote about Walden to the rather similar circumstances in which he himself is writing about Thoreau.

Second, because he is writing deliberatively and not talking impromptu, the essayist can select his words and phrases more carefully and can use a more studied and varied style than is common in speech. He can revise and polish until the language entirely satisfies him. The best essayists obviously delight in phrase-making and wit, in manner of writing as well as matter.

But here, too, the differences between the essay and the best conversation are not so great as might appear. In lively conversations sparks are often struck—inspired ideas produced—that would not have occurred to the speaker in the solitude of his study. On the other hand, after argumentative conversations, we often lie awake at night, revising when it is too late, wishing that we could withdraw a phrase which was tactless or crude, or add something brilliant and conclusive which has only now come to mind.

The essayist can combine the two, can draw upon his best moments in conversation, but add and develop in a way that is possible only in a thoughtfully composed piece of writing. It is not surprising to find that many famous essayists were also famous conversationalists: Oscar Wilde, Samuel Johnson, George Bernard Shaw, Samuel Taylor Coleridge, W. H. Auden, and Ralph Waldo Emerson.

The essayist by no means gives up the diction and rhythms of familiar speech. On the contrary, again using art to conceal art, he creates in his style the illusion of easy, natural conversation. E. B. White, for example, relishes emphatic colloquial phrases. In "A Slight Sound at Evening," we find "whack down some trees," "raised all that ruckus," "a toot on the trumpet," "batted out a magazine piece," and "Nature Boy." In E. M. Forster's "What I Believe," there are sentences that could easily occur in the unstudied speech of someone with firm ideas who is not particularly literary. He writes, "We don't know what we are like. We can't know what other people are like." Or "I hate the idea of causes, and if I had to choose between betraying my country and betraying my friend, I hope I should have the guts to betray my country."

Spontaneous though it sometimes seems, the essay is an art form. The writer imitates what is strong and effective in ordinary speech and avoids its weaknesses. He makes more vivid the qualities of colloquial terms and of poetic or technical terms by mixing them, and by shifting back and forth from conversational rhythms to those of formal eloquence. Speaking in "What I Believe" of the Ring of the Niebelung, Forster writes, "The giants there have the guns, or in other words the gold; but they do nothing with it, they do not realise that they are all-powerful, with the result that the catastrophe is delayed and the castle of Walhalla, insecure but glorious, fronts the storms." The concluding phrases "insecure but glorious" and "fronts the storms" sound well when spoken, but they would seem rather pretentious or poetic in ordinary conversation; they are more suited to deliberately heightened oratory.

In his essay on Thoreau, E. B. White writes,

> As things turned out, Thoreau, very likely without knowing quite
> what he was up to, took man's relation to Nature and man's di-
> lemma in society and man's capacity for elevating his spirit and
> he beat all these matters together, in a wild free interval of self-
> justification and delight, and produced an original omelette from
> which people can draw nourishment in a hungry day.

This sentence is both an illustration and a description of what
familiar essayists do stylistically. White begins with phrases like
"man's relation to Nature" and "man's dilemma in society" which
might appear in any conventional textbook or editorial, but he
achieves lightness and contrast with colloquial phrases like "as things
turned out" and "what he was up to," and with phrases of his own
invention like "wild free interval of self-justification and delight."
Notice that when White uses the metaphor of the omelette, he takes
it seriously. The literal act of cooking and eating is very real to
him, and he employs a whole set of terms—"beat," "nourishment,"
and "hungry"—consistent with it.

In the familiar essayist's prose there is room, as White says, citing
Thoreau, for "both Uranus and the shutter," one remote and grand,
with a classical name from the Greek for "heaven," the other near
and homely, with a functional name from Old English, "that which
shuts." Another way of using the elevated and literary with freshness and ease is to ring changes on well-known quotations. Talking
of style and remembering "Sweet are the uses of adversity" in *As
You Like It*, White says, "How sweet are the uses of brevity." Borrowing from one of Shakespeare's sonnets, Forster refers to "actions
no stronger than a flower."

The important thing is that terms and allusions never be used
tritely, mechanically, or ponderously. Words should be at once vivid
and precise. This is a matter equally of the words themselves and of
the positions in which they are placed. White and Forster have
been used for illustrations because their styles are perhaps most
characteristic of the familiar essay at its best, but all the twentieth-
century writers included in this collection show the same qualities in
varying degrees. Where writers do use trite phrases, as Frank Sullivan
does in "The Night the Old Nostalgia Burned Down," it is for satiric
purposes.

"Politics and the English Language" by George Orwell attacks jargon and the pretentious insensitivity with which a great many professionals use words—including university professors and writers of textbooks and learned articles. Since the student is bombarded by bad prose of this kind and likely to be influenced by it unaware, he would do well to absorb Orwell's teaching and apply it very consciously in his own writing. Certainly the essayists here all agree with Orwell in what they avoid. At the same time Orwell's advice, though badly needed, is largely negative. Once it is absorbed, the student can permit himself, as do most of the writers in this collection, to use any terms, no matter how learned or technical or rare, so long as they evoke the right response. But this means being very sensitive to the quality of the terms and their possible connotations. I have deliberately included the grandiloquent, *bravura* piece by De Quincey, "Levana and Our Ladies of Sorrow," to show how wide the range of effects in the essay may be. This is a highly rhetorical, visionary kind of writing, but it is also personal, evocative, and reminiscent. It is certainly an essay, though perhaps we would agree that in most senses of the word it is not a "familiar" one.

Essays are as varied in content and organization as in style, yet it is possible, in studying them, to apply some quite definite criteria.

Most of the propositions put forward by these essays are experimental to the extent, to quote the *Concise Oxford Dictionary*, that they are "based on experience, not authority or conjecture." We sometimes forget that "experience" and "experiment" are forms of the same word. First of all, then, we ask, "Whose experience is being presented, and how?"

Sometimes the experience is largely implied or implicit. "Morality and the Novel" by D. H. Lawrence makes a few references to the author's own physical activities and to his reading, but we take what he says seriously, first because it is persuasive and is in accord with our own needs and experiences, and second because we know already that Lawrence has had vast and influential experience as a critic and writer of novels. Something of the same holds for Auden's "Notes on Music and Opera," except that Auden does not speak with quite the same degree of authority. We depend more on the intrinsic plausibility and suggestiveness of what he asserts and on his use of musical references and illustrations.

Most of the essays, however, recreate experience directly, often with considerable detail, in passages of narration and description which we can judge—as to matters of language and pace and vividness and imagery—by exactly the same standards we would use for fiction. Frequently the writer is drawing on his own first-hand experience or that of others which they have shared with him, as in Aldous Huxley's visit to the laboratories of the scientist Bose in Calcutta. Sometimes he is imagining the experiences of others, though on the basis of a good deal of observation, as in Johnson's "Letter from Euphelia." Sometimes he is reporting and interpreting experiences which he has read about, as in Robert Graves' essay on Benedict Arnold and Virginia Woolf's on Poe. This last example gives us a chance to raise, if we wish, all the usual scholarly questions about the choice, reliability, and interpretation of sources.

The most characteristic kind of familiar essay draws on personal experience. The writer tells what happened to him, how he acted, thought, and felt. Though stylistically his descriptions and narration are indistinguishable from those of fiction, we assume a fundamental difference in the material used. By Aristotelian formula, we expect the author to present what *did* happen, not what *might* happen. We expect him to report, not invent. We want the authority that comes when a man is speaking on the basis of first-hand evidence.

To the extent that this is true and possible, we have one of the distinctive values of the essay. In Graham Greene's "The Lost Childhood," James Baldwin's "Notes of a Native Son," and the excerpt from *Goodbye to All That* by Robert Graves, we recognize and respect serious efforts to do justice to the quality of experience as it actually occurred. But from events which we have shared with other people, especially within the family during childhood, we know that different participants not only have different evaluations of what occurred but are convinced of quite incompatible facts. Mary McCarthy's afterword to "Yonder Peasant, Who Is He?" admits freely the transformations and distortions of fact in an account which she originally presented as straight autobiography.

Often the difference between the autobiographical essay and fiction is due not so much to the actual material presented as to the implied contract with the reader about the kind of truth that is being offered him. Does the essayist violate that contract when he selects, heightens, or even transforms the facts of his experience so as to illustrate or support an idea? Sometimes he does this simply to be more entertaining and dramatic. We can watch it happening step by step with raconteurs among our friends. The oftener they tell a story, the better it becomes. Starting as fact, it moves toward fiction, encouraged by the cries of amazement or amusement from its hearers. Autobiographical novels, on the other hand, like *A Portrait of the Artist as a Young Man, David Copperfield, The Sun Also Rises,* and *Look Homeward, Angel,* report personal experiences only slightly transformed or heightened. "A Relic" by Max Beerbohm finds its place in this collection partly because of its very amusing way of combining fiction and fact. It describes, no doubt rather fictitiously, an absurd attempt to make fiction out of very inadequate facts, but in the telling gives us the best of both worlds. By ingenious repetitions and variations ("Down below the sea rustled to and fro. . . ."), Beerbohm shows how certain basic patterning devices can be used equally well for fiction and essays.

We can only speculate about the original material for the character sketch "Will Wimble." Was Addison creating a composite type rather than painting an individual directly from life? This would be more consistent with eighteenth-century literary theory. Also the fame of the *Spectator* would make it necessary to protect any real individual by altering any details which would too readily identify him. An opposite necessity holds in the case of "Mr. More and the Mithraic Bull" by Edmund Wilson. Since More was well known to many of his readers, Wilson had to be completely faithful to the subject of his portrait.

According to the implied contract, the essayist presents experience as it actually occurred. The novelist is free to alter or invent as he pleases. But when the essayist presents no external or verifiable documentation, our ways of judging are not very different. Of experience in the novel we ask, *"Would* it happen this way, granted the characters and the situation?" Of experience in the essay we ask, *"Did* it happen this way, or did the writer distort, omit, exaggerate, rearrange?" Both cases require us to depend on internal evidence, but if we can convince ourselves that the author of an essay is telling the truth, he can make us accept with excitement and wonder many stories that would be quite unbelievable in fiction.

Both fiction and essays move back and forth between events and the ideas that the events dramatize or imply. Many novelists— Fielding, Thackeray, Melville, Hardy, Mann, Proust, Huxley, Faulkner—include in their novels long passages of reflection and analysis that are essentially essays. And essayists, as we have seen, make generous use of narration and description. At their extremes, however, the two forms are completely different. Some expository essays develop their themes primarily through logical argument and with the support of facts so generalized and statistical that they have lost all the color of immediate experience which a novelist would be bound to give them. And at the other extreme are novels of pure narrative without any commentary or generalization whatsoever.

In analyzing essays we examine both the experience and the way generalizations have been drawn from it or applied to it.

Certain experiences are intrinsically interesting. We are eager to learn from Robert Graves what it was like to take hallucinogenic drugs or fight in the muddy trenches of the First World War. The difficulties which Mary McCarthy and James Baldwin suffered with parents or parental surrogates are not so unusual, but we respond to the depth and vividness with which they recreate them and to the opportunity to compare other people's childhoods with our own. Often, as in E. B. White's "A Slight Sound at Evening," the personal experiences reported are fairly mild in themselves, but glow from the wit and charm with which they are treated or because of the larger issues which illuminate them.

Sometimes the essayist gives the impression of looking freshly at his experience to see what ideas it suggests. At other times he has clearly settled in advance on a particular approach or theme or idea which governs completely the way material is selected and presented. This is evident in "Trooper Silas Tomkyn Comberbacke" and "My Confession." In such cases notice the role played by language and use of detail.

Sometimes, as we observed of Huxley's "Copan," general ideas will be introduced in an order determined by the order of the events which suggested them. In other instances, such as "The Double Crisis" and, rather pretentiously, "The Guilty Vicarage," the order is that of systematic logical exposition. Because of the freedom of the essay form, all sorts of mixed structures are possible, as in "A Slight Sound at Evening." The sequences and transitions in such essays deserve careful study, and they may teach us to make our own writing more varied and adventurous.

Above all, of course, we are interested in what the essayists have to say. We read essays to enjoy them, to learn from them, to argue with them. When we start reading an essay, we usually have some opinions, however unformed, on the topic of discussion. What happens as we go on? Do we simply accept the author's views in place of our own? Do we reject what he says on logical grounds or be-

cause it runs counter to ideas, values, and mental habits of our own
that we are not disposed to give up? Or do we arrive dia-
lectically at a compromise in which we modify or extend some of
our own views without fully accepting his? It can be fun to watch
this dialectic developing, and valuable to write an account of it.

Any reader can argue with the writers in this collection, for on
most of the topics which they discuss they write as amateurs,
though exceedingly eloquent and well-informed amateurs. Pro-
fessionally speaking, Robert Graves is not a historian or Herbert
Gold a sociologist or Aldous Huxley a demographer or W. H.
Auden a musician. Their essays show what can be done when an intelligent man of original mind brings to bear on some particular subject the results of all his reading and writing and thinking, his full
sense of life and life's possibilities. Most of the contributors to this
volume are not scholars or technical critics even in literature. The
literary essays which I have included are addressed, like the other
essays, to the general reader. They are "polite" essays, not technical
expositions. Challenging as the evaluations are, they do not use terms
or references that require specialized preparation of the reader.
Here, too, reader and writer can meet on common ground.

What the essayists all do share to a very high degree is the ability
to write well. And with one exception—E. B. White—the writers
represented by these essays are all well-known novelists and poets.
This is not surprising, for the poet's or novelist's talents, his visual
powers and feeling for words, are almost equally useful to the essayist. But these writers also take the essay seriously as an independent
form in its own right, which lets them say things they could
not say in fiction or verse. Nearly all the contributors have been
highly productive, and show in the variety, freedom, and control of
their writing the results of vast experience in handling many kinds
of subjects.

For this reason, the ten writers chosen for the first part of the
volume are represented by three essays each. This helps us to get to
know them well—and they are well worth knowing. But more immediately, it enables us, in analyzing essays closely, to see by comparison when the tone, style, and selection of material is determined
by the theme or subject of the particular essay, and when it is
characteristic of the author's essays generally. This is especially appropriate in the approach to familiar essays, where personality plays
such a role. In some cases we learn that this personality is itself an

artistic creation which can be deliberately controlled and varied. All the essays have been selected first of all for the quality of their writing and for the intrinsic interest of what they discuss. Where an author is represented by three essays, I have also tried to suggest the kinds of topics he most likes to treat, and the range or restrictions of his mode of thought. The sequence in the appendix is not intended to show the development of the essay as a form, for we have agreed with Virginia Woolf that it sprang fully developed from the mind of Montaigne. I have simply chosen some of the liveliest and more characteristic examples from past and present centuries. But since the essay is a very personal kind of writing, highly responsive to changes in taste, diction, attitude, and habits of association, each one of this varied group evokes its author and period in both obvious and subtle ways that invite all sorts of discriminating comparisons.

Trooper Silas Tomkyn Comberbacke
The United States
What I Believe

E. M. FORSTER
(*b. 1879*)

IN 1921 E. M. Forster served as private secretary to
the native ruler of an Indian state. In 1924 he published
the novel *A Passage to India*, an imaginative, affectionate, amusing, and profoundly disturbing study of
racial and political differences among British, Hindus,
and Moslems. What he wrote applies almost equally
well to subsequent developments in Asia, Africa,
and the Middle East. *A Passage to India* can be wise
about politics because it goes much deeper than
politics. The issues evoked by the mysterious central
incident in a cave are eternal ones of lust, death,
personal identity, and religious faith.

Forster was well established as a novelist before the
First World War with *Where Angels Fear to Thread*
(1905), *The Longest Journey* (1907), *A Room with
a View* (1908), and *Howard's End* (1910). In these,
too, he had treated national differences, especially
between English and Italians, and class differences
among the English themselves, anticipating some of
the themes of young British social novelists after the
Second World War. In the delightfully readable
Aspects of the Novel (1927), perhaps the best treatise
on the novel that we have, Forster shows how
conscious is his mastery of his art.

Since his undergraduate days at Cambridge, Forster
had been friends with the Bloomsbury group of

Virginia Woolf, Bertrand Russell, Lytton Strachey,
J. M. Keynes, and Roger Fry, all brilliant stylists.
He traveled widely, was a Red Cross worker in
Alexandria during the First World War, was editor
of the Labour Party paper, the *Daily Herald*, in 1920,
and made frequent anti-Nazi broadcasts during the
Second World War. His principal collections of
essays are *Abinger Harvest* (1936) and *Two Cheers
for Democracy* (1951).

Forster's varied experience of life, his combination
of devotion and detachment, are suggested by the title,
"Two Cheers. . . ." With his wit, modesty, and love of
style, he is an ideal familiar essayist. Notice in
"Trooper Silas Tomkyn Comberbacke" the virtuosity
with which Forster quotes and paraphrases his sources,
letting characters speak for themselves, relishing odd
turns of phrase, and yet keeping the narrative moving
swiftly and a little mysteriously. The ending is more
than a trick, for it raises fascinating questions about
the relationship of romantic creativity to the everyday
world. "What I Believe" is a straightforward and
deeply moving revindication of liberal, democratic
humanism, completely free from dogma, rhetoric, or
false optimism. In "The United States" we have
an opportunity to see how we look to a friendly
Englishman well practiced in judging national
differences. It makes a good comparison with Auden's
"American Poetry."

Trooper Silas Tomkyn Comberbacke

The workhouse at Henley-on-Thames has, or rather had, a garden attached to it, in the midst of which stood a solitary hut, reserved for inmates who were suffering from infectious diseases. At the moment our eyes rest upon this hut—that is to say at a moment during the February of 1794—it was occupied by two troopers of the King's Light Dragoons. One of them was sick of the confluent smallpox; he raved in delirium, and the other, who held him down, was covered with ominous spots. The unfortunate men had been left behind by their regiment to look after themselves as best they could, and their situation was appalling, for the weather was bitter, the hut possessed four windows and little else, and though the paupers in the main building were sympathetic they approached with circumspection. We do not know the name of the trooper who had the smallpox, but the one covered with spots was called Comberbacke.

Comberbacke was a clumsy young man, with a drooping lower lip and aspiring eyes, and somewhat of a puzzle to his mates. They saw easily enough that he was a "natural" but he was a talking natural, a rare and rather agreeable species; he could speak and even write upon a variety of topics with a fluency they felt bound to admire. Although he could neither mount his horse nor groom it, he was grand when he came to the wars of the past, and he was always willing to describe them in an interminable and interesting way. There was an expedition entailing the Hellespont—probably the mouth of the Thames being a broad space of water—leading to Thermopple (*sic*) a place up north, and General Alexander—no doubt from Truro, where it is a well-known name. He talked and laughed, didn't mind being teased, changed from subject to subject; he was superb; nothing could stop him when once he had started, and if asked to write a letter for you it was the same: the ink poured out in a torrent, so that by the time he had got to the fourth page the girl couldn't do otherwise than give in. Thus he gained a curious

TROOPER SILAS TOMKYN COMBERBACKE. From *Abinger Harvest*, copyright, 1936, 1964 by E. M. Forster. Reprinted by permission of Harcourt, Brace & World, Inc., and Edward Arnold (Publishers) Ltd., London.

reputation, where even his imbecilities were admired. For instance, "Whose rusty gun is this?" the inspecting officer would ask. "Is it *very* rusty?" replied Comberbacke, "because if it is I think it must be mine." What a reply! But how successful! For the inspecting officer was dumbfounded. And again, Comberbacke's idea that a horse ought to "rub himself down and so shine in all his native beauty"—well, it was the idea of a zany, still when the letter was written and the girl on the way there or back there was no reason you shouldn't brighten his horse up for him; it didn't take long, and you knew which end kicked and which bit, more than he did. At last he proved so incompetent that his horse was withdrawn from beneath him permanently, and he was employed upon matters relating to sanitation; that was why he was in the garden-hut now. When his comrade's delirium lessened, he procured pen and ink and wrote the following letter:

> My assumed name is Silas Tomkyn Comberbacke, 15th or King's Regiment of Light Dragoons, G Troop. My number I do not know. It is of no import. The bounty I received was six guineas and a half: but a light horse man's bounty is a mere lure: it is expended for him in things which he must have had without a bounty—gaiters, a pair of leather breeches, stable jacket, and shell; horse-cloth, surcingle, watering bridle, brushes and the long etc. of military accoutrement. I enlisted the 2nd of December 1793, was attested and sworn the 4th. I am at present nurse to a sick man, and shall, I believe, stay at Henley another week. There will be a large draught from our regiment to complete our troops abroad. The men were picked out today. I suppose I am not one, being a very indocile equestrian. Farewell.

Love, extravagance, and a too reckless support of Unitarianism had combined to put him in this plight. A clergyman's son, he had been sent by his brothers up to Cambridge, where he had successfully composed a Latin declaration on Posthumous Fame, and a poem entitled *To a Young Ass*, and seemed to be settling down. Then he ran away and enlisted. He was always like that. He would start suddenly and collapse suddenly, and he was about to collapse now. The hut, his mate's illness, his own eruptive spots, were going to be too much for him, and to induce in him his favourite reaction —a sense of guilt. For the moment he played the man, and a beautiful girl even ventured into the garden and flirted with him from a distance. Though he mourned for a lost girl of his own, he was touched, and in after years he thought of writing a poem called *The Soother in Absence* to commemorate the visitor, but like so much else that he planned this was never accomplished. He seldom did what he or what others hoped, and posterity has marked him as her prey in consequence. She has never ceased to hold up her plump finger to him, and shake it and say that he has disappointed her. And he has acquiesced because he is a darling. But if one turns on posterity and says, "Well! what else do you want him to do? Would you rather have Comberbacke as he is or not at all?" she is apt to be silent or to change the conversation.

His Cambridge career included typical irregularities. "We have veal, sir, tottering on the verge of beef," he had shouted out in Hall upon one occasion; and on another, when the Master of his college met him and said, "When will you get rid of that shameful gown?" he had retorted, "Why, sir, I think I have got rid of the best part of it already." More serious was the unholy row in the Senate House on the occasion of the expulsion of a Mr. Frend for his Unitarian principles. The undergraduates sympathized with Mr. Frend, because they associated him with revolutionary ideas and they attended in great numbers to applaud his defence. Comberbacke clapped with the rest, and when the Proctor approached him he deftly exchanged places with a man who had scarcely any arms. "Sir, you were applauding," said the Proctor; the man retorted, "Would that I could," showing his stumps. And there were drinking parties. Nothing very much, but on to it all fell a love-disappointment: his affection for the sister of an old schoolfellow was not returned. So one night he crossed the court from his rooms to the entrance gate, passed down the long paved passage called "the chimney," gained the street and entered the world. It was not his first escapade. At the age of seven he had nearly killed his brother Frank in a quarrel over some toasted cheese; then, stricken with remorse, he had rushed into the twilight and had watched the river and some calves on the further side of it, and so poignant had been the misery that in later years a chance sound would invoke the whole scene: "There would come on my mind that night I slept out at Ottery and the calf across the river whose lowing so deeply impressed me. Chill and child and calf and lowing." And he was to have other escapades in the future: there was another journey—alas!

someone interrupted it—along the course of an underground river, and there was a voyage—perhaps the most marvellous any navigator has ever undertaken—into the Antarctic seas.

He went by coach from Cambridge to London, got off at Holborn, bought a ticket for the Irish Lottery (not yet illegal), composed a poem on it beginning—

> Promptress of unnumber'd sighs,
> O snatch that circling bandage from thine eyes.

—sent the poem to the *Morning Chronicle*, went to the King's mews, and enlisted.

An old schoolfellow was the first to find out what had happened; then it got round to the family; and as soon as his brothers started writing to him he fell to pieces. He rushed at once from heroics to morbidity ("Mine is a sensibility gangrened with inward corruption"), to mawkishness ("Alas, my poor mother!"—whom he did not like), to self-abasement ("Oh, my wayward soul! I have been a fool even to madness!"), to solemn fudge ("In a mind which vice has not utterly divested of sensibility, few occurrences can inflict a more acute pang than the receiving proofs of tenderness and love where only resentment and reproach were expected and deserved"), and finally to a deprecating and uneasy gaiety. But his troubles were not at an end. He had to be got out of the Dragoons, and it proved to be less easy than getting in; and he had to be got back into Cambridge, if Cambridge would receive him.

His brothers, one of whom held a commission, got in touch with the War Office, and, so far as we know, it is through this channel that he was released. But he never was very truthful, and in after years he used to tell dramatic tales. They centre round one of his own officers, a Captain Ogle. According to one of these tales, he was standing sentry outside a ballroom when Captain Ogle, who was passing in with another officer, quoted two lines in Greek, and ascribed them to Euripides. "I hope your honour will excuse me," said Trooper Comberbacke, "but the lines you have repeated are not quite accurately cited; moreover, instead of being in Euripides they will be found in the second antistrophe of the *Oedipus* of Sophocles." In another version, it is through Latin that he attracts the Captain's attention; he wrote up some pathetic lines in the stable where he had failed to groom his horse. At this point Miss Mitford, authoress of *Our Village*, takes up the thread. Captain Ogle's father and Miss Mitford's father were friends. They were at dinner at Reading and Captain Ogle was with them. To amuse them he told them of the scholar-trooper, and his yearnings for release, but, says Miss Mitford, "kind and clever as Captain Ogle was, he was so indolent a man that without a flapper the matter might have slept in his hands till the Greek Kalends." The company exerted themselves. The difficulty was to find a substitute, for troopers were scarce. One of the servants who was waiting at the table was called, and agreed to serve for a suitable honorarium. The matter was fixed up there and then, and so grateful was Comberbacke that in after years he looked through two of Miss Mitford's works, entitled *Christina* and *Blanch*, and gave her good advice, which was, however, of no use to her, she feared.

As release approached, he became more and more schoolboyish and hysterical. He was afraid of annoying his brothers further, particularly George the clergyman, and now asks advice on every detail. Should he, or should he not, order new clothes?

"They are gone irrevocably. My shirts, which I have with me, are, all but one, worn to rags, mere rags; their texture was ill adapted to the labour of the stables. . . . I have ordered therefore a pair of breeches, which will be nineteen shillings, a waistcoat at twelve shillings, a pair of shoes at seven shillings and four pence. Besides these I must have a hat. Have I done wrong in ordering these things? I have so seldom acted right that in every step I take of my own accord I tremble lest I should be wrong. I forgot in the above account to mention a flannel waistcoat; it will be six shillings. The military dress is almost oppressively warm, and so very ill as I am at present I think it imprudent to Hazard cold."

Besides the clothes, there is a terrible confession about some books; he sold books that were worth forty shillings for fourteen; he will do all he can to buy them back. Moreover, should he write a contrite letter to Dr. Pearce, the master of his College, imploring to be taken back, or would it show truer humility if he remained dumb? His brothers seem to have behaved decently—it cost them at least forty guineas to buy his discharge; and the college authorities were sympathetic and made no difficulties in receiving him. Some censure had to be administered, and, consequently, the Register of Jesus, Cambridge, contains the famous entry: "1794 Apr: Coleridge admonitus est per magistrum in praesentia sociorum." And now you know who Comberbacke is if you did not know it before.

As soon as Comberbacke felt himself Coleridge again, he began to perk up. He had really been treated most leniently, but "Dr. Pearce behaved with great asperity," he complains, and has confined him to college for a month and ordered him to translate the works of Demetrius Phalereus. "All the fellows tried to persuade the Master to leniency, but in vain." Then he turns cheeky: "Without the least affectation, I applaud his conduct and think nothing of it. The confinement is nothing. I have the field and grove of the College to walk in, and what can I wish more? What do I wish more? Nothing. The Demetrius is dry." He gets up at 5.0 A.M.; he has dropped all his old acquaintances; he is finishing a Greek Ode; really, his brothers need not worry about him any more.

The rooms he occupied at Jesus' are still to be seen. They are in the front court, on the ground floor—charming rooms—and Malthus, if one seeks for a contrast, once occupied the rooms opposite. It is natural to assume that after his military career he would settle quietly down. But it is dangerous to assume anything about Coleridge. If life is a lesson, he never learnt it. He did not settle down to his Demetrius, he did not proceed to his degree, and in the autumn of that same year the College register contains a second Latin entry, to the effect that Coleridge went away and did not return.

He had disgraced himself irretrievably, and three years later he wrote *The Ancient Mariner*.

The United States

Amerca is rather like life. You can usually find in it what you look for. If you look for skyscrapers or cowboys or cocktail parties or gangsters or business connections or political problems or women's clubs, they will certainly be there. You can be very hot there or very cold. You can explore the America of your choice by plane or train, by hitch-hike or on foot. It will probably be interesting, and it is sure to be large.

I went there for the first time at the age of sixty-eight. By sixty-eight one is so to speak a pilgrim grandfather who knows very clearly what to look for when he disembarks. I had no doubt as to what I wanted to discover in America. It was to provide me with scenery and individuals. The scenery was to be of two sorts—gigantic and homely. The individuals were not to be representative—I never could get on with representative individuals—but people who existed on their own account and with whom it might therefore be possible to be friends. That is the America I looked for and was to find. My visit was a complete success from my own point of view.

After a respectful glance at New York, I went a hundred miles north into the Berkshires. It was April. The trees were leafless— thousands and thousands of birch trees, their trunks whiter than the birch trees here, milk white, ghost white in the sharp sunshine, covering the sides of the valley and the crests of the hills; and among the birches pushed pine and hemlock—which is like a not very dark green yew. Was I in England? Almost, but not quite. That was again and again to be my sensation, and in the Arizona Desert I was to feel I was almost but not quite in India, and in the Yosemite Valley that it was not quite Switzerland. America is always throwing out these old-world hints, and then withdrawing them in favour of America. To return to the Berkshires: after a few days' quiet the snow descended and silence became absolute. The country became primeval and polar—endless purity, underspreading motionless trees. I can never be grateful enough for those opening days of silence and snow. They imposed proportion. They made me realise that America is not all town: such a generalisation would be truer of England. It is country—controlled no doubt by mechanised gadgets, still it is country. I was glad I had not gaped too long at the New York skyscrapers. Exciting as they are, they mislead. They do not epitomise what lies behind them. Presently the snow melted. Where it had lain appeared dark brown earth and occasional pale lilac hepaticas, and the spring began—in double quick time compared to our spring.

The Berkshires are homely scenery. Gigantic scenery is more difficult to describe, but I will make an attempt. Suppose yourself walking on a Surrey common near Bagshot. There are a good many fir trees about, the soil is sandy, and the prospect rather dull. Suddenly the common stops, and you are standing without any warning on the brink of a precipice which is one mile deep. One mile into the tortured earth it goes, the other side of the chasm is miles away, and the chasm is filled with unbelievable deposits of rock which resemble sphinxes draped in crimson shawls. That, as far as I can get it into a single sentence, gives you my first impression of the Grand Canyon of the Colorado River, but the Grand Canyon would need many sentences to describe and many books. It is the most astounding natural object I have ever seen. It frightens. There are many colours in it besides crimson—strata of black and of white, and rocks of ochre and pale lilac. And the Colorado River itself is, when one gets down to it, still more sinister, for it is muddy white and very swift, and it rages like an infuriated maggot between precipices of granite, gnawing at them and cutting the Canyon deeper. It was strange after two days amongst these marvels, and terrors, to return to the surface of the earth, and go bowling away in a 'bus between little fir trees.

The second item I sought in America was the human, the individual. My work lay mainly in universities, and there and elsewhere I found the individuals I sought. I had expected generosity and hospitality. I had not expected so much tact, charm and sensitiveness; here was the delightful surprise. Wherever I went I found delicate understanding of our troubles in Britain over food and clothing, and a desire to help that was never patronising. This was not confined to the highly educated classes. I recall a cheap eating-house in Nevada where some strangers came up and asked what they could send. I remember the chambermaid in the hotel at Salt Lake City who when I offered her a tip replied, "I don't like to take your money, brother, you need it more than I do." That is the sort of remark which comes from the heart and goes to the heart, and in the light of it and the warmth of it I found difficulty in examining the defects of the American character. The defects are, I suspect, lack of discrimination, emotionalism, and a tendency to narrow the idea of freedom into freedom to make money. "What else have we fought the war for?" a business acquaintance enquired. But I cannot feel these defects are basic. My friends reassure me against this, and not only my friends; the faces of strangers lighting up everywhere, compassionate, respectful, anxious to help. The individuals I met were mostly of Anglo-Saxon stock; I also knew some Swedish and some Italian farming people, made some Oriental contacts, and had one or two Mexican friends. I did not have the good fortune to get to know any Negroes. On the whole I saw as much of the human landscape as an elderly traveller may reasonably expect, and I liked it.

But now comes a qualification. Although the Americans I encountered were full of charitable feelings towards Great Britain, I cannot say that they showed much interest in us otherwise. I have often been asked since my return home: "What do they think about us over there?" Indeed, it is often the only thing English people want to know. The answer, not very flattering to our pride, is that the Americans scarcely think about us at all. They are curious about our Royal Family, they are grateful and appreciative towards Mr. Churchill, they are—or were—enthusiastic over British films. That is all. They do not discuss our Empire. India, over which they have been so critical in the past, is now scarcely in the news and seems to bore them. Even Palestine was seldom mentioned. An explanation of this indifference is that they concentrate, as we all do, on home affairs, and that when they do think of foreign affairs they think of Russia. China to some extent, but mostly Russia. Russia is always weighing on their minds. They are afraid of war, or that their standard of life may be lowered. I shall never forget a dinner party, supposedly given in my honour, at which one of the guests, a journalist, urged that atomic bombs should be dropped upon the Soviet Union without notice, and quoted with approval a remark which he inaccurately ascribed to Oliver Cromwell: "Stone dead hath no fellow." "That's good, isn't it, Tom?" he called to another journalist. "Stone dead hath no fellow." Tom agreed that it was very good, and they shouted: "Stone dead hath no fellow" in unison or antiphonically for the rest of the evening. They were cultivated men, but as soon as the idea of Russia occurred to them, their faces became blood red; they ceased to be human. No one seemed appalled by the display but myself, no one was surprised and our hostess congratulated herself afterwards on the success of her party. This obsession over Russia should be realised by all who would understand America, and it explains in part her lack of interest in us.

I did not encounter such hysteria elsewhere, and maybe did not frequent the circles where it is likeliest to occur. Most of the people I was with were not influential or highly placed: many of them were teachers, and some of them were young—students, or they practised music or painting or acting or the ballet, or they were doing small commercial jobs or working on the land. My general impression was of good temper and goodwill and hopefulness. I could darken the picture, no doubt. I do not take the Statue of Liberty in New York harbour as seriously as she takes herself. And I did encounter hints of oppression and of violence, and of snobbery. But the main verdict is favourable, and I do beg anyone who happens to have fallen into the habit of nagging at America to drop it. Nagging is so insidious. It often resides not in what is said but in the tone of voice. It proceeds not from considered criticism but from envy and from discontent—and, of course, life out there is far more comfortable for the average man than it is here. The food is nicer, if dearer, the clothes are nicer and cheaper, the cold drinks are not lukewarm, and the railway carriages are not dirty. But these advantages over ourselves should not embitter us against the people who enjoy them. Nor should we charge it against all Americans that their politicians do what our politicians tell them, and tell us, they ought not to do.

I chanced to end my three months' visit in the same district of the Berkshires where it had begun. Now it was high summer. The little spring from which I fetched water every day had already begun to flag. The meadows were full of flowers—ox-eye daisies, black-eyed susans, orchids, and an under-carpet of creeping jenny; the meadows sloped down to a brook where the farm hands bathed. There were swallow-tail butterflies and fritillaries, and the bobolink, a very agreeable bird, skipped from post to post carolling, and another bird, the phoebe, repeated "phoebe, phoebe, phoebe," whence its name. At night there were fireflies to remind us that this was in the latitude of Madrid. Thunderstorms did not disconcert them, and I would watch their flash vanish in the superior brilliancy of lightning, and reappear. Some of them flew at the level of the grass, others across the curtain of birch trees. They were extraordinarily bright; it was a good year for fireflies, and the memory of them sparking in the warm rain and the thunder is the latest of my American impressions, and the loveliest.

What I Believe

I do not believe in Belief. But this is an age of faith, and there are so many militant creeds that, in self-defence, one has to formulate a creed of one's own. Tolerance, good temper and sympathy are no longer enough in a world which is rent by religious and racial persecution, in a world where ignorance rules, and science, who ought to have ruled, plays the subservient pimp. Tolerance, good temper and sympathy—they are what matter really, and if the human race is not to collapse they must come to the front before long. But for the moment they are not enough, their action is no stronger than a flower, battered beneath a military jack-boot. They want stiffening, even if the process coarsens them. Faith, to my mind, is a stiffening process, a sort of mental starch, which ought to be applied as sparingly as possible. I dislike the stuff. I do not believe in it, for its own sake, at all. Herein I probably differ from most people, who believe in Belief, and are only sorry they cannot swallow even more than they do. My law-givers are Erasmus and Montaigne, not Moses and St. Paul. My temple stands not upon Mount Moriah but in that Elysian Field where even the immoral are admitted. My motto is: "Lord, I disbelieve—help thou my unbelief."

I have, however, to live in an Age of Faith—the sort of epoch I used to hear praised when I was a boy. It is extremely unpleasant really. It is bloody in every sense of the word. And I have to keep my end up in it. Where do I start?

With personal relationships. Here is something comparatively solid in a world full of violence and cruelty. Not absolutely solid, for Psychology has split and shattered the idea of a "Person," and has shown that there is something incalculable in each of us, which may at any moment rise to the surface and destroy our normal balance. We don't know what we are like. We can't know what other people are like. How, then, can we put any trust in personal relationships, or cling to them in the gathering political storm? In theory we cannot. But in practice we can and do. Though A is not

---

WHAT I BELIEVE. Copyright, 1939 by E. M. Forster. Reprinted from his volume *Two Cheers for Democracy* by permission of Harcourt, Brace & World, Inc., and Edward Arnold (Publishers) Ltd., London.

unchangeably A or B unchangeably B, there can still be love and loyalty between the two. For the purpose of living one has to assume that the personality is solid, and the "self" is an entity, and to ignore all contrary evidence. And since to ignore evidence is one of the characteristics of faith, I certainly can proclaim that I believe in personal relationships.

Starting from them, I get a little order into the contemporary chaos. One must be fond of people and trust them if one is not to make a mess of life, and it is therefore essential that they should not let one down. They often do. The moral of which is that I must, myself, be as reliable as possible, and this I try to be. But reliability is not a matter of contract—that is the main difference between the world of personal relationships and the world of business relationships. It is a matter for the heart, which signs no documents. In other words, reliability is impossible unless there is a natural warmth. Most men possess this warmth, though they often have bad luck and get chilled. Most of them, even when they are politicians, *want* to keep faith. And one can, at all events, show one's own little light here, one's own poor little trembling flame, with the knowledge that it is not the only light that is shining in the darkness, and not the only one which the darkness does not comprehend. Personal relations are despised today. They are regarded as bourgeois luxuries, as products of a time of fair weather which is now past, and we are urged to get rid of them, and to dedicate ourselves to some movement or cause instead. I hate the idea of causes, and if I had to choose between betraying my country and betraying my friend, I hope I should have the guts to betray my country. Such a choice may scandalise the modern reader, and he may stretch out his patriotic hand to the telephone at once and ring up the police. It would not have shocked Dante, though. Dante places Brutus and Cassius in the lowest circle of Hell because they had chosen to betray their friend Julius Caesar rather than their country Rome. Probably one will not be asked to make such an agonising choice. Still, there lies at the back of every creed something terrible and hard for which the worshipper may one day be required to suffer, and there is even a terror and a hardness in this creed of personal relationships, urbane and mild though it sounds. Love and loyalty to an individual can run counter to the claims of the State. When they do—down with the State, say I, which means that the State would down me.

This brings me along to Democracy, "even Love, the Beloved Re-

public, which feeds upon Freedom and lives." Democracy is not a
Beloved Republic really, and never will be. But it is less hateful than
other contemporary forms of government, and to that extent it deserves our support. It does start from the assumption that the individual is important, and that all types are needed to make a civilisation. It does not divide its citizens into the bossers and the bossed—
as an efficiency-regime tends to do. The people I admire most are
those who are sensitive and want to create something or discover
something, and do not see life in terms of power, and such people
get more of a chance under a democracy than elsewhere. They
found religions, great or small, or they produce literature and art, or
they do disinterested scientific research, or they may be what is
called "ordinary people," who are creative in their private lives,
bring up their children decently, for instance, or help their neighbours. All these people need to express themselves; they cannot do
so unless society allows them liberty to do so, and the society which
allows them most liberty is a democracy.

Democracy has another merit. It allows criticism, and if there is
not public criticism there are bound to be hushed-up scandals. That
is why I believe in the Press, despite all its lies and vulgarity, and
why I believe in Parliament. Parliament is often sneered at because
it is a Talking Shop. I believe in it *because* it is a talking shop. I believe in the Private Member who makes himself a nuisance. He gets
snubbed and is told that he is cranky or ill-informed, but he does
expose abuses which would otherwise never have been mentioned,
and very often an abuse gets put right just by being mentioned. Occasionally, too, a well-meaning public official starts losing his head in
the cause of efficiency, and thinks himself God Almighty. Such officials are particularly frequent in the Home Office. Well, there will
be questions about them in Parliament sooner or later, and then they
will have to mind their steps. Whether Parliament is either a representative body or an efficient one is questionable, but I value it because it criticises and talks, and because its chatter gets widely
reported.

So Two Cheers for Democracy: one because it admits variety and
two because it permits criticism. Two cheers are quite enough:
there is no occasion to give three. Only Love the Beloved Republic
deserves that.

What about Force, though? While we are trying to be sensitive
and advanced and affectionate and tolerant, an unpleasant question

pops up: does not all society rest upon force? If a government cannot count upon the police and the army, how can it hope to rule? And if an individual gets knocked on the head or sent to a labour camp, of what significance are his opinions?

This dilemma does not worry me as much as it does some. I realise that all society rests upon force. But all the great creative actions, all the decent human relations, occur during the intervals when force has not managed to come to the front. These intervals are what matter. I want them to be as frequent and as lengthy as possible, and I call them "civilisation." Some people idealise force and pull it into the foreground and worship it, instead of keeping it in the background as long as possible. I think they make a mistake, and I think that their opposites, the mystics, err even more when they declare that force does not exist. I believe that it exists, and that one of our jobs is to prevent it from getting out of its box. It gets out sooner or later, and then it destroys us and all the lovely things which we have made. But it is not out all the time, for the fortunate reason that the strong are so stupid. Consider their conduct for a moment in the Niebelung's Ring. The giants there have the guns, or in other words the gold; but they do nothing with it, they do not realise that they are all-powerful, with the result that the catastrophe is delayed and the castle of Walhalla, insecure but glorious, fronts the storms. Fafnir, coiled round his hoard, grumbles and grunts; we can hear him under Europe today; the leaves of the wood already tremble, and the Bird calls its warnings uselessly. Fafnir will destroy us, but by a blessed dispensation he is stupid and slow, and creation goes on just outside the poisonous blast of his breath. The Nietzschean would hurry the monster up, the mystic would say he did not exist, but Wotan, wiser than either, hastens to create warriors before doom declares itself. The Valkyries are symbols not only of courage but of intelligence; they represent the human spirit snatching its opportunity while the going is good, and one of them even finds time to love. Brünnhilde's last song hymns the recurrence of love, and since it is the privilege of art to exaggerate, she goes even further, and proclaims the love which is eternally triumphant and feed's upon freedom, and lives.

So that is what I feel about force and violence. It is, alas! the ultimate reality on this earth, but it does not always get to the front. Some people call its absences "decadence"; I call them "civilisation" and find in such interludes the chief justification for the human experiment. I look the other way until fate strikes me. Whether this is due to courage or to cowardice in my own case I cannot be sure. But I know that if men had not looked the other way in the past, nothing of any value would survive. The people I respect most behave as if they were immortal and as if society was eternal. Both assumptions are false: both of them must be accepted as true if we are to go on eating and working and loving, and are to keep open a few breathing holes for the human spirit. No millennium seems likely to descend upon humanity; no better and stronger League of Nations will be instituted; no form of Christianity and no alternative to Christianity will bring peace to the world or integrity to the individual; no "change of heart" will occur. And yet we need not despair, indeed, we cannot despair; the evidence of history shows us that men have always insisted on behaving creatively under the shadow of the sword; that they have done their artistic and scientific and domestic stuff for the sake of doing it, and that we had better follow their example under the shadow of the aeroplanes. Others, with more vision or courage than myself, see the salvation of humanity ahead, and will dismiss my conception of civilisation as paltry, a sort of tip-and-run game. Certainly it is presumptuous to say that we *cannot* improve, and that Man, who has only been in power for a few thousand years, will never learn to make use of his power. All I mean is that, if people continue to kill one another as they do, the world cannot get better than it is, and that since there are more people than formerly, and their means for destroying one another superior, the world may well get worse. What is good in people—and consequently in the world—is their insistence on creation, their belief in friendship and loyalty for their own sakes; and though Violence remains and is, indeed, the major partner in this muddled establishment, I believe that creativeness remains too, and will always assume direction when violence sleeps. So, though I am not an optimist, I cannot agree with Sophocles that it were better never to have been born. And although, like Horace, I see no evidence that each batch of births is superior to the last, I leave the field open for the more complacent view. This is such a difficult moment to live in, one cannot help getting gloomy and also a bit rattled, and perhaps short-sighted.

In search of a refuge, we may perhaps turn to hero-worship. But here we shall get no help, in my opinion. Hero-worship is a dangerous vice, and one of the minor merits of a democracy is that it does not encourage it, or produce that unmanageable type of citizen known as the Great Man. It produces instead different kinds of small men—a much finer achievement. But people who cannot get interested in the variety of life, and cannot make up their own minds, get discontented over this, and they long for a hero to bow down before and to follow blindly. It is significant that a hero is an integral part of the authoritarian stock-in-trade today. An efficiency-regime cannot be run without a few heroes stuck about it to carry off the dullness—much as plums have to be put into a bad pudding to make it palatable. One hero at the top and a smaller one each side of him is a favourite arrangement, and the timid and the bored are comforted by the trinity, and, bowing down, feel exalted and strengthened.

No, I distrust Great Men. They produce a desert of uniformity around them and often a pool of blood too, and I always feel a little man's pleasure when they come a cropper. Every now and then one reads in the newspapers some such statement as: "The coup d'état appears to have failed, and Admiral Toma's whereabouts is at present unknown." Admiral Toma had probably every qualification for being a Great Man—an iron will, personal magnetism, dash, flair, sexlessness—but fate was against him, so he retires to unknown whereabouts instead of parading history with his peers. He fails with a completeness which no artist and no lover can experience, because with them the process of creation is itself an achievement, whereas with him the only possible achievement is success.

I believe in aristocracy, though—if that is the right word, and if a democrat may use it. Not an aristocracy of power, based upon rank and influence, but an aristocracy of the sensitive, the considerate and the plucky. Its members are to be found in all nations and classes, and all through the ages, and there is a secret understanding between them when they meet. They represent the true human tradition, the one permanent victory of our queer race over cruelty and chaos. Thousands of them perish in obscurity, a few are great names. They are sensitive for others as well as for themselves, they are considerate without being fussy, their pluck is not swankiness but the power to endure, and they can take a joke. I give no examples—it is risky to do that—but the reader may as well consider whether this is the type of person he would like to meet and to be, and whether (going farther with me) he would prefer that this type should *not* be an ascetic one. I am against asceticism myself. I

am with the old Scotsman who wanted less chastity and more deli-
cacy. I do not feel that my aristocrats are a real aristocracy if they
thwart their bodies, since bodies are the instruments through which
we register and enjoy the world. Still, I do not insist. This is not a
major point. It is clearly possible to be sensitive, considerate and
plucky and yet be an ascetic too, if anyone possesses the first three
qualities, I will let him in! On they go—an invincible army, yet not a
victorious one. The aristocrats, the elect, the chosen, the Best People
—all the words that describe them are false, and all attempts to organise them fail. Again and again Authority, seeing their value, has
tried to net them and to utilise them as the Egyptian Priesthood or
the Christian Church or the Chinese Civil Service or the Group
Movement, or some other worthy stunt. But they slip through the
net and are gone; when the door is shut, they are no longer in the
room; their temple, as one of them remarked, is the Holiness of the
Heart's Affection, and their kingdom, though they never possess it,
is the wide-open world.

With this type of person knocking about, and constantly crossing
one's path if one has eyes to see or hands to feel, the experiment of
earthly life cannot be dismissed as a failure. But it may well be
hailed as a tragedy, the tragedy being that no device has been found
by which these private decencies can be transmitted to public
affairs. As soon as people have power they go crooked and sometimes dotty as well, because the possession of power lifts them into a
region where normal honesty never pays. For instance, the man who
is selling newspapers outside the Houses of Parliament can safely
leave his papers to go for a drink and his cap beside them: anyone
who takes a paper is sure to drop a copper into the cap. But the men
who are inside the Houses of Parliament—they cannot trust one another like that, still less can the Government they compose trust
other governments. No caps upon the pavement here, but suspicion,
treachery and armaments. The more highly public life is organised
the lower does its morality sink; the nations of today behave to each
other worse than they ever did in the past, they cheat, rob, bully
and bluff, make war without notice, and kill as many women and
children as possible; whereas primitive tribes were at all events re-
strained by taboos. It is a humiliating outlook—though the greater
the darkness, the brighter shine the little lights, reassuring one another, signalling: "Well, at all events, I'm still here. I don't like it
very much, but how are you?" Unquenchable lights of my aristoc-

racy! Signals of the invincible army! "Come along—anyway, let's have a good time while we can." I think they signal that too.

The Saviour of the future—if ever he comes—will not preach a new Gospel. He will merely utilise my aristocracy, he will make effective the good will and the good temper which are already existing. In other words, he will introduce a new technique. In economics, we are told that if there was a new technique of distribution, there need be no poverty, and people would not starve in one place while crops were being ploughed under in another. A similar change is needed in the sphere of morals and politics. The desire for it is by no means new; it was expressed, for example, in theological terms by Jacopone da Todi over six hundred years ago. "Ordina questo amore, O tu che m'ami," he said; "O thou who lovest me—set this love in order." His prayer was not granted, and I do not myself believe that it ever will be, but here, and not through a change of heart, is our probable route. Not by becoming better, but by ordering and distributing his native goodness, will Man shut up Force into its box, and so gain time to explore the universe and to set his mark upon it worthily. At present he only explores it at odd moments, when Force is looking the other way, and his divine creativeness appears as a trivial by-product, to be scrapped as soon as the drums beat and the bombers hum.

Such a change, claim the orthodox, can only be made by Christianity, and will be made by it in God's good time: man always has failed and always will fail to organise his own goodness, and it is presumptuous of him to try. This claim—solemn as it is—leaves me cold. I cannot believe that Christianity will ever cope with the present world-wide mess, and I think that such influence as it retains in modern society is due to the money behind it, rather than to its spiritual appeal. It was a spiritual force once, but the indwelling spirit will have to be restated if it is to calm the waters again, and probably restated in a non-Christian form. Naturally a lot of people, and people who are not only good but able and intelligent, will disagree here; they will vehemently deny that Christianity has failed, or they will argue that its failure proceeds from the wickedness of men, and really proves its ultimate success. They have Faith, with a large F. My faith has a very small one, and I only intrude it because these are strenuous and serious days, and one likes to say what one thinks while speech is comparatively free: it may not be free much longer.

The above are the reflections of an individualist and a liberal who has found liberalism crumbling beneath him and at first felt ashamed. Then, looking around, he decided there was no special reason for shame, since other people, whatever they felt, were equally insecure. And as for individualism—there seems no way of getting off this, even if one wanted to. The dictator-hero can grind down his citizens till they are all alike, but he cannot melt them into a single man. That is beyond his power. He can order them to merge, he can incite them to mass-antics, but they are obliged to be born separately, and to die separately, and, owing to these unavoidable termini, will always be running off the totalitarian rails. The memory of birth and the expectation of death always lurk within the human being, making him separate from his fellows and consequently capable of intercourse with them. Naked I came into the world, naked I shall go out of it! And a very good thing too, for it reminds me that I am naked under my shirt, whatever its colour.

Dance of the Sprouting Corn
Morality and the Novel
Adolf

D. H. LAWRENCE
(1885–1930)

D. H. LAWRENCE was the most ardent evangelist among
the English poets and novelists of this century. All
his writing, in whatever form, was an attempt to
reawaken in men the instinctual vitality which modern
ideas and institutions threatened to destroy. The novel
Sons and Lovers (1913) described his own efforts to
break free from the restricting influence of his mother.
In *The Rainbow* (1915) and *Women in Love* (1920),
he dramatized the inadequacies and inhibitions of
mine owners, workers, farmers, aristocrats, bohemians,
and intellectuals, in symbolism drawn from animal
life and myth. *Psychoanalysis and the Unconscious*
(1921) and *Fantasia of the Unconscious* (1922) present
very heterodox versions of modern psychoanalysis.
Studies in Classic American Literature (1923) states
dogmatically the "true" meaning of nineteenth-century
American literature. *Apocalypse* (1931) reinterprets
the Book of Revelation in the light of modern mass
politics. Lawrence explains with great vividness
and originality how and why man has lost living
connection with nature and his own collective
unconsciousness.

Like E. M. Forster, Lawrence traveled widely, but
his purpose was very different. What he felt lacking
emotionally in England he sought in Italy, Ceylon,

Australia, New Mexico, and old Mexico. From this largely fruitless quest came the novels *Kangaroo* (1923) and *The Plumed Serpent* (1926), the marvelous travel books *Sea and Sardinia* (1921), *Mornings in Mexico* (1927), and *Etruscan Places* (1932), and many great poems and short stories.

The mystic, anti-intellectualist longing in Lawrence's descriptions of nature and of primitive ritual is balanced by a capacity for exact observation and by powers of visualization, of sensory evocation, unequaled by any writer of his period.

At first the prose in "Dance of the Sprouting Corn" seems casual, repetitious, even crude. Lawrence wrote rapidly, usually without revision. If he was dissatisfied with a version, he tore it up and began afresh. His writing has some of the quality of action painting. Its shape and rhythm result from the excitement that emerges spontaneously as an experience is lived through in words. Description of a dance makes especially appropriate material. The verbal repetitions recreate the emotional effect of the repetitions in the ritual dance itself, developing steadily greater sureness, greater unity, until they culminate in the eloquent final statement of the theme—or reality—of rebirth.

"Morality and the Novel" at first seems very different. It is an intelligent, challenging, dogmatic assertion of aesthetic principles of wholeness and spontaneity. But here, too, as the argument continues, we notice the development of a special rhythm, the natural speech rhythm of oral exposition when the expositor is completely at home with his material and completely convinced of the importance of what he is saying. "Adolf" is an amusing reminiscence which shows Lawrence's sympathy with animals, especially when he can use them to gibe at human stuffiness.

Dance of the Sprouting Corn

Pale, dry, baked earth, that blows into dust of fine sand. Low hills of baked pale earth, sinking heavily, and speckled sparsely with dark dots of cedar bushes. A river on the plain of drought, just a cleft of dark, reddish-brown water, almost a flood. And over all, the blue, uneasy, alkaline sky.

A pale, uneven, parched world, where a motor-car rocks and lurches and churns in sand. A world pallid with dryness, inhuman with a faint taste of alkali. Like driving in the bed of a great sea that dried up unthinkable ages ago, and now is drier than any other dryness, yet still reminiscent of the bottom of the sea, sandhills sinking, and straight, cracked mesas, like cracks in the dry-mud bottom of the sea.

So, the mud church standing discreetly outside, just outside the pueblo, not to see too much. And on its façade of mud, under the timbered mud-eaves, two speckled horses rampant, painted by the Indians, a red piebald and a black one.

Swish! Over the logs of the ditch-bridge, where brown water is flowing full. There below is the pueblo, dried mud like mud-pie houses, all squatting in a jumble, prepared to crumble into dust and be invisible, dust to dust returning, earth to earth.

That they don't crumble is the mystery. That these little squarish mud-heaps endure for centuries after centuries, while Greek marble tumbles asunder, and cathedrals totter, is the wonder. But then, the naked human hand with a bit of new soft mud is quicker than time, and defies the centuries.

Roughly the low, square, mud-pie houses make a wide street where all is naked earth save a doorway or a window with a pale-blue sash. At the end of the street, turn again into a parallel wide, dry street. And there, in the dry, oblong aridity, there tosses a small forest that is alive: and thud—thud—thud goes the drum, and the

---

deep sound of men singing is like the deep soughing of the wind, in the depths of a wood.

You realise that you had heard the drum from the distance, also the deep, distant roar and boom of the singing, but that you had not heeded, as you don't heed the wind.

It all tosses like young, agile trees in a wind. This is the dance of the sprouting corn, and everybody holds a little, beating branch of green pine. Thud—thud—thud—thud—thud! goes the drum, heavily the men hop and hop and hop, sway, sway, sway, sway go the little branches of green pine. It tosses like a little forest, and the deep sound of men's singing is like the booming and tearing of a wind deep inside a forest. They are dancing the Spring Corn Dance.

This is the Wednesday after Easter, after Christ Risen and the corn germinated. They dance on Monday and on Tuesday. Wednesday is the third and last dance of this green resurrection.

You realise the long line of dancers, and a solid cluster of men singing near the drum. You realise the intermittent black-and-white fantasy of the hopping Koshare, the jesters, the Delight-Makers. You become aware of the ripple of bells on the knee-garters of the dancers, a continual pulsing ripple of little bells; and of the sudden wild, whooping yells from near the drum. Then you become aware of the seed-like shudder of the gourd-rattles, as the dance changes, and the swaying of the tufts of green pine-twigs stuck behind the arms of all the dancing men, in the broad green arm-bands.

Gradually come through to you the black, stable solidity of the dancing women, who poise like solid shadow, one woman behind each rippling, leaping male. The long, silky black hair of the women streaming down their backs, and the equally long, streaming, gleaming hair of the males, loose over broad, naked, orange-brown shoulders.

Then the faces, the impassive, rather fat, golden-brown faces of the women, with eyes cast down, crowned above with the green tableta, like a flat tiara. Something strange and noble about the impassive, barefoot women in the short black cassocks, as they subtly tread the dance, scarcely moving, and yet edging rhythmically along, swaying from each hand the green spray of pine-twig out—out—out—out, to the thud of the drum, immediately behind the leaping fox-skin of the men dancers. And all the emerald-green, painted tabletas, the flat wooden tiaras shaped like a castle gateway, rise steady and noble from the soft, slightly bowed heads of the women held by a band under the chin. All the tabletas down the line, emerald green, almost steady, while the bright black heads of the men leap softly up and down, between.

Bit by bit you take it in. You cannot get a whole impression, save of some sort of wood, tossing, a little forest of trees in motion, with gleaming black hair and gold-ruddy breasts that somehow do not destroy the illusion of forest.

When you look at the women, you forget the men. The bare-armed, bare-legged, barefoot women with streaming hair and lofty green tiaras, impassive, downward-looking faces, twigs swaying out-wards from subtle, rhythmic wrists; women clad in the black, pre-historic short gown fastened over one shoulder, leaving the other shoulder bare, and showing at the arm-place a bit of pink or white undershirt; belted also round the waist with a woven woollen sash, scarlet and green on the hand-woven black cassock. The noble, slightly submissive bending of the tiara-ed head. The subtle measure of the bare, breathing, bird-like feet, that are flat, and seem to cleave to earth softly, and softly lift away. The continuous outward sway-ing of the pine-sprays.

But when you look at the men, you forget the women. The men are naked to the waist, and ruddy-golden, and in the rhythmic hop-ping leap of the dance their breasts shake downwards, as the strong, heavy body comes down, down, down down, in the downward plunge of the dance. The black hair streams loose and living down their backs, the black brows are level, the black eyes look out un-changing from under the silky lashes. They are handsome, and ab-sorbed with a deep rhythmic absorption, which still leaves them awake and aware. Down, down, down they drop, on the heavy, ceaseless leap of the dance, and the great necklaces of shell-cores spring on the naked breasts, the neck-shell flaps up and down, the short white kilt of woven stuff, with the heavy woollen embroidery, green and red and black, opens and shuts slightly to the strong lift-ing of the knees: the heavy whitish cords that hang from the kilt-band at the side sway and coil forever down the side of the right leg, down to the ankle, the bells on the red-woven garters under the knees ripple without end, and the feet, in buckskin boots furred round the ankle with a beautiful band of skunk fur, black with a white tip, come down with a lovely, heavy, soft precision, first one, then the other, dropping always plumb to earth. Slightly bending forward, a black gourd rattle in the right hand, a small green bough in the left, the dancer dances the eternal drooping leap, that brings his life down, down, down, down from the mind, down from the broad, beautiful shaking breast, down to the powerful pivot of the knees, then to the ankles, and plunges deep from the ball of the foot into the earth, towards the earth's red centre, where these men belong, as is signified by the red earth with which they are smeared.

And meanwhile, the shell-cores from the Pacific sway up and down, ceaselessly on their breasts.

Mindless, without effort, under the hot sun, unceasing, yet never perspiring nor even breathing heavily, they dance on and on. Mindless, yet still listening, observing. They hear the deep, surging singing of the bunch of old men, like a great wind soughing. They hear the cries and yells of the man waving his bough by the drum. They catch the word of the song, and at a moment, shudder the black rattles, wheel, and the line breaks, women from men, they thread across to a new formation. And as the men wheel round, their black hair gleams and shakes, and the long fox-skin sways, like a tail. And always, when they form into line again, it is a beautiful long straight line, flexible as life, but straight as rain.

The men round the drum are old, or elderly. They are all in a bunch, and they wear day dress, loose cotton drawers, pink or white cotton shirt, hair tied up behind with the red cords, and banded round the head with a strip of pink rag, or white rag, or blue. There they are, solid like a cluster of bees, their black heads with the pink rag circles all close together, swaying their pine-twigs with rhythmic, wind-swept hands, dancing slightly, mostly on the right foot, ceaselessly, and singing, their black bright eyes absorbed, their dark lips pushed out, while the deep strong sound rushes like wind, and the unknown words form themselves in the dark.

Suddenly the solitary man pounding the drum swings his drum round, and begins to pound on the other end, on a higher note, pang —pang—pang! instead of the previous brumm! brumm! brumm! of the bass note. The watchful man next the drummer yells and waves lightly, dancing on bird-feet. The Koshare make strange, eloquent gestures to the sky.

And again the gleaming bronze-and-dark men dancing in the rows shudder their rattles, break the rhythm, change into a queer, beautiful two-step, the long lines suddenly curl into rings, four rings of dancers, the leaping, gleaming-seeming men between the solid, subtle, submissive blackness of the women who are crowned with emerald-green tiaras, all going subtly round in rings. Then slowly they change again, and form a star. Then again, unmingling, they come back into rows.

And all the while, all the while the naked Koshare are threading about. Of bronze-and-dark men-dancers there are some forty-two, each with a dark, crowned woman attending him like a shadow. The old men, the bunch of singers in shirts and tied-up black hair, are about sixty in number, or sixty-four. The Koshare are about twenty-four.

They are slim and naked, daubed with black and white earth, their hair daubed white and gathered upwards to a great knot on top of the head, whence springs a tuft of corn-husks, dry corn-leaves. Though they wear nothing but a little black square cloth, front and back, at their middle, they do not seem naked, for some are white with black spots, like a leopard, and some have broad black lines or zigzags on their smeared bodies, and all their faces are blackened with triangle or lines till they look like weird masks. Meanwhile their hair, gathered straight up and daubed white and sticking up from the top of the head with corn-husks, completes the fantasy. They are anything but natural. Like blackened ghosts of a dead corn-cob, tufted at the top.

And all the time, running like queer spotted dogs, they weave nakedly, through the unheeding dance, comical, weird, dancing the dance-step naked and fine, prancing through the lines, up and down the lines, and making fine gestures with their flexible hands, calling something down from the sky, calling something up from the earth, and dancing forward all the time. Suddenly as they catch a word from the singers, name of a star, of a wind, a name for the sun, for a cloud, their hands soar up and gather in the air, soar down with a slow motion. And again, as they catch a word that means earth, earth deeps, water within the earth, or red-earth-quickening, the hands flutter softly down, and draw up the water, draw up the earth-quickening, earth to sky, sky to earth, influences above to influences below, to meet in the germ-quick of corn, where life is.

And as they dance, the Koshare watch the dancing men. And if a fox-skin is coming loose at the belt, they fasten it as the man dances, or they stoop and tie another man's shoe. For the dancer must not hesitate to the end.

And then, after some forty minutes, the drum stops. Slowly the dancers file into one line, woman behind man, and move away, threading towards their kiva, with no sound but the tinkle of knee-bells in the silence.

But at the same moment the thud of an unseen drum, from beyond, the soughing of deep song approaching from the unseen. It is the other half, the other half of the tribe coming to continue the dance. They appear round the kiva—one Koshare and one dancer leading the rows, the old men all abreast, singing already in a great strong burst.

So, from ten o'clock in the morning till about four in the afternoon, first one-half then the other. Till at last, as the day wanes, the two halves meet, and the two singings like two great winds surge one past the other, and the thicket of the dance becomes a real forest. It is the close of the third day.

Afterwards, the men and women crowd on the roofs of the two low round towers, the kivas, while the Koshare run round jesting and miming, and taking big offerings from the women, loaves of bread and cakes of blue-maize meal. Women come carrying big baskets of bread and guayava, on two hands, an offering.

And the mystery of germination, not procreation, but *putting forth*, resurrection, life springing within the seed, is accomplished. The sky has its fire, its waters, its stars, its wandering electricity, its winds, its fingers of cold. The earth has its reddened body, its invisible hot heart, its inner waters and many juices and unaccountable stuffs. Between them all, the little seed: and also man, like a seed that is busy and aware. And from the heights and from the depths man, the caller, calls: man, the knower, brings down the influences and brings up the influences, with his knowledge: man, so vulnerable, so subject, and yet even in his vulnerability and subjection, a master, commands the invisible influences and is obeyed. Commands in that song, in that rhythmic energy of dance, in that still-submissive mockery of the Koshare. And he accomplishes his end, as master. He partakes in the springing of the corn, in the rising and budding and earing of the corn. And when he eats his bread at last, he recovers all he once sent forth, and partakes again of the energies he called to the corn, from out of the wide universe.

Morality and the Novel

The business of art is to reveal the relation between man and his circumambient universe, at the living moment. As mankind is always struggling in the toils of old relationships, art is always ahead of the "times", which themselves are always far in the rear of the living moment.

When van Gogh paints sunflowers, he reveals, or achieves, the vivid relation between himself, as man, and the sunflower, as sunflower, at that quick moment of time. His painting does not represent the sunflower itself. We shall never know what the sunflower itself is. And the camera will *visualise* the sunflower far more perfectly than van Gogh can.

The vision on the canvas is a third thing, utterly intangible and inexplicable, the offspring of the sunflower itself and van Gogh himself. The vision on the canvas is for ever incommensurable with the canvas, or the paint, or van Gogh as a human organism, or the sunflower as a botanical organism. You cannot weigh nor measure nor even describe the vision on the canvas. It exists, to tell the truth, only in the much-debated fourth dimension. In dimensional space it has no existence.

It is a revelation of the perfected relation, at a certain moment, between a man and a sunflower. It is neither man-in-the-mirror nor flower-in-the-mirror, neither is it above or below or across anything. It is between everything, in the fourth dimension.

And this perfected relation between man and his circumambient universe is life itself, for mankind. It has the fourth-dimensional quality of eternity and perfection. Yet it is momentaneous.

Man and the sunflower both pass away from the moment, in the process of forming a new relationship. The relation between all things changes from day to day, in a subtle stealth of change. Hence art, which reveals or attains to another perfect relationship, will be for ever new.

MORALITY AND THE NOVEL. From *Phoenix* (Viking Press, 1936) by D. H. Lawrence. All Rights Reserved. Reprinted by permission of The Viking Press, Inc.

At the same time, that which exists in the non-dimensional space of pure relationship is deathless, lifeless, and eternal. That is, it gives us the *feeling* of being beyond life or death. We say an Assyrian lion or an Egyptian hawk's head "lives". What we really mean is that it is beyond life, and therefore beyond death. It gives us that feeling. And there is something inside us which must also be beyond life and beyond death, since that "feeling" which we get from an Assyrian lion or an Egyptian hawk's head is so infinitely precious to us. As the evening star, that spark of pure relation between night and day, has been precious to man since time began.

If we think about it, we find that our life *consists in* this achieving of a pure relationship between ourselves and the living universe about us. This is how I "save my soul" by accomplishing a pure relationship between me and another person, me and other people, me and a nation, me and a race of men, me and the animals, me and the trees or flowers, me and the earth, me and the skies and sun and stars, me and the moon: an infinity of pure relations, big and little, like the stars of the sky: that makes our eternity, for each one of us, me and the timber I am sawing, the lines of force I follow; me and the dough I knead for bread, me and the very motion with which I write, me and the bit of gold I have got. This, if we knew it, is our life and our eternity: the subtle, perfected relation between me and my whole circumambient universe.

And morality is that delicate, for ever trembling and changing *balance* between me and my circumambient universe, which precedes and accompanies a true relatedness.

Now here we see the beauty and the great value of the novel. Philosophy, religion, science, they are all of them busy nailing things down, to get a stable equilibrium. Religion, with its nailed-down One God, who says *Thou shalt, Thou shan't*, and hammers home every time; philosophy, with its fixed ideas; science with its "laws": they, all of them, all the time, want to nail us on to some tree or other.

But the novel, no. The novel is the highest example of subtle interrelatedness that man has discovered. Everything is true in its own time, place, circumstance, and untrue outside of its own place, time, circumstance. If you try to nail anything down, in the novel, either it kills the novel, or the novel gets up and walks away with the nail.

Morality in the novel is the trembling instability of the balance.

When the novelist puts his thumb in the scale, to pull down the balance to his own predilection, that is immorality.

The modern novel tends to become more and more immoral, as the novelist tends to press his thumb heavier and heavier in the pan: either on the side of love, pure love: or on the side of licentious "freedom".

The novel is not, as a rule, immoral because the novelist has any dominant *idea,* or *purpose.* The immorality lies in the novelist's helpless, unconscious predilection. Love is a great emotion. But if you set out to write a novel, and you yourself are in the throes of the great predilection for love, love as the supreme, the only emotion worth living for, then you will write an immoral novel.

Because *no* emotion is supreme, or exclusively worth living for. *All* emotions go to the achieving of a living relationship between a human being and the other human being or creature or thing he becomes purely related to. All emotions, including love and hate, and rage and tenderness, go to the adjusting of the oscillating, unestablished balance between two people who amount to anything. If the novelist puts his thumb in the pan, for love, tenderness, sweetness, peace, then he commits an immoral act: he *prevents* the possibility of a pure relationship, a pure relatedness, the only thing that matters: and he makes inevitable the horrible reaction, when he lets his thumb go, towards hate and brutality, cruelty and destruction.

Life is so made that opposites sway about a trembling centre of balance. The sins of the fathers are visited on the children. If the fathers drag down the balance on the side of love, peace, and production, then in the third or fourth generation the balance will swing back violently to hate, rage, and destruction. We must balance as we go.

And of all the art forms, the novel most of all demands the trembling and oscillating of the balance. The "sweet" novel is more falsified, and therefore more immoral, than the blood-and-thunder novel.

The same with the smart and smudgily cynical novel, which says it doesn't matter what you do, because one thing is as good as another, anyhow, and prostitution is just as much "life" as anything else.

This misses the point entirely. A thing isn't life just because somebody does it. This the artist ought to know perfectly well. The ordinary bank clerk buying himself a new straw hat isn't "life" at all: it is just existence, quite all right, like everyday dinners: but not "life".

By life, we mean something that gleams, that has the fourth-dimensional quality. If the bank clerk feels really piquant about his hat, if he establishes a lively relation with it, and goes out of the shop with the new straw on his head, a changed man, be-aureoled, then that is life.

The same with the prostitute. If a man establishes a living relation to her, if only for one moment, then it is life. But if it *doesn't:* if it is just money and function, then it is not life, but sordidness, and a betrayal of living.

If a novel reveals true and vivid relationships, it is a moral work, no matter what the relationships may consist in. If the novelist *honours* the relationship in itself, it will be a great novel.

But there are so many relationships which are not real. When the man in *Crime and Punishment* murders the old woman for sixpence, although it is *actual* enough, it is never quite real. The balance between the murderer and the old woman is gone entirely; it is only a mess. It is actuality, but it is not "life", in the living sense.

The popular novel, on the other hand, dishes up a *réchauffé* of old relationships: *If Winter Comes.* And old relationships dished up are likewise immoral. Even a magnificent painter like Raphael does nothing more than dress up in gorgeous new dresses relationships which have already been experienced. And this gives a gluttonous kind of pleasure of the mass: a voluptuousness, a wallowing. For centuries, men say of their voluptuously ideal woman: "She is a Raphael Madonna." And women are only just learning to take it as an insult.

A new relation, a new relatedness hurts somewhat in the attaining; and will always hurt. So life will always hurt. Because real voluptuousness lies in re-acting old relationships, and at the best, getting an alcoholic sort of pleasure out of it, slightly depraving.

Each time we strive to a new relation, with anyone or anything, it is bound to hurt somewhat. Because it means the struggle with and the displacing of old connexions, and this is never pleasant. And moreover, between living things at least, an adjustment means also a fight, for each party, inevitably, must "seek its own" in the other, and be denied. When, in the parties, each of them seeks his own, her own, absolutely, then it is a fight to the death. And this is true of the thing called "passion". On the other hand, when, of the two parties, one yields utterly to the other, this is called sacrifice, and it also means death. So the Constant Nymph died of her eighteen months of constancy.

It isn't the nature of nymphs to be constant. She should have been constant in her nymph-hood. And it is unmanly to accept sacrifices. He should have abided by his own manhood.

There is, however, the third thing, which is neither sacrifice nor fight to the death: when each seeks only the true relatedness to the other. Each must be true to himself, herself, his own manhood, her own womanhood, and let the relationship work out of itself. This means courage above all things: and then discipline. Courage to accept the life-thrust from within oneself, and from the other person. Discipline, not to exceed oneself any more than one can help. Courage, when one has exceeded oneself, to accept the fact and not whine about it.

Obviously, to read a really new novel will *always* hurt, to some extent. There will always be resistance. The same with new pictures, new music. You may judge of their reality by the fact that they do arouse a certain resistance, and compel, at length, a certain acquiescence.

The great relationship, for humanity, will always be the relation between man and woman. The relation between man and man, woman and woman, parent and child, will always be subsidiary.

And the relation between man and woman will change for ever, and will for ever be the new central clue to human life. It is the *relation itself* which is the quick and the central clue to life, not the man, nor the woman, nor the children that result from the relationship, as a contingency.

It is no use thinking you can put a stamp on the relation between man and woman, to keep it in the *status quo*. You can't. You might as well try to put a stamp on the rainbow or the rain.

As for the bond of love, better put it off when it galls. It is an absurdity, to say that men and women *must love*. Men and women will be for ever subtly and changingly related to one another; no need to yoke them with any "bond" at all. The only morality is to have man true to his manhood, woman to her womanhood, and let the relationship form of itself, in all honour. For it is, to each, *life itself*.

If we are going to be moral, let us refrain from driving pegs through anything, either through each other or through the third thing, the relationship, which is for ever the ghost of both of us. Every sacrificial crucifixion needs five pegs, four short ones and a long one, each one an abomination. But when you try to nail down the relationship itself, and write over it *Love* instead of *This is the King of the Jews*, then you can go on putting in nails for ever. Even Jesus called it the Holy Ghost, to show you that you can't lay salt on its tail.

The novel is a perfect medium for revealing to us the changing rainbow of our living relationships. The novel can help us to live, as nothing else can: no didactic Scripture, anyhow. If the novelist keeps his thumb out of the pan.

But when the novelist *has* his thumb in the pan, the novel becomes an unparalleled perverter of men and women. To be compared only, perhaps, to that great mischief of sentimental hymns, like "Lead, Kindly Light," which have helped to rot the marrow in the bones of the present generation.

Adolf

When we were children our father often worked on the nightshift. Once it was spring-time, and he used to arrive home, black and tired, just as we were downstairs in our nightdresses. Then night met morning face to face, and the contact was not always happy. Perhaps it was painful to my father to see us gaily entering upon the day into which he dragged himself soiled and weary. He didn't like going to bed in the spring morning sunshine.

But sometimes he was happy, because of his long walk through the dewy fields in the first daybreak. He loved the open morning, the crystal and the space, after a night down pit. He watched every bird, every stir in the trembling grass, answered the whinnying of the pewits and tweeted to the wrens. If he could, he also would have whinnied and tweeted and whistled in a native language that was not human. He liked non-human things best.

One sunny morning we were all sitting at table when we heard his heavy slurring walk up the entry. We became uneasy. His was al-

ADOLPH. From *Phoenix* (Viking Press, 1936) by D. H. Lawrence. All Rights Reserved. Reprinted by permission of The Viking Press, Inc.

ways a disturbing presence, trammelling. He passed the window darkly, and we heard him go into the scullery and put down his tin bottle. But directly he came into the kitchen. We felt at once that he had something to communicate. No one spoke. We watched his black face for a second.

"Give me a drink," he said.

My mother hastily poured out his tea. He went to pour it out into his saucer. But instead of drinking he suddenly put something on the table among the teacups. A tiny brown rabbit! A small rabbit, a mere morsel, sitting against the bread as still as if it were a made thing.

"A rabbit! A young one! Who gave it you, father?"

But he laughed enigmatically, with a sliding motion of his yellow-grey eyes, and went to take off his coat. We pounced on the rabbit.

"Is it alive? Can you feel its heart beat?"

My father came back and sat down heavily in his armchair. He dragged his saucer to him, and blew his tea, pushing out his red lips under his black moustache.

"Where did you get it, father?"

"I picked it up," he said, wiping his naked forearm over his mouth and beard.

"Where?"

"It is a wild one!" came my mother's quick voice.

"Yes, it is."

"Then why did you bring it?" cried my mother.

"Oh, we wanted it," came our cry.

"Yes, I've no doubt you did——" retorted my mother. But she was drowned in our clamour of questions.

On the field path my father had found a dead mother rabbit and three dead little ones—this one alive, but unmoving.

"But what had killed them, daddy?"

"I couldn't say, my child. I s'd think she'd aten something."

"Why did you bring it!" again my mother's voice of condemnation. "You know what it will be."

My father made no answer, but we were loud in protest.

"He must bring it. It's not big enough to live by itself. It would die," we shouted.

"Yes, and it will die now. And then there'll be *another* outcry."

My mother set her face against the tragedy of dead pets. Our hearts sank.

"It won't die, father, will it? Why will it? It won't."

"I s'd think not," said my father.

"You know well enough it will. Haven't we had it all before!" said my mother.

"They dunna always pine," replied my father testily.

But my mother reminded him of other little wild animals he had brought, which had sulked and refused to live, and brought storms of tears and trouble in our house of lunatics.

Trouble fell on us. The little rabbit sat on our lap, unmoving, its eye wide and dark. We brought it milk, warm milk, and held it to its nose. It sat as still as if it was far away, retreated down some deep burrow, hidden, oblivious. We wetted its mouth and whiskers with drops of milk. It gave no sign, did not even shake off the wet white drops. Somebody began to shed a few secret tears.

"What did I say?" cried my mother. "Take it and put it down in the field."

Her command was in vain. We were driven to get dressed for school. There sat the rabbit. It was like a tiny obscure cloud. Watching it, the emotions died out of our breast. Useless to love it, to yearn over it. Its little feelings were all ambushed. They must be circumvented. Love and affection were a trespass upon it. A little wild thing, it became more mute and asphyxiated still in its own arrest, when we approached with love. We must not love it. We must circumvent it, for its own existence.

So I passed the order to my sister and my mother. The rabbit was not to be spoken to, nor even looked at. Wrapping it in a piece of flannel I put it in an obscure corner of the cold parlour, and put a saucer of milk before its nose. My mother was forbidden to enter the parlour whilst we were at school.

"As if I should take any notice of your nonsense," she cried affronted. Yet I doubt if she ventured into the parlour.

At midday, after school, creeping into the front room, there we saw the rabbit still and unmoving in the piece of flannel. Strange grey-brown neutralization of life, still living! It was a sore problem to us.

"Why won't it drink its milk, mother?" we whispered. Our father was asleep.

"It prefers to sulk its life away, silly little thing." A profound problem. Prefers to sulk its life away! We put young dandelion leaves to its nose. The sphinx was not more oblivious. Yet its eye was bright.

At tea-time, however, it had hopped a few inches, out of its flannel, and there it sat again, uncovered, a little solid cloud of muteness, brown, with unmoving whiskers. Only its side palpitated slightly with life.

Darkness came; my father set off to work. The rabbit was still unmoving. Dumb despair was coming over the sisters, a threat of tears before bedtime. Clouds of my mother's anger gathered as she muttered against my father's wantonness.

Once more the rabbit was wrapped in the old pit-singlet. But now it was carried into the scullery and put under the copper fireplace, that it might imagine itself inside a burrow. The saucers were placed about, four or five, here and there on the floor, so that if the little creature *should* chance to hop abroad, it could not fail to come upon some food. After this my mother was allowed to take from the scullery what she wanted and then she was forbidden to open the door.

When morning came and it was light, I went downstairs. Opening the scullery door, I heard a slight scuffle. Then I saw dabbles of milk all over the floor and tiny rabbit-droppings in the saucers. And there the miscreant, the tips of his ears showing behind a pair of boots. I peeped at him. He sat bright-eyed and askance, twitching his nose and looking at me while not looking at me.

He was alive—very much alive. But still we were afraid to trespass much on his confidence.

"Father!" My father was arrested at the door. "Father, the rabbit's alive."

"Back your life it is," said my father.

"Mind how you go in."

By evening, however, the little creature was tame, quite tame. He was christened Adolf. We were enchanted by him. We couldn't really love him, because he was wild and loveless to the end. But he was an unmixed delight.

We decided he was too small to live in a hutch—he must live at large in the house. My mother protested, but in vain. He was so tiny. So we had him upstairs, and he dropped his tiny pills on the bed and we were enchanted.

Adolf made himself instantly at home. He had the run of the

house, and was perfectly happy, with his tunnels and his holes behind the furniture.

We loved him to take meals with us. He would sit on the table humping his back, sipping his milk, shaking his whiskers and his tender ears, hopping off and hobbling back to his saucer, with an air of supreme unconcern. Suddenly he was alert. He hobbled a few tiny paces, and reared himself up inquisitively at the sugar basin. He fluttered his tiny fore-paws, and then reached and laid them on the edge of the basin, whilst he craned his thin neck and peeped in. He trembled his whiskers at the sugar, then did his best to lift down a lump.

"*Do* you think I will have it! Animals in the sugar pot!" cried my mother, with a rap of her hand on the table.

Which so delighted the electric Adolf that he flung his hindquarters and knocked over a cup.

"It's your own fault, mother. If you left him alone——"

He continued to take tea with us. He rather liked warm tea. And he loved sugar. Having nibbled a lump, he would turn to the butter. There he was shooed off by our parent. He soon learned to treat her shooing with indifference. Still, she hated him to put his nose in the food. And he loved to do it. And one day between them they overturned the cream-jug. Adolf deluged his little chest, bounced back in terror, was seized by his little ears by my mother and bounced down on the hearth-rug. There he shivered in momentary discomfort, and suddenly set off in a wild flight to the parlour.

This last was his happy hunting ground. He had cultivated the bad habit of pensively nibbling certain bits of cloth in the hearth-rug. When chased from this pasture he would retreat under the sofa. There he would twinkle in Buddhist meditation until suddenly, no one knew why, he would go off like an alarm clock. With a sudden bumping scuffle he would whirl out of the room, going through the doorway with his little ears flying. Then we would hear his thunderbolt hurtling in the parlour, but before we could follow, the wild streak of Adolf would flash past us, on an electric wind that swept him round the scullery and carried him back, a little mad thing, flying possessed like a ball round the parlour. After which ebullition he would sit in a corner composed and distant, twitching his whiskers in abstract meditation. And it was in vain we questioned him about his outbursts. He just went off like a gun, and was as calm after it as a gun that smokes placidly.

Alas, he grew up rapidly. It was almost impossible to keep him from the outer door.

One day, as we were playing by the stile, I saw his brown shadow loiter across the road and pass into the field that faced the houses. Instantly a cry of "Adolf!"—a cry he knew full well. And instantly a wind swept him away down the sloping meadow, his tail twinkling and zigzagging through the grass. After him we pelted. It was a strange sight to see him, ears back, his little loins so powerful, flinging the world behind him. We ran ourselves out of breath, but could not catch him. Then somebody headed him off, and he sat with sudden unconcern, twitching his nose under a bunch of nettles.

His wanderings cost him a shock. One Sunday morning my father had just been quarrelling with a pedlar, and we were hearing the aftermath indoors, when there came a sudden unearthly scream from the yard. We flew out. There sat Adolf cowering under a bench, whilst a great black and white cat glowered intently at him, a few yards away. Sight not to be forgotten. Adolf rolling back his eyes and parting his strange muzzle in another scream, the cat stretching forward in a slow elongation.

Ha, how we hated that cat! How we pursued him over the chapel wall and across the neighbours' gardens.

Adolf was still only half grown.

"Cats!" said my mother. "Hideous detestable animals, why do people harbour them?"

But Adolf was becoming too much for her. He dropped too many pills. And suddenly to hear him clumping downstairs when she was alone in the house was startling. And to keep him from the door was impossible. Cats prowled outside. It was worse than having a child to look after.

Yet we would not have him shut up. He became more lusty, more callous than ever. He was a strong kicker, and many a scratch on face and arms did we owe to him. But he brought his own doom on himself. The lace curtains in the parlour—my mother was rather proud of them—fell on the floor very full. One of Adolf's joys was to scuffle wildly through them as though through some foamy undergrowth. He had already torn rents in them.

One day he entangled himself altogether. He kicked, he whirled round in a mad nebulous inferno. He screamed—and brought down the curtain-rod with a smash, right on the best beloved pelargonium, just as my mother rushed in. She extricated him, but she never for-

gave him. And he never forgave either. A heartless wildness had
come over him.

Even we understood that he must go. It was decided, after a long
deliberation, that my father should carry him back to the wild-
woods. Once again he was stowed into the great pocket of the pit-
jacket.

"Best pop him i' th' pot," said my father, who enjoyed raising the
wind of indignation.

And so, next day, our father said that Adolf, set down on the edge
of the coppice, had hopped away with utmost indifference, neither
elated nor moved. We heard it and believed. But many, many were
the heartsearchings. How would the other rabbits receive him?
Would they smell his tameness, his humanized degradation, and
rend him? My mother pooh-poohed the extravagant idea.

However, he was gone, and we were rather relieved. My father
kept an eye open for him. He declared that several times passing the
coppice in the early morning, he had seen Adolf peeping through
the nettle-stalks. He had called him, in an odd, high-voiced, cajoling
fashion. But Adolf had not responded. Wildness gains so soon upon
its creatures. And they become so contemptuous then of our tame
presence. So it seemed to me. I myself would go to the edge of the
coppice, and call softly. I myself would imagine bright eyes between the nettle-stalks, flash of a white, scornful tail past the
bracken. That insolent white tail, as Adolf turned his flank on us! It
reminded me always of a certain rude gesture, and a certain unprint-
able phrase, which may not even be suggested.

But when naturalists discuss the meaning of the rabbit's white tail,
that rude gesture and still ruder phrase always come to my mind.
Naturalists say that the rabbit shows his white tail in order to guide
his young safely after him, as a nursemaid's flying strings are the
signal to her toddling charges to follow on. How nice and naïve!
I only know that my Adolf wasn't naïve. He used to whisk his flank
at me, push his white feather in my eye, and say *"Merde!"* It's a
rude word—but one which Adolf was always semaphoring at me,
flag-wagging it with all the derision of his narrow haunches.

That's a rabbit all over—insolence, and the white flag of spiteful
derision. Yes, and he keeps his flag flying to the bitter end, sporting,
insolent little devil that he is. See him running for his life. Oh, how
his soul is fanned to an ecstasy of fright, a fugitive whirlwind of
panic. Gone mad, he throws the world behind him, with astonishing

hind legs. He puts back his head and lays his ears on his sides and rolls the white of his eyes in sheer ecstatic agony of speed. He knows the awful approach behind him; bullet or stoat. He knows! He knows, his eyes are turned back almost into his head. It is agony. But it is also ecstasy. Ecstasy! See the insolent white flag bobbing. He whirls on the magic wind of terror. All his pent-up soul rushes into agonized electric emotion of fear. He flings himself on, like a falling star swooping into extinction. White heat of the agony of fear. And at the same time, bob! bob! bob! goes the white tail, *merde! merde! merde!* it says to the pursuer. The rabbit can't help it. In his utmost extremity he still flings the insult at the pursuer. He is the inconquerable fugitive, the indomitable meek. No wonder the stoat becomes vindictive.

And if he escapes, this precious rabbit! Don't you see him sitting there, in his earthly nook, a little ball of silence and rabbit triumph? Don't you see the glint on his black eye? Don't you see, in his very immobility, how the whole world is *merde* to him? No conceit like the conceit of the meek. And if the avenging angel in the shape of the ghostly ferret steals down on him, there comes a shriek of terror out of that little hump of self-satisfaction sitting motionless in a corner. Falls the fugitive. But even fallen, his white feather floats. Even in death it seems to say: "I am the meek, I am the righteous, I am the rabbit. All you rest, you are evil doers, and you shall be *bien emmerdés!*"

ALDOUS HUXLEY
(1894–1963)

ALDOUS HUXLEY began his career with a series of light-hearted comic novels: *Crome Yellow* (1921), *Antic Hay* (1923), and *Those Barren Leaves* (1925). His first major work, *Point Counter Point* (1928), a satire on artists and intellectuals, displays the immense erudition to be expected of the grandson of the biologist Thomas Henry Huxley, the grandnephew of the critic-poet Matthew Arnold, and the brother of the anthropologist Julian Huxley. *Point Counter Point* plays off artistic, political, religious, moral, and scientific ideas against each other until no certainties are left. Its most positive character is based on D. H. Lawrence, whose *Letters* (1932) Huxley later edited. Huxley used his knowledge ever more frighteningly in the anti-utopia, *Brave New World* (1932). Published long before George Orwell's *Nineteen Eighty-Four*, it imagined with great ingenuity what might happen to humanity if a totalitarian regime set psychologists and biologists to work transforming everything.

Like Forster and Lawrence, Huxley was an inveterate traveler. His accounts of his experiences, *Along the Road* (1925), *Jesting Pilate* (1926), and *Beyond the Mexique Bay* (1934), show a novelist's feeling for situation, a philosopher's hunger for truth. After 1938 Huxley lived mostly in California. Like Lawrence he sought a new basis for life, but his search, perhaps

because of three years of near-blindness in youth,
took the more introspective direction of pacificism,
nonattachment, yoga, and other forms of psychosomatic experimentation, sometimes with the aid of
hallucinogenic drugs. The stages of this quest are
recorded in *Ends and Means* (1937), *The Art of Seeing*
(1942), *The Perennial Philosophy* (1945), and *Doors
of Perception* (1954). Huxley was incredibly productive, publishing fifty separate volumes of poems,
plays, essays, novels, and short stories.

"Copan" makes a delightful combination of geography,
archaeology, and personal adventure. The commentary
plays freely with allusions and ideas, expressed in
such formulations as "Numinosity is in inverse ratio
to luminosity" or "Before the door of the cabin
stood half a dozen ruffians looking like the Second
Murderers of Elizabethan drama . . . ."

In "Calcutta," on the other hand, the writing is
simple. In clear, expert, almost conversational
expository prose, Huxley gives an exact account of
Bose's dramatic experiments and their implications.
What seem to be metaphors, when he describes
vegetable and mineral life in terms ordinarily employed for animals and human beings, are meant
literally. The differences among the natural kingdoms
are of degree more than of kind: man should feel
deep communion with all creation.

"The Double Crisis" is the longest essay in this
collection, but justifiably so, since it covers a large
range of world problems in their basic interrelationship. Though Huxley's essay was published
in 1949, before China broke with Russia and began
going its own imperialist way in Asia and Africa,
the situation is now even more urgent, and Huxley's
proposals for meeting the "Martian invasion" are
even more relevant. This masterly essay is at once
farseeing and hardheaded. "Non-attached" to anything except human welfare, Huxley was free to be

thoroughly scientific and realistic in his diagnosis.

Copan

To the ordinary Englishman, how little the aeroplane still means! He lives as though the Wright brothers had never existed, moves and almost uninterruptedly has his being in a pre-Blériot world. When he travels it is always by train or car, over a network of rails and metalled roads. The plane is for him superfluous, an unjustifiable and slightly inconvenient luxury.

Profoundly different is the state of things in Central America. The plane has come and, quite suddenly, transformed an immemorial mode of life. There are hardly any railways in the Five Republics, and the roads are mostly mere bridle paths. Over the greater part of the country one travelled, until very recently, as the Britons travelled before the coming of Julius Caesar. Maudslay possessed but one advantage over the Old Empire Mayas, whose ruined cities he explored—he had a horse to ride and pack mules to carry his luggage. In Maya times his beasts of burden and his mounts would all have been bipeds. (Even under the Spanish dispensation some people preferred the human beast of burden. Stephens thus describes the mode of travel favoured by distinguished ecclesiastics in 1840. "He set off on the back of an Indian in a *silla,* or chair with a high back and top to protect him from the sun. Three other Indians followed as relay carriers, and a noble mule for his relief if he should become tired of the chair. The Indian was bent almost double, but the *canonigo* was in high spirits, smoking his cigar, and waving his hand till he was out of sight.")

Mules, porters, mud-tracks through the jungle. . . . Then, from one day to another, people were hurtling through space in tri-motored air liners. A long, laborious epoch of history was suppressed, and without transition men passed from a neolithic technique of transportation to the most advanced twentieth-century practice.

Measured on the map, distances in Guatemala are absurdly small. Measured by human effort and fatigue, they are enormous. Ten years ago, for example, it took you anything from twelve days to three weeks to travel from Guatemala City to Flores in the northeastern corner of the country. You had to go down to Puerto Barrios on the Atlantic, take ship to Belize in British Honduras, paddle up the Belize river in a canoe for four, six, seven, even ten days—it depended on the amount of water that was coming down —and finish up with four or five days on a mule, riding through the jungles of Peten. Now you step into your plane at half-past ten and step out again at Flores in comfortable time for lunch.

By rail and what, by courtesy, we will call road, Copan is about four days from Guatemala City; by aeroplane, about an hour and a quarter. Unfortunately there is, for political reasons, no regular service between the two points. Copan is a village just across the frontier in Honduras. In the Five Republics the local air services are all strictly national; and Pan-American Airways, which are responsible for the long-distance international services, call only at the more important towns. The gulf dividing Copan from Guatemala City seemed therefore impassable. But an enterprising acquaintance, Dr. Harris, the American biologist, had discovered that the journey could be made. True, no pilot from Guatemala had ever landed at Copan; but it was reported to possess a flying field. A plane could be chartered from the local company, and, armed with the necessary visas, vaccination certificates, flying permits, and what not, we could drop down into the neighbouring republic, look at the ruins and be back, if necessary, in time for lunch.

The theory of nationalism is one of the grandest labour-creating devices ever invented. To fly from point A to another point B a hundred miles away is, physically, a simple matter. But if the two points lie on opposite sides of a national boundary, how difficult the business at once becomes! The theory of nationalism makes it necessary for each State to create huge, expensive organizations, whose function is, first to prevent and then, at a price and under absurd conditions, to allow, the performance of such physically simple acts as flying from A to B. And how much time and trouble must be wasted by innocent individuals in circumventing the obstacles which are so carefully put in their way! A mitigation of nationalism would save the world millions of hours of wasted time and an incalculable expense of spirit, physical energy, and money.

To the rare travellers who visit these far-away countries of Central America, the resident diplomats show a boundless kindness. Mr.

Lee, the British consul and acting minister, wrote me a letter of recommendation so glowing that, when at last I found the Honduranean minister, he gave me all the necessary visas at once and—what I thought uncommonly handsome—free of all charge. I was grateful; and would have been a good deal more grateful if I had not had to make about four blisteringly hot journeys to his legation before finding him at home. Meanwhile, the officials of the aeroplane company had not been idle. Through the Guatemalan Foreign Office they had approached the Honduranean Foreign Office at Tegucicalpa; the Honduranean Foreign Office had communicated with the Honduranean Ministry of War; and after due consideration it had been decided that the safety of the State would not be seriously imperilled by our visit to Copan. Telegraphically, we were authorized to go. The arranging of our little trip had consumed about six man-hours of valuable official time and about as many of (I flatter myself) still more valuable unofficial time.

The sun had just risen when we took off from the airport of Guatemala. We climbed into a flawless sky, but down in the valleys the mist lay impenetrably white. There was sunlight only above four thousand feet. The mountains were islands, and here and there the cone of a volcano rose like Stromboli from the level expanse of that shining sea. We flew on. The valley of the Motagua wound away beneath us, a fjord between mountains. In the interminable and meaningless wilderness of peaks and *barrancas* and volcanoes, it was the only clear and significant geographical feature.

Time passed; we were approaching our destination. Somewhere below us lay the ruins. But where? Which of these narrow rivers of white mist was the valley of Copan? There was nothing for it but to go down and look. Three times our pilot swooped down out of the blue—two thousand feet of steep and sickening descent—down into the fog between the closely crowding mountains. But there was nothing to be seen and after the third attempt he turned back. Twenty minutes away, in Guatemalan territory, was the landing field of Esquipulas—a plateau lying high enough to be free of mist. We landed. In an hour the sun would have scoured the lowest valleys and we could start again.

Esquipulas is the home of a Black Christ of such extraordinary sanctity that every January pilgrims came, and still come, from enormous distances to worship at his shrine. It seems that in the eyes of all the aboriginal American races, black is traditionally a sacred colour; so that what draws the worshippers from as far as Mexico in the north, and as Ecuador in the south, and even as Peru, is probably less the saintliness of the historic Jesus than the magical sootiness of his image. With us, black is symbolical only of grief. The black uniform of our clergy is a kind of chronic mourning that is meant, I suppose, to testify to the essential *sérieux* of their official character. It has no magical significance; for on all ceremonial occasions it is discarded for a praying costume of white linen, or of cloth of gold, or of gaudily embroidered silk. But though black is not with us a sacred colour, black images of exceeding holiness are none the less fairly common in Europe. The reason, I suspect, is that such statues have a somewhat sinister appearance. (The Holy Face of Lucca is very nearly black and, with its glittering jewelled eyes, is one of the strangest and most terrifying sculptures ever made.) In Otto's terminology, black idols are intrinsically more "numinous" than white. Numinosity is in inverse ratio to luminosity.

Most regrettably we were unable to see the image. The village of Esquipulas stands some two or three miles from the landing field, and to have walked there and back would have taken too long. Our pilot was anxious to reach Copan as soon as possible, so that we could get away again before the afternoon wind sprang up and made starting difficult. We had to content ourselves with a distant bird's-eye view of the huge white church, towering high above the almost invisible huts of its attendant village, a landmark in the wilderness.

An hour passed; the sun was already high in the sky and very hot. We climbed into the plane again and started off. The mist had all melted away and, in a little while, there below us, clear as a map, was the valley of Copan, narrow between hills, with its village, its fields of dust-coloured stubble, its winding river, its tree-grown Maya acropolis rising sheer in a great wall from the water's edge. We came spiralling down. A small bald patch not far from the ruins was evidently the landing field. A herd of cows scattered in hysterical agitation as we descended. Avoiding these animals as best he could, and steering clear of the larger of the numerous rocks with which the air-port was strewn, our pilot, who was fortunately a most skilful flyer, brought us safely to land. We stepped out and, accompanied by some small boys who offered to be our guides, walked off to see the ruins. Our pilot took the road to the village; the local authorities would be anxious, he knew, to prove their importance by lengthily examining his paper. If he did not indulge them, they might turn savage.

Time and its allies in destruction, vegetation and weather, play curious tricks on the works of man. A city left to their tender mercies is generally destroyed as an architectural and engineering whole, but spared in its decorative details. The great masses of masonry are buried and disrupted; tend, if the vegetation is strong, to vanish altogether, dissolved into their component parts; the statues, the reliefs, the fragile pots and jewels survive, very often, almost intact. At Copan, for example, a few mounds covered with trees, a wall here and there, some rubbish heaps of tumbled stones, are all that remain of the great complex of pyramids, of platforms, of walls and terraces, of sunken courtyards, which once occupied the site. Buried and, under the mould, disintegrated by the thrusting roots of the tropical vegetation, a sacred city of pure geometrical forms once stood here. Its sharp-edged planes of hewn stone, of white or painted stucco, shone smooth, like the surfaces of a crystal, in the perpendicular sunlight. But toiling up and down through the scrub, among the fallen stones, I found it all but impossible to reconstruct in my imagination the Mayas' huge embodiment of a mathematician's dream. I had read the writings of the archaeologists and knew what sort of monument had been raised at Copan. But these almost shapeless barrows supplied my fancy with no visible foundations on which to rebuild the Mayas' prodigious works. Only the plastic decorations with which their mountains of solid geometry had been incidentally trimmed were still there, in unequivocal existence, before my eyes. The whole had gone; but a few of the ornamental parts remained. In a maize field at the foot of the wooded mounds —the mounds were the acropolis and principal pyramid, the maize field had been a great forum—stood a group of magnificent stelae, floridly carved in such deep relief that the stone was sometimes pierced from side to side. Using neolithic tools, the Maya sculptors had displayed an almost contemptuous mastery of their material; they had treated their twenty-foot monoliths as a Chinese craftsman might treat a piece of ivory. One is left bewildered by the spectacle of so much technical accomplishment displayed by people having such inadequate technical resources.

The stelae are not Copan's only monuments. Scrambling among the ruins, we found an astonishing wealth of carved stones. Here was a great cubic skull-symbol, its eye sockets glaring, its teeth deep in the grass and weeds; here, at the base of a broken wall, a dado of small death's heads in low relief; here the famous altar with its frieze of fantastically adorned astronomer-priests in scientific conference; here, carved in the round, a giant's head, grotesquely open-mouthed; here a pair of statues, broken, but still violently alive. The finest specimens of sculpture in the round are no longer at Copan. I saw nothing to compare in grace, in plastic subtlety, in emotional expressiveness, with the torso of the maize god at the British Museum, or with the lovely head of the same god now at Boston. These two pieces and certain others in American museums, are stylistically so close to one another that one is tempted to think of them as the works of a single sculptor of outstanding ability. Of the other carvings in the round still at Copan, none exhibited the kind of approach to reality exemplified in these extraordinary statues. The beauty of most Mayan sculpture is felt by us to be profoundly, incommensurably alien. But with this particular group of carvings from Copan one feels suddenly at home, on familiar emotional ground. The mind of the man, or men, who made them seems to have been gifted with the same kind of sensibilities as ours. Now that these works have been taken away, the European visitor to Copan enjoys no such comforting conviction. He looks at the astonishing works around him, but looks at them from across a gulf; they exist in a universe of sentiment and discourse that it not his universe. Those colossal skulls, for example—they have nothing to do with the macabre of our later middle ages, or the florid horrors of baroque sepulchral art.

> The flesh is bruckle, the fiend is slee
> *Timor mortis conturbat me.*

So wailed our ancestors. But I doubt if the Mayas were saying anything of the kind. In these great cubic monoliths, adorned (with what an unerring sense of the significantly decorative effect!) with eye sockets, nose hole, teeth, one finds no trace of our European lament for transience, our personal terror of extinction and decay. One finds—what? Confronted by the extraordinary objects themselves one can only ask the question, not hope to answer it. It is impossible to know by personal experience what the people who made such things felt and thought. Each life has its own private logic, and the logics of all the lives of people living at a given time, under a given cultural dispensation, have, at some point, a certain resemblance among themselves. The Mayas' life-logic was not the same as ours. The admiration with which we look at their works of art is tinged with a speculative incomprehension. What were they really up to? *Quien sabe?*

We came back from the ruins to find the entire population of Copan clustered round our aeroplane, like a crowd of Breughel's peasants round a crucifixion. Some were standing; some with the air of people who had come out for a long day's pleasure, were sitting in the shade of our wings and picnicking. They were a villainous set of men and women; not indian, but low *ladino*, squalid and dirty as only a poverty-stricken half-caste, with a touch of white blood and a sense of superiority to all the traditional decencies of the inferior race, can be dirty and squalid. Before the door of the cabin stood half a dozen ruffians, looking like the Second Murderers of Elizabethan drama, and armed with genuinely antique muskets of the American Civil War pattern. The local police. We were criminals.

It was, of course, our old friend nationalism at work once more, creating labour and discomfort with a punctual fidelity—creating also, it must be admitted, a great deal of gratuitous amusement for the inhabitants of Copan. Our license to land at Copan had been issued by the central authorities in Tegucicalpa. But the central authorities had omitted to tell the local authorities of what they had done; so that when we dropped out of the blue, our arrival must have had, for the *alcalde* of Copan and the General in charge of the department, to whom he had immediately telegraphed, all the exciting characteristics of an unprovoked outrage, a wanton piece of Guatemalan sabre-rattling. "*Aux armes, citoyens! formez vos bataillons!*" The Copanese had responded manfully to the call. Those Second Murderers, with their muskets, offensively refusing to allow us to sit in the cabin of our own aeroplane, were animated, I am sure, by the purest patriotism.

The hours passed, it grew hotter and hotter. Our pilot had telegraphed to Guatemala; but goodness only knew how long it would take for the telegram to produce any effect in Copan. I began to wonder uncomfortably whether we should have to spend the night behind the bars of the local prison, in intimate companionship with the local bugs, ticks, lice and fleas. But happily, half-way through the afternoon, deliverance came. On the receipt of our telegram the aeroplane company had appealed to the Guatemalan Foreign Office, and the Guatemalan Foreign Office, justly indignant, had tele-

graphed to Tegucicalpa, and Tegucicalpa had telegraphed to the
General at the head of the department, and the General had
telegraphed to the *alcalde* of Copan. There was nothing for it but to
let us go. With obvious reluctance the Copanese prepared to obey
the orders from above. But, as though he could not bear to be deprived so soon of the exquisite pleasure of being offensive to his bet-
ters, the young man in charge of the Second Murderers insisted on
having yet one more look at our passports, and kept them a quarter
of an hour, while he copied down all the names he could find, from
our own to those of the Foreign Secretaries by whom the passports
had been issued. Then, when there was really nothing more he
could do to annoy us, he called away his men. We climbed into the
cabin; the pilot started up his engines and, after having paid—the
final outrage—fifteen dollars for the use of the landing-field, and a
dollar a head for the privilege of photographing the ruins, shut the
door behind us and prepared to take off.

A field not more than three hundred yards long, strewn with
rocks and infested with cows; at the end of it a river, with mountains rising steeply from the further bank. . . . Ignorance is bliss;
but even I could see that this was not the ideal taking-off place for
an aeroplane. Our pilot, however, knew his job superbly well, and
the plane was powerfully engined. We left the stony field in an
astonishingly short space of time, wheeled round to avoid the rising
ground beyond the river, and, corkscrewing up, were soon in the
open sky a thousand feet above the mountains. Little more than an
hour later we were in Guatemala.

"They told me," said the pilot, as we walked towards the waiting
car, "that this was the second ship that ever landed at Copan." He
paused to light a cigarette. "Well so far as I'm concerned," he went
on, "it's the last."

Calcutta

The experimenter's is a curious and special talent. Armed with a tea canister and some wire, with silk, a little sealing-wax, and two or three jam-pots, Faraday marched forth against the mysterious powers of electricity. He returned in triumph with their captured secrets. It was just a question of suitably juxtaposing the wax, the glass jars, the wires. The mysterious powers couldn't help surrendering. So simple—if you happened to be Faraday.

And if you happened to be Sir J. C. Bose, it would be so simple, with a little clockwork, some needles and filaments, to devise machines that would make visible the growth of plants, the pulse of their vegetable "hearts," the twitching of their nerves, the processes of their digestion. It would be so simple—though it cost even Bose long years of labour to perfect his instruments.

At the Bose Institute in Calcutta, the great experimenter himself was our guide. Through all an afternoon we followed him from marvel to marvel. Ardently and with an enthusiasm, with a copiousness of ideas that were almost too much for his powers of expression and left him impatiently stammering with the effort to elucidate methods, appraise results, unfold implications, he expounded them one by one. We watched the growth of a plant being traced out automatically by a needle on a sheet of smoked glass; we saw its sudden, shuddering reaction to an electric shock. We watched a plant feeding; in the process it was exhaling minute quantities of oxygen. Each time the accumulation of exhaled oxygen reached a certain amount, a little bell, like the bell that warns you when you are nearly at the end of your line of typewriting, automatically rang. When the sun shone on the plant, the bell rang often and regularly. Shaded, the plant stopped feeding; the bell rang only at long intervals, or not at all. A drop of stimulant added to the water in which the plant was standing set the bell wildly tinkling, as though some record-breaking typist were at the machine. Near it—for the plant

CALCUTTA. From *The Jesting Pilate* by Aldous Huxley. Copyright, 1926, 1954 by Aldous Huxley. Reprinted by permission of Harper & Row, Publishers, and Chatto and Windus Ltd., London.

was feeding out of doors—stood a large tree. Sir J. C. Bose told us that it had been brought to the garden from a distance. Transplanting is generally fatal to a full-grown tree; it dies of shock. So would most men if their arms and legs were amputated without an anaesthetic. Bose administered chloroform. The operation was completely successful. Waking, the anaesthetised tree immediately took root in its new place and flourished.

But an overdose of chloroform is as fatal to a plant as to a man. In one of the laboratories we were shown the instrument which records the beating of a plant's "heart." By a system of levers, similar in principle to that with which the self-recording barometer has made us familiar, but enormously more delicate and sensitive, the minute pulsations, which occur in the layer of tissue immediately beneath the outer rind of the stem, are magnified—literally millions of times—and recorded automatically in a dotted graph on a moving sheet of smoked glass. Bose's instruments have made visible things that it has been hitherto impossible to see, even with the aid of the most powerful microscope. The normal vegetable "heart beat," as we saw it recording itself, point by point on the moving plate, is very slow. It must take the best part of a minute for the pulsating tissue to pass from maximum contraction to maximum expansion. But a grain of caffeine or of camphor affects the plant's "heart" in exactly the same way as it affects the heart of an animal. The stimulant was added to the plant's water, and almost immediately the undulations of the graph lengthened out under our eyes and, at the same time, came closer together: the pulse of the plant's "heart" had become more violent and more rapid. After the pick-me-up we administered poison. A mortal dose of chloroform was dropped into the water. The graph became the record of a death agony. As the poison paralysed the "heart," the ups and downs of the graph flattened out into a horizontal line half-way between the extremes of undulation. But so long as any life remained in the plant, this medial line did not run level, but was jagged with sharp irregular ups and downs that represented in a visible symbol the spasms of a murdered creature desperately struggling for life. After a little while, there were no more ups and downs. The line of dots was quite straight. The plant was dead.

The spectacle of a dying animal affects us painfully; we can see its struggles and, sympathetically, feel something of its pain. The unseen agony of a plant leaves us indifferent. To a being with eyes a million times more sensitive than ours, the struggles of a dying plant would be visible and therefore distressing. Bose's instrument endows us with this more than microscopical acuteness of vision. The poisoned flower manifestly writhes before us. The last moments are so distressingly like those of a man, that we are shocked by the newly revealed spectacle of them into a hitherto unfelt sympathy.

Sensitive souls, whom a visit to the slaughterhouse has converted to vegetarianism, will be well advised, if they do not want to have their menu still further reduced, to keep clear of the Bose Institute. After watching the murder of a plant, they will probably want to confine themselves to a strictly mineral diet. But the new self-denial would be as vain as the old. The ostrich, the sword-swallower, the glass-eating fakir are as cannibalistic as the frequenters of chop-houses, take life as fatally as do the vegetarians. Bose's earlier researches on metals—researches which show that metals respond to stimuli, are subject to fatigue and react to poisons very much as living vegetable and animal organisms do—have deprived the conscientious practitioners of *ahimsa* of their last hope. They must be cannibals, for the simple reason that everything, including the "inanimate" is alive.

This last assertion may seem—such is the strength of inveterate prejudice—absurd and impossible. But a little thought is enough to show that it is, on the contrary, an assertion of what is *a priori* probable. Life exists. Even the most strict and puritanical physicists are compelled, albeit grudgingly, to admit the horridly disquieting fact. Life exists, manifestly, in a small part of the world we know. How did it get there? There are two possible answers. Either it was, at a given moment, suddenly introduced into a hitherto completely inanimate world from outside and by a kind of miracle. Or else it was, with consciousness, inherent in the ultimate particles of matter and, from being latent, gradually extrinsicated itself in ever increasingly complicated and perfect forms. In the present state of knowledge—or ignorance, put it how you will—the second answer seems the more likely to be correct. If it is correct, then one might expect that inanimate matter would behave in the same way as does matter which is admittedly animate. Bose has shown that it does. It reacts to stimuli, it suffers fatigue, it can be killed. There is nothing in this that should astonish us. If the conclusion shocks our sense of fitness, that is only due to the fact that we have, through generations, made a habit of regarding matter, as something dead; a lump that can be moved, and whose only real attribute is extension. Motion and extension are easily measured and can be subjected to mathematical treatment. Life, especially in its higher, conscious forms, cannot. To deny life to matter and concentrate only on its measurable qualities was a sound policy that paid by results. No wonder we made a habit of it. Habits easily become a part of us. We take them for granted, as we take for granted our hands and feet, the sun, falling downstairs instead of up, colours and sounds. To break a physical habit may be as painful as an amputation; to question the usefulness of an old-established habit of thought is felt to be an outrage, an indecency, a horrible sacrilege.

Crains dans le mur aveugle un regard qui t'épie.

It was all very well from a poet. One could smile indulgently at a pleasing and childish fancy. But when it came to laboratory experiments and graphs, things, it was felt, were getting more serious. It was time to make a protest.

Personally, I make no protest. Being only a literary man and not one of those physicists, whose professional interest it is to keep matter in its place, with only such attributes as render it amenable to mathematics, I am delighted. I love matter, I find it miraculous, and it pleases me when a serious man, like Bose, comes along and gives it a new certificate of merit.

In the philosophy books matter is generally spoken of slightingly, as something lumpish and crude. To the sublety of their own minds, on the other hand, the metaphysicians can never pay a sufficiently glowing tribute. But in reality—if I may be pardoned the philosophically gross expression—it is to matter, not mind, that the attributes of subtlety, fineness, complexity belong. Our mental picture of the world and its component parts is a crude symbolical affair, having about as much relation to the original as a New Guinea idol to the human body. It is precisely because it is so crude and simple that the thought-picture is valuable to us. Reality—again I apologise—is infinitely too complicated for our understanding. We must simplify. But having simplified, we ought not to say that those Papuan images of the world, which are our philosophical and religious systems, our scientific hypotheses, are subtle; they are not. They are crude, compared with the original, and it is, precisely, their crudeness which gives them value, for us. Year by year, our world-picture becomes increasingly complicated. More details are noted in the original and are incorporated, symbolically into the image. If the mind of man develops and grows more subtle, that is due to the fact that each succeeding generation is brought up with a progressively more complete and elaborate thought-picture of the world and all its details. We think, we also feel, more subtly and multifariously than did the ancients. To our posterity, a thousand years from now, our subtleties will seem, no doubt, most barbarously crude. Perfection will be attained when mind has completely understood matter and is therefore as delicate, as complex, as variously rich as it. That is to say, perfection will never be attained.

The Double Crisis

The human race is passing through a time of crisis, and that crisis exists, so to speak, on two levels—an upper level of political and economic crisis and a lower level of demographic and ecological crisis. That which is discussed at international conferences and in the newspapers is the upper-level crisis—the crisis whose immediate causes are the economic breakdown due to the War and the struggle for power between national groups possessing, or about to possess, the means of mass extermination. Of the low-level crisis, the crisis in population and world resources, hardly anything is heard in the press, on the radio or at the more important international conferences. The Big Threes and Big Fours do not deign to discuss it; leaving the matter to the subaltern and unauthoritative delegations to conferences on health or food, they devote their entire energies to the question of who shall bully whom. And yet the low-level crisis is at least as serious as the crisis in the political and economic field. Moreover, the problems on the upper level cannot be solved without reference to the problems that are shaping up in the cosmic and biological basement. If it is ignored, the low-level crisis is bound to exacerbate the crisis on the political and economic levels. At the same time, a concentration of attention and energy on power politics and power economics will make a solution of the low-level problems not merely difficult, but impossible. In what follows I propose to discuss certain aspects of the low-level crisis and to point out how the obscure happenings in the basement have affected and are likely to go on affecting the lives of private individuals, the policies of statesmen and the conduct of nations.

It has been fashionable for some time past to talk about "poverty in the midst of plenty." The phrase implies that the planet possesses abundant resources to feed, clothe, house and provide amenities for its existing population and for any immediately foreseeable increase in that population, and that the present miseries of the human race are due entirely to faulty methods of production and, above all, of distribution. Given currency reform, socialism, communism, unrestricted capitalism, distributism, or whatever the favourite remedy may be, humanity, like the prince and princess in the fairy stories, will be able to live happily ever after. Want and hunger will be transformed into abundance and the whole earth will become one vast Land of Cockayne.

Such are the miracles to be achieved by political and economic planning. But when we pass from these high-level considerations to a study of what is going on at the biological and ecological levels, our optimism is apt to seem a little premature, to say the least of it. Instead of poverty in the midst of plenty, we find that there is poverty in the midst of poverty. World resources are inadequate to world population. At the present time, our planet supports a little less than two and a quarter billions of human beings, and the area of food-producing land is in the neighbourhood of four billion acres. It has beeen calculated that two and a half acres of land are needed to provide a human being with a diet which nutritionists would regard as adequate. Thus, even if all the available productive land were good—and much of it is of very poor quality—the existing population could not be assured of an adequate diet. Actually, in order to guarantee an adequate diet for all of the world's two and a quarter billions of men, women and children, the present food supply would have to be doubled. But this cannot be accomplished overnight. In the words of Dr. Thomas Parran, the U.S. Surgeon-General, "the greatest possible increase in food production will not for decades be enough to meet the minimum adequate diet." And meanwhile world population is rising. It is rising at the rate of about two hundred millions every ten years. This means that, by the time the food supply is doubled, there will be, not two and a quarter billions of mouths to feed, but well over three billions. In spite of all that may have been achieved in the interval, malnutrition will be just as serious and just as widespread as it is today.

Moreover, while population goes up, the fertility of the soil declines. "Modern man," writes Ward Shepard in his *Food or Famine*, "has perfected two devices, either of which is capable of annihilating civilization. One is atomic war, the other is world soil-erosion. Of the two, soil-erosion is the more insidiously destructive. War disrupts or destroys the social environment, which is the matrix of civilization. Soil-erosion destroys the natural environment, which is its foundation." In other words, atomic war may destroy one particular civilization—the Western-Industrial variety, for example; soil-erosion, if unchecked, can put an end to the possibility of any civilization whatsoever.

The catalogue of man's crimes against his environment is long and dismal. In Africa the Sahara is advancing; the habitable mountains and table-lands of the equator are rapidly eroding; the southern plains are over-grazed dust-bowls. Central America is in process of becoming a desert. Much of South America is being washed down unterraced mountain slopes into the sea. With every drought vast areas of Australia and the United States turn into wind-blown dust. In Asia it is the same lamentable story. As population goes up, the fertility of the ever more ruthlessly exploited land goes down. There is spreading and deepening human poverty in the midst of spreading and deepening natural poverty.

In certain respects the European picture is decidedly brighter. Thanks to sound agricultural practices and a climate that is without extremes, the farmers of Western Europe can produce good crops, and go on producing them, without, in the process, ruining their land. But however good these crops may be, they are insufficient to provide the present population of the territory with its minimum food requirements. In relation to the local resources Western Europe is overpopulated. In England, Belgium, Holland, Italy and the Western zones of Germany, there is less than one acre of food-producing land for each inhabitant. And even where the density of population is lower than in these countries the productive land available is still insufficient to provide a full diet (to say nothing of the necessary timber and fibres) for the local inhabitants. According to some competent authorities, even Russia is overpopulated. The short northern summer severely limits the size of the crops, and the long northern winter severely limits the number of animals that can be kept alive on stored-up fodder. And over the greater part of the country precipitation is low and irregular. In these circumstances even a low population density may be excessive. And the birth-rate is high, modern hygiene and medicine are prolonging the expectation of life, numbers are rapidly increasing. But meanwhile new methods of arctic agriculture have been devised; ambitious schemes of irrigating Central Asia are under study; and, having abolished the laws of 'reactionary genetics,' Lysenko promises a revolution in plant-breeding. Will the tundras, the deserts and ideologically correct science be able to feed and clothe the two hundred and fifty millions who will inhabit the U.S.S.R. in 1970? Let us hope so; for the alternative is a crusade for more *lebensraum*.

Since 1800 Western Europe has more than trebled its population. This huge increase was made possible by elementary hygiene and the exploitation of the virgin territories of the New World. Today hygiene and medicine are keeping more Europeans alive; but the New World has a large and rapidly increasing population of its own and, after more than a century of abuse, not a little of its soil has lost or is in process of losing its fertility. In a good year there is still a very large exportable surplus. But not every season is a good season. During the lean years of the thirties, the United States had very little to sell abroad. And here we may remark that the success of the Marshall Plan and, indeed, the whole outcome of the Cold War depend, among other things, on the weather. Consider, for example, this by no means impossible contingency: for three years in succession Russia has bumper wheat crops, while the harvests of Western Europe, North America, Australia and the Argentine are ruined by drought or excessive rains. In these circumstances, who will control the world—the people with the atomic bombs, or the people with bread? Obviously, the people with bread.

Up to the present, Western Eruope has contrived to pay for the food imported from the New World by selling manufactured articles and technical services. With the industrialization of the New World, these are becoming less and less acceptable. Europe will find it increasingly difficult to pay for supplies which, as the population pressure on the New World's eroded soils increases, are bound to diminish. And this will happen at a time when Asia, newly industrialized and overcrowded as never before, will be desperately competing for whatever surpluses of food the New World can still make available to the Old.

Food is a renewable commodity. If the soil is not abused, this year's harvest will be succeeded next year by another harvest no less bountiful. But the vein of tin or copper, which was the source of this year's supply of ore, will not be renewed in years to come. When the lode has been worked out, the miner must move on to another deposit of the mineral. And if he can find no other deposits? *Après moi le déluge.* Industrialism is the systematic exploitation of wasting assets. In all too many cases, the thing we call progress is merely an acceleration in the rate of that exploitation. Such prosperity as we have known up to the present is the consequence of rapidly spending the planet's irreplaceable capital.

How long can the accelerating dissipation of capital go on? How soon will the wasting assets of the world be exhausted? We do not know. All that is certain is that the supplies of many hitherto essential commodites are limited and that, in many places, very rich and easily available deposits of those commodities have been, or are in process of being, worked out. And this is happening at a time when a rising population with steadily improving methods of production is calling for ever increasing quantities of consumer goods—in other words, is making ever heavier demands on the limited reserves of our planetary capital.

Up to this point, I have dealt with world population as a single undifferentiated whole. The problem thus posed is that of increasing pressure upon diminishing resources. But this basic problem of our time is deepened and complicated by the fact that rates of increase are not uniform throughout the world's population. Differential birth-rates as between the various peoples of the earth, and as between classes within a people, are rapidly engendering a host of new problems.

In Western Europe and North America, the over-all birth-rate has sharply declined in the course of the last fifty or sixty years. Because of the lowered death-rate and the relatively large numbers of persons within the reproductive age-groups, this decline in the birth-rate has not yet manifested itself in a net decline of population. But the onset of such a decline is close at hand. For example, by 1970 the population of France and Great Britain will have declined by about four millions apiece, and the number of persons over sixty-five will be approximately equal to the number of those under fifteen. Similar declines are due, at a slightly later date, in the other countries of Western Europe and in the New World (except South America). Meanwhile, in spite of much higher death-rates, the population of Eastern Europe and of Asia is destined to go on increasing. By the end of the present century, Asia alone will have a population of about two billions. And in 1970, when Western Europe will have some nine million fewer inhabitants than it possesses today, Russia will have gained upwards of fifty millions.

Within any nation whose birth-rate is declining, there is a tendency for the decline to be most rapid among the most accomplished and gifted members of the population, least rapid among those whose hereditary and educational endowment is the lowest. The higher the Intelligence Quotient and the level of education, the smaller the family; and vice versa. The future population of Western Europe and North America will be constituted, in the main, by the descendants of the least intelligent persons now living in those areas. Among the lower animals, biological degeneration, involving the heritable qualities of whole populations, is a slow and gradual process. But human beings differ from other animals in possessing self-consciousness and a measure of free-will, and in being the inhabitants of a man-made universe within the greater natural order. Reacting to what goes on in this man-made universe, they use their free-will to modify their basic patterns of animal behaviour. And when the nature of the human universe is such as to discourage the more sensitive, intelligent and prudent individuals from reproducing their kind, the deterioration of entire societies comes about with an almost explosive rapidity. Thus an eminent English authority, Sir Cyril Burt, foresees that by the end of the present century, there will be, in Great Britain, half as many children of scholarship ability as there are at present, and twice as many defectives; while the average intelligence of the population as a whole will have declined by five IQ points. And the case of Britain is not unique. Throughout Western Europe, and, a little later, in North America, the decline in numbers is destined to be accompanied by a rapid deterioration in the quality of the population.

We have now to consider the ways in which these untoward biological happenings have affected, or are likely in the future to affect, our behaviour on the levels of domestic and international politics. The nature of the low-level crisis is such that it must necessarily take a very long time to remove its underlying causes. The best we can do is to palliate the more dangerous symptoms and to draw up plans for a genuinely etiological treatment.

Differential birth-rates within any national community lead, as we have seen, to a qualitative deterioration of the population as a whole. The effects of such a deterioration have not yet made themselves felt, and it is hard to foresee in detail what they will be. We must be content merely to pose a question. Is it possible for democratic institutions to flourish in a community in which the incidence of outstanding ability is falling, while that of mental defect is rising? Fifty years from now our grandchildren will know the answer. In the interval it will be necessary to develop new types of training designed to get the best out of worsening human material and to find means for inducing the congenitally gifted to reproduce their kind.

Where the birth-rate of an entire nation declines sharply, while that of its neighbours remains high, we must expect, in the world as it is now constituted, a more or less serious threat to peace. Regardless of what faiths may currently be professed, the real and effective religion of twentieth-century man is nationalistic idolatry. Nominally we may be Christians or Buddhists or Hindus or Moslems or Jews; but in actual fact we worship, not one God, but fifty or sixty godlets, each of whom is, by definition, the enemy, actual or potential, of all the rest. In ever country where there is no established church, the only religion taught in the public schools is some local variant of Shintoism—a saluting of flags, a cult of the State and, very often, of the men who control its machinery, a glorification of the national prowess, as set forth in the official history books. Entities which are the accidental and transient products of history are treated as though they were divine, as though they embodied principles of eternal and universal validity. From childhood the citizen is taught that his highest duty is to work for the greater glory of the local idol. But since this glory is expressed mainly in terms of political and military power, it follows that no individual can do his nationalistic duty without inflicting harm on some at least of his fellow men. In the context of nationalistic idolatry, any shift in the balance of power constitutes a temptation to wage war, aggressive on the part of those nations which are becoming stronger, defensive or preventive on the part of those whose situation is changing for the worse. Such a shift will take place wherever the birth-rates of two equally industrialized nations change in such a way that one has an increasing and predominantly youthful population, while the other has a population that is growing smaller, older and perhaps also less intelligent.

Populations increase and decrease relatively not only to one another, but also to natural resources. In most parts of the world, as we have seen, the relation between population and resources is already unfavourable and will probably become even more unfavourable in the future. This growing poverty in the midst of growing poverty constitutes a permanent menace to peace. And not only to peace, but also to democratic institutions and personal liberty. For overpopulation is not compatible with freedom. An unfavourable relationship between numbers and resources tends to make the earning of a living almost intolerably difficult. Labour is more abundant than goods, and the individual is compelled to work long hours for little pay. No surplus of accumulated purchasing power stands between him and the tyrannies of unfriendly nature or of the equally unfriendly wielders of political and economic power. Democracy is, among other things, the ability to say No to the boss. But a man cannot say No to the boss, unless he is sure of being able to eat when the boss's favour has been withdrawn. And he cannot be certain of his next meal unless he owns the means of producing enough wealth for his family to live on, or has been able to accumulate a surplus out of past wages, or has a chance of moving away to virgin territories, where he can make a fresh start. In an overcrowded country, very few people own enough to make them financially independent; very few are in a position to accumulate purchasing power; and there is no free land. Moreover, in any country where population presses hard upon natural resources, the general economic situation is apt to be so precarious that government control of capital and labour, production and consumption, becomes inevitable. It is no accident that the twentieth century should be the century of highly centralized governments and totalitarian dictatorships; it had to be so for the simple reason that the twentieth century is the century of planetary overcrowding. It is childish to imagine that we can "plant democratic institutions" in India, or China, or "teach the Germans to take their place among the democratic nations of the world." So long as the relationship between population and natural resources remains as hopelessly unfavourable as it now is throughout Asia and in the greater part of Europe, above all in defeated Germany, it will be for all practical purposes impossible for democratic institutions to take root and develop. Wherever Malthus's nightmare has come true, political institutions tend inevitably towards totalitarianism. In Western Europe, where the tradition of democracy is still strong, the new totalitarianism will be for some time benevolent and humane. It remains to be seen how long it will be before their almost absolute power corrupts the politicians who wield it.

In the political field, the greatest enemy to liberty is war. That is why, from time immemorial, all tyrants have been so fond of war, or at least of the preparation for war. Universal military conscription puts every individual at the mercy of the central government. An aggressive foreign policy evokes reactions in kind, and these reactions are then used as an excuse for more militarism and a further curtailment of civil and personal liberties. Dictators can always consolidate their tyranny by an appeal to patriotism. Meanwhile, the danger of war is made a pretext for a policy, not of reducing, but actually increasing the birth-rate—a policy which was vigorously pursued by Hitler and Mussolini and is being even more vigorously pursued today by the rulers of Soviet Russia. More babies mean more cannon fodder, more colonists for conquered territories, and also more misery, more need for centralized 'planning' and more power for the political bosses, less liberty for the masses. Overcrowding and militarism are the guarantees of dictatorship.

In our days war on any considerable scale can be waged only by a highly industrialized nation. There can be no successful aggression without the copious and complicated armaments which are the modern means of aggression. Lacking these means, the people of an overpopulated country are confronted with only two alternatives. They can either stop breeding, and so reduce the population. Or else they can go on breeding until famine, disease, political unrest and civil war combine to raise the death-rate to the point where a decreased population can re-establish a favourable relationship with natural resources. But some overpopulated countries are also industrialized; and for these there is a third alternative: to enslave or exterminate their neighbours, and so acquire more land, food, raw materials and markets.

It should be added that, though they cannot themselves wage large-scale war, industrially weak nations can provoke and assist in the waging of war by industrially powerful nations. An unfavourable relationship between numbers and resources is experienced, by the less fortunate citizens of an overpopulated nation, as chronic hunger, low wages, long hours, lack of freedom and opportunity. The resulting discontent is apt to be expressed in political unrest and revolt against constituted authority. At the present time all political unrest, whatever its cause, tends to be rationalized in terms of Communist theory and organized in terms of Communist power politics. But at this moment of history Communism is, among other things, the instrument of Russian nationalism, and Russia is an industrialized country, capable of waging large-scale war and committed in advance to a permanent crusade against the West.

Let us consider a concrete example. Throughout Asia a misery, whose basic cause is the unfavourable relation between numbers and resources, finds its expression in political unrest. Canalized by professional Communists, this unrest may be expected to result in the setting up of governments which will do everything in their power to aid Russia and to thwart the plans of the Western Powers. Merely by withholding essential raw materials, a communist Asia could delay or even completely prevent European recovery. The West would then find itself confronted by the alternatives of surrender or preventive war. Thus we see that the overpopulation even of industrially feeble nations may constitute a grave threat to world peace.

In the world as we know it nation A will collaborate wholeheartedly with nation B only when both are menaced by C. During a war that is being waged to preserve their national sovereignty, a group of allies will consent to sacrifice a part of that sovereignty for the sake of victory. But as soon as victory has been achieved, the allied nations return to their normal condition of more or less hostile symbiosis, ready, however, to collaborate again, either with the same or with some other partners, against the same or another enemy.

On the international level, union here is always the product of disunion somewhere else; there is no unrestricted mutual aid except against a third party. Hence the old despairing jest to the effect that those who desire peace on earth should pray for an invasion from Mars. But, fortunately in one respect, unfortunately in another, we do not have to wait for an attack across interplanetary space. Man is his own Martian, at war against himself. Overbreeding and extractive agriculture are his weapons and, though he may not know it, his war aims are the ravaging of his planet, the destruction of his civilization and the degradation of his species.

That the nations have not yet united against this common enemy within their own ranks is due partly to the distracting influence of nationalistic idolatry, partly to ignorance, and partly to men's habit of thinking about the problem in wholly inappropriate terms. Time, energy and money that could be better spent are everywhere devoted to power politics and preparations for war. And meanwhile, throughout the more fortunate regions of the earth, most persons are still unaware of the fact that the general condition of mankind is one of poverty in the midst of growing poverty; and in the less fortunate regions, where the harsh facts are inescapable, there is a tendency to believe that the remedy for such poverty is a violent and radical change of government. The inhabitants of countries, in which there is an unfavourable relationship between numbers and resources, can easily be persuaded that the causes of their misery are political and that, as soon as their present rulers are replaced by others trained in Moscow, all will be well. But one-party government is no cure for overpopulation, and the collectivization of agriculture will not increase the area of productive land.

It has been fashionable for a long time past to maintain that the reformer's primary concern is with questions of ownership and distribution. And, in effect, distribution is often inefficient and unfair, and there can be no moral or utilitarian justification for that outright and irresponsible ownership of land which permits a man to withhold or destroy at his pleasure the natural resources upon which the life of a whole society depends.

We need a new system of money that will deliver us from servitude to the banks and permit people to buy what they are able to produce; and we need a new system of ownership that will check the tendency towards monopoly in land and make it impossible for individuals to lay waste the planetary resources which belong to all mankind. But changes in social and economic organization are not enough, of themselves, to solve our problem. Production is inadequate to present population, and population, over large areas, is rapidly rising. A change in the laws governing the ownership of land will not change its quantity or quality. The equitable distribution of too little may satisfy men's desire for justice; it will not stay their hunger. In a world where population is growing at the rate of about fifty-six thousand a day, and where erosion is daily ruining an equal or perhaps greater number of productive acres, our primary concern must be with reducing numbers and producing more food with less damage to the soil.

Sooner or later mankind will be forced by the pressure of circumstances to take concerted action against its own destructive and suicidal tendencies. The longer such action is postponed, the worse it will be for all concerned. To delay is to risk the spread and intensification of misery, to invite revolution, war and tyranny. But if we start at once to resolve the low-level crisis, there is at least a chance that we may escape the most disastrous consequences of nationalistic idolatry and power politics.

The history of the League of Nations and of the United Nations Organization proves conclusively that, on the basis of nationalistic idolatry and power politics, there cannot possibly be co-operation between all the world's sovereign states; there can only be co-operation of one group against another group. Overpopulation and erosion constitute a Martian invasion of the planet. Against this invasion the alliance can be world-wide and the fight can be waged without war. This is the first reason why the low-level crisis should take its place at the top of the agenda of every international conference.

Here is another reason. There is nobody who does not wish to have enough to eat. In the face of this universal agreement any government which, for merely political or ideological reasons, refuses to join the crusade against the Martian in our midst is likely to become exceedingly unpopular.

A third good reason is to be found in the fact that this crusade is mainly a technological affair. Differences of opinion over technoglogical problems rarely result in bloodshed; differences of opinion over political and ideological problems have been the cause of uncounted murders, feuds, wars and revolutions. Here violence is in direct proportion to ignorance. About technological problems we either know enough already, or if we do not, we know how to set about acquiring the necessary knowledge. But where politics and ideologies are concerned the case is very different. For example, nobody knows enough to be able to decide whether a certain theory of history is true or false or meaningless. And nobody knows enough to be able to say which among all the possible alternatives is the form of government best suited to human societies. In regard to the theory of history it seems very unlikely that the necessary knowledge will ever be accumulated. And in regard to any given form of government, knowledge can come only with the passage of time. Future events in the material universe can, to some extent, be foreseen; but our ability to predict psychological events is practically non-existent. How will our children and grandchildren react to forms of organizations which, to ourselves, seem the last word in beneficent efficiency? Will they like what we like, or will they detest it? Will an arrangement which works well enough for us work equally well for them? We do not and we cannot know. That is why we must never take the practical application of a principle as seriously as the principle which is being applied. Thus, we may take very seriously the principle that the State exists in order to make possible the development of individuals as free and responsible persons. But we must not take too seriously any particular plan for applying that principle in political and economic practice. The mere passage of time may demonstrate the unsoundness of any particular application of first principles. To treat political expedients as though they were sacred and inviolable is to commit an idolatry that can only result in totalitarian coercion. Thus, in our ignorance, we do not know whether the Webbs were right in advocating centralized planning as the best means to the desired end, or whether Belloc was right in warning us against the evils of the Servile State. Time alone will show; and when it begins to show, we must be ready, in the name of our principles, to modify the policy which, in our ignorance, we once regarded as the most effective application of those principles. Unfortunately there are very many persons to whom the admission of ignorance is intolerable. Laying claim to certainty in spheres where certainty is impossible, to infallibility concerning matters where even a Pope admits that he can err, they rationalize faith, passion and self-interest into a simulacrum of knowledge. Hence the wars, the revolutions, the tyrannies, the wholesale enslavement of political heretics. A pseudo-knowledge compounded of faith, passion and self-interest cannot convince doubters or the exponents of another system of pseudo-knowledge, except by force. Real knowledge is based upon observation and experiment; and those who possess such knowledge are always able to appeal to facts and the tested rules of scientific procedure. In the technological sphere there can be unforced agreement and persuasion without resort to threats or open violence. We should therefore give approval to any international project which may distract the attention of the world's rulers from the insoluble and war-provoking problems of power politics in order to focus it upon problems which, being technological, admit of some solution and do not necessarily commit all those concerned to fratricide and self-destruction. And in the case of a project which cannot be delayed except at grave risk to the entire human species, our approval should be whole-hearted and enthusiastic.

That the Russians have been 'winning the peace' is due, at least in part, to the fact that they profess and teach, as absolutely true, a clear-cut philosophy of man and nature. This philosophy permits them to predict the future and to affirm (with a confidence which, though unjustified and baseless, is none the less deeply impressive) that, if a certain kind of political and economic revolution is made, general well-being will inevitably follow. In the West we neither impose, nor have we voluntarily accepted, any coherent conception of the world; we lay no claims to understand History from the inside; we do not profess to know in advance what is going to happen fifty or a hundred years from now; and when we are called upon to frame world policies, we find it easier, because of our lack of a philosophy, to be *against* the Russians than to be *for* anything which the great masses of suffering humanity are likely to find either plausible or attractive. The Western refusal to assert an infallibility or to impose an orthodoxy is something of which we need not be ashamed. Less creditable, however, is the fact that we have failed to develop a generally acceptable philosophy for ourselves and for those whom we would like to draw to our side; and still more discreditable is our failure to formulate any policy sensible and beneficent enough to seem more attractive than the policies of Communism. The nearest approach to such a positive policy was the Marshall Plan. But the Marshall Plan has now (1949) been overlaid by military alliance, and military alliances seem attractive only to those immediately involved and (in view of the past history of military alliances) not wildly attractive even to them.

The positive, realistic and universally attractive policy of which the Western Powers are so desperately in need can easily be found. It is a policy aimed at palliating the effects and removing the causes of that low-level crisis through which the entire human species is passing. If the Russians are willing to co-operate in the framing and carrying out of this policy, so much the better. If they refuse and the Cold War is to persist, this policy can be made into a powerful diplomatic and propagandist weapon in the hands of the democracies. Its adoption will not, of course, guarantee peace in our time; but it may perhaps decrease the probabilities of war in the immediate and, still more, in the remoter future. Let us consider in detail the lines along which our policy should be framed.

The world's economic and political crisis has its origin, at least in part, in the underlying demographical crisis. In most countries the relationship between numbers and resources is unfavourable. Nature has her own methods for re-establishing a favourable balance; but, applied to human beings living under twentieth-century conditions, such methods involve not merely intense and widespread misery, but also the gravest threat to civilization. Stated in its most general terms, the problem is to reconcile biological facts with human values.

Our first task is to create a general awareness of the danger. At every opportunity we must insist upon the fact that man is his own Martian, that the invasion of the planet is already under way, and that fresh cohorts are constantly arriving to swell the ranks simultaneously of the enemy and of his victims. At the same time we have to proclaim no less insistently that the miseries resulting from this Martian invasion cannot be removed by any revolution, however radical. Overpopulation and erosion do their destructive work on a plane which is not that of politics. A concerted attempt to cope with events on the demographical and agricultural plane may indirectly exercise a salutary effect upon international politics. But an attempt to impose one kind of political system upon all the peoples of the earth will do nothing whatever to resolve the low-level crisis, but on the contrary will prevent men from doing anything about it and thereby increase the sum and intensity of preventable misery. The low-level crisis can be resolved in only two ways—by controlling world population and by increasing food production, while restoring and preserving the earth's fertility.

Man cannot live by bread alone; but still less can he live exclusively by idealism. To talk about the Rights of Man and the Four Freedoms in connection, for example, with India is merely a cruel joke. In a country where two-thirds of the people succumb to the consequences of malnutrition before they reach the age of thirty, but where, none the less, the population increases by fifty millions every decade, most men possess neither rights nor any kind of freedom. The 'giant misery of the world' is only aggravated by mass violence and cannot be mitigated by inspirational twaddle. Misery will yield only to an intelligent attack upon the causes of misery.

It is, of course, a great deal easier to talk about a world population policy than it is to get such a policy accepted by the various national governments; and it will be easier to get the policy accepted than to get it implemented. Moreover, even if it should, by some miracle, come to be accepted and implemented immediately, the beneficent results could not, in the nature of things, be apparent for several generations. Let us elaborate a little on this depressing theme.

So long as idolatrous nationalism remains the effective religion of mankind, and so long as it is taken for granted that war is right, proper and inevitable, no government of a country with a high birth-rate will pledge itself to the reduction of that rate; and no government of a country with a low birth-rate will forgo in advance the privilege of trying to increase that rate with a view to increasing the size of its armed forces.

Assuming now, for the sake of argument, that, in spite of nationalism and militarism, a world population policy should be agreed upon, how easy would it be to get that policy implemented? The answer is that, in the countries where its immediate implementation would be most desirable, it would be exceedingly difficult, indeed almost impossible, to do so. For a variety of reasons, material and psychological, birth-control cannot be practised by persons whose standard of living falls below a level which, for the great majority of Asiatics and even of Eastern Europeans, is unattainably high. To obtain any conscious or deliberate reduction of the high birth-rates prevailing in the East would be a task requiring many years of education and technological advance.

Finally, even if a substantial cut in the present high birth-rates of the world were to be agreed upon and successfully implemented tomorrow, the number of persons in the reproductive age-groups is at present so large that, despite the reduced birth-rate, over-all population would continue to increase until at least the end of the present century. In the most favourable circumstances we can reasonably imagine, world population is bound to rise to at least three billions before it starts to decline. This means that, whatever happens, the next half-century will be a time of the gravest political and economic danger. If a world population policy should be agreed upon and implemented in the near future, this danger may be expected to grow less acute after about the year 2000. If no such policy is adopted, the crisis is likely, unless something startlingly good or something startlingly bad should happen in the interval, to persist for many years thereafter. So far as we can now judge, the human situation is likely to be more than ordinarily difficult and precarious for at least two generations, and perhaps for much longer. The sooner we can get a reasonable population policy adopted and implemented, the shorter will be the period of special danger through which, it would seem, mankind must inevitably pass.

Here a brief parenthesis is in order. In this matter of population we are on the horns of a dilemma. For what is good for us in one way, is bad in another; and what is bad in one way, in another is good. Biologically and historically speaking, the large family is more normal than the small. A woman who has borne five or six children is 'nearer to nature' than one who has artificially restricted the number to one or two. In countries where the birth-rate is sharply declining, there has been, during the last forty years, a marked increase in the incidence of neurosis and even of insanity. In part this increase is attributable to the industrialization and urbanization with which, in modern times, a falling birth-rate has always been associated; in part, to the fact that birth-control has created patterns of sexual and familial life which are in some way profoundly unsatisfactory to adults and children alike. Wherever biologically normal behaviour has been sacrificed to modern civilization, we tend to become maladjusted and unbalanced. But wherever biologically normal behaviour patterns have not been sacrificed to modern civilization, we find ourselves growing hungrier, less free and in acuter danger of being involved in war and revolution. On which of these two horns shall we choose to be impaled? To my mind, the first is the lesser evil. Overpopulation, with its accompaniments of extractive agriculture, tyranny and mass murder, can cause irreparable disasters. Of the bad psychological consequences of birth-control some perhaps may yield to appropriate medication, others may be prevented, by appropriate social arrangements, from ever arising. Departure from biologically normal behaviour is always dangerous; but the dangers involved in birth-control are not so great as those which arise when individuals retain their natural breeding habits in a world where hygiene, insecticides, antibiotics and false teeth have radically changed their natural dying habits. If we interfere with the forces that bring death, we must also interfere with those that bring life. Otherwise we shall have overpopulation, an unfavourable relationship between man and his environment, wholesale destruction of planetary resources, hunger, revolution, war and wholesale extermination. Given sewage systems, aureomycin and plastic dentures, contraception becomes a necessity and the adoption of a world population policy a matter of the most urgent importance. Unfortunately, as we have seen, a world population policy cannot be expected to show results for many years to come. But while we are waiting for it to take effect we can set to work immediately on the task of checking erosion, preserving the fertility of the soil and increasing the production of food.

At the present time most nations are quite incapable of undertaking this task single-handed. They live from hand to mouth; and the mouth is for ever growing larger, the hand, as it desperately tries to extract more food from a limited area of exhausted soil, becomes increasingly destructive. For these nations there is no margin of time, or land, or resources. Everything, and more than everything, that their territory can produce has to be used up now. Future fertility must be sacrificed to prevent hunger. In a country where population presses heavily upon resources self-preservation results in self-destruction.

If the Western Powers had a positive instead of a mainly negative international policy, they would come forward with a plan to check this rake's progress towards human and planetary bankruptcy. Or rather they would come forward with several plans. First, a plan to repair the damage already done to the earth's cultivated lands; second, a plan to replace destructive methods of farming and forestry by methods more in harmony with the laws of nature; and, third, a plan to discover and develop new sources of supply.

The cost of carrying out the first two plans would be high—though certainly no higher than the cost of preparing to win the Third World War and crush the First World Revolution. It would be high because, in order to give eroded land a chance to recover its fertility, it would be necessary for a period of years to relieve the pressure imposed upon it by an excessive population. In other words, it would be necessary to provide over-crowded countries with an amount of food equal to the difference between what they might have extracted from the soil by ruinous exploitation and what, under the plan, they are able to extract, while checking erosion and preparing the shift to better agricultural methods. It would also be necessary to subsidize the migration to safer areas of those persons now living on specially vulnerable watersheds. Additional funds would have to be found for supplying experts to technologically backward countries, for training nationals of those countries in sound agriculture and the theory and practice of conservation, and for undertaking a world-wide survey of soils, climates and natural resources.

The third plan would be in the nature of a vast international project for research and experimentation. To men of science and technicians recruited from every part of the world would be assigned the task of discovering new ways, not of murdering their fellows, but of feeding and clothing them. Let us consider a few of the more obvious possibilities that will have to be explored.

Large areas of the earth's surface are uninhabited because, under present conditions, they are uninhabitable. But in some of these areas the expenditure of much capital and hard work might render the land productive. At present the development of deserts, tundras and tropical forests is prohibitively costly; but as population rises and the demand for food and fibres yet further outstrips supply, what is now uneconomic may come to be a 'business proposition.' It will be the business of our hypothetical board of experts to decide which areas are to be developed, when the development shall take place, and at what expenditure of international funds.

It is desirable that the world's total food supply should be increased, and increased in any way whatsoever. But let us always remember that, from a political point of view, the most satisfactory kind of increase is one which does not involve a natural monopoly by specially favoured nations. In the context of nationalism, a natural monopoly in food surpluses can become an instrument by means of which one nation, or group of nations, may coerce other nations less fortunate than themselves. Ideally, the world's food supply should be increased in such a way that the increase shall not strengthen existing natural monoplies, or create new ones, but shall permit every nation to live on supplies grown on its own land or coming from sources equally available to all mankind. Under existing circumstances, international trade is as much of a curse as a blessing. It will become an unmitigated blessing only when nationalistic idolatry shall have ceased to be the effective religion of mankind.

Meanwhile we should do everything in our power to foster national, or at least regional, self-sufficiency in the prime necessities of existence. A step in this direction would be taken if we could develop means for getting more food from the sea. At the present time most of the seas in the neighbourhood of densely populated areas are being over-fished. More effort has to be put forth in order to obtain a diminishing harvest of fish—and this at a time when we need more food to satisfy the growing population. Can the oceans be made to yield new sources of supply? Can sea-weeds be processed into fodder and manure? What about plankton? What about the enclosure and fertilizing of landlocked bays and inlets?

But some countries have no access to the sea. Even salt water is a natural monopoly. Our international board of researchers must consider yet other ways of achieving regional self-sufficiency. What about the transformation of poor land into productive fish-ponds? What about the cultivation of fresh-water algae for fodder? What about the conversion of sawdust and vegetable wastes into sugar solutions for the cultivation of edible yeasts? And the bacteria with their tremendous capacity for bringing about chemical transformations—can any of these be domesticated and set to work producing food for man?

Natural monopolies in minerals are perhaps even more dangerous, politically speaking, than natural monopolies in food surpluses. When located in the territory of a strong nation with a culture orientated towards aggressive enterprise, deposits of coal, petroleum and the metals necessary to heavy industry are a standing temptation to imperialist expansion. When located in the territory of a weak nation, they are a standing invitation to aggression from abroad. Research should be systematically directed to the development of universally available surrogates for the present sources of power and industrial production—for example, wind-power and sun-power, in combination with an efficient storage battery, as a supplement and partial substitute for power derived from coal and petroleum; glass, plastics, light metals derived from clay and sea-water as partial substitutes for the capriciously distributed minerals upon which industry at present depends. By these means we might perhaps succeed in breaking the natural monoplies which are so politically dangerous; and at the same time we should be doing something to shift our industrial civilization from its precarious basis in the exploitation of rapidly wasting assets to a more secure, a more nearly permanent foundation.

We now come to the henceforth inescapable fact of nuclear fission. For us the question is simple: how can nuclear fission help us in resolving the low-level crisis? In the immediate future its greatest contribution will probably be made in the field of genetics. By exposing seeds to the gamma rays emanating from an atomic pile, we can produce large numbers of unprecedented mutations. The overwhelming majority of these mutations will be harmful; but a few may result in varieties not merely viable, but even economically useful—varieties yielding more of this or that food element, varieties capable of maturing under climatic conditions which would be fatal to the parent strain, varieties resistant to certain diseases and parasites, and so forth.

Theoretically and ideally, nuclear fission should provide cheap power for developing territories too arid, or too cold, or too rugged, or too remote from the conventional sources of power to be worth exploiting under present conditions. In practice, however, atomic power is likely to remain for some time to come a very expensive luxury. Twenty years from now it may be that the dream of almost costless power will have been realized. It will be none too soon; for twenty years from now the planet will have to support a population greater by four hundred millions than its population today. And meanwhile every lunatic in a position of power, every fanatic, every idealist, every patriot will be under chronic temptation to use the new source of energy for political purposes, in a war of aggression, or prevention, or defence. To purchase advantages which, in the short and middle run, are not likely to be very great, we must run risks so enormous as to be incommensurable with a conceivable gain. One is reminded of Pascal's wager. We are betting on a strictly finite good against the far from remote possibility of an evil that, for practical purposes, may be regarded as infinite.

In a world where nationalism is axiomatic and where the differences between politico-religious ideologies are as irreconcilable as they were in the days of the Crusades, an international project for the relief of hunger and the conservation of our planetary resources seems to offer the best and perhaps the only hope for peace and international co-operation. At this point, the sponsors of world federation will object that our project cannot be carried out except by a world government. Political union, they will say, must come first; economic and technological collaboration will then follow as a matter of course. But at the present time, unfortunately, the governments of most nations do not want union. Or, to be more accurate, they want union, but do not want the means to union. For the means to political union entail immediate sacrifices which it would not be pleasant to make. For example, in a politically federated Europe many local industries, which have been fostered and protected by national tariffs, would prove to be redundant and would either have to be suppressed by government fiat, or would find themselves ruined by the competition of industries more efficiently managed or more favourably situated in relation to raw materials and markets. The suppression of redundant industries would cause much hardship among owners, managers and workers alike. And this is only one of the costs of political union. Enormous advantages in the long run can be secured only by a number of rather painful sacrifices in the short run. Political union can be imposed by force, under a military dictatorship; or under the pressure of circumstances. During periods of 'normalcy' the political union of sovereign, democratic states is much harder to achieve. Men and women will not vote for a policy which entails the immediate loss of their jobs and a disturbing change in their habits. As a general rule, it is only in times of crisis that people are willing to make sacrifices now for the sake of a good in the future. All the higher religions are, among other things, devices for convincing human beings that their every moment is a moment of crisis, involving matters of spiritual life and death, and that therefore it is reasonable as well as right to make certain sacrifices. On quite another level every moment in the life of human beings on an overcrowded and eroding planet is also a moment of crisis. To explain the nature of man's Martian aggression against himself and to convince the masses of the necessity of concerted action against the invasion should not be too difficult, all the more so as the immediate sacrifices involved will not be excessive and the advantages to be expected in the long and middle run are so concrete, evident and appealing. Once established, this primarily technological alliance against the Martian forces of overpopulation and erosion can be expected to develop into a political and economic collaboration which, in its turn, may prove to be the precursor of genuine world federation under a single authority. If, in the meantime, federation can be achieved by purely political means, so much the better. It does not matter which comes first, the political chicken or the technological egg. What is important is that, in some way or other, we should get both, and get them with the least possible delay.

And meanwhile we may hope that the habit of collaboration upon a project that so obviously concerns the whole of mankind may do something to undermine, among rulers as well as ruled, that nationalistic idolatry which is the prime political cause of all our high-level crises. Nationalism is an artificial thing, but an artificial thing which has its roots in the individual's quasi-instinctive attachment to the environment of his childhood—to a place, to a dietary, to a set of habits, customs and conventions, to a language and the people who speak that language. Such local patriotism is found on the subhuman level. Birds, for example, will fight for their territory; the sentries at the entrance to a hive will attack and kill any bee belonging to another swarm. The first is an example of rugged individualism—"an Englishman's home is his castle"; the second, of collective xenophobia—"every Western visitor is a class-enemy of the U.S.S.R." Among human beings, tribal sentiment is the nearest approach to a natural and unsophisticated expression of the quasi-instinct of local patriotism. Tribes have now given place to nations; and this has happened because rulers found that it was possible, by means of suitable education and propaganda, to transfer the quasi-instinctive sentiment of tribalism from its natural object to a new, artificial object —the nation. The home place and the home people can be touched, seen, directly experienced. It is therefore possible for a man to love them in an almost physiological way. The nation is too large to be an object of immediate acquaintance and, for any given individual within the nation, is hardly more than an abstraction. But the abstraction can be symbolically represented by an object (the flag), by a person (the King, the Leader), by a tune and a form of words (the Star-spangled Banner, the Internationale). These symbolic representations can be immediately experienced and loved, not merely with the head, but also with the heart, the yearning bowels. It is by means of symbols that men and women have been educated out of tribal patriotism and into nationalistic idolatry. And symbols, no doubt, will be used when the moment comes to educate them out of nationalistic idolatry and into world-patriotism. In Western Europe it took several centuries for capitalistic thought-patterns to replace the thought-patterns of feudal society. How many years will pass before humanity at large can be made to forget the nationalistic axioms on which so much of its current thinking and feeling is based and to accept in their place the axioms of a non-nationalistic system? Anyone who would hazard a guess must take into account two facts: first, that we have more effective instruments of propaganda and instruction than were possessed by our ancestors; but, second, that man's life-span is three-score years and ten, that we find it hard to change the thought-patterns formed in our childhood, and that all governments are at present engaged in implanting nationalistic thought-patterns in the minds of their subjects, young and old alike. As soon as we and our rulers desire it, modern methods of propaganda can be used to effect a change of thought-patterns within a single lifetime. Meanwhile nationalistic idolatry is likely to remain the religion for which men will lay down their lives in wars which, but for that religion, would never have been declared.

On the ideological level, the best antidote to nationalistic idolatry is a monotheism with its corollary (since God's fatherhood implies men's brotherhood) of monoanthropism. At present we have pentakosiotheism and as many varieties of mutually hostile humans as there are of Heinz's soups and pickles. That any system of monotheism will come, in the near future, to be generally accepted seems very unlikely. But it should not be impossible to secure the wide and immediate acceptance of a form of what may be called cosmic ethics; and this, perhaps, might serve as a basis for a future monotheism. At present men think and act as though they had no duties towards Nature. The Catholic Church, for example, officially teaches that sub-human lives may be treated as though they were things. But to any realistic observer it is surely obvious that not only do we have no right to treat living things as things; we have no right to treat even things as mere things. Things must be treated as though they were parts of a complex and beautifully co-ordinated living organism. We are beginning to discover that to treat them in any other way may be to condemn the whole human experiment to failure. The Golden Rule is to be applied to animate and inanimate Nature as well as to our fellow men. Treat Nature with charity and understanding, and Nature will repay you with unfailing gifts. Treat Nature aggressively, with greed and violence and incomprehension: wounded Nature will turn and destroy you. Theoretically, at least, the ancients understood these truths better than ourselves. The Greeks, for example knew very well that hubris against the essentially divine order of Nature would be followed by its appropriate nemesis. The Chinese taught that the Tao, or indwelling Logos, was present on every level from the physical and the biological up to the spiritual; and they knew that outrages against Tao, in Nature no less than in man, would lead to fatal results. We have to recapture some of this old lost wisdom. If we fail to do this—if, presumptuously imagining that we can 'conquer' Nature, we continue to live on our planet like a swarm of destructive parasites—we condemn ourselves and our children to misery and deepening squalor and the despair that finds expression in the frenzies of collective violence.

Was Benedict Arnold a Traitor?
From *Goodbye to All That*
The Poet's Paradise

ROBERT GRAVES
(*b. 1895*)

ROBERT GRAVES has learning as prodigious as Huxley's
and has published as many volumes. His erudition is
more concentratedly mythico-historical but extends
over the course of some thirty centuries. This is the
more remarkable because he spent many of his
creative years on the island of Majorca, far from
libraries and scholarly companionship.

In his indispensable two-volume handbook *The
Greek Myths*, Graves retells the myths in all their
variants with scrupulous faithfulness to classic
sources, then explains each one according to his
own speculative but exciting theories of cultural
conquest and diffusion and of the relations of myth to
ritual, magic, and matriarchy. These theories are set
forth in *The White Goddess*, where Graves, whose
own family background is Irish and Welsh, draws
also on very recondite druidical lore, including a tree
alphabet. Graves believes that true poetry is genuine
magic, literally inspired by the Muse, or White
Goddess.

He never fears to attack poetry of repute when
he considers it inauthentic. Though often unfair,
these attacks are witty and instructive, for Graves has
a highly trained sensitivity in all matters of literary

technique. He has lectured frequently in American and British universities and was elected Professor of Poetry at Oxford. Among his many works on literature and writing are *A Survey of Modernist Poetry*, with Laura Riding (1927), *A Pamphlet Against Anthologies*, with Laura Riding (1928), *The Reader over Your Shoulder*, with Alan Hodge (1943), *Common Asphodel: Collected Essays on Poetry, 1922–1943* (1949), *The Crowning Privilege* (1955), and *Oxford Addresses on Poetry* (1962).

Graves has published a long series of historical novels, basing them less on academic scholarship than on his own research and original theories. These include two on prehistoric Greece, *Hercules, My Shipmate* (1944) and *Homer's Daughter* (1955); two on imperial Rome, *I, Claudius* (1934) and *Claudius the God* (1934); two on the American Revolutionary War, *Sergeant Lamb's America* (1940) and *Proceed, Sergeant Lamb* (1941); and a heterodox, controversial interpretation of the missions of Jesus and Judas, *King Jesus* (1946).

"Was Benedict Arnold a Traitor?" shows the zest with which Graves takes some well-known historical incident and, on the basis of facts that most people do not know or have ignored, reinterprets it in a way that raises all sorts of moral and social questions.

With his autobiographical *Goodbye to All That* (1929) Graves became one of the literary men whose books on the First World War helped create the political attitudes of the 1930s. The responses to war, violence, and sudden death described in the excerpt reprinted here are common material for fiction but seldom receive this kind of thoughtful treatment in essay form.

"The Poet's Paradise" is both a personal adventure and a vivid summary of Graves' theories about poetic inspiration and its relation to myth.

Was Benedict Arnold a Traitor?

The American Revolution brought into being a new way of life which, after nearly two centuries of refinement, can now be confidently offered as a model to the civilized world; if only because the United States has at last succeeded Great Britain, which similarly succeeded France at the close of the Napoleonic Wars, as the richest, most progressive, most envied of all nations. We British accept this change calmly enough, recognizing it as a natural consequence of the United States' energy, size, unity, and geographical separation from the storm-centres of Europe; and feel grateful that armed American intervention saved us, in two wars, from conquest by Germany. Then, since nobody with a sense of realism would suggest that the United States should re-enter the British Commonwealth, or that Great Britain should apply for membership of the United States, and since the two countries have become close allies, it is surely high time to revise the irreconcilable accounts of the Revolutionary War commonly presented to British and American schoolchildren. Nothing but good could come of discarding ancient historical propaganda which continues to embitter Anglo-American relations, and particularly of settling once and for all the crucial question: 'Was General Benedict Arnold a traitor to his country?'

The first sense of 'traitor' in English is 'a man who for base personal motives plots to deliver a master, or liege, into the power of his enemies.' The best-known popular example is Judas; though his happens not to be a very convincing case. One can hardly exculpate Judas of presumption and officiousness; yet the New Testament evidence, examined in the light of contemporary history, suggests that he foresaw an abortive Messianic revolt against the Romans, and arranged to have his Master placed in protective custody. Thus Judas's kiss seems to have conveyed a friendly reassurance: 'I have done this for your own good!' When, however, he realized that his plan had miscarried: that the High Priests had handed over Jesus to

WAS BENEDICT ARNOLD A TRAITOR? From *Food for Centaurs*. Reprinted by permission of Willis Kingsley Wing. Copyright © 1960 by International Authors N. V. Published by Doubleday & Company, 1960.

the Romans instead of waiting until the Feast of Passover ended and then bringing him before the Jewish Supreme Court (which would doubtless have adjourned the case *sine die*), Judas tried to pay back the thirty pieces of silver, and committed suicide. I mention Judas because the second meaning of 'traitor' is 'a man who for base personal motives plots to deliver his native country into the power of its enemies'; and because 'Judas' was a favourite insult cast at Benedict Arnold after his defection. Yet if Judas had been a traitor in the agreed sense, he could have demanded at least thirty thousand pieces of silver for his betrayal. The very fact that, when asked to name his reward, he chose precisely thirty (an ironical reference to the Temple Treasurers in Zechariah XI, who insulted a prophet of God by valuing him at the lowest legal sum) proves that he was not a traitor. A dishonest treasurer, as Judas is represented as being, would not have sold out at that petty price. He could have continued to amass large sums by quietly pocketing the donations which came flowing in from rich sympathizers, among them the wife of King Herod Antipas's finance minister (Luke XIII:3). Precisely the same argument holds good for Benedict Arnold. He may have been wrong-headed or presumptuous, but his motives seem to have been far from base, and his financial honesty beyond question. Like Judas, he accepted a mere token payment for an act which he hoped would save his nation from disaster.

Traitors are to be closely distinguished from rebels. Oliver Cromwell, though rebelliously taking arms against King Charles I, did not call in the Dutch to win his battles, and cannot therefore be called a traitor to England. General Lee, who took arms against the Federal Government in the Civil War, was a rebel, no traitor; because Jefferson Davis and his Congress did not apply to the British for aid. It is indeed difficult to find, in modern history, traitors comparable with the Spartan king who went over to Xerxes during the Persian War, or Alcibiades, the Athenian general who went over to Sparta during the Peloponnesian War. True, the British hanged Sir Roger Casement as a traitor for his clandestine dealings with Germany in World War I, but Casement was an Irish patriot rather than a British traitor. They also hanged William Joyce ('Lord Haw-Haw') for treasonably broadcasting German propaganda in World War II; but Joyce did not regard himself as a British subject and, except on a doubtful technicality, was not one. Joyce can in fact be considered hardly more of a traitor to King George VI than Napoleon, whose

native island had for a short period of his youth been a British possession, was a traitor to King George III. A stronger case might be
made out against Goethe for traitorously eulogizing Napoleon, the
invader of Germany; though it is usual to regard Goethe as a col-
laborationist who prudently kept his own small region from the
depredations of the French 'army of enlightenment.' Or, yet more
kindly, as an internationalist; a title, however, which should then in
justice be conferred on Burgess and Maclean, the British Foreign
Office officials who deserted to Russia during the Cold War: with
the avowed, if foolish, intention of improving Anglo-Soviet relations.

Between 1775 and 1783, every native American was confronted
with the alternatives of being called a rebel for his disloyalty to
King George, and being called a rebel for his objection to the Revolution. The sides were pretty evenly divided in this earlier Civil
War, several 'Loyalist' regiments assisting the British throughout
the struggle. A man might then obey the dictates of his political conscience and, should he not at first possess such a thing, it was soon
forced on him. Probably three out of every four colonists would
have declared in 1775 that, little as they felt themselves bound by
the laws of a far-distant London Parliament, and loth as they were
to be taxed for the upkeep of British armed forces, even as protective garrisons against possible attack by the French and Indians, they
had no intention of going beyond civil disobedience in their attempt to secure independence of the Crown. But the Revolutionary
Committees organized a newspaper and pamphlet propaganda campaign of the most inventive and sensational sort, as a means of incit-
ing the luke-warms and the don't-cares into active rebellion. It was
a technique carefully studied by the Sinn Feiners during the 'Troubles' a century and a half later, and finally perfected by Hitler and
Goebbels when they set themselves to impose their Nazi creed on all
Germans everywhere.

At the close of the Revolution, Samuel Adams had written:

Here in my retreat, like another Catiline, the collar around my
neck, in danger of the severest punishment, I laid down the plan
of revolt: I endeavoured to persuade my timid accomplices that
a most glorious revolution might be the result of our efforts, but
I scarcely dared to hope it; and what I have seen realized appears
to me like a dream. You know by what obscure intrigues, by
what unfaithfulness to the mother-country a powerful party was

formed; how the minds of the people were irritated before we could provoke the insurrection.

Yet, though fear of having their houses burned down or their ships scuttled, or being given 'a Marblehead Ride' in a coat of tar and feathers, obliged even the most peace-loving colonists to join the local militia, companies that would face a British command of equal numbers were few. Had it not been for Washington's capture at Trenton of a thousand elderly, homesick, forcibly enlisted Hessians, and his subsequent surprise and repulse of a small British column at Princeton, no standing army would have been left him by February 1777. Yet, as Lord Chatham pointed out, sensibly enough, one could not conquer a map. The British Government must in the end have granted the colonists their independence—even if this meant approving Congress's summary sequestration of royal and noble estates, to the value of forty million dollars, for the benefit of land-hungry settlers. As it happened, however, things had to get far worse before they could get better.

Benedict Arnold was a native American: the great-grandson, and fourth in direct descent, of his seventeenth-century namesake, three times Royal Governor of Rhode Island. Why he joined the Revolutionary forces, despite his Tory background, is no mystery. As a wide-awake merchant, he realized that Royal Governorships and an Established Church were anachronisms; so also were the immense estates of the Phillips, Pepperell, Morris, Penn, and Fairfax families; and the royal ban on free settlement of the lands beyond the Alleghenies. Only an all-American Parliament could solve outstanding problems of trade, revenue, defence, public works; and recent British commercial policy in Northern Ireland suggested that overseas interests were, as a rule, subordinated to those of the mother country. Arnold's decision to fight was coloured perhaps by a feeling that the British had undervalued him during his early service against the French in a New York company (1758–1759)—he deserted them in a huff and went home—and an ambition to prove himself a real soldier after all, despite thirteen years spent in trade. No one, indeed, understood better than he how to handle American volunteers: namely by leading them rather than by giving them directives. His phenomenal courage and energy shamed the least bellicose into heroism; and if he held a high opinion of himself, why, so did almost every man who served under him. Yet his successes, though approved by Washington, always caused jealousy, hatred and backbiting among senior officers whose military uselessness could not escape the shrewd censure of their free-spoken troops.

Washington's decision to fight the British was based on similarly common-sense grounds. He agreed with a view afterwards expressed by Tom Paine that the Colonists were morally entitled to break their allegiance as soon as it proved a burden, and held that Virginia's prosperity, threatened by a steep fall in tobacco prices at the close of the Seven Years' War, and the dumping of British goods, could be ensured only by secession. True, he bore a private grudge against the British: they had made light of his services in the French War and declined to give him a regular commission. At that time American militia officers, however exalted, ranked junior to the youngest ensign of a British line-regiment. Washington wrote to a Colonial official in 1754: 'If you think me capable of holding a commission that has neither rank nor emoluments, you must entertain a very contemptible opinion of my weakness, and believe me to be more empty than the commission itself.'

A personal grudge does not necessarily imply faulty political judgement; it merely spurs a man to action. Washington, however, consistently misunderstood the kind of war which he had been called upon to fight. American militiamen could not hope to beat trained European troops in pitched battles. The frontiermen, the best fighting material available, were adept at Indian warfare, sniping from behind trees at troops on the march, or picking off stragglers, but did not take kindly to volley-firing or 'push of bayonet.' It never dawned on Washington, as a would-be British regular, that there was no real reason why his men should fight any pitched battles at all. They could best wear the enemy down by guerrilla tactics: swift, well-planned raids; a scorched-earth policy; harassing of vulnerable supply lines—the British could not transport everything by sea or river. When, in July 1776, five hundred Connecticut men volunteered to form an irregular cavalry commando, which was what Washington needed most, he replied that owing to a lack of forage he could use them only as infantry. When they would not give up their horses, he dismissed them; and it was years before the commandos led by Sumter, Marion and Pickens on the Revolutionary side, and on the British by Tarleton's Greens, a Loyalist force, proved how foolish he had been. Washington, in fact, shared the military creed of his generals, Horatio Gates and Charles Lee, who had held regular commissions respectively as major and lieutenant in the British Army. As a Virginian gentleman, not a populist, he believed in a system of command based on social differences rather than capacity for leadership, and supported by the savage old-world punishments of lashes, riding the wooden horse, and running the gauntlet. His difficulties in recruiting convinced patriots were largely due to their natural resentment at this most un-American way of soldiering. Those who did volunteer considered themselves the equals of their officers, whom they 'valued no higher than broomsticks.'

Arnold's first important assignment was to assist in the invasion of Canada, and there raise a revolt of the French peasantry. A hopeless task, since the *habitants* were perfectly content with the liberties granted them after the British conquest of Canada: such as the abolition of *corvée*, a forced-labour system which had so irked them under French rule. Besides, Congress had unwisely protested to London against the British toleration of Catholicism in Canada; and religious freedom had been among the most welcome benefits bestowed on the *habitants*. Arnold reached the Canadian border after a two-months' march with 1,100 men through the woods of Maine in conditions of fearful privation and hardship, and made straight for Quebec. There he found the British on the alert, and had to call a halt until his colleague Montgomery arrived with 2,000 men from Montreal. The assault, delivered on the last day of 1775, failed. Montgomery lost his life; Arnold was severely wounded in the leg. The ravages of smallpox, lack of hard money to buy food, the expiration of numerous enlistments, and desperately cold weather, forced the Americans to retreat; reinforcements sent by Congress caught the smallpox too, and gave way before the British advance. Of an original 9,000 American invaders only 3,000 left Canada; the last man to cross the frontier being Arnold, who had ridden back to reconnoitre and narrowly escaped capture by the British vanguard.

The naval battle fought on Lake Champlain in October 1776 was the most spectacular event of the war. Arnold, who had strengthened the American fleet of schooners by building four new galleys and eight gondolas, could outgun the British; but General Carleton, his opponent, fetched sailors form the Royal Navy to man another extemporized flotilla and, with their help, would have gained an absolute victory at Valcour Island but for Arnold's fantastic courage. When his flagship, *The Royal Savage*, was clumsily handled and came under fire from the *Inflexible* frigate, the largest vessel engaged, he decided to abandon her while he could, and transfer to the *Congress* galley. Most of his officers on the *Congress* were soon killed or wounded and, for want of trained gunners, he pointed and discharged every gun himself, stepping from one to the other 'like a man touching off fireworks for the King's birthday.' That night he brought his shattered fleet away under cover of mist and darkness, and the next day fought a desperate battle at Split Rock. He beached the *Congress* only after she caught fire, and was the last man to climb along her bowsprit to safety. He had even succeeded in saving a small part of his fleet.

In April 1777, Arnold was in the forefront of a vigorous attack on Governor Tryon's force which had raided Danbury; and chased them back to their ships. For this, Washington recommended Congress to appoint Arnold a major-general; but meanwhile Arnold's personal enemies charged him with wrongfully commandeering goods from Montreal merchants for the use of his troops. In May these charges were investigated by the Board of War. The verdict, confirmed by Congress, was that his character and conduct had been 'cruelly and groundlessly aspersed.'

In August, Arnold, now serving under General Philip Schuyler, marched up the Mohawk Valley and raised the siege of Fort Stanwix; but Schuyler was soon superseded by the egregious General Gates. When Burgoyne moved his army down the Hudson from Lake Champlain and, in September, came upon Gates at Bemis Heights, he could count himself unlucky not to have defeated him at the first encounter by seizing a hill a short distance away and cutting his communications. Arnold, realizing danger, had asked Gates's permission to take out part of his division and prevent this manoeuvre, which would have forced the Americans either to surrender or to swim the river. Gates told Arnold to mind his own business, but Arnold won the support of another born soldier—Colonel Dan Morgan, of the Virginian Rifles, who had come very close to storming Quebec two years previously. Together they raised such a storm at Headquarters, clapping hands to pistols and swearing terribly, that Gates gave way in alarm: he let Arnold lead forward half a brigade of New England militia, stiffened by Morgan's riflemen. These riflemen, now mostly Pennsylvanians of Northern Irish stock, were the best troops in America. They could march forty miles a day, subsist on jerked beef and corn porridge and, for mere sport, would take turns to shoot apples off one another's heads at sixty paces. Arnold's command broke the resistance of the Canadians and American Loyalists on the British flank and, though repulsed with heavy loss by British regulars, quickly switched their attack to the centre. There they would have got through, had Gates supplied the reinforcements demanded of him. When Arnold's horse fell dead, he fought on foot, urging the weary men to a final effort. His exploits, which saved Bemis Heights and kept Burgoyne from breaking through to Albany, provoked anger and jealousy at Headquarters. Gates's chief of staff even circulated a story that Arnold had stayed out of the battle and spent the whole day at Camp drinking! In disgust, he resigned his command, which Gates accepted, allowing him to remain with the army only as a private person.

The second and decisive battle of Saratoga took place on October 7th, 1777. Arnold, forbidden by Gates to leave Camp, drew his sword and wounded the officer ordered to detain him, then galloped into the thick of the melee, bareheaded and in undress. The New England militia followed, cheering enthusiastically; he managed to carry three regiments of Massachusetts infantry against Burgoyne's centre. These scattered the German troops, forcing the British to fight a stiff rearguard action and abandon all their guns. Later, Arnold attacked the enemy camp with a brigade of Continental troops, but came up against British regulars, as in the previous battle, and was repulsed. Again switching his attack, he advanced in fading light towards a redoubt which protected the right of the camp, scattered a force of Canadians, and captured the entire garrison of Brunswickers. As Arnold entered the sally-port he had another horse shot under him, and a wounded German, firing at point-blank range, shattered his thigh-bone.

Here he was finally overtaken by the aide-de-camp who, pursuing him all day with an order from Gates to return at once, had been led into some very hot spots. Arnold paid him no attention and summoned a surgeon. The surgeon recommended amputation, but Arnold cried: 'Goddam it, sir, if that is all you can do with me, I shall see the battle out on another horse.' The battle, however, was already won; but by no action of Gate's, who, it is said, had spent the greater part of the day preaching to a dying prisoner, Sir Francis Clark, the righteousness of the American cause. Sir Francis, unconvinced, reproached him for spoiling the last hours of his life. Gates then turned to one of his aides: 'Did you ever hear such an impudent son of a bitch?'

Burgoyne, outnumbered, cut off from Canada, and dangerously short of provisions and ammunition, chose to capitulate. Gates could have insisted on an unconditional surrender, but was scared by news of Clinton's move up the Hudson and had so little trust in his subordinates that he readily signed the proposals put forward by Burgoyne. These allowed the British to march away with the honours of war, on condition that the whole force engaged—only 2,000 British troops were left alive—would abandon their arms and agree never to serve in America again.

One Sergeant Downing, a New England militiaman, wrote after the battle:

> Arnold was our fighting general and a bloody fellow he was. He didn't care for nothing. He'd ride right in. He's as brave a man as ever lived and they didn't treat him right. *He* ought to have Burgoyne's sword.

Washington persuaded Congress to thank Arnold for his services, and gave him the Governorship of Philadelphia, which the British had recently evacuated. A dangerous honour, since it did not carry with it the entertainment allowance which he would need to uphold the dignity of his office in that elegant town. There he married Margaret Shippen, daughter of a moderate Loyalist, and necessarily lived beyond his means. In February 1779, the Executive Council of Pennsylvania, under the presidency of Joseph Reed, an enemy of Arnold's, laid before Congress eight charges of misconduct, all of them trifling. A Congressional Committee exonerated Arnold, but in April, Reed obtained a reconsideration. Congress threw out four charges and referred the others to a court martial, which was left hanging over Arnold's head for eight months longer. In January 1780, the Court absolved him of all wrongful intent—the two main charges being those of giving a pass to a trading vessel on the Delaware River without first consulting General Washington, and using certain Army wagons, then lying idle, to move the property of private citizens beyond the reach of enemy foragers. To save Reed's face, the Court directed Washington to reprimand Arnold for his impudence. Washington did so, using the phrases 'peculiarly reprehensible, imprudent and improper.'

Arnold had originally taken arms against the British because this seemed the only way to obtain redress of American grievances. Three public events now combined to alter his opinion. The first was the decision of Congress not to ratify the Capitulation articles signed by General Gates at Saratoga; thus the British troops, though granted the honours of war, found themselves placed in prison camps instead of being repatriated. There they were starved, ill-treated, and constantly offered bribes to desert. So open a breach of faith seemed to Arnold and other men of honour most disgraceful —especially since Congress still employed Gates.

The second event was Congress's rejection of the peace offer conveyed by the King's Commissioners. Arnold thought these terms highly generous: a native American Parliament of two houses, to settle all domestic affairs of the colonies; free trade; and the assistance of the British fleet and army in time of need, without any obligation to pay for their upkeep.

The third event was the French alliance, which in so far as it involved the despatch of French troops to America, Arnold thought plain treason. Military convention permitted the hiring of mercenaries to serve under a national flag—the present French and Spanish 'Foreign Legions' are a relic of this—but it was a very different matter to sign a military pact with Britain's hereditary foe: an enemy against whom Washington, Schuyler, Gates and Arnold himself had all fought, and with whom most Americans had nothing in common, either politically, religiously or culturally. The French were, indeed, despised as the tools of a tyranny far more absolute than King George's. If Congress had treated men like Arnold and Dan Morgan generously, and let them conduct the war in true American fashion, rather than rely on foreigners who forced inappropriate Continental strategy, tactics and discipline on the revolutionaries, there would have been no need to call in the French. (Dan Morgan, consistently overpassed for promotion, remained a mere 'bird-colonel,' despite his remarkable victory at Cowpens, which he won when crippled by arthritis. He continued to be snubbed by the Board of War, and finally retired to his farm in disgust.)

These three events, combined with the misery and destitution that were now afflicting his native country, and the general war-weariness that surrounded him, decided Arnold to 'do a General Monk'—Monk being, of course, the Cromwellian who brought over the British Commonwealth Army bloodlessly to King Charles II's side at the Restoration and won great acclaim in consequence. The war had long ceased to be an American popular revolution. Joseph Galloway, a Pennsylvanian Congressman who had gone over to the British, reported that not one soldier in four of Washington's Continental Army, the only force continuously under arms, was a native-born American. Records show that most of them were Irishmen, the remainder British, with some German deserters and an average quota of fifty-eight freed Negroes to each battalion. Nathaniel Greene, the ablest American general after Arnold and (as Washington handsomely admitted) the true victor of Trenton, said that at the close of the war his army consisted largely of British deserters.

Arnold obtained from Washington the command of West Point, the Gibraltar of America, and in a secret correspondence with General Sir Henry Clinton, then at New York, offered to surrender it; an act which, he believed, would end the war at a blow, and bloodlessly. He had initialled this correspondence signing himself 'Monk' in May 1779, while commanding in Philadelphia; with the full approval, even perhaps at the instigation, of his wife. The first overture to Arnold is extant, so far as I can discover, only in a French version:

. . . Render then, brave general, this important service to your country. The colonies cannot sustain much longer the unequal strife. Your troops are perishing in misery. They are badly armed, half naked, and crying for bread. The efforts of Congress are futile against the languor of the people. Your fields are untilled, trade languishes, learning dies. The neglected education of a whole generation is an irreparable loss to society. Your youth, torn by thousands from their rustic pursuits or useful employments, are mown down by war. Such as survive have lost the vigour of their prime, or are maimed in battle: the greater part bring back to their families the idleness and the corrupt manners of the camp. Let us put an end to so many calamities; you and ourselves have the same origin, the same language, the same laws. We are inaccessible in our island; and you, the masters of a vast and fertile territory, have no other neighbours than the people of our loyal colonies . . . From the northern to the southern pole, from the east to the west, our vessels find everywhere a neighbouring harbour belonging to Great Britain. So many islands, so many countries acknowledging our sway, are all ruled by a uniform system that bears on every feature the stamp of liberty, yet is as well adapted to the genius of different nations and of various climes. . . .

Beware of breaking forever the links and ties of a friendship whose benefits are proven by the experience of a hundred and fifty years. Time gives to human institutions a strength which what is new can only attain, in its turn, by the lapse of ages. . . .

United in equality we will rule the universe: we will hold it bound, not by arms and violence, but by the ties of commerce; the lightest and most gentle bands that humankind can wear.

Arnold had at first demanded as his recompense no more than the value of the private property which he would forfeit by the action, namely £10,000; and the same substantive rank in the British forces as he held in the American. This was routine procedure: in 1775, General Charles Lee had stipulated that Congress should grant him a similar compensation when he transferred from the British to the American Army. Later, when Arnold found himself commanding this critical fortress, he raised his demand to £20,000. The increase is perhaps a measure not so much of greed, as of increased resentment at what he believed to be the dishonesty of Congress in delaying payment of moneys due to him, while the Continental currency steadily declined in value. In effect, he accepted £6,319. But had he asked a couple of million dollars for the surrender of West Point, it would have been cheap at the price. Benjamin Franklin scoffed:

Judas sold only one man, Arnold three millions. Judas got for his one man thirty pieces of silver, Arnold not a halfpenny a head.

It happened that Major André, the British agent sent to meet Arnold between the lines and secretly arrange for the surrender of the fortress, was captured by a group of marauding 'Skinners' who coveted his fine riding boots. In the heel of one of them they found the incriminating correspondence, and marched André off to American Headquarters for examination. Arnold escaped to the British lines before his fellow-officers could arrest him; André was convicted as a spy and sentenced to death by a court martial of French and American generals.

Sir Henry Clinton tried to exchange six captured American colonels against André, but without success. Arnold thereupon offered to present himself at Washington's headquarters as a willing sacrifice, on condition that André's life would be spared. According to a letter published by Captain James Battersby of the 29th Foot, Clinton refused to let him go: 'Your proposal, sir, does you great honour; but were Major André my own brother I would not consent to such a transaction.' Washington dared not intervene to save André, for fear of being charged with complicity in the plot—Congress knew that he had planned to visit West Point at the time of its proposed surrender. André was therefore hanged. The British comment, voiced by Clinton himself, was: 'The horrid deed is done. Washington has committed premeditated murder and must answer for the consequences.' The fierce indignation which a discovery of treason always excites among luke-warm patriots revived the flagging cause of American liberty. Arnold was everywhere burned in effigy, and any man unfortunate enough to have the same surname, whether related to him or not, must needs adopt another. A plan was sponsored by Washington for Arnold's kidnapping by one Sergeant Champe, who was persuaded to desert and enter the British service with that main object, though incidentally to investigate the supposed treason of another American general. Washington promised Champe 100 guineas, five hundred acres of land, and three slaves. Jefferson believed that a bribe of 5,000 guineas would tempt a partisan unit to raid Arnold's camp and carry him off. An official order was issued denying Arnold the rights due to a prisoner of war if captured. All attempts to abduct him proved fruitless, however.

In command of Loyalists forces under the Earl of Cornwallis, Arnold showed his grasp of strategic principles by raids on Richmond, Norfolk and Petersburgh, where he burned most of the tobacco which Congress had offered the French in payment for their services; but in vain. By the cynical incompetence of the Earl of Sandwich, First Lord of the Admiralty, the British fleet had been allowed to fall far below safety level. The Spanish, Dutch and French, joining in arms against Britain, began to prey on her inadequately protected merchant convoys. Three thousand vessels were captured or sunk before she regained command of the sea. Meanwhile, the French landed large forces in America. Washington re-equipped and paid his poor tattered Continental Army, now long immobilized at Valley Forge, and in May 1781 led his new allies southward to Yorktown, where Cornwallis with some six thousand sick and hungry British were cornered by the French. Encouraged by this unexpected turn of fortune, American patriots who had retired from active warfare some years previously, flocked up to the kill. This put

30,000 men at Washington's disposal: 20,000 being French soldiers and sailors. Cornwallis presently surrendered for lack of food and ammunition; the war ended.

In December 1781, Arnold had been invited to visit England and advise King George on American affairs. He was never afterwards employed as a soldier. Twenty years later he died; not, like Judas, by his own hand, but of melancholia, assisted by gout, dropsy and asthma.

It would be unjust for an American to call Benedict Arnold a traitor; as it would be discourteous for an Englishman to call George Washington a traitor. Washington erased the stigma of treason in 1783, when the Peace Treaty conceded the colonists all their demands, and he became the Father of his Country. In 1791, moreover, he sternly rebuffed Genêt, the French Revolutionary envoy, who came pleading for a renewed American alliance against Britain. As the proverb says:

> *Treason doth never prosper; what's the reason?*
> *If treason prospers, 'tis no longer treason!*

Washington's coat-of-arms, by the way, the stars and stripes (or *bars* and *mullets*) of which appear in the United States flag, bore the motto: *Exitus Acta Probat*—which can mean either 'the result is a test of the means employed' or, in a more cynical sense, 'the end justifies the means.' His obduracy in keeping the war going has since allowed the United States to develop a classless republican society, now their chief distinction; for it freed them from the incubus of a hereditary nobility with which the British intended to endow them. Not that Washington hankered after a classless society. Like John Adams, he believed in government by an aristocracy of wealth and talents. In fact, he hated the Republicans so bitterly that he tried to exclude them from the American armed forces; and it took a second Civil War to break the power of the Southern slave-owning gentry whose champion he had been.

Goodbye to All That

The first night I was in trenches my company commander asked me to go out on patrol; it was the regimental custom to test new officers in this way. My orders for this patrol were to see whether a German sap-head was occupied by night or not.

I went out from Red Lamp Corner with Sergeant Townsend at about ten o'clock. We both had revolvers. We pulled socks, with the toes cut off, over our bare knees, to prevent them showing up in the dark and to make crawling easier. We went ten yards at a time, slowly, not on all fours, but wriggling flat along the ground. After each movement we lay and watched for about ten minutes. We crawled through our own wire entanglements and along a dry ditch; ripping our clothes on more barbed wire, glaring into the darkness till it began turning round and round (once I snatched my fingers in horror from where I had planted them on the slimy body of an old corpse), nudging each other with rapidly beating hearts at the slightest noise or suspicion, crawling, watching, crawling, shamming dead under the blinding light of enemy flares and again crawling, watching, crawling. (A Second Battalion officer who revisited these Laventie trenches after the war was over told me of the ridiculously small area of No Man's Land compared with the size it seemed on the long, painful journeys that he made over it. 'It was like the real size of the hollow in a tooth compared with the size it feels to the tongue.')

We found a gap in the German wire and came at last to within five yards of the sap-head that was our objective. We waited quite twenty minutes listening for any signs of its occupation. Then I nudged Sergeant Townsend and, revolvers in hand, we wriggled quickly forward and slid into it. It was about three feet deep and unoccupied. On the floor were a few empty cartridges and a wicker basket containing something large and smooth and round, twice as

---

large as a football. Very, very carefully I groped and felt all around
it in the dark. I couldn't guess what it was. I was afraid that it was
some sort of infernal machine. Eventually I dared to lift it out and
carry it back. I had a suspicion that it might be one of the German
gas-cylinders that we had heard so much about. We got back after
making the journey of perhaps two hundred yards in rather more
than two hours. The sentries passed along the word that we were in
again. Our prize turned out to be a large glass container quarter-
filled with some pale yellow liquid. This was sent down to battalion
headquarters and from there sent along to the divisional intelligence
office. Everybody was very interested in it. The theory was that the
vessel contained a chemical for re-damping gas masks. I now believe
it was the dregs of country wine mixed with rainwater. I never
heard the official report. The colonel, however, told my company
commander in the hearing of the Surrey-man: 'Your new wart
seems to have more guts than the others.' After this I went out
fairly often. I found that the only thing that the regiment respected
in young officers was personal courage.

Besides, I had worked it out like this. The best way of lasting the
war out was to get wounded. The best time to get wounded was at
night and in the open, because a wound in a vital spot was less likely.
Fire was more or less unaimed at night and the whole body was exposed. It was also convenient to be wounded when there was no
rush on the dressing-station services, and when the back areas were
not being heavily shelled. It was most convenient to be wounded,
therefore, on a night patrol in a quiet sector. You could usually
manage to crawl into a shell-hole until somebody came to the rescue. Still, patrolling had its peculiar risks. If you were wounded and
a German patrol got you, they were as likely as not to cut your
throat. The bowie-knife was a favourite German patrol weapon; it
was silent. (At this time the British inclined more to the 'cosh', a
loaded stick.) The most important information that a patrol could
bring back was to what regiment and division the troops opposite
belonged. So if a wounded man was found and it was impossible to
get him back without danger to oneself, the thing to be done was to
strip him of his badges. To do that quickly and silently it might be
necessary first to cut his throat or beat in his skull.

Sir P. Mostyn, a lieutenant who was often out patrolling at
Laventie, had a feud on with a German patrol on the left of the battalion frontage. (Our patrols usually consisted of an officer and one

or, at the most, two men. German patrols were usually six or seven men under an N.C.O. German officers left as much as they decently could to their N.C.O.'s. They did not, as one of our sergeant-majors put it, believe in 'keeping a dog and barking themselves.') One night Mostyn caught sight of his opponents; he had raised himself on one knee to throw a percussion bomb at them when they fired and wounded him in the arm, which immediately went numb. He caught the bomb before it hit the ground and threw it with his left hand, and in the confusion that followed managed to return to the trench.

Like every one else I had a carefully worked out formula for taking risks. We would all take any risk, even the certainty of death, to save life or to maintain an important position. To take life we would run, say, a one-in-five risk, particularly if there was some wider object than merely reducing the enemy's man-power; for instance, picking off a well-known sniper, or getting fire ascendancy in trenches where the lines were dangerously close. I only once refrained from shooting a German I saw, and that was at Cuinchy about three weeks after this. When sniping from a knoll in the support line where we had a concealed loop-hole I saw a German, about seven hundred yards away, through my telescopic sights. He was having a bath in the German third line. I somehow did not like the idea of shooting a naked man, so I handed the rifle to the sergeant who was with me and said: 'Here, take this. You're a better shot than me.' He got him, he said; but I had not stayed to watch.

About saving the lives of enemy wounded there was disagreement; the convention varied with the division. Some divisions, like the Canadians and a division of Lowland territorials, who had, they claimed, atrocities to avenge, would not only take no risks to rescue enemy wounded, but would go out of their way to finish them off. The Royal Welch Fusiliers were gentlemanly: perhaps a one-in-twenty risk to get a wounded German to safety would be considered justifiable. An important factor in taking risks was our own physical condition. When exhausted and wanting to get quickly from one point in the trenches to another without collapse, and if the enemy were not nearer than four or five hundred yards, we would sometimes take a short cut over the top. In a hurry we would take a one-in-two-hundred risk, when dead tired a one-in-fifty risk. In some battalions where the *morale* was not high, one-in-fifty risks were often taken in mere laziness or despair. The Munsters in the

First Division were said by the Welsh to 'waste men wicked' by not keeping properly under cover when in the reserve lines. In the Royal Welch there was no wastage of this sort. At no time in the war did any of us allow ourselves to believe that hostilities could possibly continue more than nine months or a year more, so it seemed almost worth while taking care; there even seemed a chance of lasting until the end absolutely unhurt.

The Second Royal Welch, unlike the Second Welsh, believed themselves better trench fighters than the Germans. With the Second Welsh it was not cowardice but modesty. With the Second Royal Welch it was not vainglory but courage: as soon as they arrived in a new sector they insisted on getting fire ascendancy. Having found out from the troops they relieved all possible information as to enemy snipers, machine-guns, and patrols, they set themselves to deal with them one by one. They began with machine-guns firing at night. As soon as one started traversing down a trench the whole platoon farthest removed from its fire would open five rounds rapid at it. The machine-gun would usually stop suddenly but start again after a minute or two. Again five rounds rapid. Then it usually gave up.

The Welsh seldom answered a machine-gun. If they did, it was not with local organized fire, beginning and ending in unison, but in ragged confused protest all along the line. There was almost no firing at night in the Royal Welch, except organized fire at a machine-gun or a persistent enemy sentry, or fire at a patrol close enough to be distinguished as a German one. With all other battalions I met in France there was random popping off all the time; the sentries wanted to show their spite against the war. Flares were rarely used in the Royal Welch; most often as signals to our patrols that it was time to come back.

As soon as enemy machine-guns had been discouraged, our patrols would go out with bombs to claim possession of No Man's Land. At dawn next morning came the struggle for sniping ascendancy. The Germans, we were told, had special regimental snipers, trained in camouflaging themselves. I saw one killed once at Cuinchy who had been firing all day from a shell-hole between the lines. He had a sort of cape over his shoulders of imitation grass, his face was painted green and brown, and his rifle was also green fringed. A number of empty cartridges were found by him, and his cap with the special oak-leaf badge. Few battalions attempted to get control of the sniping situation. The Germans had the advantage of having many times more telescopic sights than we did, and steel loopholes that our bullets could not pierce. Also a system by which the snipers were kept for months in the same sector until they knew all the loopholes and shallow places in our trenches, and the tracks that our ration-parties used above-ground by night, and where our traverses came in the trench, and so on, better than we did ourselves. British snipers changed their trenches, with their battalions, every week or two, and never had time to learn the German line thoroughly. But at least we counted on getting rid of the unprofessional German sniper. Later we had an elephant-gun in the battalion that would pierce the German loopholes, and if we could not locate the loophole of a persistent sniper we did what we could to dislodge him by a volley of rifle-grenades, or even by ringing up the artillery.

It puzzled us that if a sniper were spotted and killed, another sniper would begin again next day from the same position. The Germans probably underrated us and regarded it as an accident. The willingness of other battalions to let the Germans have sniping ascendancy helped us; enemy snipers often exposed themselves unnecessarily, even the professionals. There was, of course, one advantage of which no advance or retreat of the enemy could rob us, and that was that we were always facing more or less East; dawn broke behind the German lines, and they seldom realized that for several minutes every morning we could see them though still invisible ourselves. German night wiring-parties often stayed out too long, and we could get a man or two as they went back; sunsets were against us, but sunset was a less critical time. Sentries at night were made to stand with their head and shoulders above the trenches and their rifles in position on the parapet. This surprised me at first. But it meant greater vigilance and self-confidence in the sentry, and it put the top of his head above the level of the parapet. Enemy machine-guns were trained on this level, and it was safer to be hit in the chest or shoulders than in the top of the head. The risk of unaimed fire at night was negligible so this was really the safest plan. It often happened in battalions like the Second Welsh, where the head-and-shoulder rule was not in force and the sentry just took a peep now and then, that an enemy patrol would sneak up unseen to the British wire, throw a few bombs and get safely back. In the Royal Welch the barbed-wire entanglement was the responsibility of the company behind it. One of our first acts on taking over trenches was to inspect and repair it. We did a lot of work on the wire.

Thomas was an extremely silent man; it was not sullenness but shyness. 'Yes' and 'no' was the limit of his usual conversation; it was difficult for us subalterns. He never took us into his confidence about company affairs, and we did not like asking him too much. His chief interests seemed to be polo and the regiment. He was most conscientious in taking his watch at night, a thing that the other company commanders did not always do. We enjoyed his food-hampers sent every week from Fortnum and Mason; we messed by companies when in the trenches. Our only complaint was that Buzz Off, who had a good nose for a hamper, used to spend more time than he would otherwise have done in the company mess. This embarrassed us. Thomas went on leave to England about this time. I heard about it accidentally. He walked about the West End astonished at the amateur militariness that he met everywhere. To be more in keeping with it he gave elaborate awkward salutes to newly-joined second-lieutenants and raised his cap to dug-out colonels and generals. It was a private joke at the expense of the war.

I used to look forward to our spells in trenches at Laventie. Billet life meant battalion mess, also riding-school, which I found rather worse than the Surrey-man had described it. Parades were carried out with peace-time punctiliousness and smartness, especially the daily battalion guard-changing which every now and then, when I was orderly officer, it was my duty to supervise. On one occasion, after the guard-changing ceremony and inspection were over and I was about to dismiss the old guard, I saw Buzz Off cross the village street from one company headquarters to another. As he crossed I called the guard to attention and saluted. I waited for a few seconds and then dismissed the guard, but he had not really gone into the billet; he had been waiting in the doorway. As soon as I dismissed the guard he dashed out with a great show of anger. 'As you were, as you were, stand fast!' he shouted to the guard. And then to me: 'Why in hell's name, Mr. Graves, didn't you ask my permission to dismiss the parade? You've read the King's Regulations, haven't you? And where the devil are your manners, anyhow?' I apologized. I said that I thought he had gone into the house. This made matters worse. He bellowed at me for arguing; then he asked me where I had learned to salute. 'At the depot, sir,' I answered. 'Then, by heaven, Mr. Graves, you'll have to learn to salute as the battalion does. You will parade every morning before breakfast for a month under Staff-sergeant Evans and do an hour's saluting drill.' Then he turned to the guard and dismissed them himself. This was not a particular act of spite against me but the general game of 'chasing the warts,' at which all the senior officers played. It was honestly intended to make us better soldiers.

I had been with the Royal Welch about three weeks when the Nineteenth Brigade was moved down to the Béthune sector to fill a gap in the Second Division; the gap was made by taking out the brigade of Guards to go into the Guards Division which was then being formed. On the way down we marched past Lord Kitchener. Kitchener, we were told, commented to the brigadier on the soldierlike appearance of the leading battalion—which was ourselves—but said cynically: 'Wait until they've been a week or two in the trenches; they will lose some of that high polish.' He apparently mistook us for one of the new-army battalions.

The first trenches we went into on our arrival were the Cuinchy brick-stacks. The company I was with was on the canal-bank frontage, a few hundred yards to the left of where I had been with the Welsh Regiment at the end of May. The Germans opposite wished to be sociable. They sent messages over to us in undetonated riflegrenades. One of these messages was evidently addressed to the Irish battalion we had relieved:

We all German korporals wish you English korporals a good day and invite you to a good German dinner to-night with beer (ale) and cakes. You little dog ran over to us and we keep it safe; it became no food with you so it run to us. Answer in the same way, if you please.

Another message was a copy of the *Neueste Nachrichten,* a German army newspaper printed at Lille. It gave sensational details of Russian defeats around Warsaw and immense captures of prisoners and guns. But we were more interested in a full account in another column of the destruction of a German submarine by British armed trawlers; no details of the sinking of German submarines had been allowed to appear in any English papers. The battalion cared no more about the successes or reverses of our Allies than it did about the origins of the war. It never allowed itself to have any political feelings about the Germans. A professional soldier's job was to fight whomsoever the King ordered him to fight; it was as simple as that. With the King as colonel-in-chief of the regiment it was even simpler. The Christmas 1914 fraternization, in which the battalion was among the first to participate, was of the same professional simplicity; it was not an emotional hiatus but a commonplace of military tradition—an exchange of courtesies between officers of opposite armies.

Cuinchy was one of the worst places for rats. They came up from the canal and fed on the many corpses and multiplied. When I was here with the Welsh a new officer came to the company, and, as a token of his welcome, he was given a dug-out containing a spring-bed. When he turned in that night he heard a scuffling, shone his torch on the bed, and there were two rats on his blankets tussling for the possession of a severed hand. This was thought a great joke.

The colonel called for a patrol to go out along the side of the tow-path, where we had heard suspicious sounds on the previous night, to see whether a working-party was out. I volunteered to go when it was dark. But there was a moon that night so bright and full that it dazzled the eyes to look at it. Between us and the Germans was a flat stretch of about two hundred yards, broken only by shell-craters and an occasional patch of coarse grass. I was not with my own company, but lent to B, which had two officers away on leave. Childe-Freeman, the company commander, said: 'You're not going out on patrol to-night, are you? It's almost as bright as day.' I said: 'All the more reason for going; they won't be expecting me. Will you please have everything as usual? Let the men fire an occasional rifle and send up a flare every half hour. If I go carefully they'll not see me.' But I was nervous, and while we were having supper I clumsily knocked over a cup of tea, and after that a plate. Freeman said: 'Look here, I'll 'phone through to battalion and tell them it's too bright for you to go out.' But I knew Buzz Off would accuse me of cold feet, so Sergeant Williams and I put on our crawlers and went out by way of a mine-crater at the side of the tow-path. There was no need that night for the usual staring business. We could see only too clearly. All we had to do was to wait for an opportunity to move quickly, stop dead and trust to luck, then move on quickly again. We planned our rushes from shell-hole to shell-hole; the opportunities were provided by artillery or machine-gun fire which would distract the sentries. Many of the craters contained corpses of men who had been wounded and crept in and died. Some of them were skeletons, picked clean by the rats. We got to within thirty yards of a big German working-party who were digging a trench ahead of their front line. Between them and us we could count a covering party of ten men lying on the grass in their great-coats. We had gone far enough. There was a German lying on his back about twelve yards away humming a tune. It was the 'Merry Widow' waltz. The sergeant, who was behind me, pressed my foot with his hand and showed me the revolver he was carrying. He raised his eyebrows inquiringly. I gave him the signal for 'no.' We turned to go back; it was hard not to go back too quickly. We had got about half-way back when a German machine-gun opened traversing fire along the top of our trenches. We immediately jumped to our feet; the bullets were brushing the grass, so it was safer to be standing up. We walked the rest of the way back, but moving irregularly to distract the aim of the covering party if they saw us. Back in the trench I rang up the artillery and asked them to fire as much shrapnel as they could spare fifty yards short of where the German front trench touched the tow-path; I knew that one of the night-lines of the battery supporting us was trained near enough to this point. A minute and a quarter later the shells started coming over. We heard the clash of downed tools and distant shouts and cries; we reckoned the probable casualties. The next morning at stand-to Buzz Off came up to me: 'I hear you were on patrol last night?' I said: 'Yes, sir.' He asked me for particulars. When I had told him about the covering party he cursed me for 'not scuppering them with that revolver of yours. Cold feet,' he snorted as he turned away.

One day while we were here the Royal Welch were instructed to shout across to the enemy and induce them to take part in a conversation. The object was to find out how strongly the German front trenches were manned at night. A German-speaking officer in the company among the brick-stacks was provided with a megaphone. He shouted: 'Wie gehts ihnen, kamaraden?' Somebody shouted back in delight: 'Ah, Tommee, hast du den deutsch gelernt?' Firing stopped and a conversation began across the fifty yards or so of No Man's Land. The Germans refused to say what regiment they were. They would not talk any military shop. One of them shouted out: 'Les sheunes madamoiselles de La Bassée bonnes pour coucher avec. Les madamoiselles de Béthune bonnes aussi, hein?' Our spokesman refused to discuss this. In the pause that followed he asked how the Kaiser was. They replied respectfully that he was in excellent

health, thank you. 'And how is the Crown Prince?' he asked them.
'Oh, b—r the Crown Prince,' shouted somebody in English, and was
immediately suppressed by his comrades. There was a confusion of
angry voices and laughter. Then they all began singing the 'Wacht
am Rhein.' The trench was evidently very well held indeed.

The Poet's Paradise

We have narrowed our minds by a neglect of the physical senses:
relying on reason, we no longer see, hear, taste, smell or feel anything like so acutely as our primitive ancestors did, or as most little
children still do before their education hardens. Henry Vaughan's
The Retreat, imitated by Wordsworth in his better known *Intima-
tions of Immortality,* begins:

> Happy those early days when I
> Shin'd in my angel-infancy,
> Before I understood this place
> Appointed for my second race
> Or taught my soul to fancy aught
> But a white celestial thought,
> When yet I had not walked above
> A mile or two from my first love
> And looking back (at that short space),
> Could see a glimpse of his bright face
> When on some gilded cloud or flower
> My gazing soul would dwell an hour . . . .

Civilized man notices a gilded cloud and, at best, mutters 'cumulus'
or 'cirrus' or 'mare's tail', speculating on the weather it portends;
notices a flower and dismisses it with a casual recognition of the variety. To gaze at a wild rose or buttercup for even a minute and find
illumination in the sight, would never occur to him; if only because
all his senses are blunted by a persistent disregard of the ugly smells,
ugly sounds, ugly sights and unpalatable tastes which the struggle

THE POET'S PARADISE. From *Oxford Addresses on Poetry.* Reprinted by permission
of Willis Kingsley Wing. Copyright © 1961, 1962 by International Authors
N. V. Published by Doubleday & Company (United States) and Cassell & Co.,
Ltd. (Great Britain).

for existence entails. His spirit, also, has lost touch with the ideas of mystery, grace and love that originally informed it: intellect and habit starve out imagination. How to awaken these dormant capacities is a problem seldom raised, except by mystics, who usually suggest a daunting formula of spiritual exercises designed to tame bodily lusts. Some claim to have themselves visited Paradise in a state of trance so induced, and to have found it the seat of true felicity and perfect wisdom. Here is a typical passage from Thomas Traherne's *Centuries of Meditation* (he was a contemporary of Vaughan's):

> The corn was orient and immortal wheat, which never should be reaped nor ever was sown. I thought it had stood from everlasting to everlasting. The dust and stones of the street were as precious gold: the gates were at first the end of the world. The green trees when I first saw them through one of the gates transported and ravished me: their sweetness and unusual beauty made my heart to leap, and almost mad with ecstasy, they were such strange and beautiful things . . . all things abided eternally as they were in their proper places. Eternity was manifest in the light of the day and something infinite behind everything appeared, which talked with my expectation and moved my desire.

Today, the main alleviations for the stress of commercial and industrial life are organized religion, organized entertainment, drink. Organized religion may sober the spirit, but except among the more ecstatic sects, rarely purges it. Organized entertainment, distracts, but does not illuminate, the mind. Though some poems, melodies, works of art, love-affairs and fever dreams may give glimpses of a lost magical reality, their spell is short-lasting: it does not create such a permanent nostalgia for the fairyland of childhood as possessed, say, John Clare in Northampton Asylum. The hard, dirty, loveless, synthetic world re-asserts itself as the sole factual truth. Yet a superstitious dream that, somehow, happiness, love, glory, magic lie hidden close at hand, protects the world from the nervous breakdown of which recent wars have been symptomatic; a dream that, when fostered by films and family magazines, becomes optimistically attached to personal success in a career or in marriage and, when fostered by the Church, optimistically attached to a Paradisal afterworld.

In ancient times, 'Paradise' was strictly reserved for an illuminated aristocracy, until the Church at last threw open the gates to all converts, however brutish or feeble-minded, who would accept baptism. Priests then preached Heaven's glories (attainable only by a belief in Christ) as the reward of patience and humility after traversing this vale of tears. Yet St John's Apocalyptic Paradise is borrowed from chapters of the pre-Christian *Book of Enoch*, which are themselves based on the 'Eden' chapters of *Ezekiel* and *Genesis;* and these, again, on the Babylonian Paradise described in the Gilgamesh Epic and elsewhere. The Persians knew a similar Paradise; and their name for it, *paridaeza*, yields the Syrian-Greek word *paradeisos* and the Hebrew *pardess*. Those middle-Eastern Paradises, so far back as the Sumerian, are reported as being delightful mountain-top gardens watered by a four-headed crystal river, their fruit-trees laden with flashing jewels; and a wise serpent always haunts them. Rare humans who enter Paradise while in a state of grace are granted 'perfect wisdom' by the Serpent—'knowledge of good and evil' means knowledge of 'all things that exist'—and only the herb of immortality is denied them. Thus Gilgamesh, having visited the jewelled Babylonian Paradise, dived to the sea-bottom and drew up a herb of immortality; but the Serpent took it from him, and he meekly resigned himself to death. Adam and Eve were driven out of Eden ('pleasure') by God lest they might discover and eat the fruit of immortality; the Cherub, on guard at the gate thereafter with a flaming sword, is the very Serpent who gave them the fruit of knowledge. The King of Tyre, though perfect in beauty and wisdom, is figuratively expelled from Eden (*Ezekiel* xxviii) for claiming to be an immortal god with a seat in the heart of the sea. *Enoch* mentions both the tree of wisdom and the tree of life; and *the Secrets of Enoch* places the latter in the Third Heaven, a paradise to which St Paul claimed that he had been caught up.

Greek mythographers told of a Paradise on Mount Atlas, the 'Garden of the Hesperides', guarded by a hundred-headed Serpent; but made Heracles shoot the Serpent, take away some of the jewelled fruit, and become immortal. This Paradise, like the Sumerian one that antedates Gilgamesh's 'Garden of Delights', belonged to a Mother-goddess—it was Hera's before she married Zeus—not to a male god. Christians chose to identify the serpent in Eden with Satan; they preached that Jesus Christ, a 'Second Adam', lives permanently in Paradise, having expelled the Serpent, and is ready there to welcome all believers when it has finally been destroyed on the Day of Judgment.

Why do paradises follow a traditional pattern, wide-spread and persistent enough to be shared even by Polynesians and pre-Columbian Mexicans? The evidence suggests that, originally, a common drug causes the paradisal visions and provides the remarkable mental illumination described as 'perfect wisdom'. One such drug, a hallucigenic mushroom, was certainly used in Central America before the Spanish conquest. Professor Roger Heim and R. G. Wasson's massive work, *Les Champignons Hallucigènes de Mexique* (Paris, 1958), contains a coloured reproduction of a fresco from the Aztec city of Tepantitla, dated between 300 and 600 A.D., which shows a soul visiting Paradise. The usual elements are there: a river (stocked with fish), bordered with flowers and bejewelled trees, haunted by bright-coloured butterflies and a spectacular serpent. The soul stands open-mouthed, weeping tears of joy and wonder, his body connected to the river by a blue thread. This river is shaped like a mushroom and, at its source—the centre of the mushroom head—lurks Tlalóc, God of Mysteries, in toad form, the water issuing from his mouth. Tlalóc, who often wore a serpent head-dress, was a god of lightning. He used a sea-shell as another emblem, and 'had his seat in the midst of the seas': at the bottom of the fresco an underwater grotto appears, marked with a cross, the four heads of which are mushrooms. Nobody who has been admitted to the rite thus pictured will find much difficulty in deciphering the symbolism.

R. G. Wasson's ritual experience came as the culmination of a study on which he and his wife had been engaged for years: that of mycophobia. Mycophobia, the unreasoning fear of mushrooms, affects whole populations in Europe, Asia and Africa, being total in some regions, in others modified by certain exceptions (such as the white field mushroom among the English), elsewhere non-existent. Now, a few mushrooms, easily distinguished from edible varieties, do contain a mortal poison; but most are palatable, if not delicious. Why, the Wassons asked, when wholesome fruit and vegetables are eaten freely, with a disregard for the poisonous or the inedible, should this selectivity be denied the mushroom? Why should horrible and obscene names be applied to edible mushrooms? Perhaps mycophobia pointed to an ancient taboo, like that which has given Jews and Moslems a disgust of pork, and Northern Europeans a disgust of horse-flesh—nutritious and tasty meat—both pig and horse having once been holy animals. And, since mushrooms figured alongside toads, snakes and devils in numerous late mediaeval paintings, and still bear popular names connected with toads, snakes and devils, it looked as if they might have been sacred food in a pagan rite, preserved by witches of Western Europe who kept toads and snakes as diabolic 'familiars'.

A particular variety of mushroom, the *amanita muscaria*, in Britain called 'fly-cap', grows under birch-trees in Northern countries, where it is scarlet, with white spots; but under conifers to the southward, where its scarlet becomes fox-colour. Fly-cap induces in the Korjaks, a Palaeo-Siberian tribe of Kamchatka, and among the Mongol Hazaras of Afghanistan, a boisterous ecstasy which helps them to consult ancestral spirits and utter prophecies. R. G. Wasson guessed that the mushroom had been similarly used in Europe, though reserved for the priesthood; that, for security reasons, the taboo had been extended to cover the eating of all mushrooms, on pain of death; and that this taboo hung on long after the rites came to an end—except in countries where famine forced the common people to defy it and become positive mycophiles, as all Slavonic peoples now are. The name 'toadstool', particularly applied to fly-cap, is apt; because it contains a poison, *bufotenine*, which is also exuded by toads from their 'warts' when frightened.

Moreover, early Spanish archives mentioned Mexican mushroom-oracles that, though officially extinct, were still rumored to operate in secret far from civilization. A certain mushroom was known as 'God's Body' by the Mazateks of Oaxaca Province, because sacramentally eaten. The Wassons, learning of this, visited Oaxaca during the June mushroom season, and were able to attend an oracular meeting at which the *curandero* ('healer') who took charge, ceremoniously ate certain small ill-tasting mushrooms and, speaking for the god, gave an unexpected, surprising and accurate answer to the question they had asked him. Later, when invited by a *curandera* to eat the mushrooms themselves, they understood the solemn local tradition about the feast: 'One knows all; one even sees where God dwells.' Their visions recalled the heaven shown on the Tepantitla fresco, and it became clear that they had been symbolically eating the body not of Christ, but of the god Tlalóc.

In the different regions of Mexico where the cult survives, certain religious rules are common to all. Devotees, before partaking of a mushroom feast, must fast, abstain from sexual intercourse, and be at peace with the world and themselves. Whoever disregards these rules (the *curanderos* and *curanderas* agreed) may see such demonic visions as to wish they had never been born. The Christian, Jewish, Greek and Babylonian Heavens, it should be recalled, have a Hell which complements Paradise; and the usual vision is of innumerable demon faces grinning from lurid caverns. But those who attend such a feast while in a state of grace, report that the mushrooms not only sharpen their intelligence, so that they seem to possess 'perfect wisdom', but shower on them what Christians call 'the peace and love that passes all understanding'—a strong, non-erotic sense of spiritual comradeship.

The Roman Catholic Church teaches that Paradise cannot be attained except by repentance; and prepares every sinner for the journey with the *viaticum*, a symbolic consumption of Jesus Christ's body and blood, after asking him to purge his soul by a sincere confession. From what religion, it should be asked, did St Paul borrow this rite, since it is not attested in the Gospels and is an infringement of the Hebrew law against the drinking of blood? A question that leads to another: in what pre-Christian cult did a god deliver oracles when his flesh was symbolically eaten—as the Mazateks now believe that Tlalóc-Christ does? Tlalóc, we know, was the Spirit of lightning-engendered toadstool. More questions arise. What European god claimed this nativity? Or had associations with the serpent or the toad? Or possessed an underwater retreat? Or assisted at mysteries where ineffable visions were witnessed?

The sole European deity known to have matched Tlaloc in these respects was Dionysus. Born as a serpent-crowned child from the Earth-goddess Semele, whom a flash of lightning had impregnated, he went through a variety of transformations, was then torn to shreds and eaten by the Titans, but restored to life by his grandmother, the Goddess Rhea, Creatrix of the world; possessed an underwater retreat in the grottoes of the Sea-goddess Thetis; and assisted at the chief Greek Mysteries, under the protection of goddesses.

The Greek poets tell how when Dionysus' Maenads tore off Orpheus' head, it continued to prophesy. The head of Pentheus, another figure in the Dionysus myth, was torn off by his own mother Agave; both incidents could refer to the practice of tearing the mushroom-head from its stalk—heads alone are used at Mexican oracles. The Eleusinian Mysteries, sacred to the goddesses Demeter and Persephone, and also to Dionysus, were preceded by fasting and a ritual bathe in the sea, where devotees transferred their sins to scape-pigs. They then entered a temple, drank mint-water and ate pastries baked in magical shapes and carried in baskets. As a result, they saw celestial visions which could never afterwards be forgotten. The meaning of the Greek word *mysterion* ('mystery') is disputed, but since the mysteries were an autumnal festival complementary to the spring *anthesterion*, and since this means 'flower-springing', *mysterion* may well mean *myko-sterion*, or 'mushroom-springing'.

A distinction should here be drawn between the wild Dionysian orgies of Maenads who went raging over the hills, often in the company of Satyrs (a pre-Hellenic mountain tribe), and the decently conducted temple-mysteries, where no violence occurred. Pliny's remark that an awed hush 'descends on people if a toad is placed among them' suggests that Dionysus, like Tlalóc, had a toad epiphany. But the celestial visions of the mysteries are unlikely to have been produced by fly-cap, which loses its toxic quality when cooked, and could not well be introduced raw into food and drink. However, the toxic qualities of *panaeolus papilionaceus*, a hallucigenic toadstool shown on an early Greek vase and now known to have figured in the European witch cult, resist cooking; its liquor may have been mixed in the mint-water, and its flesh baked in the magical pastries. I believe, but cannot prove, that fly-cap, which appears on a carved Etruscan mirror at the feet of the criminal Ixion, was the original mushroom sacred to the universal Toad-god, and that the more tranquil and equally delightful properties of *panaeolus papilionaceus* and *psilocybe*, were discovered by later experiment and also placed under the Toad-god's charge. Fly-cap grows in both hemispheres, and the ancient mushroom-stones of Guatemala show Tlalóc in toad shape, seated underneath a mushroom which appears to be a fly-cap, not a *psilocybe*.

Some of the Eleusinian pastries had phallic shapes, and indeed, *mykes* ('mushroom') also means 'phallus' in Greek; others were baked like piglings (a widespread term for mushrooms); some perhaps like toads and serpents. A common name for the toad in European folklore is 'the cripple', because of his clumsy feet; and 'Dionysus' means 'the lame god'. One Greek hero who, according to the myths, at first resisted Dionysus, but presently saw the light, was Perseus, King of Argos and founder of Mycenae. Punished for his obduracy with an outbreak of madness among the Argive women —they began eating their own babies raw, as also happened at Thebes when Pentheus resisted the cult—Perseus dedicated a temple to Dionysus at Mycenae. Argos had a toad as its badge, and Perseus is said to have named Mycenae after a mushroom found on the site, 'from which proceeded a stream of water'. He also made visionary flights through the air, paid a visit to the 'Stygian nymphs' on the slopes of Mount Atlas—presumably the Hesperides, who were later kind to his descendant Heracles—and claimed the same sort of nativity as Dionysus, having been engendered by Zeus in a shower of gold. Phryneus, the Toadstool-Dionysus to which these myths point, lay securely hidden behind the Wine-Dionysus and the Grain-Dionysus. Apart from a menacing Greek proverb 'Mushrooms are the food of the gods', nobody mentioned the subject. Greek peasants are mycophobes.

Baby-eating, a practice not associated with any Greek cult except that of Dionysus, also figured (according to Catholic missionaries) in the Aztec rain-making rites of Tlalóc. This god's name meant 'Pulp of the Earth' (i.e. mushroom?), and he lived at Tlalócan, a mountain paradise, with certain Grain-goddesses and his gentle sister-spouse Chalchiuthlicue, patroness of streams and family-life. Some centuries before the Spanish conquest, matriarchy and clan-totemism had been superseded among the Aztecs by patriarchy and individual totemism. Tlalóc thus officially escaped from the tutelage of goddesses, just as Dionysus did in Classical Greece when he was raised to the Olympic Council of Twelve and took over the Barley-goddess Demeter's winnowing festival, the Haloa. Yet in the Mysteries, Dionysus seems still to have been subservient to Demeter and Persephone. Similarly, the Mazatec *curandera* who initiated the Wassons addressed the Christianized Tlalóc as if he were her wayward son, and she a goddess. It is possible that, alike in Greece and Mexico, the 'babies' eaten in sacred pictures were really mushrooms.

The Christian sacrament of bread and wine was a love-feast in Hellenistic style. Initiates of the Lesser Eleusinian Mysteries, who had to undergo a period of probation before being admitted to the Greater Mysteries, saw no celestial visions. Presumably, the mystagogues withheld the sacred hallucigenic agent until sure of a candidate's worthiness; he received bread and wine only, symbols of the Grain-Dionysus and the Wine-Dionysus. The Church has indeed banished the Serpent from Paradise. Her sacramental elements give the communicant no visionary foretaste of the new Jerusalem. The disappointment often felt by Protestant adolescents at their first communion is a natural one—the priest promises more than they are able to experience. I learned only last week, from an Arabic scholar, that the root-word F.T.R. means, in Arabic, first 'toadstool', then 'divine rapture', then 'sacred pellets of bread'. This points to a pre-Islamic hallucigenic practice of immense age.

Granted, many Christian mystics and Jewish mystics have undoubtedly seen Paradisal sights, but always after a life of intense spiritual struggle; and these often alternate with terrifying visions of Hell. It is now therefore usual to treat mystics as schizophrenics, arresting them and prescribing electric-shock treatment if their enthusiasm has caused a breach of the peace. The Church herself is apt to discourage a mystic who claims to have seen sights denied to his ecclesiastical superiors; suspecting him, at best, of spiritual pride. This type of schizophrenia is chronic, uncontrollable, and what is called 'anti-social'. Only when mystics have written poems, or painted pictures, in which the illumination cannot be denied, and only when they have been dead some years—for example St John of the Cross, El Greco, Blake, van Gogh—are they likely to be valued as great souls.

The use of hallucigenic mushrooms, on the other hand, induces a temporary, controllable schizophrenia within the Mazatek social scheme, and the sole religious demand on participants is that they shall enter the circle fasting, with a clear conscience and a quiet mind. When I ate *psilocybe* on 31 January 1960, a recording of the *curandera's* invocation to Tlaloc as Christ gave the rite a decent solemnity. *Psilocybe* must be eaten in complete darkness—because the least light, even strained through the eyelids, becomes painful as soon as the drug takes effect. The visions last for some four and a half hours. According to the Mazateks, a novice seldom sees persons or historical scenes: he finds it enough to enter the 'Garden of Delights'. The second and third feast may widen his experiences. Adepts learn to direct their mind wherever they please, visit the past, foretell the future.

Here is the account I wrote of my experience:

That evening, four of us gathered in Gordon Wasson's apartment overlooking the East River, prepared to set out for Paradise under his guidance. He had advised us to fast beforehand, drink no liquor, and try to achieve a state of grace. At seven-thirty he gave us the mushrooms in crystalline form washed down with water and, at eight, began turning out the lights one by one, while we settled down in easy chairs. Soon no sound was heard except the swish-

swish of cars passing in an endless stream along the Drive between us and the river: a noise not unlike the sound of waves on a beach.

By eight o'clock I felt a numbness in my arms, and a pricking at the nape of my neck. In the half-light that filtered through the shutters, coloured dots appeared on the ceiling; they shone brighter when I closed my eyes. We all began to shiver, our pulses slowed down, and Masha Wasson brought in blankets. Since she is a trained nurse and had twice made this journey herself, we welcomed the reassuring pressure of her hand. I remembered a warning quotation: 'You are going where God dwells; and will be granted all knowledge. . . . Whoever nurses evil in his heart sees hideous demons and nameless horrors, more proper to Hell than to Paradise, and wishes he had never been born.' I anxiously considered my own motives. How honest were they? Would I see demons? Though not a saint, I was at least a dedicated historian and poet; with luck I might be spared punishment.

Since even the half-light had become uncomfortably strong for my eyes, I kept them closed. I knew that the road to Paradise often begins under the sea, or from a lake-bottom; so the greenish water now lapping around me came as no surprise. I entered a marble grotto, passing a pile of massive sunken statuary, and found myself in a high-roofed tunnel lit by brilliantly coloured lamps. The sea lay behind.

This was perfect schizophrenia. My corporeal self reclined in a chair, fully conscious, exchanging occasional confidences with friends: but another 'I' had entered the tunnel—perhaps the same tunnel through which, four thousand years before, the epic hero Gilgamesh made his approach to the Babylonian Paradise?

Still worrying about the demons, I glanced up at the roof. Thousands of pink, green or yellow faces, like carnival masks, grimaced horribly down; but I dismissed them with a wave of my hand, and they obediently vanished. . . . A turn in the tunnel brought me to the domed Treasury, without which no Paradise is complete, whether Hindu, Babylonian, Hebrew, Icelandic, Irish, Greek or Chinese. As the prophet Ezekiel wrote:

> Every precious stone was thy covering: the sardius, topaz and the diamond; the beryl, the onyx and the jasper; the sapphire, the emerald, the carbuncle and gold.

Her Majesty's Crown Jewels at the Tower of London would have looked tawdry by comparison with the fantastic treasure now heaped before me: diadems, tiaras, necklaces, crosses, breast-plates, goblets, ephods, cups, platters, sceptres, blazing or twinkling. But, even richer than these jewels, were the royal silks spread out for my inspection in blue, mulberry and white: vast lengths, miraculously brocaded with birds, beasts, flowers. . . . My closest experience to this had been in early childhood when, after waiting endlessly in the cold, dark hall, my sisters and I saw the drawing-room door suddenly flung open, and there blazed the Christmas tree: all its candles lighted, its branches glistening with many-coloured tinsel.

I reached for a notebook and wrote: '9 p.m. Visions of . . .' but got no further: things were happening too fast. Besides, the pen felt strange in my hand, and its scratch on paper sounded offensively loud. I remember saying after awhile: 'I have seen enough treasure for a lifetime. Is there no human beauty in Paradise?' At once the diadems, tiaras, necklaces, crosses and sceptres vanished, as the demons had done. Instead, a row of lovely, live, naked Caryatids appeared, lined along the wall, as if supporting the dome. Their faces were shrouded. Yet I hesitated to indulge in erotic fancies, lest the Caryatids turned into filthy, deformed devilkins like the ones in Flemish pictures of St Anthony's Temptations. Blushing, I dismissed them too, and came out from the tunnel into daylight. What I had been taught at school and in church proved true enough, though the truth enormously transcended the account. Around me lay a mountain-top Eden, with its jewel-bright trees, its flowers and its pellucid streams. And I experienced not only the bliss of innocence, but also the 'knowledge of good and evil'. Most Christians understand this phrase as meaning the power to distinguish right from wrong; in Hebrew, however, it signifies a universal understanding of all things, whether good or evil. Indeed, my mind suddenly became so agile and unfettered that I felt capable of solving any problem in the world; it was as if I had immediate access to all knowledge everywhere. But the sensation of wisdom sufficed—why should I trouble to exploit it?

Gordon Wasson had switched on the tape-recorder and the *curandera's* voice was now invoking Tlaloc as 'Christo'. She chanted, scolded, entreated, commanded, coaxed him to do what she required; it might have been the Goddess Aphrodite addressing her froward son Eros. . . . Every now and then she would change her mood and song; would mourn, triumph, or laugh. I fell wholly under her spell, and presently enjoyed the curious experience of *seeing* sound. The song-notes became intricate links of a round golden chain that coiled and looped in serpentine fashion among jade-green bushes: the only serpent I met in Eden. . . . Each song was followed by a pause, and always I waited in a lover's agony for her to begin again, tears pricking at my eyelids. Once the *curandera* seemed to sing off-key. Perhaps this was quarter-tone music; at any rate, my ear was not offended: I knew what she meant when I saw one edge of the golden chain band now formed by the sound spread out into a spectrum; and laughed for pleasure. Towards the end came a quick, breathless, cheerful song of creation and growth. The notes fell to earth but rose once more in green shoots which soared swiftly up, putting on branches, leaves, flowers —until it dominated the sky like the beanstalk in the fairytale.

My spirit followed after into the clear blue air, gazing down on cornfields, fields of poppies, and the spires of a heavenly city, and Thomas Traherne's orient and immortal wheat, 'which never should be reaped nor ever was sown'.

At last the music ended. The visions were fading now. My corporeal self sighed, stretched luxuriously, and looked around. Most of the company had left the room. Only one friend remained. I asked him: 'So the journey seems to be over?'

'Ah, but close your eyes, and you can get back at once,' he said.

'How do you feel?'

'My mind has never been so clear! Did you hear such music in all your life?'

We joined the others in the kitchen, ate cold turkey sandwiches and compared notes. . . . 'I saw huge slow-moving fish in the sea; did you?'—'. . . The demons scared me nearly to death! I wept and sobbed; maybe I wasn't in a state of grace. And when I looked at my hand, O God!'—'. . . Weren't those buildings *enormous?* But I couldn't place their architectural style.'—'. . . Me, I'd take the journey all over again—this minute, if I could!'

A curious bond of affection had been established between us: so strong that I felt nothing could ever break it. At two o'clock in the morning we said good-bye. By eight I was on my way to Idlewild, headed for Europe: profoundly refreshed, and (in Wordsworth's phrase) 'trailing clouds of glory'—wisps of celestial memory which persisted nearly a month.

*

Civilized consciences revolt against the abuse of hallucigenic drugs—most of them habit-forming, dangerous, and unobtainable except by prescription, or in the black market. Spirits, tobacco, tranquillizers—all harmful if habitually taken—are however on unrestricted sale and, because they provide no visions (apart from the fearful hell of *delirium tremens*), the Churches condone their use;

for hard liquor merely depresses the senses, tobacco and tranquillizers merely dull them.

Psilocybin, the active principle of *psilocybe*, is now synthetically
made in Switzerland. At present, the medical profession controls the
supply, and uses it for the diagnosis of mental illness. But, since the
formula has been published, not even severe legislation will prevent
the general public from access to the product. It seems likely, therefore, that what was for thousands of years a sacred and secret element, entrusted only to persons chosen for their good conduct and
integrity, will soon be snatched at by jaded sensation-seekers. They
will be disappointed. The word 'drug', originally applied to all in-
gredients used in chemistry, pharmacy, dyeing and so on, has acquired a particular connotation in modern English, which cannot
apply to *psilocybin*: 'to drug' is to stupefy, rather than to quicken,
the senses. *Psilocybin* provides no welcome semi-death in drunken
stupor: though the body is relaxed, the mind is conscious throughout, indeed, supra-conscious. Psychiatrists at the Lexington Addiction Centre, Kentucky, who give *psilocybin* to alcoholics as a means
of discovering why they are trying to escape from reality by drink,
find that it intensifies and lays bare mental conflict. Experimentalists
are therefore likely to see visions evoked by their own uneasy consciences: weeping for grief, not joy; or even shuddering aghast.

Good and evil alternate in most people's hearts. Few are habitually
at peace with themselves; and whoever prepares to eat hallucigenic
mushroom should take as careful stock of his mental and moral well-
being as initiates took before attending the Eleusinian Mysteries.
The friend who ate mushrooms with us while not in a state of peace
watched his hand turn corpse-like and slowly disintegrate into a
dusty skeleton. This peculiar virtue of *psilocybin*, the power to enhance personal reality, turns 'Know thyself!' into a practical pre-
cept; and may commend it as the sacramental food of some new religion. *Peyotl*, made from cactus buds, another sacred hallucigenic
agent—but, it seems, not in such early religious use among the
Mexicans as mushrooms—has already been sanctified by a 'Christian
church' of two hundred thousand members, extending from Central
America to Canada. The Catholic and main Protestant churches can
never, of course, accept visions that either *peyotl* or *psilocybin* excites as anything but diabolical and illusory. They may even put
pressure on public-health authorities to outlaw *psilocybin*, arguing
that, although the *psilocybe* mushroom does not make for addiction

among the Mazateks, and seems to have no harmful effect on their minds and bodies, this may be due to its short season and a loss of virtue when dried; whereas the virtue is stable in *psilocybin,* and the results of long-term dosing are unknown—a permanent schizophrenia might occur. Liquor and tobacco interests would, no doubt, wholeheartedly support the Churches' plea.

My single experience of *psilocybe* was wholly good: an illumination of the mind, a re-education of sight and hearing, and even of touch, as I handled small objects beside me. The perfect sensory control which I could enjoy, confirmed, by analogy, my life-long faith in the poetic trance: a world where words come to life and combine, under the poet's supra-conscious guidance, into inevitable and true rhythmic statements. But I find one main difference between the two conditions: a mushroom trance is relatively passive; a poetic trance, active—the pen running briskly across paper.

Research should show how far the similarity of most people's visits to Eden or Tlalócan depends on the mushrooms' toxic properties, and how far on suggestion. I think it unnecessary, here, to cite Jung's theory of the Collective Unconscious, since a common tradition of Paradise may be attributed to ancient cultural contact even between distant civilizations, especially if these experiences can be shown to correspond with the physical action of a common toxin. A distinct lowering of body-temperature occurs an hour after eating *psilocybe,* which would explain both the cool sea-grottoes and Gilgamesh's search for the herb of immortality at the sea bottom; it is also followed by a considerable heightening of colour sensitivity, which would account for the jewels. After all, such writhing and creeping things as torment sufferers from *delirium tremens* are clearly not products of the Collective Unconscious, but due to a characteristic tremor of the optic nerve and an irritation of the skin, caused by alcohol.

Paradise, in fact, seems to be a subjective vision. As Jesus himself said: 'The Kingdom of Heaven is within you.' He might have added: 'So is the Kingdom of Hell.' The jewelled 'Garden' can be attained by the pure of heart without undergoing so austere a regimen as to become alienated from their friends; many young women have a secret garden which they frequently visit. The love-feast, for all who attend it in a state of grace and with complete mutual trust —by no means a simple condition—strengthens human friendship and at the same time bestows spiritual enlightenment: which are the twin purposes of most religions. Whether the soul visits a non-subjective Paradise or Hell on quitting its body, let theologians dispute.

The natural poetic trance, however, as I have experienced it on different levels—sometimes light, sometimes so deep that the slightest disturbance causes acute distress—means a good deal more to me than any trance induced by artificial means. I understand Coleridge's depreciation of *Kubla Khan*, which he wrote almost automatically after stupefying his mind with laudanum. It was, as it were, a demon's gift; not earned (like his other poems) by active poetic thought. True, I have survived enough operations to know the difference in kind between an opiate dream, where one is the dazed victim, and a mushroom vision that can, I know, be consciously assessed and even controlled. Since I found myself capable of dismissing that vision of Crown Jewels and Caryatids, and since one or two of my companions found it possible to visit particular places when under the influence of *psilocybe*, I hesitate to challenge the claim that Tlalóc's adepts can use their liberation of mental forces for oracular research. Nevertheless, it seems established that Tlalocan, for all its sensory marvels, contains no palace of words presided over by the Living Muse, and no small white-washed cell (furnished with only a table, a chair, pen, ink and paper) to which a poet may retire and actively write poems in her honour—rather than bask sensuously under her spell.

Farewell, My Lovely!
A Slight Sound at Evening
The Shape of the U.N.

E. B. WHITE
(*b. 1899*)

IN THE LATER twenties and early thirties, *The New Yorker* magazine raised American standards of taste and wit, especially in matters of language. Though he had some formidable fellow-contributors—Dorothy Parker, Robert Benchley, Ogden Nash, James Thurber, Clarence Day, Frank Sullivan, and S. J. Perelman —E. B. White perhaps did most to set the tone of the magazine. As principal author of the department "Talk of the Town," he began each issue with editorials that defined the position of the magazine and expressed its style and mood. He wrote in a spirit of apparently naive inquiry which was welcomed as a new and satisfying kind of sophistication. White collaborated with James Thurber on a spoof (*Is Sex Necessary?* 1929) of the articles of advice based on psychoanalysis which then, as now, filled the popular publications. He and his wife, Katherine, also an editor of *The New Yorker*, collaborated on *A Subtreasury of American Humor* (1941), an anthology which by its discriminating choices will always be helpful to anyone who tries to define what is distinctively our own in this important genre.

Early in his career White published in periodicals two glowing tributes to New York City as a place to live. Later he wrote *Here Is New York* (1949), a guidebook based on very personal responses to the city. For all his loyality, though, by 1937 he had left New York to spend most of the next seven years with his wife and child at his farm on the seacoast of Maine. He had always been a devoted Thoreauvian; the Maine adventure was his personal Walden. During this period he wrote a monthly column, "One Man's Meat," for *Harper's Magazine,* in which he reflected, with a good many side glances at his own daily life, on such themes as farming, New England neighbors, nature, and war.

At Cornell University, where White was editor of the student paper during the First World War, he had the luck and the sensitivity to come under the influence of Professor William Strunk, who wrote *The Elements of Style.* In 1959 White arranged for a new edition of this brief text, adding an introduction and a chapter of his own on the art of writing. Even a practiced author will find this book helpful in keeping his style pure.

White has published two volumes of light verse, *The Lady Is Cold* (1929) and *The Fox of Peapack* (1938), and two children's books, *Stuart Little* (1945) and *Charlotte's Web* (1952). Fables and parables are mixed with the essays in his principal collections: *Every Day Is Saturday* (1934), *Quo Vadimus* (1939), *One Man's Meat* (1942), *The Second Tree from the Corner* (1954), and *Points of My Compass* (1962).

"Farewell, My Lovely!" was originally published in *The New Yorker* under the pseudonym Lee Strout White, because it is White's rewriting or recreation of a piece submitted by Richard Lee Strout of *The Christian Science Monitor.* As an imaginative revival of life with the Model T Ford, it parallels in words the enthusiasm with which hobbyists keep antique automobiles resplendent and running. But it is also a record of American folkways, and is amusingly ingenious in the phrases it invents to humanize machinery.

"A Slight Sound at Evening," written on the hundredth anniversary of the publication of Thoreau's *Walden*, has already been discussed in the Introduction as an ideal example, in structure and style, of the familiar essay at its best. "The Shape of the U. N." may seem to use too many homely colloquial metaphors, especially in the first part. But this deliberate contrast with the noncommittal abstractions of diplomacy is more than stylistic in its implications. White, as a "word man," sees how the Charter's contradictory insistence on the indefinable word "aggression" is a key to the whole problem of international organization. What he wrote in 1956 became even more pertinent ten years later during the controversies over American intervention in Santo Domingo and Viet Nam.

Farewell, My Lovely!

(An aging male kisses an old flame goodbye, circa 1936)

I see by the new Sears Roebuck catalogue that it is still possible to buy an axle for a 1909 Model T Ford, but I am not deceived. The great days have faded, the end is in sight. Only one page in the current catalogue is devoted to parts and accessories for the Model T; yet everyone remembers springtimes when the Ford gadget section was larger than men's clothing, almost as large as household furnishings. The last Model T was built in 1927, and the car is fading from what scholars call the American scene—which is an understatement, because to a few million people who grew up with it, the old Ford practically *was* the American scene.

It was the miracle God had wrought. And it was patently the sort

FAREWELL, MY LOVELY. This essay originally appeared in *The New Yorker* over the pseudonym Lee Strout White. It was suggested by a manuscript submitted to the magazine by Richard Lee Strout, and was written by E. B. White. Reprinted by permission. Copyright © 1936, 1964, The New Yorker Magazine, Inc.; published in book form by G. P. Putnam under the title *Farewell to Model T*, 1936. Reprinted under its original title in *The Second Tree from the Corner* by E. B. White, Harper & Bros., 1954.

of thing that could only happen once. Mechanically uncanny, it was like nothing that had ever come to the world before. Flourishing industries rose and fell with it. As a vehicle, it was hardworking, commonplace, heroic; and it often seemed to transmit those qualities to the persons who rode in it. My own generation identifies it with Youth, with its gaudy, irretrievable excitements; before it fades into the mist, I would like to pay it the tribute of the sigh that is not a sob, and set down random entries in a shape somewhat less cumbersome than a Sears Roebuck catalogue.

The Model T was distinguished from all other makes of cars by the fact that its transmission was of a type known as planetary—which was half metaphysics, half sheer fiction. Engineers accepted the word "planetary" in its epicyclic sense, but I was always conscious that it also meant "wandering," "erratic." Because of the peculiar nature of this planetary element, there was always, in Model T, a certain dull rapport between engine and wheels, and even when the car was in a state known as neutral, it trembled with a deep imperative and tended to inch forward. There was never a moment when the bands were not faintly egging the machine on. In this respect it was like a horse, rolling the bit on its tongue, and country people brought to it the same technique they used with draft animals.

Its most remarkable quality was its rate of acceleration. In its palmy days the Model T could take off faster than anything on the road. The reason was simple. To get under way, you simply hooked the third finger of the right hand around a lever on the steering column, pulled down hard, and shoved your left foot forcibly against the low-speed pedal. These were simple, positive motions; the car responded by lunging forward with a roar. After a few seconds of this turmoil, you took your toe off the pedal, eased up a mite on the throttle, and the car, possessed of only two forward speeds, catapulted directly into high with a series of ugly jerks and was off on its glorious errand. The abruptness of this departure was never equalled in other cars of the period. The human leg was (and still is) incapable of letting in a clutch with anything like the forthright abandon that used to send Model T on its way. Letting in a clutch is a negative, hesitant motion, depending on delicate nervous control; pushing down the Ford pedal was a simple, country motion—an expansive act, which came as natural as kicking an old door to make it budge.

The driver of the old Model T was a man enthroned. The car, with top up, stood seven feet high. The driver sat on top of the gas tank, brooding it with his own body. When he wanted gasoline, he alighted, along with everything else in the front seat; the seat was pulled off, the metal cap unscrewed, and a wooden stick thrust down to sound the liquid in the well. There were always a couple of these sounding sticks kicking around in the ratty sub-cushion regions of a flivver. Refuelling was more of a social function then, because the driver had to unbend, whether he wanted to or not. Directly in front of the driver was the windshield—high, uncompromisingly erect. Nobody talked about air resistance, and the four cylinders pushed the car through the atmosphere with a simple disregard of physical law.

There was this about a Model T: the purchaser never regarded his purchase as a complete, finished product. When you bought a Ford, you figured you had a start—a vibrant, spirited framework to which could be screwed an almost limitless assortment of decorative and functional hardware. Driving away from the agency, hugging the new wheel between your knees, you were already full of creative worry. A Ford was born naked as a baby, and a flourishing industry grew up out of correcting its rare deficiencies and combatting its fascinating diseases. Those were the great days of lily-painting. I have been looking at some old Sears Roebuck catalogues, and they bring everything back so clear.

First you bought a Ruby Safety Reflector for the rear, so that your posterior would glow in another's car's brilliance. Then you invested thirty-nine cents in some radiator Moto Wings, a popular ornament which gave the Pegasus touch to the machine and did something godlike to the owner. For nine cents you bought a fan-belt guide to keep the belt from slipping off the pulley.

You bought a radiator compound to stop leaks. This was as much a part of everybody's equipment as aspirin tablets are of a medicine cabinet. You bought special oil to prevent chattering, a clamp-on dash light, a patching outfit, a tool box which you bolted to the running board, a sun visor, a steering-column brace to keep the column rigid, and a set of emergency containers for gas, oil, and water—three thin, disc-like cans which reposed in a case on the running board during long, important journeys—red for gas, gray for water, green for oil. It was only a beginning. After the car was

about a year old, steps were taken to check the alarming disintegra-
tion. (Model T was full of tumors, but they were benign.) A set of
anti-rattlers (ninety-eight cents) was a popular panacea. You
hooked them on to the gas and spark rods, to the brake pull rod, and
to the steering-rod connections. Hood silencers, of black rubber,
were applied to the fluttering hood. Shock-absorbers and snubbers
gave "complete relaxation." Some people bought rubber pedal pads,
to fit over the standard metal pedals. (I didn't like these, I remember.) Persons of a suspicious or pugnacious turn of mind bought a
rear-view mirror; but most Model T owners weren't worried by
what was coming from behind because they would soon enough see
it out in front. They rode in a state of cheerful catalepsy. Quite a
large mutinous clique among Ford owners went over to a foot ac-
celerator (you could buy one and screw it to the floor board), but
there was a certain madness in these people, because the Model T,
just as she stood, had a choice of three foot pedals to push, and there
were plenty of moments when both feet were occupied in the routine performance of duty and when the only way to speed up the
engine was with the hand throttle.

Gadget bred gadget. Owners not only bought ready-made gadgets, they invented gadgets to meet special needs. I myself drove my
car directly from the agency to the blacksmith's, and had the smith
affix two enormous iron brackets to the port running board to support an army trunk.

People who owned closed models builded along different lines:
they bought ball grip handles for opening doors, window anti-
rattlers, and de-luxe flower vases of the cut-glass anti-splash type.
People with delicate sensibilities garnished their car with a device
called the Donna Lee Automobile Disseminator—a porous vase
guaranteed, according to Sears, to fill the car with a "faint clean
odor of lavender." The gap between open cars and closed cars was
not as great then as it is now: for $11.95, Sears Roebuck converted
your touring car into a sedan and you went forth renewed. One
agreeable quality of the old Fords was that they had no bumpers,
and their fenders softened and wilted with the years and permitted
the driver to squeeze in and out of tight places.

Tires were 30 x 3½, cost about twelve dollars, and punctured
readily. Everybody carried a Jiffy patching set, with a nutmeg
grater to roughen the tube before the goo was spread on. Every-

body was capable of putting on a patch, expected to have to, and did have to.

During my association with Model T's, self-starters were not a prevalent accessory. They were expensive and under suspicion. Your car came equipped with a serviceable crank, and the first thing you learned was how to Get Results. It was a special trick, and until you learned it (usually from another Ford owner, but sometimes by a period of appalling experimentation) you might as well have been winding up an awning. The trick was to leave the ignition switch off, proceed to the animal's head, pull the choke (which was a little wire protruding through the radiator) and give the crank two or three nonchalant upward lifts. Then, whistling as though thinking about something else, you would saunter back to the driver's cabin, turn the ignition on, return to the crank, and this time, catching it on the down stroke, give it a quick spin with plenty of That. If this procedure was followed, the engine almost always responded—first with a few scattered explosions, then with a tumultuous gunfire, which you checked by racing around to the driver's seat and retarding the throttle. Often, if the emergency brake hadn't been pulled all the way back, the car advanced on you the instant the first explosion occurred and you would hold it back by leaning your weight against it. I can still feel my old Ford nuzzling me at the curb, as though looking for an apple in my pocket.

In zero weather, ordinary cranking became an impossibility, except for giants. The oil thickened, and it became necessary to jack up the rear wheels, which, for some planetary reason, eased the throw.

The lore and legend that governed the Ford were boundless. Owners had their own theories about everything; they discussed mutual problems in that wise, infinitely resourceful way old women discuss rheumatism. Exact knowledge was pretty scarce, and often proved less effective than superstition. Dropping a camphor ball into the gas tank was a popular expedient; it seemed to have a tonic effect on both man and machine. There wasn't much to base exact knowledge on. The Ford driver flew blind. He didn't know the temperature of his engine, the speed of his car, the amount of his fuel, or the pressure of his oil (the old Ford lubricated itself by what was amiably described as the "splash system"). A speedometer cost money and was an extra, like a windshield-wiper. The dashboard of the early models was bare save for an ignition key; later models, grown effete, boasted an ammeter which pulsated alarmingly with the throbbing of the car. Under the dash was a box of coils, with vibrators which you adjusted, or thought you adjusted. Whatever the driver learned of his motor, he learned not through instruments but through sudden developments. I remember that the timer was one of the vital organs about which there was ample doctrine. When everything else had been checked, you "had a look" at the timer. It was an extravagantly odd little device, simple in construction, mysterious in function. It contained a roller, held by a spring, and there were four contact points on the inside of the case against which, many people believed, the roller rolled. I have had a timer apart on a sick Ford many times. But I never really knew what I was up to—I was just showing off before God. There were almost as many schools of thought as there were timers. Some people, when things went wrong, just clenched their teeth and gave the timer a smart crack with a wrench. Other people opened it up and blew on it. There was a school that held that the timer needed large amounts of oil; they fixed it by frequent baptism. And there was a school that was positive it was meant to run dry as a bone; these people were continually taking it off and wiping it. I remember once spitting into a timer; not in anger, but in a spirit of research. You see, the Model T driver moved in the realm of metaphysics. He believed his car could be hexed.

One reason the Ford anatomy was never reduced to an exact science was that, having "fixed" it, the owner couldn't honestly claim that the treatment had brought about the cure. There were too many authenticated cases of Fords fixing themselves—restored naturally to health after a short rest. Farmers soon discovered this, and it fitted nicely with their draft-horse philosophy: "Let 'er cool off and she'll snap into it again."

A Ford owner had Number One Bearing constantly in mind. This bearing, being at the front end of the motor, was the one that always burned out, because the oil didn't reach it when the car was climbing hills. (That's what I was always told, anyway.) The oil used to recede and leave Number One dry as a clam flat; you had to watch that bearing like a hawk. It was like a weak heart—you could hear it start knocking, and that was when you stopped to let her cool off. Try as you would to keep the oil supply right, in the end Number One always went out. "Number One Bearing burned out on me and I had to have her replaced," you would say, wisely; and your companions always had a lot to tell about how to protect and pamper Number One to keep her alive.

Sprinkled not too liberally among the millions of amateur witch doctors who drove Fords and applied their own abominable cures were the heaven-sent mechanics who could really make the car talk. These professionals turned up in undreamed-of spots. One time, on the banks of the Columbia River in Washington, I heard the rear end go out of my Model T when I was trying to whip it up a steep incline onto the deck of a ferry. Something snapped; the car slid backward into the mud. It seemed to me like the end of the trail, But the captain of the ferry, observing the withered remnant, spoke up.

"What's got her?" he asked.

"I guess it's the rear end," I replied, listlessly. The captain leaned over the rail and stared. Then I saw that there was a hunger in his eyes that set him off from other men.

"Tell you what," he said, carelessly, trying to cover up his eagerness, "let's pull the son of a bitch up onto the boat, and I'll help you fix her while we're going back and forth on the river."

We did just this. All that day I plied between the towns of Pasco and Kennewick, while the skipper (who had once worked in a Ford garage) directed the amazing work of resetting the bones of my car.

Springtime in the heyday of the Model T was a delirious season. Owning a car was still a major excitement, roads were still wonderful and bad. The Fords were obviously conceived in madness: any car which was capable of going from forward into reverse without any perceptible mechanical hiatus was bound to be a mighty challenging thing to the human imagination. Boys used to veer them off the highway into a level pasture and run wild with them, as though they were cutting up with a girl. Most everybody used the reverse pedal quite as much as the regular foot brake—it distributed the wear over the bands and wore them all down evenly. That was the big trick, to wear all the bands down evenly, so that the final chattering would be total and the whole unit scream for renewal.

The days were golden, the nights were dim and strange. I still recall with trembling those loud, nocturnal crises when you drew up to a signpost and raced the engine so the lights would be bright enough to read destinations by. I have never been really planetary since. I suppose it's time to say goodbye. Farewell, my lovely!

A Slight Sound at Evening

Allen Cove, Summer, 1954

In his journal for July 10–12, 1841, Thoreau wrote: "A slight sound at evening lifts me up by the ears, and makes life seem inexpressibly serene and grand. It may be in Uranus, or it may be in the shutter." The book into which he later managed to pack both Uranus and the shutter was published in 1854, and now, a hundred years having gone by, *Walden*, its serenity and grandeur unimpaired, still lifts us up by the ears, still translates for us that language we are in danger of forgetting, "which all things and events speak without metaphor, which alone is copious and standard."

Walden is an oddity in American letters. It may very well be the oddest of our distinguished oddities. For many it is a great deal too odd, and for many it is a particular bore. I have not found it to be a well-liked book among my acquaintances, although usually spoken of with respect, and one literary critic for whom I have the highest regard can find no reason for anyone's giving *Walden* a second thought. To admire the book is, in fact, something of an embarrassment, for the mass of men have an indistinct notion that its author was a sort of Nature Boy.

I think it is of some advantage to encounter the book at a period in one's life when the normal anxieties and enthusiasms and rebellions of youth closely resemble those of Thoreau in that spring of 1845 when he borrowed an ax, went out to the woods, and began to whack down some trees for timber. Received at such a juncture, the book is like an invitation to life's dance, assuring the troubled recipient that no matter what befalls him in the way of success or failure he will always be welcome at the party—that the music is played for

A SLIGHT SOUND AT EVENING. From *The Points of My Compass* (Allen Cove, Summer, 1954) by E. B. White. Copyright, 1954 by E. B. White. Originally published in *The Yale Review*, under the title "Walden—1954," and reprinted with the permission of Harper & Row, Publishers.

him, too, if he will but listen and move his feet. In effect, that is what the book is—an invitation, unengraved; and it stirs one as a young girl is stirred by her first big party bid. Many think it a sermon; many set it down as an attempt to rearrange society; some think it an exercise in nature-loving; some find it a rather irritating collection of inspirational puffballs by an eccentric show-off. I think it none of these. It still seems to me the best youth's companion yet written by an American, for it carries a solemn warning against the loss of one's valuables, it advances a good argument for travelling light and trying new adventures, it rings with the power of positive adoration, it contains religious feeling without religious images, and it steadfastly refuses to record bad news. Even its pantheistic note is so pure as to be noncorrupting—pure as the flute-note blown across the pond on those faraway summer nights. If our colleges and universities were alert, they would present a cheap pocket edition of the book to every senior upon graduating, along with his sheepskin, or instead of it. Even if some senior were to take it literally and start felling trees, there could be worse mishaps: the ax is older than the Dictaphone and it is just as well for a young man to see what kind of chips he leaves before listening to the sound of his own voice. And even if some were to get no farther than the table of contents, they would learn how to name eighteen chapters by the use of only thirty-nine words and would see how sweet are the uses of brevity.

If Thoreau had merely left us an account of a man's life in the woods or if he had simply retreated to the woods and there recorded his complaints about society, or even if he had contrived to include both records in one essay, *Walden* would probably not have lived a hundred years. As things turned out, Thoreau, very likely without knowing quite what he was up to, took man's relation to Nature and man's dilemma in society and man's capacity for elevating his spirit and he beat all these matters together, in a wild free interval of self-justification and delight, and produced an original omelette from which people can draw nourishment in a hungry day. *Walden* is one of the first of the vitamin-enriched American dishes. If it were a little less good than it is, or even a little less queer, it would be an abominable book. Even as it is, it will continue to baffle and annoy the literal mind and all those who are unable to stomach its caprices and imbibe its theme. Certainly the plodding economist will continue to have rough going if he hopes to emerge from the book with a clear system of economic thought. Thoreau's assault on the Concord society of the mid-nineteenth century has the quality of a modern Western: he rides into the subject at top speed, shooting in all directions. Many of his shots ricochet and nick him on the rebound, and throughout the melee there is a horrendous cloud of inconsistencies and contradictions, and when the shooting dies down and the air clears, one is impressed chiefly by the courage of the rider and by how splendid it was that somebody should have ridden in there and raised all that ruckus.

When he went to the pond, Thoreau struck an attitude and did so deliberately, but his posturing was not to draw the attention of others to him but rather to draw his own attention more closely to himself. "I learned this at least by my experiment: that if one advances confidently in the direction of his dreams, and endeavors to live the life which he has imagined, he will meet with a success unexpected in common hours." The sentence has the power to resuscitate the youth drowning in his sea of doubt. I recall my exhilaration upon reading it, many years ago, in a time of hesitation and despair. It restored me to health. And now in 1954 when I salute Henry Thoreau on the hundredth birthday of his book, I am merely paying off an old score—or an installment on it.

In his journal for May 3-4, 1838—Boston to Portland—he wrote: "Midnight—head over the boat's side—between sleeping and waking—with glimpses of one or more lights in the vicinity of Cape Ann. Bright moonlight—the effect heightened by seasickness." The entry illuminates the man, as the moon the sea on that night in May. In Thoreau the natural scene was heightened, not depressed, by a disturbance of the stomach, and nausea met its match at last. There was a steadiness in at least one passenger if there was none in the boat. Such steadiness (which in some would be called intoxication) is at the heart of *Walden*—confidence, faith, the discipline of looking always at what is to be seen, undeviating gratitude for the life-everlasting that he found growing in his front yard. "There is nowhere recorded a simple and irrepressible satisfaction with the gift of life, any memorable praise of God." He worked to correct that deficiency. *Walden* in his acknowledgment of the gift of life. It is the testament of a man in a high state of indignation because (it seemed to him) so few ears heard the uninterrupted poem of creation, the morning wind that forever blows. If the man sometimes wrote as though all his readers were male, unmarried, and well-connected, it is because he gave his testimony during the callow years, and, for that matter, never really grew up. To reject the book because of the immaturity of the author and the bugs in the logic is to throw away a bottle of good wine because it contains bits of the cork.

Thoreau said he required of every writer, first and last, a simple and sincere account of his own life. Having delivered himself of this chesty dictum, he proceeded to ignore it. In his books and even in his enormous journal, he withheld or disguised most of the facts from which an understanding of his life could be drawn. *Walden*, subtitled "Life in the Woods," is not a simple and sincere account of a man's life, either in or out of the woods; it is an account of a man's journey into the mind, a toot on the trumpet to alert the neighbors. Thoreau was well aware that no one can alert his neighbors who is not wide-awake himself, and he went to the woods (among other reasons) to make sure that he would stay awake during his broadcast. What actually took place during the years 1845–47 is largely unrecorded, and the reader is excluded from the private life of the author, who supplies almost no gossip about himself, a great deal about his neighbors and about the universe.

As for me, I cannot in this short ramble give a simple and sincere account of my own life, but I think Thoreau might find it instructive to know that this memorial essay is being written in a house that, through no intent on my part, is the same size and shape as his own domicile on the pond—about ten by fifteen, tight, plainly finished, and at a little distance from my Concord. The house in which I sit this morning was built to accommodate a boat, not a man, but by long experience I have learned that in most respects it shelters me better than the larger dwelling where my bed is, and which, by design, is a manhouse not a boathouse. Here in the boathouse I am a wilder and, it would appear, a healthier man, by a safe margin. I have a chair, a bench, a table, and I can walk into the water if I tire of the land. My house fronts a cove. Two fishermen have just arrived to spot fish from the air—an osprey and a man in a small yellow plane who works for the fish company. The man, I have noticed, is less well equipped than the hawk, who can dive directly on his fish and carry it away, without telephoning. A mouse and a squirrel share the house with me. The building is, in fact, a multiple dwelling, a semidetached affair. It is because I am semidetached while here that I find it possible to transact this private business with the fewest obstacles.

There is also a woodchuck here, living forty feet away under the wharf. When the wind is right, he can smell my house; and when the wind is contrary, I can smell his. We both use the wharf for sunning, taking turns, each adjusting his schedule to the other's convenience. Thoreau once ate a woodchuck. I think he felt he owed it to his readers, and that it was little enough, considering the indignities they were suffering at his hands and the dressing-down they were taking. (Parts of *Walden* are pure scold.) Or perhaps he ate the woodchuck because he believed every man should acquire strict business habits, and the woodchuck was destroying his market beans. I do not know. Thoreau had a strong experimental streak in him. It is probably no harder to eat a woodchuck than to construct a sentence that lasts a hundred years. At any rate, Thoreau is the only writer I know who prepared himself for his great ordeal by eating a woodchuck; also the only one who got a hangover from drinking too much water. (He was drunk the whole time, though he seldom touched wine or coffee or tea.)

Here in this compact house where I would spend one day as deliberately as Nature if I were not being pressed by the editor of a magazine, and with a woodchuck (as yet uneaten) for neighbor, I can feel the companionship of the occupant of the pond-side cabin in Walden woods, a mile from the village, near the Fitchburg right of way. Even my immediate business is no barrier between us: Thoreau occasionally batted out a magazine piece, but was always suspicious of any sort of purposeful work that cut into his time. A man, he said, should take care not to be thrown off the track by every nutshell and mosquito's wing that falls on the rails.

There has been much guessing as to why he went to the pond. To set it down to escapism is, of course, to misconstrue what happened. Henry went forth to battle when he took to the woods, and *Walden* is the report of a man torn by two powerful and opposing drives— the desire to enjoy the world (and not be derailed by a mosquito wing) and the urge to set the world straight. One cannot join these two successfully, but sometimes, in rare cases, something good or even great results from the attempt of the tormented spirit to reconcile them. Henry went forth to battle, and if he set the stage himself, if he fought on his own terms and with his own weapons, it was because it was his nature to do things differently from most men, and to act in a cocky fashion. If the pond and the woods seemed a more plausible site for a house than an in-town location, it was because a cowbell made for him a sweeter sound than a churchbell. *Walden*, the book, makes the sound of a cowbell, more than a churchbell, and proves the point, although both sounds are in it, and both remarkably clear and sweet. He simply preferred his churchbell at a little distance.

I think one reason he went to the woods was a perfectly simple and commonplace one—and apparently he thought so, too. "At a certain season of our life," he wrote, "we are accustomed to consider every spot as the possible site of a house." There spoke the young man, a few years out of college, who had not yet broken away from home. He hadn't married, and he had found no job that measured up to his rigid standards of employment, and like any young man, or young animal, he felt uneasy and on the defensive until he had fixed himself a den. Most young men, of course, casting about for a site, are content merely to draw apart from their kinfolks. Thoreau, convinced that the greater part of what his neighbors called good was bad, withdrew from a great deal more than family: he pulled out of everything for a while, to serve everybody right for being so stuffy, and to try his own prejudices on the dog.

The house-hunting sentence above, which starts the chapter called "Where I Lived, and What I Lived For," is followed by another passage that is worth quoting here because it so beautifully illustrates the offbeat prose that Thoreau was master of, a prose at once strictly disciplined and wildly abandoned. "I have surveyed the country on every side within a dozen miles of where I live," continued this delirious young man. "In imagination I have bought all the farms in succession, for all were to be bought, and I knew their price. I walked over each farmer's premises, tasted his wild apples, discoursed on husbandry with him, took his farm at his price, at any price, mortgaging it to him in my mind; even put a higher price on it—took everything but a deed of it—took his word for his deed, for I dearly love to talk—cultivated it, and him too to some extent, I trust, and withdrew when I had enjoyed it long enough, leaving him to carry it on." A copy-desk man would get a double hernia trying to clean up that sentence for the management, but the sentence needs no fixing, for it perfectly captures the meaning of the writer and the quality of the ramble.

"Wherever I sat, there I might live, and the landscape radiated from me accordingly." Thoreau, the home-seeker, sitting on his hummock with the entire State of Massachusetts radiating from him, is to me the most humorous of the New England figures, and *Walden* the most humorous of the books, though its humor is almost continuously subsurface and there is nothing deliberately funny anywhere, except a few weak jokes and bad puns that rise to the surface like the perch in the pond that rose to the sound of the maestro's flute. Thoreau tended to write in sentences, a feat not every writer is capable of, and *Walden* is, rhetorically speaking, a collection of certified sentences, some of them, it would now appear, as indestructible as they are errant. The book is distilled from the vast journals, and this accounts for its intensity: he picked out bright particles that pleased his eye, whirled them in the kaleidoscope of his content, and produced the pattern that has endured—the color, the form, the light.

On this its hundredth birthday, Thoreau's *Walden* is pertinent and timely. In our uneasy season, when all men unconsciously seek a retreat from a world that has got almost completely out of hand, his house in the Concord woods is a haven. In our culture of gadgetry and the multiplicity of convenience, his cry "Simplicity, simplicity, simplicity!" has the insistence of a fire alarm. In the brooding atmosphere of war and the gathering radioactive storm, the innocence and serenity of his summer afternoons are enough to burst the remembering heart, and one gazes back upon that pleasing interlude—its confidence, its purity, its deliberateness—with awe and wonder, as one would look upon the face of a child asleep.

"This small lake was of most value as a neighbor in the intervals of a gentle rain-storm in August, when, both air and water being perfectly still, but the sky overcast, midafternoon had all the serenity of evening, and the wood-thrush sang around, and was heard from shore to shore." Now, in the perpetual overcast in which our days are spent, we hear with extra perception and deep gratitude that song, tying century to century.

I sometimes amuse myself by bringing Henry Thoreau back to life and showing him the sights. I escort him into a phone booth and let him dial Weather. "This is a delicious evening," the girl's voice says, "when the whole body is one sense, and imbibes delight through every pore." I show him the spot in the Pacific where an island used to be, before some magician made it vanish. "We know not where we are," I murmur. "The light which puts out our eyes is darkness to us. Only that day dawns to which we are awake." I thumb through the latest copy of *Vogue* with him. "Of two patterns which differ only by a few threads more or less of a particular color," I read, "the one will be sold readily, the other lie on the shelf, though it frequently happens that, after the lapse of a season, the latter becomes the most fashionable." Together we go outboarding on the Assabet, looking for what we've lost—a hound, a bay horse, a turtledove. I show him a distracted farmer who is trying to repair a hay baler before the thunder shower breaks. "This farmer," I remark, "is endeavoring to solve the problem of a livelihood by a formula more complicated than the problem itself. To get his shoestrings he speculates in herds of cattle."

I take the celebrated author to Twenty-One for lunch, so the waiters may study his shoes. The proprietor welcomes us. "The gross feeder," remarks the proprietor, sweeping the room with his arm, "is a man in the larva stage." After lunch we visit a classroom in one of those schools conducted by big corporations to teach their superannuated executives how to retire from business without serious injury to their health. (The shock to men's systems these days when relieved of the exacting routine of amassing wealth is very great and must be cushioned.) "It is not necessary," says the teacher to his pupils, "that a man should earn his living by the sweat of his brow, unless he sweats easier than I do. We are determined to be starved before we are hungry."

I turn on the radio and let Thoreau hear Winchell beat the red hand around the clock. "Time is but the stream I go a-fishing in," shouts Mr. Winchell, rattling his telegraph key. "Hardly a man takes a half hour's nap after dinner, but when he wakes he holds up his head and asks, 'What's the news?' If we read of one man robbed, or murdered, or killed by accident, or one house burned, or one vessel wrecked, or one steamboat blown up, or one cow run over on the Western Railroad, or one mad dog killed, or one lot of grasshoppers in the winter—we need never read of another. One is enough."

I doubt that Thoreau would be thrown off balance by the fantastic sights and sounds of the twentieth century. "The Concord nights," he once wrote, "are stranger than the Arabian nights." A four-engined airliner would merely serve to confirm his early views on travel. Everywhere he would observe, in new shapes and sizes, the old predicaments and follies of men—the desperation, the impedimenta, the meanness—along with the visible capacity for elevation of the mind and soul. "This curious world which we inhabit is more wonderful than it is convenient; more beautiful than it is useful; it is more to be admired and enjoyed than used." He would see that today ten thousand engineers are busy making sure that the world shall be convenient even if it is destroyed in the process, and others are determined to increase its usefulness even though its beauty is lost somewhere along the way.

At any rate, I'd like to stroll about the countryside in Thoreau's company for a day, observing the modern scene, inspecting today's snowstorm, pointing out the sights, and offering belated apologies for my sins. Thoreau is unique among writers in that those who admire him find him uncomfortable to live with—a regular hairshirt of a man. A little band of dedicated Thoreauvians would be a sorry sight indeed: fellows who hate compromise and have compromised, fellows who love wildness and have lived tamely, and at their side, censuring them and chiding them, the ghostly figure of this upright man, who long ago gave corroboration to impulses they perceived were right and issued warnings against the things they instinctively knew to be their enemies. I should hate to be called a Thoreauvian, yet I wince every time I walk into the barn I'm pushing before me, seventy-five feet by forty, and the author of *Walden* has served as my conscience through the long stretches of my trivial days.

Hairshirt or no, he is a better companion than most, and I would not swap him for a soberer or more reasonable friend even if I could. I can reread his famous invitation with undiminished excitement. The sad thing is that not more acceptances have been received, that so many decline for one reason or another, pleading some previous engagement or ill health. But the invitation stands. It will beckon as long as this remarkable book stays in print—which will be as long as there are August afternoons in the intervals of a gentle rainstorm, as long as there are ears to catch the faint sounds of the orchestra. I find it agreeable to sit here this morning, in a house of correct proportions, and hear across a century of time his flute, his frogs, and his seductive summons to the wildest revels of them all.

The Shape of the U.N.

Turtle Bay, December 1, 1956

My most distinguished neighbor in Turtle Bay, as well as my most peculiar one, is the U.N., over on the East River. Its fame has soared in the past month, on the wings of its spectacular deeds, and its peculiarities have become more and more apparent. Furthermore, the peculiarities have taken on an added importance, because of President Eisenhower's determination to make United States foreign policy jibe with the U.N. Charter. In many respects, I would feel easier if he would just make it jibe with the Classified Telephone Directory, which is clear and pithy.

The Charter was a very difficult document to draft and get accepted. The nations were still at war and the founding fathers were doubtful about whether a world organization could be made to work at all, so they inserted a clause or two to cover themselves in case it didn't. Every member went in with his fingers crossed, and the Charter reflects this. It derives a little from the Ten Commandments, a little from the Covenant of the League of Nations, and a little from the fine print on a bill of lading. It is high in purpose, low in calories. Portions of it are sheer double-talk and, as a result, support double-dealing, but membership in a league is an exercise in double-dealing anyway, because the stern fact is that each sovereign nation has one foot in, one foot out. When the United States, for example, found itself up to its neck in the Middle East dilemma, it subscribed to the Charter's pledge to suppress aggression in the common interest; it also issued an order to the commander of the 6th Fleet: "Take no guff from anyone!" You won't find such words in the Charter, but they are implicit in the Charter, and that is one of its peculiarities.

In shape the U.N. is like one of the very early flying machines—a breath-taking sight as it takes to the air, but full of bugs. It is obvi-

---

THE SHAPE OF THE U.N. From *The Points of My Compass* (Turtle Bay, December 1, 1956) by E. B. White, with postscript (May, 1962). Copyright © 1956, 1962 by E. B. White. Originally published in *The New Yorker* without its postscript, and reprinted with the permission of Harper & Row, Publishers.

ously in the experimental stage, which is natural. Since many readers have probably never examined the Charter, I will give a quick run-down, covering merely the Preamble and Chapter One, where the gist of the political structure is to be found.

The Preamble awards honorable mention to the following: human rights, equal rights, justice, respect for treaties (the Charter itself is a treaty, so it is just whistling to keep up its courage here), tolerance, peace, neighborliness, economic and social advancement. The Preamble is *against:* war, and the use of armed force except in the common interest.

Chapter One deals with (1) Purposes, (2) Principles. The *purposes* are, in summarized form: to maintain peace; to suppress aggression; to develop friendly relations among nations on the principle of equal rights and self-determination (which I presume includes cannibalism); to cooperate; to harmonize actions of nations. The *principles* are: sovereign equality; members shall fulfill obligations in good faith; settle disputes by peaceful means; refrain from the threat or use of force against the territorial integrity or political independence of any state; cooperate; and never, never intervene in matters which are essentially within the domestic jurisdiction of any state.

As you can see, the thing has bugs. There are some truly comical ones, like Chapter I, Article 2, Paragraph 5, which, if I interpret it correctly, commands a member to help deliver a public whipping to himself. But I shall not dwell on the funny ones. Let us just stare for a few moments at two of the more serious bugs.

One: In a fluid world, the Charter affirms the *status quo.* By its use of the word "aggression" and by other devices it makes the *status quo* the test of proper international conduct.

Two: Aimed at building a moral community, of peace, order, and justice, the Charter fails to lay down rules of conduct as a condition of membership. Any nation can enjoy the sanctuary of the Charter while violating its spirit and letter. A member, for example, is not required to allow the organization to examine its internal activities. Mr. Shepilov can come to Turtle Bay, but can Mr. Hammarskjöld go to Budapest? The world waits to see. Even if he makes it, he will arrive awfully late.

Despite its faults, the U.N. has just emerged from a great month in world history, and emerged all in one piece. It pulled England and France out of a shooting war and sent the constabulary to replace them in Egypt. It failed in Hungary, but in the General Assembly the Soviet Union took a rhetorical shellacking that really counted. The U.N. is our most useful international device, but it is built on old-fashioned ideas. The Charter is an extremely tricky treaty. Its trickiness is dangerous to the world because, for one thing, it leads idealistic nations like ours into situations that suddenly become sticky and queer. This very thing happened when, in order to "condemn aggression" in the Middle East, in conformity with our Charter obligations, we deserted England and France and took up with the dictator of the Arab world and his associate the Soviet Union.

Some people, perhaps most people, think words are not really important, but I am a word man and I attach the very highest importance to words. I even think it was dishonest to call the world organization the "United Nations," when everybody knew the name was a euphemism. Why start on a note of phonyness, or wistfulness? The newspapers, with their sloppy proofreading, sometimes call the world organization the United Notions, sometimes the Untied Nations. Neither of these typos would make a serviceable title, but curiously enough, both are pat. Dr. Luns, of the Netherlands, recently described the U.N. Charter as "the expression of an attitude of mind." He said some countries used it merely as a juke box—they put in their nickel and the box would light up and play. That is about it. The Charter is an accommodating box and can produce a remarkable variety of tunes.

When Hungary erupted, the world was shocked beyond measure at what was taking place. But under the Charter of the United Nations the Hungarian government was in a position to put up just as noisy an argument as the oppressed people who were in rebellion. "Nothing contained in the present Charter shall authorize the United Nations to intervene in matters which are essentially within the domestic jurisdiction of any state." (Chapter I, Article 2, Paragraph 7.) And when the U.N. wanted to send observers in, it received a polite no. This is palpably ridiculous, and it boils down to a deficiency in the Charter, a deficiency that is in the nature of an eleven-year-old appeasement. The Charter says that a member shall encourage "respect for human rights." That is laudable but fluffy. One way a Charter can advance human rights is to insist that the rights themselves (such as they are) remain visible to the naked eye, remain open to inspection. One of the preconditions of membership in the United Nations should be that the member himself not shut his door in the face of the Club. If the member won't agree to that, let him look elsewhere, join some other club.

Many will argue that if you are dealing with Iron Curtain countries, you have to take them on their own terms or you don't get them at all. That may be true. But who agreed to that amount of appeasement in the first place? And were they right? The appeasement was agreed to eleven years ago by charter writers who were trying to put together a world organization while a world war was still in progress. Their eye was not always on the ball, and they were looking back more than ahead. They were playing with century-old ideas: nonaggression (which is undefinable), self-determination (which includes the determination to send people to the salt mines), sovereign equality (which means that all nations are equal in the sight of God but the big ones are equal in the Security Council). The Charter bravely tries to keep these threadbare ideas alive, but they will not stay alive in the modern world of hydrogen and horror, and unless the Charter is brought up to date, it may fail us.

Much has happened in eleven years. Almost everything that has happened indicates that the United Nations should never have admitted the Communist nations on *their* terms; that is, freedom to operate behind a wall. If nations are to cooperate, the first condition must be that they have social and political intercourse. The Soviet Union held out for cooperation without intercourse, which is a contradiction in terms and which is as unworkable for nations as for spouses. A marriage can be annulled on the ground of denial of intercourse. A world organization can blow up on account of it.

The subtlest joker in the Charter is the word "aggression." There are other jokers, but none so far-reaching. When the United States was confronted with the Middle East crisis, it was surprised and bewildered to discover itself backing Nasser and Russia against France and England. One reason for this queer turn of events was that Britain and France had "aggressed," and therefore had violated the Charter of the United Nations. Actually, our government did not take its stand solely, or even principally, on the basis of its U.N. membership, but it did use its U.N. membership to justify its decision and lend it a high moral tone.

The word "aggression" pops up right at the very beginning of the Charter: Chapter I, Article 1, Paragraph 1. Aggression is the keystone of the Charter. It is what every member is pledged to suppress. It is also what nobody has been able to define. In 1945, the founding fathers agreed among themselves that it would be unwise to include a definition of aggression in the Charter, on the score that somebody would surely find a loophole in it. But in 1954 a special U.N. committee was appointed to see if it could arrive at a definition of aggression. The committee was called the United Nations Special Committee on the Question of Defining Aggression. It huffed and it puffed, but it did not come up with a definition, and around the first of last month it adjourned. So one of the great peculiarities of the Charter is that all nations are pledged to oppose what no nation is willing to have defined. I think it can fairly be said that the one subject the seventy-nine members of the United Nations are in silent agreement on is aggression: they are agreed that each nation shall reserve the right to its own interpretation, when the time comes.

This isn't surprising. To define aggression, it is necessary to get into the realm of right and wrong, and the Charter of the United Nations studiously avoids this delicate area. It is also necessary to go back a way. Webster says of aggression, "A first or unprovoked attack." And that, you see, raises the old, old question of which came first, the hen or the egg. What, we must ask, came first in the Middle East clash between Arab and Jew? You could go back two thousand years, if you wanted to. You could certainly go back beyond October 29, 1956, when the Israelis came streaming across the Sinai desert.

Not only has no member, in eleven years, accepted a definition of aggression, no member has admitted that it has committed an aggressive act, although many members have used arms to get their way and at least one member, the U.S.S.R., employs the threat of force as a continuing instrument of national policy. The Charter of the U.N. is a treaty signed by sovereign nations, and the effect of a treaty written around the concept of aggression is to equate the use of arms with wrongdoing and to assume that the world is static, when, of course, that is not so—the world is fluid and (certainly at this point in history) riddled with revolutionary currents at work everywhere. The tendency of any document founded on the idea of nonaggression is to freeze the world in its present mold and command it to stand still.

The world has seen a lot happen lately; it hasn't been standing still. And you will get as many definitions of aggression as there are parties to the event. Ask the delegate of the Soviet Union what happened in Hungary and he will say, "Remnants of Fascist bands aggressed." And he will cite Chapter I, Article 2, Paragraph 4: "All members shall refrain . . . from the threat or use of force against the territorial integrity or political independence of any state." Ask a citizen of Budapest what happened and he will say, "We couldn't take it any longer. We threw stones." And he will cite the Preamble on fundamental human rights and the dignity and worth of the human person. Under the Charter, it is possible to condemn both these aggressive acts—you just take your choice. Is the aggressor the man who throws stones at a tank, or is the aggressor the man who drives the tank into the angry crowd? The world was quick to form an opinion about this, but it got little help from the Charter. The Charter affirms the integrity of Hungary as a political entity, and officially designates both the Hungarian government and the Soviet government as "peace-loving." But that's not the way it looked to most of the world.

When the Israelis were asked what had happened, Eban replied, "The Israeli forces took security measures in the Sinai Peninsula in the exercise of Israel's inherent right of self-defense" (Chapter VII, Article 51). When the Arabs were asked what had happened, the heads of the Arab League issued a statement applauding Egypt's "glorious defense of the safety of her territories and sovereignty" (same chapter, same verse).

Neither England nor France has admitted to an aggression, although the two nations mounted an assault and carried it out—two permanent members of the Security Council shooting their way into Egypt before breakfast. It is, in fact, inconceivable that any nation will ever admit to having aggressed.

In the *Herald Tribune* the other morning, Walter Lippmann wrote, "In the past few days, the U.N. has been pushed into a position where its main function seems to be that of restoring conditions as they were before the explosion." That is certainly true, and one reason for it is that the Charter condemns aggression, sight unseen, and then turns over to the forum the task of studying the events leading up to the tragedy and the atmosphere in which it occurred. To condemn aggression is to decide *in advance of an event* the merits of the dispute. Since this is absurd, the subject of aggression should not be made part of a charter. The business of a charter is not to decide arguments in advance, it is to diagram the conditions under which it may be possible, with luck, to settle the argument when it arises. Surely one of those conditions is the right to observe at close hand.

Another peculiarity of the U.N. is its police. These are now famous, and rightly so. A couple of weeks ago, ninety-five Danish and Norwegian riflemen, wearing emergency blue, dropped out of the sky to keep the peace of the world. They were the advance unit of the United Nations Emergency Force. The men were reported looking "tired," and I should think they might. One editorial writer described them as "symbolic soldiers"; the label is enough in itself to tire a man. The *Times* correspondent in Abu Suweir, where the troops landed, described the policemen's task as "most delicate."

Their task is more than merely delicate; it is primeval. This force (it now numbers about two thousand) is the true dawn patrol, and these Scandinavian riflemen are dawn men. They are the police who are charged with enforcing the laws that do not yet exist. They are clothed with our universal good intentions, armed with the hopes and fears of all the years. They have been turned loose in a trouble spot with the instructions "Enforce the absence of law! Keep us all safe!" Behind them is the authority of the United Nations, all of whose members are "peace-loving" and some of whose members have just engaged in war. It is a confusing scene to a young policeman. It is confusing for people everywhere. One of the first things that happened on the arrival of UNEF was that General Burns, the commander, had to fly back to First Avenue to find out what the Chief of Police had in mind. Another thing that happened was that the Secretary General of the U.N. had to fly to Cairo to get permission from the Egyptian government to let the world be policed in its bailiwick.

It is confusing, but it is not hopeless. Police (so-called) have sometimes been known to antedate the laws that they enforce. It is again a case of the egg and the hen—law enforcers preceding law itself, like the vigilantes of our frontier West.

The U.N. has from the very start stirred people's imaginations and hopes. There seems little doubt that the very existence of a world organization is a help. I read in the *Times* magazine section the other day a good analysis of the U.N. by Ambassador Henry Cabot Lodge, who praised it because it "mobilizes world opinion" and because it shows "midnight courage." All this is certainly true. The

U.N. is the shaky shape of the world's desire for order. If it is to establish order, though, it will have to muster the right words as well as the midnight courage. The words of the Charter are soft and punky. The Charter makes "aggression" synonymous with "wrongdoing" but drops the matter there, as though everyone understood the nature of sin. Yet it would appear from recent events that the users of force rarely think they are aggressing, and never admit they are. To simplify an idea this way is bad writing.

A league of sovereign nations—some of them much sovereigner than others—is not in a good position to keep order by disciplining a member in the middle of a fracas. Discipline can mean war itself, as we saw in Korea, and the U.N. is physically puny. But a league *is* in a position to do other things. One thing it can do is lay down conditions of membership. In its own house the U.N. has unlimited power and authority. Its bylaws should not appease anybody or make life easy for bad actors. The U.N. swings very little weight in Moscow or in Budapest, but it swings a lot of weight in Turtle Bay, and that's where it should start to bear down. Whether the U.N. could have been effective in Hungary is anybody's guess, but certainly its chances of operating effectively, for human rights and humankind, were diminished by the softness of the Charter and the eleven-year-old accommodation to the Communists, who from the very start showed that they intended to eat their forum and have it, too. Munich has nothing on San Francisco in this matter.

Ambassador Lodge, in his article, pointed out that the U.N., contrary to what a few Americans hope and a few Americans fear, is not a world government. He wrote, "As for the future, a world government which free men could accept is as far off as a worldwide common sense of justice—without which world government would be world tyranny."

True enough. And the world is a long way from a common sense of justice. But the way to cut down the distance is to get on the right track, use the right words. Our Bill of Rights doesn't praise free speech, it forbids Congress to make any law abridging it. The U.N. could profit from that kind of tight writing. The Charter sings the praises of the dignity of man, but what it lacks is a clause saying, "A member shall make no move abridging the right of the Secretary General to stop by for a drink at any hour of the day or night."

Raffles and Miss Blandish
Politics and the English Language
Marrakech

GEORGE ORWELL
(1903-1950)

IN AN INTRODUCTION to *Homage to Catalonia* (1938),
Orwell's account of his experiences during the Spanish
Civil War, Lionel Trilling applied to Orwell the
old-fashioned word "virtuous," having in mind Orwell's stubborn fortitude in trying both to define and
to practice the good.

Orwell's intellectual honesty and clarity of vision
were not a matter simply of ideas. In fact, because he
had had an extremely complex and varied experience
of life which he had tried to confront squarely, he
quarreled with the ideas of others, particularly those
of the leftist liberals in the thirties and forties, when
they were in conflict with what he himself had suffered and observed.

Orwell, whose real name was Eric Hugh Blair, was
born into the home of a very minor British official
in Bengal. After experiencing the bitterness of being
a poor boy in fashionable English schools, including
Eton, he went to Burma and served five years
in the Imperial Police. The novel *Burmese Days*
(1934) describes this painful instruction in cultural
conflict and in the nature and necessities of power. He
left India in 1927 and held a series of unsatisfactory
jobs in France and England until he began to establish

[167]

himself as a writer. His first publication was the autobiographical *Down and Out in Paris and London*
(1933), followed by a series of realistic social novels.
Best known among them is *Keep the Aspidistra Flying*
(1936). Once his literary career began, Orwell published a book nearly every year until his early death
from tuberculosis.

The Spanish Civil War was crucial for Orwell. In
1936 the rebel General Franco, many of whose troops
were Moorish, set out to overthrow the democratically
elected government. Franco was supported by Hitler
and Mussolini; the government, or Loyalist, forces
were supported by international volunteer brigades
with the help of some Russian arms and advisers.
Enlisting as a volunteer in a mood generally sympathetic with the communists, Orwell chanced to serve
in a Catalonion anarchist regiment which the Russians
regarded as Trotskyite. He saw at first hand the
ruthlessness and dishonesty with which the communists
eliminated those whom they could not use for their
own political purposes. To escape from them Orwell
himself, after being wounded in battle, had to flee
Spain.

After his Spanish experiences, the theorizing of the
English leftists struck him as extremely naive, for
reasons explained in his pamphlet *The Lion and the
Unicorn* (1941). His anti-Stalinism deepened with the
war years and their aftermath, and was dramatized
in two popular political satires. *Animal Farm* (1945)
analyzed leftist totalitarianism in the guise of an animal
fable. *Nineteen Eighty-Four* (1949) projected some
of the more extreme tendencies of Stalinism into a
nightmarish future. The language of this future is
Newspeak, a brutal jargon in which the lies of communist propaganda are built into the structure of
language itself.

"Raffles and Miss Blandish" demonstrates a socio-
psychological approach to the themes of popular art

that has been increasingly applied since Orwell wrote. His remains one of the best studies of the amoral sadism of mass entertainment, even more conspicuous recently in the period of James Bond and the later Hitchcock. "Politics and the English Language" is rich in specific, badly needed and readily useful advice, but could only have been written by someone with Orwell's grasp of the relationship between political realism and verbal reality. As a vivid attempt really to see the people in a colonial country and guess at what they are feeling, "Marrakech" provides the necessary emotional complement to Huxley's "The Double Crisis."

Raffles and Miss Blandish

Nearly half a century after his first appearance, Raffles, "the amateur cracksman," is still one of the best-known characters in English fiction. Very few people would need telling that he played cricket for England, had bachelor chambers in the Albany and burgled the Mayfair houses which he also entered as a guest. Just for that reason he and his exploits make a suitable background against which to examine a more modern crime story such as *No Orchids for Miss Blandish*. Any such choice is necessarily arbitrary—I might equally well have chosen *Arsene Lupin*, for instance—but at any rate *No Orchids* and the Raffles books [1] have the common quality of being crime stories which play the limelight on the criminal rather than the policemen. For sociological purposes they can be compared. *No Orchids* is the 1939 version of glamorised crime, *Raffles* the 1900

---

[1] *Raffles, A Thief in the Night* and *Mr. Justice Raffles*, by E. W. Hornung. The third of these is definitely a failure, and only the first has the true Raffles atmosphere. Hornung wrote a number of crime stories, usually with a tendency to take the side of the criminal. A successful book in rather the same vein as *Raffles* is *Stingaree*.

---

version. What I am concerned with here is the immense difference in moral atmosphere between the two books, and the change in the popular attitude that this probably implies.

At this date, the charm of *Raffles* is partly in the period atmosphere and partly in the technical excellence of the stories. Hornung was a very conscientious and on his level a very able writer. Anyone who cares for sheer efficiency must admire his work. However, the truly dramatic thing about Raffles, the thing that makes him a sort of byword even to this day (only a few weeks ago, in a burglary case, a magistrate referred to the prisoner as "a Raffles in real life"), is the fact that he is a *gentleman*. Raffles is presented to us—and this is rubbed home in countless scraps of dialogue and casual remarks —not as an honest man who has gone astray, but as a public-school man who has gone astray. His remorse, when he feels any, is almost purely social; he has disgraced "the old school," he has lost his right to enter "decent society," he has forfeited his amateur status and become a cad. Neither Raffles nor Bunny appears to feel at all strongly that stealing is wrong in itself, though Raffles does once justify himself by the casual remark that "the distribution of property is all wrong anyway." They think of themselves not as sinners but as renegades, or simply as outcasts. And the moral code of most of us is still so close to Raffles' own that we do feel his situation to be an especially ironical one. A West End club man who is really a burglar! That is almost a story in itself, is it not? But how if it were a plumber or a greengrocer who was really a burglar? Would there be anything inherently dramatic in that? No—although the theme of the "double life," of respectability covering crime, is still there. Even Charles Peace in his clergyman's dog-collar seems somewhat less of a hypocrite than Raffles in his Zingari blazer.

Raffles, of course, is good at all games, but it is peculiarly fitting that his chosen game should be cricket. This allows not only of endless analogies between his cunning as a slow bowler and his cunning as a burglar, but also helps to define the exact nature of his crime. Cricket is not in reality a very popular game in England—it is nowhere near so popular as football, for instance—but it gives expression to a well-marked trait in the English character, the tendency to value "form" or "style" more highly than success. In the eyes of any true cricket-lover it is possible for an innings of ten runs to be "better" (*i.e.* more elegant) than an innings of a hundred runs: cricket is also one of the very few games in which the amateur can excel the professional. It is a game full of forlorn hopes and sudden dramatic changes of fortune, and its rules are so ill-defined that their interpretation is partly an ethical business. When Larwood, for instance, practised body line bowling in Australia he was not actually breaking any rule: he was merely doing something that was "not cricket." Since cricket takes up a lot of time and is rather an expensive game to play, it is predominantly an upper-class game, but for the whole nation it is bound up with such concepts as "good form," "playing the game," etc., and it has declined in popularity just as the tradition of "don't hit a man when he's down" has declined. It is not a twentieth-century game, and nearly all modern-minded people dislike it. The Nazis, for instance, were at pains to discourage cricket, which had gained a certain footing in Germany before and after the last war. In making Raffles a cricketer as well as a burglar, Hornung was not merely providing him with a plausible disguise; he was also drawing the sharpest moral contrast that he was able to imagine.

Raffles, no less than *Great Expectations* or *Le Rouge et le Noir,* is a story of snobbery, and it gains a great deal from the precariousness of Raffles's social position. A cruder writer would have made the "gentleman burglar" a member of the peerage, or at least a baronet. Raffles, however, is of upper-middle-class origin and is only accepted by the aristocracy because of his personal charm. "We were in Society but not of it," he says to Bunny towards the end of the book; and "I was asked about for my cricket." Both he and Bunny accept the values of "Society" unquestionably, and would settle down in it for good if only they could get away with a big enough haul. The ruin that constantly threatens them is all the blacker because they only doubtfully "belong." A duke who has served a prison sentence is still a duke, whereas a mere man about town, if once disgraced, ceases to be "about town" for evermore. The closing chapters of the book, when Raffles has been exposed and is living under an assumed name, have a twilight of the gods feeling, a mental atmosphere rather similar to that of Kipling's poem, "Gentleman Rankers":

> "Yes, a trooper of the forces—
> Who has run his own six horses!" etc.

Raffles now belongs irrevocably to the "cohorts of the damned." He can still commit successful burglaries, but there is no way back into

Paradise, which means Piccadilly and the M.C.C. According to the public-school code there is only one means of rehabilitation: death in battle. Raffles dies fighting against the Boers (a practised reader would foresee this from the start), and in the eyes of both Bunny and his creator this cancels his crimes.

Both Raffles and Bunny, of course, are devoid of religious belief, and they have no real ethical code, merely certain rules of behaviour which they observe semi-instinctively. But it is just here that the deep moral difference between *Raffles* and *No Orchids* becomes apparent. Raffles and Bunny, after all, are gentlemen, and such standards as they do have are not to be violated. Certain things are "not done," and the idea of doing them hardly arises. Raffles will not, for example, abuse hospitality. He will commit a burglary in a house where he is staying as a guest, but the victim must be a fellow-guest and not the host. He will not commit murder,[2] and he avoids violence wherever possible and prefers to carry out his robberies unarmed. He regards friendship as sacred, and is chivalrous though not moral in his relations with women. He will take extra risks in the name of "sportsmanship," and sometimes even for æsthetic reasons. And above all, he is intensely patriotic. He celebrates the Diamond Jubilee ("For sixty years, Bunny, we've been ruled over by absolutely the finest sovereign the world has ever seen") by despatching to the Queen, through the post, an antique gold cup which he has stolen from the British Museum. He steals, from partly political motives, a pearl which the German Emperor is sending to one of the enemies of Britain, and when the Boer War begins to go badly his one thought is to find his way into the fighting line. At the front he unmasks a spy at the cost of revealing his own identity, and then dies gloriously by a Boer bullet. In this combination of crime and patriotism he resembles his near-contemporary Arsene Lupin, who also scores off the German Emperor and wipes out his very dirty past by enlisting in the Foreign Legion.

It is important to note that by modern standards Raffles's crimes are very petty ones. Four hundred pounds' worth of jewellery seems to him an excellent haul. And though the stories are convincing in their physical detail, they contain very little sensationalism—

[2] 1945. Actually Raffles does kill one man and is more or less consciously responsible for the death of two others. But all three of them are foreigners and have behaved in a very reprehensible manner. He also, on one occasion, contemplates murdering a blackmailer. It is, however, a fairly well-established convention in crime stories that murdering a blackmailer "doesn't count."

very few corpses, hardly any blood, no sex crimes, no sadism, no perversions of any kind. It seems to be the case that the crime story, at any rate on its higher levels, has greatly increased in blood-thirstiness during the past twenty years. Some of the early detective stories do not even contain a murder. The Sherlock Holmes stories, for instance, are not all murders, and some of them do not even deal with an indictable crime. So also with the John Thorndyke stories, while of the Max Carrados stories only a minority are murders. Since 1918, however, a detective story not containing a murder has been a great rarity, and the most disgusting details of dismember-ment and exhumation are commonly exploited. Some of the Peter Wimsey stories, for instance, display an extremely morbid interest in corpses. The Raffles stories, written from the angle of the crimi-nal, are much less anti-social than many modern stories written from the angle of the detective. The main impression that they leave be-hind is of boyishness. They belong to a time when people had stand-ards, though they happened to be foolish standards. Their key-phrase is "not done." The line that they draw between good and evil is as senseless as a Polynesian taboo, but at least, like the taboo, it has the advantage that everyone accepts it.

So much for *Raffles*. Now for a header into the cesspool. *No Orchids for Miss Blandish*, by James Hadley Chase, was published in 1939, but seems to have enjoyed its greatest popularity in 1940, dur-ing the Battle of Britain and the blitz. In its main outlines its story is this:

Miss Blandish, the daughter of a millionaire, is kidnapped by some gangsters who are almost immediately surprised and killed off by a larger and better organised gang. They hold her to ransom and ex-tract half a million dollars from her father. Their original plan had been to kill her as soon as the ransom-money was received, but a chance keeps her alive. One of the gang is a young man named Slim, whose sole pleasure in life consists in driving knives into other peo-ple's bellies. In childhood he has graduated by cutting up living ani-mals with a pair of rusty scissors. Slim is sexually impotent, but takes a kind of fancy to Miss Blandish. Slim's mother, who is the real brains of the gang, sees in this the chance of curing Slim's impo-tence, and decides to keep Miss Blandish in custody till Slim shall have succeeded in raping her. After many efforts and much persua-sion, including the flogging of Miss Blandish with a length of rubber hosepipe, the rape is achieved. Meanwhile Miss Blandish's father has hired a private detective, and by means of bribery and torture the detective and the police manage to round up and exterminate the whole gang. Slim escapes with Miss Blandish and is killed after a final rape, and the detective prepares to restore Miss Blandish to her family. By this time, however, she has developed such a taste for Slim's caresses [3] that she feels unable to live without him, and she jumps out of the window of a sky-scraper.

Several other points need noticing before one can grasp the full implications of this book. To begin with, its central story bears a very marked resemblance to William Faulkner's novel, *Sanctuary*. Secondly, it is not, as one might expect, the product of an illiterate hack, but a brilliant piece of writing, with hardly a wasted word or a jarring note anywhere. Thirdly, the whole book, *récit* as well as dialogue, is written in the American language; the author, an Englishman who has (I believe) never been in the United States, seems to have made a complete mental transference to the American underworld. Fourthly, the book sold, according to its publishers, no less than half a million copies.

I have already outlined the plot, but the subject-matter is much more sordid and brutal than this suggests. The book contains eight full-dress murders, an unassessable number of casual killings and woundings, an exhumation (with a careful reminder of the stench), the flogging of Miss Blandish, the torture of another woman with red-hot cigarette-ends, a strip-tease act, a third-degree scene of unheard-of cruelty and much else of the same kind. It assumes great sexual sophistication in its readers (there is a scene, for instance, in which a gangster, presumably of masochistic tendency, has an orgasm in the moment of being knifed), and it takes for granted the most complete corruption and self-seeking as the norm of human behaviour. The detective, for instance, is almost as great a rogue as the gangsters, and actuated by nearly the same motives. Like them, he is in pursuit of "five hundred grand." It is necessary to the machinery of the story that Mr. Blandish should be anxious to get his daughter back, but apart from this, such things as affection, friendship, good nature or even ordinary politeness simply do not enter. Nor, to any great extent, does normal sexuality. Ultimately only one

---

[3] 1945. Another reading of the final episode is possible. It may mean merely that Miss Blandish is pregnant. But the interpretation I have given above seems more in keeping with the general brutality of the book.

motive is at work throughout the whole story: the pursuit of power.

It should be noticed that the book is not in the ordinary sense pornography. Unlike most books that deal in sexual sadism, it lays the emphasis on the cruelty and not on the pleasure. Slim, the ravisher of Miss Blandish, has "wet, slobbering lips": this is disgusting, and it is meant to be disgusting. But the scenes describing cruelty to women are comparatively perfunctory. The real highspots of the book are cruelties committed by men upon other men: above all, the third-degreeing of the gangster, Eddie Schultz, who is lashed into a chair and flogged on the windpipe with truncheons, his arms broken by fresh blows as he breaks loose. In another of Mr. Chase's books, *He Won't Need It Now*, the hero, who is intended to be a sympathetic and perhaps even noble character, is described as stamping on somebody's face, and then, having crushed the man's mouth in, grinding his heel round and round in it. Even when physical incidents of this kind are not occurring, the mental atmosphere of these books is always the same. Their whole theme is the struggle for power and the triumph of the strong over the weak. The big gangsters wipe out the little ones as mercilessly as a pike gobbling up the little fish in a pond; the police kill off the criminals as cruelly as the angler kills the pike. If ultimately one sides with the police against the gangsters, it is merely because they are better organised and more powerful, because, in fact, the law is a bigger racket than crime. Might is right: *voe victis*.

As I have mentioned already, *No Orchids* enjoyed its greatest vogue in 1940, though it was successfully running as a play till some time later. It was, in fact, one of the things that helped to console people for the boredom of being bombed. Early in the war the *New Yorker* had a picture of a little man approaching a news-stall littered with papers with such headlines as "Great Tank Battles in Northern France," "Big Naval Battle in the North Sea," "Huge Air Battles over the Channel," etc. etc. The little man is saying, "*Action Stories*, please." That little man stood for all the drugged millions to whom the world of the gangsters and the prize-ring is more "real," more "tough," than such things as wars, revolutions, earthquakes, famines and pestilences. From the point of view of a reader of *Action Stories*, a description of the London blitz, or of the struggles of the European underground parties, would be "sissy stuff." On the other hand, some puny gun-battle in Chicago, resulting in perhaps half a dozen deaths, would seem genuinely "tough." This habit of mind is now extremely widespread. A soldier sprawls in a muddy trench, with the machine-gun bullets crackling a foot or two over-head, and whiles away his intolerable boredom by reading an Amer-ican gangster story. And what is it that makes that story so exciting? Precisely the fact that people are shooting at each other with machine-guns! Neither the soldier nor anyone else sees anything cu-rious in this. It is taken for granted that an imaginary bullet is more thrilling than a real one.

The obvious explanation is that in real life one is usually a passive victim, whereas in the adventure story one can think of oneself as being at the centre of events. But there is more to it than that. Here it is necessary to refer again to the curious fact of *No Orchids* being written—with technical errors, perhaps, but certainly with consid-erable skill—in the American language.

There exists in America an enormous literature of more or less the same stamp as *No Orchids*. Quite apart from books, there is the huge array of "pulp magazines," graded so as to cater to different kinds of fantasy, but nearly all having much the same mental atmos-phere. A few of them go in for straight pornography, but the great majority are quite plainly aimed at sadists and masochists. Sold at threepence a copy under the title of Yank Mags,[4] these things used to enjoy considerable popularity in England, but when the supply dried up owing to the war, no satisfactory substitute was forthcom-ing. English imitations of the "pulp magazine" do now exist, but they are poor things compared with the original. English crook films, again, never approach the American crook film in brutality. And yet the career of Mr. Chase shows how deep the American in-fluence has already gone. Not only is he himself living a continuous fantasy-life in the Chicago underworld, but he can count on hun-dreds of thousands of readers who know what is meant by a "clip-shop" or the "hotsquat," do not have to do mental arithmetic when confronted by "fifty grand," and understand at sight a sentence like "Johnnie was a rummy and only two jumps ahead of the nut-factory." Evidently there are great numbers of English people who are partly Americanised in language and, one ought to add, in moral

[4] They are said to have been imported into this country as ballast, which accounted for their low price and crumpled appearance. Since the war the ships have been ballasted with something more useful, probably gravel.

outlook. For there was no popular protest against *No Orchids*. In the end it was withdrawn, but only retrospectively, when a later work, *Miss Callaghan Comes to Grief*, brought Mr. Chase's books to the attention of the authorities. Judging by casual conversations at the time, ordinary readers got a mild thrill out of the obscenities of *No Orchids*, but saw nothing undesirable in the book as a whole. Many people, incidentally, were under the impression that it was an American book reissued in England.

The thing that the ordinary reader *ought* to have objected to—almost certainly would have objected to, a few decades earlier—was the equivocal attitude towards crime. It is implied throughout *No Orchids* that being a criminal is only reprehensible in the sense that it does not pay. Being a policeman pays better, but there is no moral difference, since the police use essentially criminal methods. In a book like *He Won't Need It Now* the distinction between crime and crime-prevention practically disappears. This is a new departure for English sensational fiction, in which till recently there has always been a sharp distinction between right and wrong and a general agreement that virtue must triumph in the last chapter. English books glorifying crime (modern crime, that is—pirates and highwaymen are different) are very rare. Even a book like *Raffles*, as I have pointed out, is governed by powerful taboos, and it is clearly understood that Raffles's crimes must be expiated sooner or later. In America, both in life and fiction, the tendency to tolerate crime, even to admire the criminal so long as he is successful, is very much more marked. It is, indeed, ultimately this attitude that has made it possible for crime to flourish upon so huge a scale. Books have been written about Al Capone that are hardly different in tone from the books written about Henry Ford, Stalin, Lord Northcliffe and all the rest of the "log cabin to White House" brigade. And switching back eighty years, one finds Mark Twain adopting much the same attitude towards the disgusting bandit Slade, hero of twenty-eight murders, and towards the Western desperadoes generally. They were successful, they "made good," therefore he admired them.

In a book like *No Orchids* one is not, as in the old-style crime story, simply escaping from dull reality into an imaginary world of action. One's escape is essentially into cruelty and sexual perversion. *No Orchids* is aimed at the power-instinct, which *Raffles* or the Sherlock Holmes stories are not. At the same time the English attitude towards crime is not so superior to the American as I may have seemed to imply. It too is mixed up with power-worship, and has become more noticeably so in the last twenty years. A writer who is worth examining is Edgar Wallace, especially in such typical books as *The Orator* and the Mr. J. G. Reeder stories. Wallace was one of the first crime-story writers to break away from the old tradition of the private detective and make his central figure a Scotland Yard official. Sherlock Holmes is an amateur, solving his problems without the help and even, in the earlier stories, against the opposition of the police. Moreover, like Lupin, he is essentially an intellectual, even a scientist. He reasons logically from observed fact, and his intellectuality is constantly contrasted with the routine methods of the police. Wallace objected strongly to this slur, as he considered it, on Scotland Yard, and in several newspaper articles he went out of his way to denounce Holmes by name. His own ideal was the detective inspector who catches criminals not because he is intellectually brilliant but because he is part of an all-powerful organisation. Hence the curious fact that in Wallace's most characteristic stories the "clue" and the "deduction" play no part. The criminal is always defeated either by an incredible coincidence, or because in some unexplained manner the police know all about the crime beforehand. The tone of the stories makes it quite clear that Wallace's admiration for the police is pure bully-worship. A Scotland Yard detective is the most powerful kind of being that he can imagine, while the criminal figures in his mind as an outlaw against whom anything is permissible, like the condemned slaves in the Roman arena. His policemen behave much more brutally than British policemen do in real life—they hit people without provocation, fire revolvers past their ears to terrify them and so on—and some of the stories exhibit a fearful intellectual sadism. (For instance, Wallace likes to arrange things so that the villain is hanged on the same day as the heroine is married.) But it is sadism after the English fashion: that is to say, it is unconscious, there is not overtly any sex in it, and it keeps within the bounds of the law. The British public tolerates a harsh criminal law and gets a kick out of monstrously unfair murder trials: but still this is better, on any count, than tolerating or admiring crime. If one must worship a bully, it is better that he should be a policeman than a gangster. Wallace is still governed to some extent by the concept of "not done." In *No Orchids* anything is "done" so long as it leads on to power. All the barriers are down, all the motives are out in the open. Chase is a worse symptom than Wallace, to the extent that all-in wrestling is worse than boxing, or Fascism is worse than capitalist democracy.

In borrowing from William Faulkner's *Sanctuary*, Chase only took the plot; the mental atmosphere of the two books is not similar. Chase really derives from other sources, and this particular bit of borrowing is only symbolic. What it symbolises is the vulgarisation of ideas which is constantly happening, and which probably happens faster in an age of print. Chase has been described as "Faulkner for the masses," but it would be more accurate to describe him as Carlyle for the masses. He is a popular writer—there are many such in America, but they are still rarities in England—who has caught up with what is now fashionable to call "realism," meaning the doctrine that might is right. The growth of "realism" has been the great feature of the intellectual history of our own age. Why this should be so is a complicated question. The interconnection between sadism, masochism, success-worship, power-worship, nationalism and totalitarianism is a huge subject whose edges have barely been scratched, and even to mention it is considered somewhat indelicate. To take merely the first example that comes to mind, I believe no one has ever pointed out the sadistic and masochistic element in Bernard Shaw's work, still less suggested that this probably has some connection with Shaw's admiration for dictators. Fascism is often loosely equated with sadism, but nearly always by people who see nothing wrong in the most slavish worship of Stalin. The truth is, of course, that the countless English intellectuals who kiss the arse of Stalin are not different from the minority who give their allegiance to Hitler or Mussolini, nor from the efficiency experts who preached "punch," "drive," "personality" and "learn to be a Tiger man" in the nineteen-twenties, nor from that older generation of intellectuals, Carlyle, Creasey and the rest of them, who bowed down before German militarism. All of them are worshipping power and successful cruelty. It is important to notice that the cult of power tends to be mixed up with a love of cruelty and wickedness *for their own sakes*. A tyrant is all the more admired if he happens to be a bloodstained crook as well, and "the end justifies the means" often becomes, in effect, "the means justify themselves provided they are dirty enough." This idea colours the outlook of all sympathisers with totalitarianism, and accounts, for instance, for the positive delight with which many English intellectuals greeted the Nazi-Soviet pact. It was a step only doubtfully useful to the U.S.S.R., but it was entirely unmoral, and for that reason to be admired; the explanations of it, which were numerous and self-contradictory, could come afterwards.

Until recently the characteristic adventure stories of the English-speaking peoples have been stories in which the hero fights *against odds*. This is true all the way from Robin Hood to Pop-eye the Sailor. Perhaps the basic myth of the Western world is Jack the Giant-killer, but to be brought up to date this should be renamed Jack the Dwarf-killer, and there already exists considerable literature which teaches, either overtly or implicitly, that one should side with the big man against the little man. Most of what is now written about foreign policy is simply an embroidery on this theme, and for several decades such phrases as "Play the game," "Don't hit a man when he's down" and "It's not cricket" have never failed to draw a snigger from anyone of intellectual pretensions. What is comparatively new is to find the accepted pattern according to which (*a*) right is right and wrong is wrong, whoever wins, and (*b*) weakness must be respected, disappearing from popular literature as well. When I first read D. H. Lawrence's novels, at the age of about twenty, I was puzzled by the fact that there did not seem to be any classification of the characters into "good" and "bad." Lawrence seemed to sympathise with all of them about equally and this was so unusual as to give me the feeling of having lost my bearings. Today no one would think of looking for heroes and villains in a serious novel, but in lowbrow fiction one still expects to find a sharp distinction between right and wrong and between legality and illegality. The common people, on the whole, are still living in the world of absolute good and evil from which the intellectuals have long since escaped. But the popularity of *No Orchids* and the American books and magazines to which it is akin shows how rapidly the doctrine of "realism" is gaining ground.

Several people, after reading *No Orchids*, have remarked to me, "It's pure Fascism." This is a correct description, although the book has not the smallest connection with politics and very little with social or economic problems. It has merely the same relation to Fascism as, say, Trollope's novels have to nineteenth-century capitalism. It is a day dream appropriate to a totalitarian age. In his imagined world of gangsters Chase is presenting, as it were, a distilled version of the modern political scene, in which such things as mass bombing of civilians, the use of hostages, torture to obtain confessions, secret prisons, execution without trial, floggings with rubber truncheons, drownings in cesspools, systematic falsification of records and statistics, treachery, bribery and quislingism are normal and morally neutral, even admirable when they are done in a large and bold way. The average man is not directly interested in politics, and when he reads, he wants the current struggles of the world to be translated into a simple story about individuals. He can take an interest in Slim and Fenner as he could not in the G.P.U. and the Gestapo. People worship power in the form in which they are able to understand it. A twelve-year-old boy worships Jack Dempsey. An adolescent in a Glasgow slum worships Al Capone. An aspiring pupil at a business college worships Lord Nuffield. A *New Statesman* reader worships Stalin. There is a difference in intellectual maturity, but none in moral outlook. Thirty years ago the heroes of popular fiction had nothing in common with Mr. Chase's gangsters and detectives, and the idols of the English liberal intelligentsia were also comparatively sympathetic figures. Between Holmes and Fenner on the one hand, and between Abraham Lincoln and Stalin on the other, there is a similar gulf.

One ought not to infer too much from the success of Mr. Chase's books. It is possible that it is an isolated phenomenon, brought about by the mingled boredom and brutality of war. But if such books should definitely acclimatise themselves in England, instead of being merely a half-understood import from America, there would be good grounds for dismay. In choosing *Raffles* as a background for *No Orchids* I deliberately chose a book which by the standards of its time was morally equivocal. Raffles, as I have pointed out, has no real moral code, no religion, certainly no social consciousness. All he has is a set of reflexes—the nervous system, as it were, of a gentleman. Give him a sharp tap on this reflex or that (they are called "sport," "pal," "woman," "king and country" and so forth), and you get a predictable reaction. In Mr. Chase's books there are no gentlemen and no taboos. Emancipation is complete, Freud and Machiavelli have reached the outer suburbs. Comparing the schoolboy atmosphere of the one book with the cruelty and corruption of the other, one is driven to feel that snobbishness, like hypocrisy, is a check upon behaviour whose value from a social point of view has been underrated.

Politics and the English Language

Most people who bother with the matter at all would admit that the English language is in a bad way, but it is generally assumed that we cannot by conscious action do anything about it. Our civilization is decadent and our language—so the argument runs—must inevitably share in the general collapse. It follows that any struggle against the abuse of language is a sentimental archaism, like preferring candles to electric light or hansom cabs to aeroplanes. Underneath this lies the half-conscious belief that language is a natural growth and not an instrument which we shape for our own purposes.

Now, it is clear that the decline of a language must ultimately have political and economic causes: it is not due simply to the bad influence of this or that individual writer. But an effect can become a cause, reinforcing the original cause and producing the same effect in an intensified form, and so on indefinitely. A man may take to drink because he feels himself to be a failure, and then fail all the more completely because he drinks. It is rather the same thing that is happening to the English language. It becomes ugly and inaccurate because our thoughts are foolish, but the slovenliness of our language makes it easier for us to have foolish thoughts. The point is that the process is reversible. Modern English, especially written English, is full of bad habits which spread by imitation and which can be avoided if one is willing to take the necessary trouble. If one gets rid of these habits one can think more clearly, and to think clearly is a necessary first step towards political regeneration: so that the fight against bad English is not frivolous and is not the exclusive concern of professional writers. I will come back to this presently, and I hope that by that time the meaning of what I have said here will have become clearer. Meanwhile, here are five specimens of the English language as it is now habitually written.

These five passages have not been picked out because they are especially bad—I could have quoted far worse if I had chosen—but because they illustrate various of the mental vices from which we now suffer. They are a little below the average, but are fairly representative samples. I number them so that I can refer back to them when necessary:

(1) I am not, indeed, sure whether it is not true to say that the Milton who once seemed not unlike a seventeenth-century Shelley had not become, out of an experience ever more bitter in each year, more alien [sic] to the founder of that Jesuit sect which nothing could induce him to tolerate.

Professor Harold Laski
(Essay in *Freedom of Expression*).

(2) Above all, we cannot play ducks and drakes with a native battery of idioms which prescribes such egregious collocations of vocables as the Basic *put up with* for *tolerate* or *put at a loss* for *bewilder*.

Professor Lancelot Hogben (*Interglossa*).

(3) On the one side we have the free personality: by definition it is not neurotic, for it has neither conflict nor dream. Its desires, such as they are, are transparent, for they are just what institutional approval keeps in the forefront of consciousness; another institutional pattern would alter their number and intensity; there is little in them that is natural, irreducible, or culturally dangerous. But *on the other side*, the social bond itself is nothing but the mutual reflection of these self-secure integrities. Recall the definition of love. Is not this the very picture of a small academic? Where is there a place in this hall of mirrors for either personality or fraternity?

Essay on psychology in *Politics* (New York).

(4) All the "best people" from the gentlemen's clubs, and all the frantic fascist captains, united in common hatred of Socialism and bestial horror of the rising tide of the mass revolutionary movement, have turned to acts of provocation, to foul incendiarism, to medieval legends of poisoned wells, to legalize their own destruction of proletarian organizations, and rouse the agitated petty-bourgeoisie to chauvinistic fervor on behalf of the fight against the revolutionary way out of the crisis.

Communist pamphlet.

(5) If a new spirit is to be infused into this old country, there is one thorny and contentious reform which must be tackled, and that is the humanization and galvanization of the B.B.C. Timidity here will bespeak canker and atrophy of the soul. The heart of Britain may be sound and of strong beat, for instance, but the British lion's roar at present is like that of Bottom in Shakespeare's *Midsummer Night's Dream*—as gentle as any sucking dove. A virile new Britain cannot continue indefinitely to be traduced in the eyes, or rather ears, of the world by the effete languors of Langham Place, brazenly masquerading as "standard English." When the Voice of Britain is heard at nine o'clock, better far and infinitely less ludicrous to hear aitches honestly dropped than the present priggish, inflated, inhibited school-ma'amish arch braying of blameless bashful mewing maidens!

Letter in Tribune.

Each of these passages has faults of its own, but, quite apart from avoidable ugliness, two qualities are common to all of them. The first is staleness of imagery; the other is lack of precision. The writer either has a meaning and cannot express it, or he inadvertently says something else, or he is almost indifferent as to whether his words mean anything or not. This mixture of vagueness and sheer incompetence is the most marked characteristic of modern English prose, and especially of any kind of political writing. As soon as certain topics are raised, the concrete melts into the abstract and no one seems able to think of turns of speech that are not hackneyed: prose consists less and less of *words* chosen for the sake of their meaning, and more and more of *phrases* tacked together like the sections of a prefabricated hen-house. I list below, with notes and examples, various of the tricks by means of which the work of prose-construction is habitually dodged:

Dying metaphors. A newly invented metaphor assists thought by evoking a visual image, while on the other hand a metaphor which is technically "dead" (e.g. *iron resolution*) has in effect reverted to being an ordinary word and can generally be used without loss of vividness. But in between these two classes there is a huge dump of worn-out metaphors which have lost all evocative power and are merely used because they save people the trouble of inventing phrases for themselves. Examples are: *Ring the changes on, take up the cudgels for, toe the line, ride roughshod over, stand shoulder to shoulder with, play into the hands of, no axe to grind, grist to the mill, fishing in troubled waters, on the order of the day, Achilles' heel, swan song, hotbed.* Many of these are used without knowledge of their meaning (what is a "rift," for instance?), and incompatible metaphors are frequently mixed, a sure sign that the writer is not interested in what he is saying. Some metaphors now current have been twisted out of their original meaning without those who use them even being aware of the fact. For example, *toe the line* is sometimes written *tow the line.* Another example is *the hammer and the anvil,* now always used with the implication that the anvil gets the worst of it. In real life it is always the anvil that breaks the hammer, never the other way about: a writer who stopped to think what he was saying would be aware of this, and would avoid perverting the original phrase.

Operators or verbal false limbs. These save the trouble of picking out appropriate verbs and nouns, and at the same time pad each sentence with extra syllables which give it an appearance of symmetry. Characteristic phrases are *render inoperative, militate against, make contact with, be subjected to, give rise to, give grounds for, have the effect of, play a leading part (role) in, make itself felt, take effect, exhibit a tendency to, serve the purpose of, etc., etc.* The keynote is the elimination of simple verbs. Instead of being a single word, such as *break, stop, spoil, mend, kill,* a verb becomes a *phrase,* made up of a noun or adjective tacked on to some general-purposes verb such as *prove, serve, form, play, render.* In addition, the passive voice is wherever possible used in preference to the active, and noun constructions are used instead of gerunds (*by examination of* instead of *by examining*). The range of verbs is further cut down by means of the *-ize* and *de-* formations, and the banal statements are given an appearance of profundity by means of the *not un-* formation. Simple conjunctions and prepositions are replaced by such phrases as *with respect to, having regard to, the fact that, by dint of, in view of, in the interests of, on the hypothesis that;* and the ends of sentences are saved by anticlimax by such resounding common-places as *greatly to be desired, cannot be left out of account, a development to be expected in the near future, deserving of serious consideration, brought to a satisfactory conclusion,* and so on and so forth.

Pretentious diction. Words like *phenomenon, element, individual* (as noun), *objective, categorical, effective, virtual, basic, primary, promote, constitute, exhibit, exploit, utilize, eliminate, liquidate,* are used to dress up simple statement and give an air of scientific impartiality to biased judgments. Adjectives like *epoch-making, epic, historic, unforgettable, triumphant, age-old, inevitable, inexorable, veritable,* are used to dignify the sordid processes of international politics, while writing that aims at glorifying war usually takes on an archaic color, its characteristic words being: *realm, throne, chariot, mailed fist, trident, sword, shield, buckler, banner, jackboot, clarion.* Foreign words and expressions such as *cul de sac, ancien régime, deus ex machina, mutatis mutandis, status quo, gleichschaltung, weltanschauung,* are used to give an air of culture and elegance. Except for the useful abbreviations *i.e., e.g.,* and *etc.,* there is no real need for any of the hundreds of foreign phrases now current in English. Bad writers, and especially scientific, political and sociological writers, are nearly always haunted by the notion that Latin or Greek words are grander than Saxon ones, and unnecessary words like *expedite, ameliorate, predict, extraneous, deracinated, clandestine, subaqueous* and hundreds of others constantly gain ground from their Anglo-Saxon opposite numbers.[1] The jargon peculiar to Marxist writing (*hyena, hangman, cannibal, petty bourgeois, these gentry, lacquey, flunkey, mad dog, White Guard,* etc.) consists largely of words and phrases translated from Russian, German or French; but the normal way of coining a new word is to use a Latin or Greek root with the appropriate affix and, where necessary, the size formation. It is often easier to make up words of this kind (*deregionalize, impermissible, extramarital, nonfragmentary* and so forth) than to think up the English words that will cover one's meaning. The result, in general, is an increase in slovenliness and vagueness.

Meaningless words. In certain kinds of writing, particularly in art criticism and literary criticism, it is normal to come across long passages which are almost completely lacking in meaning.[2] Words like

[1] An interesting illustration of this is the way in which the English flower names which were in use till very recently are being ousted by Greek ones, *snapdragon* becoming *antirrhinum, forget-me-not* becoming *myosotis,* etc. It is hard to see any practical reason for this change of fashion: it is probably due to an instinctive turning-away from the more homely word and a vague feeling that the Greek word is scientific.
[2] Example: "Comfort's catholicity of perception and image, strangely Whitmanesque in range, almost the exact opposite in aesthetic compulsion, continues to

romantic, plastic, values, human, dead, sentimental, natural, vitality, as used in art criticism, are strictly meaningless, in the sense that they not only do not point to any discoverable object, but are hardly ever expected to do so by the reader. When one critic writes, "The outstanding feature of Mr. X's work is its living quality," while another writes, "The immediately striking thing about Mr. X's work is its peculiar deadness," the reader accepts this as a simple difference of opinion. If words like *black* and *white* were involved, instead of the jargon words *dead* and *living,* he would see at once that language was being used in an improper way. Many political words are similarly abused. The word *Fascism* has now no meaning except in so far as it signifies "something not desirable." The words *democracy, socialism, freedom, patriotic, realistic, justice,* have each of them several different meanings which cannot be reconciled with one another. In the case of a word like *democracy,* not only is there no agreed definition, but the attempt to make one is resisted from all sides. It is almost universally felt that when we call a country democratic we are praising it: consequently the defenders of every kind of régime claim that it is a democracy, and fear that they might have to stop using the word if it were tied down to any one meaning. Words of this kind are often used in a consciously dishonest way. That is, the person who uses them has his own private definition, but allows his hearer to think he means something quite different. Statements like *Marshal Pétain was a true patriot, The Soviet Press is the freest in the world, The Catholic Church is opposed to persecution,* are almost always made with intent to deceive. Other words used in variable meanings, in most cases more or less dishonestly, are: *class, totalitarian, science, progressive, reactionary, bourgeois, equality.*

Now that I have made this catalogue of swindles and perversions, let me give another example of the kind of writing that they lead to. This time it must of its nature be an imaginary one. I am going to translate a passage of good English into modern English of the worst sort. Here is a well-known verse from *Ecclesiastes:*

"I returned and saw under the sun, that the race is not to the

evoke that trembling atmospheric accumulative hinting at a cruel, an inexorably serene timelessness. . . . Wrey Gardiner scores by aiming at simple bull's-eyes with precision. Only they are not so simple, and through this contented sadness runs more than the surface bitter-sweet of resignation." (Poetry Quarterly.)

swift, nor the battle to the strong, neither yet bread to the wise, nor yet riches to men of understanding, nor yet favour to men of skill; but time and chance happeneth to them all."

Here it is in modern English:

"Objective consideration of contemporary phenomena compels the conclusion that success or failure in competitive activities exhibits no tendency to be commensurate with innate capacity, but that a considerable element of the unpredictable must invariably be taken into account."

This is a parody, but not a very gross one. Exhibit (3), above, for instance, contains several patches of the same kind of English. It will be seen that I have not made a full translation. The beginning and ending of the sentence follow the original meaning fairly closely, but in the middle the concrete illustrations—race, battle, bread—dissolve into the vague phrase "success or failure in competitive activities." This had to be so, because no modern writer of the kind I am discussing—no one capable of using phrases like "objective consideration of contemporary phenomena"—would ever tabulate his thoughts in that precise and detailed way. The whole tendency of modern prose is away from concreteness. Now analyse these two sentences a little more closely. The first contains forty-nine words but only sixty syllables, and all its words are those of everyday life. The second contains thirty-eight words of ninety syllables: eighteen of its words are from Latin roots, and one from Greek. The first sentence contains six vivid images, and only one phrase ("time and chance") that could be called vague. The second contains not a single fresh, arresting phrase, and in spite of its ninety syllables it gives only a shortened version of the meaning contained in the first. Yet without a doubt it is the second kind of sentence that is gaining ground in modern English. I do not want to exaggerate. This kind of writing is not yet universal, and outcrops of simplicity will occur here and there in the worst-written page. Still, if you or I were told to write a few lines on the uncertainty of human fortunes, we should probably come much nearer to my imaginary sentence than to the one from *Ecclesiastes*.

As I have tried to show, modern writing at its worst does not consist in picking out words for the sake of their meaning and inventing images in order to make the meaning clearer. It consists in gumming together long strips of words which have already been set in order by someone else, and making the results presentable by sheer humbug. The attraction of this way of writing is that it is easy. It is easier—even quicker, once you have the habit—to say *In my opinion it is not an unjustifiable assumption that* than to say *I think*. If you use ready-made phrases, you not only don't have to hunt about for words; you also don't have to bother with the rhythms of your sentences, since these phrases are generally so arranged as to be more or less euphonious. When you are composing in a hurry— when you are dictating to a stenographer, for instance, or making a public speech—it is natural to fall into a pretentious, Latinized style. Tags like *a consideration which we should do well to bear in mind* or *a conclusion to which all of us would readily assent* will save many a sentence from coming down with a bump. By using stale metaphors, similes, and idioms, you save much mental effort, at the cost of leaving your meaning vague, not only for your reader but for yourself. This is the significance of mixed metaphors. The sole aim of a metaphor is to call up a visual image. When these images clash—as in *The Fascist octopus has sung its swan song, the jackboot is thrown into the melting pot*—it can be taken as certain that the writer is not seeing a mental image of the objects he is naming; in other words he is not really thinking. Look again at the examples I gave at the beginning of this essay. Professor Laski (1) uses five negatives in fifty-three words. One of these is superfluous, making nonsense of the whole passage, and in addition there is the slip *alien* for akin, making further nonsense, and several avoidable pieces of clumsiness which increase the general vagueness. Professor Hogben (2) plays ducks and drakes with a battery which is able to write prescriptions, and, while disapproving of the everyday phrase *put up with*, is unwilling to look *egregious* up in the dictionary and see what it means; (3), if one takes an uncharitable attitude towards it, is simply meaningless: probably one could work out its intended meaning by reading the whole of the article in which it occurs. In (4), the writer knows more or less what he wants to say, but an accumulation of stale phrases chokes him like tea leaves blocking a sink. In (5), words and meaning have almost parted company. People who write in this manner usually have a general emotional meaning—they dislike one thing and want to express solidarity with another—but they are not interested in the detail of what they are saying. A scrupulous writer, in every sentence that he writes, will ask himself at least four questions, thus: What am I trying to say? What words will express it? What image or idiom will make it clearer? Is this image fresh enough to have an effect? And he will probably ask himself two more: Could I put it more shortly? Have I said anything that is avoidably ugly? But you are not obliged to go to all this trouble. You can shirk it by simply throwing your mind open and letting the ready-made phrases come crowding in. They will construct your sentences for you—even think your thoughts for you, to a certain extent—and at need they will perform the important service of partially concealing your meaning even from yourself. It is at this point that the special connection between politics and the debasement of language becomes clear.

In our time it is broadly true that political writing is bad writing. Where it is not true, it will generally be found that the writer is some kind of rebel, expressing his private opinions and not a "party line." Orthodoxy, of whatever color, seems to demand a lifeless, imitative style. The political dialects to be found in pamphlets, leading articles, manifestos, White Papers and the speeches of undersecretaries do, of course, vary from party to party, but they are all alike in that one almost never finds in them a fresh, vivid, homemade turn of speech. When one watches some tired hack on the platform mechanically repeating the familiar phrases—*bestial atrocities, iron heel, bloodstained tyranny, free peoples of the world, stand shoulder to shoulder*—one often has a curious feeling that one is not watching a live human being but some kind of dummy: a feeling which suddenly becomes stronger at moments when the light catches the speaker's spectacles and turns them into blank discs which seem to have no eyes behind them. And this is not altogether fanciful. A speaker who uses that kind of phraseology has gone some distance towards turning himself into a machine. The appropriate noises are coming out of his larynx, but his brain is not involved as it would be if he were choosing his words for himself. If the speech he is making is one that he is accustomed to make over and over again, he may be almost unconscious of what he is saying, as one is when one utters the responses in church. And this reduced state of consciousness, if not indispensable, is at any rate favorable to political conformity.

In our time, political speech and writing are largely the defence of the indefensible. Things like the continuance of British rule in India, the Russian purges and deportations, the dropping of the atom bombs on Japan, can indeed be defended, but only by arguments which are too brutal for most people to face, and which do not square with the professed aims of political parties. Thus political language has to consist largely of euphemism, question-begging and sheer cloudy vagueness. Defenceless villages are bombarded from the air, the inhabitants driven out into the countryside, the cattle machine-gunned, the huts set on fire with incendiary bullets: this is called *pacification*. Millions of peasants are robbed of their farms and sent trudging along the roads with no more than they can carry: this is called *transfer of population* or rectification of frontiers. People are imprisoned for years without trial, or shot in the back of the neck or sent to die of scurvy in Arctic lumber camps: this is called *elimination of unreliable elements*. Such phraseology is needed if one wants to name things without calling up mental pictures of them. Consider for instance some comfortable English professor defending Russian totalitarianism. He cannot say outright, "I believe in killing off your opponents when you can get good results by doing so." Probably, therefore, he will say something like this:

"While freely conceding that the Soviet régime exhibits certain features which the humanitarian may be inclined to deplore, we must, I think, agree that a certain curtailment of the right to political opposition is an unavoidable concomitant of transitional periods, and that the rigors which the Russian people have been called upon to undergo have been amply justified in the sphere of concrete achievement."

The inflated style is itself a kind of euphemism. A mass of Latin words falls upon the facts like soft snow, blurring the outlines and covering up all the details. The great enemy of clear language is insincerity. When there is a gap between one's real and one's declared aims, one turns as it were instinctively to long words and exhausted idioms, like a cuttlefish squirting out ink. In our age there is no such thing as "keeping out of politics." All issues are political issues, and politics itself is a mass of lies, evasions, folly, hatred and schizophrenia. When the general atmosphere is bad, language must suffer. I should expect to find—this is a guess which I have not sufficient knowledge to verify—that the German, Russian and Italian languages have all deteriorated in the last ten or fifteen years, as a result of dictatorship.

But if thought corrupts language, language can also corrupt thought. A bad usage can spread by tradition and imitation, even among people who should and do know better. The debased language that I have been discussing is in some ways very convenient. Phrases like *a not unjustifiable assumption, leaves much to be desired, would serve no good purpose, a consideration which we should do well to bear in mind,* are a continuous temptation, a packet of aspirins always at one's elbow. Look back through this essay, and for certain you will find that I have again and again committed the very faults I am protesting against. By this morning's post I have received a pamphlet dealing with conditions in Germany. The author tells me that he "felt impelled" to write it. I open it at random, and here is almost the first sentence that I see: "[The Allies] have an opportunity not only of achieving a radical transformation of Germany's social and political structure in such a way as to avoid a nationalistic reaction in Germany itself, but at the same time of laying the foundations of a co-operative and unified Europe." You see, he "feels impelled" to write—feels, presumably, that he has something new to say—and yet his words, like cavalry horses answering the bugle, group themselves automatically into the familiar dreary pattern. This invasion of one's mind by ready-made phrases (*lay the foundations, achieve a radical transformation*) can only be prevented if one is constantly on guard against them, and every such phrase anaesthetizes a portion of one's brain.

I said earlier that the decadence of our language is probably curable. Those who deny this would argue, if they produced an argument at all, that language merely reflects existing social conditions, and that we cannot influence its development by any direct tinkering with words and constructions. So far as the general tone or spirit of a language goes, this may be true, but it is not true in detail. Silly words and expressions have often disappeared, not through any evolutionary process but owing to the conscious action of a minority. Two recent examples were *explore every avenue* and *leave no stone unturned,* which were killed by the jeers of a few journalists. There is a long list of flyblown metaphors which could similarly be got rid of if enough people would interest themselves in the job; and it should also be possible to laugh the *not un-* formation out of existence,[3] to reduce the amount of Latin and Greek in the average sentence, to drive out foreign phrases and strayed scientific words, and, in general, to make pretentiousness unfashionable. But

---

[3] One can cure oneself of the *not un-* formation by memorizing this sentence: *A not unblack dog was chasing a not unsmall rabbit across a not ungreen field.*

all these are minor points. The defence of the English language implies more than this, and perhaps it is best to start by saying what it does *not* imply.

To begin with it has nothing to do with archaism, with the salvaging of obsolete words and turns of speech, or with the setting up of a "standard English" which must never be departed from. On the contrary, it is especially concerned with the scrapping of every word or idiom which has outworn its usefulness. It has nothing to do with correct grammar and syntax, which are of no importance so long as one makes one's meaning clear, or with the avoidance of Americanisms, or with having what is called a "good prose style." On the other hand it is not concerned with fake simplicity and the attempt to make written English colloquial. Nor does it even imply in every case preferring the Saxon word to the Latin one, though it does imply using the fewest and shortest words that will cover one's meaning. What is above all needed is to let the meaning choose the word, and not the other way about. In prose, the worst thing one can do with words is to surrender to them. When you think of a concrete object, you think wordlessly, and then, if you want to describe the thing you have been visualizing you probably hunt about till you find the exact words that seem to fit it. When you think of something abstract you are more inclined to use words from the start, and unless you make a conscious effort to prevent it, the existing dialect will come rushing in and do the job for you, at the expense of blurring or even changing your meaning. Probably it is better to put off using words as long as possible and get one's meaning as clear as one can through pictures or sensations. Afterwards one can choose—not simply *accept*—the phrases that will best cover the meaning, and then switch round and decide what impression one's words are likely to make on another person. This last effort of the mind cuts out all stale or mixed images, all prefabricated phrases, needless repetitions, and humbug and vagueness generally. But one can often be in doubt about the effect of a word or a phrase, and one needs rules that one can rely on when instinct fails. I think the following rules will cover most cases:

(i) Never use a metaphor, simile or other figure of speech which you are used to seeing in print.
(ii) Never use a long word where a short one will do.
(iii) If it is possible to cut a word out, always cut it out.

(iv) Never use the passive where you can use the active.
(v) Never use a foreign phrase, a scientific word or a jargon word if you can think of an everyday English equivalent.
(vi) Break any of these rules sooner than say anything outright barbarous.

These rules sound elementary, and so they are, but they demand a deep change of attitude in anyone who has grown used to writing in the style now fashionable. One could keep all of them and still write bad English, but one could not write the kind of stuff that I quoted in those five specimens at the beginning of this article.

I have not here been considering the literary use of language, but merely language as an instrument for expressing and not for concealing or preventing thought. Stuart Chase and others have come near to claiming that all abstract words are meaningless, and have used this as a pretext for advocating a kind of political quietism. Since you don't know what Fascism is, how can you struggle against Fascism? One need not swallow such absurdities as this, but one ought to recognize that the present political chaos is connected with the decay of language, and that one can probably bring about some improvement by starting at the verbal end. If you simplify your English, you are freed from the worst follies of orthodoxy. You cannot speak any of the necessary dialects, and when you make a stupid remark its stupidity will be obvious, even to yourself. Political language—and with variations this is true of all political parties, from Conservatives to Anarchists—is designed to make lies sound truthful and murder respectable, and to give an appearance of solidity to pure wind. One cannot change this all in a moment, but one can at least change one's own habits, and from time to time one can even, if one jeers loudly enough, send some worn-out and useless phrase—some *jackboot, Achilles' heel, hotbed, melting pot, acid test, veritable inferno* or other lump of verbal refuse—into the dustbin where it belongs.

Marrakech

As the corpse went past the flies left the restaurant table in a cloud and rushed after it, but they came back a few minutes later. The little crowd of mourners—all men and boys, no women— threaded their way across the market-place between the piles of pomegranates and the taxis and the camels, wailing a short chant over and over again. What really appeals to the flies is that the corpses here are never put into coffins, they are merely wrapped in a piece of rag and carried on a rough wooden bier on the shoulders of four friends. When the friends get to the burying-ground they hack an oblong hole a foot or two deep, dump the body in it and fling over it a little of the dried-up, lumpy earth, which is like broken brick. No gravestone, no name, no identifying mark of any kind. The burying-ground is merely a huge waste of hummocky earth, like a derelict building-lot. After a month or two no one can even be certain where his own relatives are buried.

When you walk through a town like this—two hundred thousand inhabitants, of whom at least twenty thousand own literally nothing except the rags they stand up in—when you see how the people live, and still more how easily they die, it is always difficult to believe that you are walking among human beings. All colonial empires are in reality founded upon that fact. The people have brown faces— besides, there are so many of them! Are they really the same flesh as yourself? Do they even have names? Or are they merely a kind of undifferentiated brown stuff, about as individual as bees or coral insects? They rise out of the earth, they sweat and starve for a few years, and then they sink back into the nameless mounds of the graveyard and nobody notices that they are gone. And even the graves themselves soon fade back into the soil. Sometimes, out for a walk, as you break your way through the prickly pear, you notice that it is rather bumpy underfoot, and only a certain regularity in the bumps tells you that you are walking over skeletons.

MARRAKECH. From *Such, Such Were the Joys* by George Orwell, copyright, 1945, 1952, 1953 by Sonia Brownell Orwell. Reprinted by permission of Harcourt, Brace & World, Inc., and Martin Secker & Warburg Ltd., Publishers, London.

I was feeding one of the gazelles in the public gardens.

Gazelles are almost the only animals that look good to eat when they are still alive, in fact, one can hardly look at their hindquarters without thinking of mint sauce. The gazelle I was feeding seemed to know that this thought was in my mind, for though it took the piece of bread I was holding out it obviously did not like me. It nibbled rapidly at the bread, then lowered its head and tried to butt me, then took another nibble and then butted again. Probably its idea was that if it could drive me away the bread would somehow remain hanging in mid-air.

An Arab navvy working on the path nearby lowered his heavy hoe and sidled slowly towards us. He looked from the gazelle to the bread and from the bread to the gazelle, with a sort of quiet amazement, as though he had never seen anything quite like this before. Finally he said shyly in French:

"*I* could eat some of that bread."

I tore off a piece and he stowed it gratefully in some secret place under his rags. This man is an employee of the Municipality.

When you go through the Jewish quarters you gather some idea of what the medieval ghettoes were probably like. Under their Moorish rulers the Jews were only allowed to own land in certain restricted areas, and after centuries of this kind of treatment they have ceased to bother about overcrowding. Many of the streets are a good deal less than six feet wide, the houses are completely windowless, and sore-eyed children cluster everywhere in unbelievable numbers, like clouds of flies. Down the centre of the street there is generally running a little river of urine.

In the bazaar huge families of Jews, all dressed in the long black robe and little black skull-cap, are working in dark fly-infested booths that look like caves. A carpenter sits crosslegged at a prehistoric lathe, turning chair-legs at lightning speed. He works the lathe with a bow in his right hand and guides the chisel with his left foot, and thanks to a lifetime of sitting in this position his left leg is warped out of shape. At his side his grandson, aged six, is already starting on the simpler parts of the job.

I was just passing the coppersmiths' booths when somebody noticed that I was lighting a cigarette. Instantly, from the dark holes all round, there was a frenzied rush of Jews, many of them old grandfathers with flowing grey beards, all clamouring for a cigarette. Even a blind man somewhere at the back of one of the booths heard a rumour of cigarettes and came crawling out, groping in the air with his hand. In about a minute I had used up the whole packet. None of these people, I suppose, works less than twelve hours a day, and every one of them looks on a cigarette as a more or less impossible luxury.

As the Jews live in self-contained communities they follow the same trades as the Arabs, except for agriculture. Fruit-sellers, potters, silversmiths, blacksmiths, butchers, leatherworkers, tailors, water-carriers, beggars, porters—whichever way you look you see nothing but Jews. As a matter of fact there are thirteen thousand of them, all living in the space of a few acres. A good job Hitler wasn't here. Perhaps he was on his way, however. You hear the usual dark rumours about the Jews, not only from the Arabs but from the poorer Europeans.

"Yes, mon vieux, they took my job away from me and gave it to a Jew. The Jews! They're the real rulers of this country, you know. They've got all the money. They control the banks, finance—everything."

"But," I said, "isn't it a fact that the average Jew is a labourer working for about a penny an hour?"

"Ah, that's only for show! They're all moneylenders really. They're cunning, the Jews."

In just the same way, a couple of hundred years ago, poor old women used to be burned for witchcraft when they could not even work enough magic to get themselves a square meal.

All people who work with their hands are partly invisible, and the more important the work they do, the less visible they are. Still, a white skin is always fairly conspicuous. In northern Europe, when you see a labourer ploughing a field, you probably give him a second glance. In a hot country, anywhere south of Gibraltar or east of Suez, the chances are that you don't even see him. I have noticed this again and again. In a tropical landscape one's eye takes in everything except the human beings. It takes in the dried-up soil, the prickly pear, the palm tree and the distant mountain, but it always misses the peasant hoeing at his patch. He is the same colour as the earth, and a great deal less interesting to look at.

It is only because of this that the starved countries of Asia and Africa are accepted as tourist resorts. No one would think of running cheap trips to the Distressed Areas. But where the human beings have brown skins their poverty is simply not noticed. What does Morocco mean to a Frenchman? An orange-grove or a job in Government service. Or to an Englishman? Camels, castles, palm trees, Foreign Legionnaires, brass trays, and bandits. One could probably live there for years without noticing that for nine-tenths of the people the reality of life is an endless, back-breaking struggle to wring a little food out of an eroded soil.

Most of Morocco is so desolate that no wild animal bigger than a hare can live on it. Huge areas which were once covered with forest have turned into a treeless waste where the soil is exactly like broken-up brick. Nevertheless a good deal of it is cultivated, with frightful labour. Everything is done by hand. Long lines of women, bent double like inverted capital L's, work their way slowly across the fields, tearing up the prickly weeds with their hands, and the peasant gathering lucerne for fodder pulls it up stalk by stalk instead of reaping it, thus saving an inch or two on each stalk. The plough is a wretched wooden thing, so frail that one can easily carry it on one's shoulder, and fitted underneath with a rough iron spike which stirs the soil to a depth of about four inches. This is as much as the strength of the animals is equal to. It is usual to plough with a cow and a donkey yoked together. Two donkeys would not be quite strong enough, but on the other hand two cows would cost a little more to feed. The peasants possess no harrows, they merely plough the soil several times over in different directions, finally leaving it in rough furrows, after which the whole field has to be shaped with hoes into small oblong patches to conserve water. Except for a day or two after the rare rainstorms there is never enough water. Along the edges of the fields channels are hacked out to a depth of thirty or forty feet to get at the tiny trickles which run through the subsoil.

Every afternoon a file of very old women passes down the road outside my house, each carrying a load of firewood. All of them are mummified with age and the sun, and all of them are tiny. It seems to be generally the case in primitive communities that the women, when they get beyond a certain age, shrink to the size of children. One day a poor old creature who could not have been more than four feet tall crept past me under a vast load of wood. I stopped her and put a five-sou piece (a little more than a farthing) into her hand. She answered with a shrill wail, almost a scream, which was partly gratitude but mainly surprise. I suppose that from her point of view, by taking any notice of her, I seemed almost to be violating a law of nature. She accepted her status as an old woman, that is to say as a beast of burden. When a family is travelling it is quite usual to see a father and a grown-up son riding ahead on donkeys, and an old woman following on foot, carrying the baggage.

But what is strange about these people is their invisibility. For several weeks, always at about the same time of day, the file of old women had hobbled past the house with their firewood, and though they had registered themselves on my eyeballs I cannot truly say that I had seen them. Firewood was passing—that was how I saw it. It was only that one day I happened to be walking behind them, and the curious up-and-down motion of a load of wood drew my attention to the human being beneath it. Then for the first time I noticed the poor old earth-coloured bodies, bodies reduced to bones and leathery skin, bent double under the crushing weight. Yet I suppose I had not been five minutes on Moroccan soil before I noticed the overloading of the donkeys and was infuriated by it. There is no question that the donkeys are damnably treated. The Moroccan donkey is hardly bigger than a St. Bernard dog, it carries a load which in the British Army would be considered too much for a fifteen-hands mule, and very often its pack-saddle is not taken off its back for weeks together. But what is peculiarly pitiful is that it is the most willing creature on earth, it follows its master like a dog and does not need either bridle or halter. After a dozen years of devoted work it suddenly drops dead, whereupon its master tips it into the ditch and the village dogs have torn its guts out before it is cold.

This kind of thing makes one's blood boil, whereas—on the whole —the plight of the human beings does not. I am not commenting, merely pointing to a fact. People with brown skins are next door to invisible. Anyone can be sorry for the donkey with its galled back, but it is generally owing to some kind of accident if one even notices the old woman under her load of sticks.

As the storks flew northward the Negroes were marching southward—a long, dusty column, infantry, screw-gun batteries, and then more infantry, four or five thousand men in all, winding up the road with a clumping of boots and a clatter of iron wheels.

They were Senegalese, the blackest Negroes in Africa, so black that sometimes it is difficult to see whereabouts on their necks the hair begins. Their splendid bodies were hidden in reach-me-down khaki uniforms, their feet squashed into boots that looked like blocks of wood, and every tin hat seemed to be a couple of sizes too small. It was very hot and the men had marched a long way. They slumped under the weight of their packs and the curiously sensitive black faces were glistening with sweat.

As they went past a tall, very young Negro turned and caught my eye. But the look he gave me was not in the least the kind of look you might expect. Not hostile, not contemptuous, not sullen, not even inquisitive. It was the shy, wide-eyed Negro look, which actually is a look of profound respect. I saw how it was. This wretched boy, who is a French citizen and has therefore been dragged from the forest to scrub floors and catch syphilis in garrison towns, actually has feelings of reverence before a white skin. He has been taught that the white race are his masters, and he still believes it.

But there is one thought which every white man (and in this connection it doesn't matter twopence if he calls himself a socialist) thinks when he sees a black army marching past. "How much longer can we go on kidding these people? How long before they turn their guns in the other direction?"

It was curious, really. Every white man there had this thought stowed somewhere or other in his mind. I had it, so had the other onlookers, so had the officers on their sweating chargers and the white N.C.O.'s marching in the ranks. It was a kind of secret which we all knew and were too clever to tell; only the Negroes didn't know it. And really it was like watching a flock of cattle to see the long column, a mile or two miles of armed men, flowing peacefully up the road, while the great white birds drifted over them in the opposite direction, glittering like scraps of paper.

The Guilty Vicarage
American Poetry
Notes on Music and Opera

W. H. AUDEN

(*b. 1907*)

W. H. AUDEN began as the most brilliant poet of his generation in England. Sometimes his poems were in an easy conversational style, with witty allusions to politics, Freud, and science; sometimes they were ingeniously experimental in form, influenced by German expressionism, Anglo-Saxon alliterative verse, and such little-known poets like John Skelton. As his career continued, Auden undertook so many kinds of cultural activities, often collaboratively, and performed them all so exceedingly well, that he became better known through these than through his later poetry.

College groups still perform two surrealist verse vaudevilles, *The Dog Beneath the Skin* (1935) and *The Ascent of F6* (1936) which he wrote with Christopher Isherwood. Trips to Iceland with Louis MacNeice and to China with Christopher Isherwood resulted in *Letters From Iceland* (1937) and *Journey to a War* (1939), unusual medleys of poetry and reportage. The long poem *Spain* reflects on his experience of the civil war there. The subsequent world war and its consequences inspired *The Age of Anxiety: A Baroque Eclogue* (1947).

For professional performances Auden wrote with Chester Kallman English versions of *The Magic Flute* (1956) and *Don Giovanni* (1961) and an original opera, *The Rake's Progress,* to the music of his close friend Stravinsky. *The Enchafèd Flood: The Romantic Iconography of the Sea* (1950) is an ideal guide for anyone who wishes to discover and appreciate thematic symbols in literature.

Since 1939 Auden has lived mostly in the United States, teaching at a long list of leading institutions and editing a long list of textbooks, among them comprehensive anthologies of verse, light and serious, and collections, called "readers," of Greek and medieval prose and poetry.

As editor of the Yale Series of Younger Poets, Auden helped other poets find publication and often wrote discerning introductions to their works. With Lionel Trilling and Jacques Barzun, he was director of two different book clubs. In addition he produced a steady stream of reviews and essays for most of the influential magazines. Some of the best of these were published in *The Dyer's Hand* (1962). *Selected Poetry* had already appeared in 1958. Auden is a member of the American Academy of Arts and Letters, was Professor of Poetry at Oxford, 1956–61, and has received the Bollingen and Pulitzer Prizes and the National Book Award.

Because of this varied cultural activity and because his essays are seldom "familiar" in the intimate sense, Auden is represented here by three comprehensive but incisive essays treating different kinds and levels of art. "The Guilty Vicarage" is a fascinating demonstration of formal analysis by division and classification, with the consequent establishment of "laws." This is convincing but amusing, since it is applied to a fairly low level of literature. The assumptions are very different from Orwell's in "Raffles and Miss Blandish." Both men shared and then reacted against the unsatisfactory ideologies of the thirties, but Auden's reaction took an Anglo-Catholic and Kierkegaardian direction. From Kierkegaard comes the strange application of the word "aesthetic" to individual uniqueness. The striking literary comparisons with which "American Poetry" begins could only have been supplied by someone with Auden's almost total knowledge of the two national traditions, and only Auden could then have turned the essay into such an erudite and original explanation of why Americans are as they are. "Notes on Music and Opera" shows how a man of intelligence as well as talent can analyze his artistic experiences and derive testable theories from them. In all three essays Auden's procedure is, in a proper sense of the word, scientific.

The Guilty Vicarage

I had not known sin, but by the law.

ROMANS: VII, 7

A CONFESSION

For me, as for many others, the reading of detective stories is an addiction like tobacco or alcohol. The symptoms of this are: firstly, the intensity of the craving—if I have any work to do, I must be careful not to get hold of a detective story for, once I begin one, I cannot work or sleep till I have finished it. Secondly, its specificity —the story must conform to certain formulas (I find it very difficult, for example, to read one that is not set in rural England). And, thirdly, its immediacy. I forget the story as soon as I have finished it, and have no wish to read it again. If, as sometimes happens, I start reading one and find after a few pages that I have read it before, I cannot go on.

Such reactions convince me that, in my case at least, detective stories have nothing to do with works of art. It is possible, however, that an analysis of the detective story, i.e., of the kind of detective story I enjoy, may throw light, not only on its magical function, but also, by contrast, on the function of art.

DEFINITION

The vulgar definition, "a Whodunit," is correct. The basic formula is this: a murder occurs; many are suspected; all but one suspect, who is the murderer, are eliminated; the murderer is arrested or dies.

This definition excludes:

1) Studies of murderers whose guilt is known, e.g., *Malice Afore-thought*. There are borderline cases in which the murderer is known and there are no false suspects, but the proof is lacking, e.g., many of the stories of Freeman Wills Crofts. Most of these are permissible.

2) Thrillers, spy stories, stories of master crooks, etc., when the identification of the criminal is subordinate to the defeat of his criminal designs.

The interest in the thriller is the ethical and characteristic conflict between good and evil, between Us and Them. The interest in the study of a murderer is the observation, by the innocent many, of the sufferings of the guilty one. The interest in the detective story is the dialectic of innocence and guilt.

As in the Aristotelian description of tragedy, there is Concealment (the innocent seem guilty and the guilty seem innocent) and Manifestation (the real guilt is brought to consciousness). There is also peripeteia, in this case not a reversal of fortune but a double reversal from apparent guilt to innocence and from apparent innocence to guilt. The fomula may be diagrammed as follows.

In Greek tragedy the audience knows the truth; the actors do not, but discover or bring to pass the inevitable. In modern, e.g., Elizabethan, tragedy the audience knows neither less nor more than the most knowing of the actors. In the detective story the audience does not know the truth at all; one of the actors—the murderer—does; and the detective, of his own free will, discovers and reveals what the murderer, of his own free will, tries to conceal.

Greek tragedy and the detective story have one characteristic in common in which they both differ from modern tragedy, namely, the characters are not changed in or by their actions: in Greek tragedy because their actions are fated, in the detective story because the decisive event, the murder, has already occurred. Time and space therefore are simply the when and where of revealing either what has to happen or what has actually happened. In consequence, the detective story probably should, and usually does, obey the classical unities, whereas modern tragedy, in which the characters develop with time, can only do so by a technical tour de force; and the thriller, like the picaresque novel, even demands frequent changes of time and place.

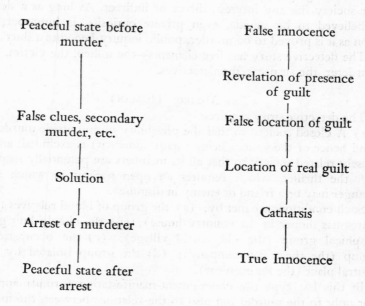

Peaceful state before
murder

False clues, secondary
murder, etc.

Solution

Arrest of murderer

Peaceful state after
arrest

False innocence

Revelation of presence
of guilt

False location of guilt

Location of real guilt

Catharsis

True Innocence

WHY MURDER

There are three classes of crime: (A) offenses against God and one's neighbor or neighbors; (B) offenses against God and society; (C) offenses against God. (All crimes, of course, are offenses against oneself.)

Murder is a member and the only member of Class B. The character common to all crimes in Class A is that it is possible, at least theoretically, either that restitution can be made to the injured party (e.g., stolen goods can be returned), or that the injured party can forgive the criminal (e.g., in the case of rape). Consequently, society as a whole is only indirectly involved; its representatives (the police, etc.) act in the interests of the injured party.

Murder is unique in that it abolishes the party it injures, so that society has to take the place of the victim and on his behalf demand restitution or grant forgiveness; it is the one crime in which society has a direct interest.

Many detective stories begin with a death that appears to be suicide and is later discovered to have been murder. Suicide is a crime belonging to Class C in which neither the criminal's neighbors nor society has any interest, direct or indirect. As long as a death is believed to be suicide, even private curiosity is improper; as soon as it is proved to be murder, public inquiry becomes a duty.

The detective story has five elements—the milieu, the victim, the murderer, the suspects, the detectives.

THE MILIEU (HUMAN)

The detective story requires:

1) A closed society so that the possibility of an outside murderer (and hence of the society being totally innocent) is excluded; and a closely related society so that all its members are potentially suspect (*cf.* the thriller, which requires an open society in which any stranger may be a friend or enemy in disguise).

Such conditions are met by: (a) the group of blood relatives (the Christmas dinner in the country house); (b) the closely knit geographical group (the old world village); (c) the occupational group (the theatrical company); (d) the group isolated by the neutral place (the Pullman car).

In this last type the concealment-manifestation formula applies not only to the murder but also to the relations between the members of the group who first appear to be strangers to each other, but are later found to be related.

2) It must appear to be an innocent society in a state of grace, i.e., a society where there is no need of the law, no contradiction between the aesthetic individual and the ethical universal, and where murder, therefore, is the unheard-of-act which precipitates a crisis (for it reveals that some member has fallen and is no longer in a state of grace). The law becomes a reality and for a time all must live in its shadow, till the fallen one is identified. With his arrest, innocence is restored, and the law retires forever.

The characters in a detective story should, therefore, be eccentric (aesthetically interesting individuals) and good (instinctively ethical)—good, that is, either in appearance, later shown to be false, or in reality, first concealed by an appearance of bad.

It is a sound instinct that has made so many detective story writers choose a college as a setting. The ruling passion of the ideal professor is the pursuit of knowledge for its own sake so that he is related to other human beings only indirectly through their common relation to the truth; and those passions, like lust and avarice and envy, which relate individuals directly and may lead to murder are, in his case, ideally excluded. If a murder occurs in a college, therefore, it is a sign that some colleague is not only a bad man but also a bad professor. Further, as the basic premise of academic life is that truth is universal and to be shared with all, the *gnosis* of a concrete crime and the *gnosis* of abstract ideas nicely parallel and parody each other.

(The even more ideal contradiction of a murder in a monastery is excluded by the fact that monks go regularly to confession and, while the murderer might well not confess his crime, the suspects who are innocent of murder but guilty of lesser sins cannot be supposed to conceal them without making the monastery absurd. Incidentally, is it an accident that the detective story has flourished most in predominantly Protestant countries?)

The detective story writer is also wise to choose a society with an elaborate ritual and to describe this in detail. A ritual is a sign of harmony between the aesthetic and the ethical in which body and mind, individual will and general laws, are not in conflict. The murderer uses his knowledge of the ritual to commit the crime and can be caught only by someone who acquires an equal or superior familiarity with it.

THE MILIEU (NATURAL)

In the detective story, as in its mirror image, the Quest for the Grail, maps (the ritual of space) and timetables (the ritual of time) are desirable. Nature should reflect its human inhabitants, i.e., it should be the Great Good Place; for the more Eden-like it is, the greater the contradiction of murder. The country is preferable to the town, a well-to-do neighborhood (but not too well-to-do—or there will be a suspicion of ill-gotten gains) better than a slum. The corpse must shock not only because it is a corpse but also because, even for a corpse, it is shockingly out of place, as when a dog makes a mess on a drawing room carpet.

Mr. Raymond Chandler has written that he intends to take the body out of the vicarage garden and give the murder back to those who are good at it. If he wishes to write detective stories, i.e., stories where the reader's principal interest is to learn who did it, he could not be more mistaken, for in a society of professional criminals, the only possible motives for desiring to identify the murderer are blackmail or revenge, which both apply to individuals, not to the group as a whole, and can equally well inspire murder. Actually, whatever he may say, I think Mr. Chandler is interested in writing, not detective stories, but serious studies of a criminal milieu, the Great Wrong Place, and his powerful but extremely depressing books should be read and judged, not as escape literature, but as works of art.

THE VICTIM

The victim has to try to satisfy two contradictory requirements. He has to involve everyone in suspicion, which requires that he be a bad character; and he has to make everyone feel guilty, which requires that he be a good character. He cannot be a criminal because he could then be dealt with by the law and murder would be unnecessary. (Blackmail is the only exception.) The more general the temptation to murder he arouses, the better; e.g., the desire for freedom is a better motive than money alone or sex alone. On the whole, the best victim is the negative Father or Mother Image.

If there is more than one murder, the subsequent victims should be more innocent than the initial victim, i.e., the murderer should start with a real grievance and, as a consequence of righting it by illegitimate means, be forced to murder against his will where he has no grievances but his own guilt.

THE MURDERER

Murder is negative creation, and every murderer is therefore the rebel who claims the right to be omnipotent. His pathos is his refusal to suffer. The problem for the writer is to conceal his demonic pride from the other characters and from the reader, since, if a person has this pride, it tends to appear in everything he says and does. To surprise the reader when the identity of the murderer is revealed, yet at the same time to convince him that everything he has previously been told about the murderer is consistent with his being a murderer, is the test of a good detective story.

As to the murderer's end, of the three alternatives—execution, suicide, and madness—the first is preferable; for if he commits suicide he refuses to repent, and if he goes mad he cannot repent, but if he does not repent society cannot forgive. Execution, on the other hand, is the act of atonement by which the murderer is forgiven by society. In real life I disapprove of capital punishment, but in a detective story the murderer must have no future.

(*A Suggesion for Mr. Chandler:* Among a group of efficient professional killers who murder for strictly professional reasons, there is one to whom, like Leopold and Loeb, murder is an *acte gratuite*. Presently murders begin to occur which have not been commissioned. The group is morally outraged and bewildered; it has to call in the police to detect the amateur murderer, rescue the professionals from a mutual suspicion which threatens to disrupt their organization, and restore their capacity to murder.)

THE SUSPECTS

The detective story society is a society consisting of apparently innocent individuals, i.e., their aesthetic interest as individuals does not conflict with their ethical obligations to the universal. The murder is the act of disruption by which innocence is lost, and the individual and the law become opposed to each other. In the case of the murderer this opposition is completely real (till he is arrested and consents to be punished); in the case of the suspects it is mostly apparent.

But in order for the appearance to exist, there must be some element of reality; e.g., it is unsatisfactory if the suspicion is caused by chance or the murderer's malice alone. The suspects must be guilty of something, because, now that the aesthetic and the ethical are in opposition, if they are completely innocent (obedient to the ethical) they lose their aesthetic interest and the reader will ignore them.

For suspects, the principal causes of guilt are:

1) the wish or even the intention to murder;
2) crimes of Class A or vices of Class C (e.g., illicit amours) which the suspect is afraid or ashamed to reveal;
3) a *hubris* of intellect which tries to solve the crime itself and despises the official police (assertion of the supremacy of the aesthetic over the ethical). If great enough, this *hubris* leads to its subject getting murdered;
4) a *hubris* of innocence which refuses to cooperate with the investigation;

5) a lack of faith in another loved suspect, which leads its subject to hide or confuse clues.

THE DETECTIVE

Completely satisfactory detectives are extremely rare. Indeed, I only know of three: Sherlock Holmes (Conan Doyle), Inspector French (Freeman Wills Crofts), and Father Brown (Chesterton). The job of detective is to restore the state of grace in which the aesthetic and the ethical are as one. Since the murderer who caused their disjunction is the aesthetically defiant individual, his opponent, the detective, must be either the official representative of the ethical or the exceptional individual who is himself in a state of grace. If he is the former, he is a professional; if he is the latter, he is an amateur. In either case, the detective must be the total stranger who cannot possibly be involved in the crime; this excludes the local police and should, I think, exclude the detective who is a friend of one of the suspects. The professional detective has the advantage that, since he is not an individual but a representative of the ethical, he does not need a motive for investigating the crime; but for the same reason he has the disadvantage of being unable to overlook the minor ethical violations of the suspects, and therefore it is harder for him to gain their confidence.

Most amateur detectives, on the other hand, are unsatisfactory either because they are priggish supermen, like Lord Peter Wimsey and Philo Vance, who have no motive for being detectives except caprice, or because, like the detectives of the hard-boiled school, they are motivated by avarice or ambition and might just as well be murderers.

The amateur detective genius may have weaknesses to give him aesthetic interest, but they must not be of a kind which outrage ethics. The most satisfactory weaknesses are the solitary oral vices of eating and drinking or childish boasting. In his sexual life, the detective must be either celibate or happily married.

Between the amateur detective and the professional policeman stands the criminal lawyer whose *telos* is, not to discover who is guilty, but to prove that his client is innocent. His ethical justification is that human law is ethically imperfect, i.e., not an absolute manifestation of the universal and divine, and subject to chance aesthetic limitations, e.g., the intelligence or stupidity of individual policemen and juries (in consequence of which an innocent man may sometimes be judged guilty).

To correct this imperfection, the decision is arrived at through an aesthetic combat, i.e., the intellectual gifts of the defense versus those of the prosecution, just as in earlier days doubtful cases were solved by physical combat between the accused and the accuser.

The lawyer-detective (e.g., Joshua Clunk) is never quite satisfactory, therefore, because of his commitment to his client, whom he cannot desert, even if he should really be the guilty party, without ceasing to be a lawyer.

SHERLOCK HOLMES

Holmes is the exceptional individual who is in a state of grace because he is a genius in whom scientific curiosity is raised to the status of a heroic passion. He is erudite but his knowledge is absolutely specialized (e.g., his ignorance of the Copernican system), he is in all matters outside his field as helpless as a child (e.g., his untidiness), and he pays the price for his scientific detachment (his neglect of feeling) by being the victim of melancholia which attacks him whenever he is unoccupied with a case (e.g., his violin playing and cocaine taking).

His motive for being a detective is, positively, a love of the neutral truth (he has no interest in the feelings of the guilty or the innocent), and negatively, a need to escape from his own feelings of melancholy. His attitude towards people and his technique of observation and deduction are those of the chemist or physicist. If he chooses human beings rather than inanimate matter as his material, it is because investigating the inanimate is unheroically easy since it cannot tell lies, which human beings can and do, so that in dealing with them, observation must be twice as sharp and logic twice as rigorous.

INSPECTOR FRENCH

His class and culture are those natural to a Scotland Yard inspector. (The old Oxonian Inspector is insufferable.) His motive is love of duty. Holmes detects for his own sake and shows the maximum indifference to all feelings except a negative fear of his own. French detects for the sake of the innocent members of society, and is indifferent only to his own feelings and those of the murderer. (He would much rather stay at home with his wife.) He is exceptional only in his exceptional love of duty which makes him take exceptional pains; he does only what all could do as well if they had the same patient industry (his checking of alibis for tiny flaws which careless hurry had missed). He outwits the murderer, partly because the latter is not quite so painstaking as he, and partly because the murderer must act alone, while he has the help of all the innocent people in the world who are doing their duty, e.g., the postmen, railway clerks, milkmen, etc., who become, accidentally, witnesses to the truth.

FATHER BROWN

Like Holmes, an amateur; yet, like French, not an individual genius. His activities as a detective are an incidental part of his activities as a priest who cares for souls. His prime motive is compassion, of which the guilty are in greater need than the innocent, and he investigates murders, not for his own sake, nor even for the sake of the innocent, but for the sake of the murderer who can save his soul if he will confess and repent. He solves his cases, not by approaching them objectively like a scientist or a policeman, but by subjectively imagining himself to be the murderer, a process which is good not only for the murderer but for Father Brown himself because, as he says, "it gives a man his remorse beforehand."

Holmes and French can only help the murderer as teachers, i.e., they can teach him that murder will out and does not pay. More they cannot do since neither is tempted to murder; Holmes is too gifted, French too well trained in the habit of virtue. Father Brown can go further and help the murderer as an example, i.e., as a man who is also tempted to murder, but is able by faith to resist temptation.

THE READER

The most curious fact about the detective story is that it makes its greatest appeal precisely to those classes of people who are most immune to other forms of daydream literature. The typical detective story addict is a doctor or clergyman or scientist or artist, i.e., a fairly successful professional man with intellectual interests and well-read in his own field, who could never stomach the *Saturday Evening Post* or *True Confessions* or movie magazines or comics. If I ask myself why I cannot enjoy stories about strong silent men and lovely girls who make love in a beautiful landscape and come into millions of dollars, I cannot answer that I have no fantasies of being handsome and loved and rich, because of course I have (though my life is, perhaps, sufficiently fortunate to make me less envious in a naïve way than some). No, I can only say that I am too conscious of the absurdity of such wishes to enjoy seeing them reflected in print.

I can, to some degree, resist yielding to these or similar desires which tempt me, but I cannot prevent myself from having them to resist; and it is the fact that I have them which makes me feel guilty, so that instead of dreaming about indulging my desires, I dream about the removal of the guilt which I feel at their existence. This I still do, and must do, because guilt is a subjective feeling where any further step is only a reduplication—feeling guilty about guilt. I suspect that the typical reader of detective stories is, like myself, a person who suffers from a sense of sin. From the point of view of ethics, desires and acts are good and bad, and I must choose the good and reject the bad, but the I which makes this choice is ethically neutral; it only becomes good or bad in its choice. To have a sense of sin means to feel guilty at there being an ethical choice to make, a guilt which, however "good" I may become, remains unchanged. It is sometimes said that detective stories are read by respectable law-abiding citizens in order to gratify in fantasy the violent or murderous wishes they dare not, or are ashamed to, translate into action. This may be true for the reader of thrillers (which I rarely enjoy), but it is quite false for the reader of detective stories. On the contrary, the magical satisfaction the latter provide (which makes them escape literature, not works of art) is the illusion of being dissociated from the murderer.

The magic formula is an innocence which is discovered to contain guilt; then a suspicion of being the guilty one; and finally a real innocence from which the guilty other has been expelled, a cure effected, not by me or my neighbors, but by the miraculous intervention of a genius from outside who removes guilt by giving knowledge of guilt. (The detective story subscribes, in fact, to the Socratic daydream: "Sin is ignorance.")

If one thinks of a work of art which deals with murder, *Crime and Punishment* for example, its effect on the reader is to compel an identification with the murderer which he would prefer not to recognize. The identification of fantasy is always an attempt to avoid one's own suffering: the identification of art is a sharing in the suffering of another. Kafka's *The Trial* is another instructive example of the difference between a work of art and the detective story.

In the latter it is certain that a crime has been committed and, temporarily, uncertain to whom the guilt should be attached; as soon as this is known, the innocence of everyone else is certain. (Should it turn out that after all no crime has been committed, then all would be innocent.) In *The Trial*, on the other hand, it is the guilt that is certain and the crime that is uncertain; the aim of the hero's investigation is not to prove his innocence (which would be impossible for he knows he is guilty), but to discover what, if anything, he has done to make himself guilty. K, the hero, is, in fact, a portrait of the kind of person who reads detective stories for escape.

The fantasy, then, which the detective story addict indulges is the fantasy of being restored to the Garden of Eden, to a state of innocence, where he may know love as love and not as the law. The driving force behind this daydream is the feeling of guilt, the cause of which is unknown to the dreamer. The fantasy of escape is the same, whether one explains the guilt in Christian, Freudian, or any other terms. One's way of trying to face the reality, on the other hand, will, of course, depend very much on one's creed.

American Poetry

The land was ours before we were the land's.
She was our land more than a hundred years
Before we were her people. She was ours
In Massachusetts, in Virginia,
But we were England's, still colonials,
Possessing what we still were unpossessed by,
Possessed by what we now no more possessed.
Something we were withholding made us weak
Until we found out that it was ourselves
We were withholding from our land of living,
And forthwith found salvation in surrender.
Such as we were we gave ourselves outright
(The deed of gift was many deeds of war)
To the land vaguely realizing westward,
But still unstoried, artless, unenhanced,
Such as she was, such as she would become.

ROBERT FROST [1]

O ne often hears it said that only in this century have the writers of the United States learned to stand on their own feet and be truly American, that, previously, they were slavish imitators of British literature. Applied to the general reading public and academic circles, this has a certain amount of truth but, so far as the writers themselves are concerned, it is quite false. From Bryant on there is scarcely one American poet whose work, if unsigned, could be mistaken for that of an Englishman. What English poet, for example, in need of emotive place names for a serious poem, would have employed, neither local names nor names famous in history or mythology, but names made up by himself as Poe did in "Ulalume"? Would an English poet have conceived the idea of writing a scientific cosmological prose poem and of prefacing it thus: "I offer this

[1] From *Complete Poems of Robert Frost*. Copyright, 1942 by Robert Frost. Reprinted by permission of Holt, Rinehart & Winston, Inc.

Book of Truths, not in its character of Truth-teller, but for the Beauty that abounds in its Truth, constituting it true. . . . *What I here propound is true:* therefore it cannot die. . . . Nevertheless it is as a Poem only that I wish this work to be judged after I am dead." (Poe, Preface to "Eureka")?

Maud, The Song of Hiawatha and the first edition of *Leaves of Grass* all appeared in the same year, 1855: no two poets could be more unlike each other than Longfellow and Whitman—such diversity is in itself an American phenomenon—yet, when compared with Tennyson, each in his own way shows characteristics of the New World. Tennyson and Longfellow were both highly skillful technicians in conventional forms and both were regarded by their countrymen as the respectable mouthpieces of their age, and yet, how different they are. There is much in Tennyson that Longfellow would never have dared to write, for the peculiar American mixture of Puritan conscience and democratic license can foster in some cases a genteel horror of the coarse for which no Englishman has felt the need. On the other hand Longfellow had a curiosity about the whole of European literature compared with which Tennyson, concerned only with the poetry of his own land and the classical authors on whom he was educated, seems provincial. Even if there had been Red Indians roaming the North of Scotland, unsubjugated and unassimilable, one cannot imagine Tennyson sitting down to write a long poem about them and choosing for it a Finnish meter. Leaving aside all questions of style, there is a difference between Tennyson's *Ode on the Death of the Duke of Wellington* and Whitman's elegy for President Lincoln *When lilacs last in the dooryard bloom'd* which is significant. Tennyson, as one would expect from the title of his poem, mourns for a great public official figure, but it would be very hard to guess from the words of Whitman's poem that the man he is talking of was the head of a State; one would naturally think that he was some close personal friend, a private individual.

To take one more example—two poets, contemporaries, both women, both religious, both introverts preoccupied with renunciation—Christina Rossetti and Emily Dickinson; could anyone imagine either of them in the country of the other? When I try to fancy such translations, the only Americans I can possibly imagine as British are minor poets with a turn for light verse like Lowell and Holmes; and the only British poets who could conceivably have been American are eccentrics like Blake and Hopkins.

Normally, in comparing the poetry of two cultures, the obvious and easiest point at which to start is with a comparison of the peculiar characteristics, grammatical, rhetorical, rhythmical, of their respective languages, for even the most formal and elevated styles of poetry are more conditioned by the spoken tongue, the language really used by the men of that country, than by anything else. In the case of British and American poetry, however, this is the most subtle difference of all and the hardest to define. Any Englishman, with a little effort, can learn to pronounce "the letter *a* in psalm and calm . . . with the sound of *a* in candle," to say *thumb-tacks* instead of *drawing-pins* or twenty-minutes-*of*-one instead of twenty-minutes-*to*-one, and discover that, in the Middle West, *bought* rhymes with *hot*, but he will still be as far from speaking American English as his Yankee cousin who comes to England will be from speaking the Queen's. No dramatist in either country who has introduced a character from the other side, has, to my knowledge, been able to make his speech convincing. What the secret of the difference is, I cannot put my finger on; William Carlos Williams, who has thought more than most about this problem, says that "Pace is one of its most important manifestations" and to this one might add another, Pitch. If undefinable, the difference is, however, immediately recognizable by the ear, even in verse where the formal conventions are the same.

> He must have had a father and a mother—
> In fact I've heard him say so—and a dog,
> As a boy should, I venture; and the dog,
> Most likely, was the only man who knew him.
> A dog, for all I know, is what he needs
> As much as anything right here today,
> To counsel him about his disillusions,
> Old aches, and parturitions of what's coming—
> A dog of orders, an emeritus,
> To wag his tail at him when he comes home,
> And then to put his paws up on his knees
> And say, 'For God's sake, what's it all about?'
>
> E. A. ROBINSON
> ("Ben Jonson Entertains a
> Man from Stratford")

Whatever this may owe to Browning, the fingering is quite different and un-British. Again, how American in rhythm as well as in sensibility is this stanza by Robert Frost:

But no, I was out for stars:
I would not come in.
I meant not even if asked,
And I hadn't been.
                    ("Come In")

Until quite recently an English writer, like one of any European
country, could presuppose two conditions, a nature which was
mythologized, humanized, on the whole friendly, and a human society which had become in time, whatever succession of invasions
it may have suffered in the past, in race and religion more or less
homogeneous and in which most people lived and died in the local-
ity where they were born.

Christianity might have deprived Aphrodite, Apollo, the local
genius, of their divinity, but as figures for the forces of nature, as a
mode of thinking about the creation, they remained valid for poets
and their readers alike. Descartes might reduce the nonhuman universe to a mechanism but the feelings of Europeans about the sun
and moon, the cycle of the seasons, the local landscape remained unchanged. Wordsworth might discard the mythological terminology
but the kind of relation between nature and man which he described
was the same personal one. Even when nineteenth-century biology
began to trouble men's minds with the thought that the universe
might be without moral values, their immediate experience was
still of a friendly and lovable nature. Whatever their doubts and
convictions about the purpose and significance of the universe as a
whole, Tennyson's Lincolnshire or Hardy's Dorset were places
where they felt completely at home, landscapes with faces of their
own which a human being could recognize and trust.

But in America, neither the size nor the condition nor the climate
of the continent encourages such intimacy. It is an unforgettable
experience for anyone born on the other side of the Atlantic to take
a plane journey by night across the United States. Looking down he
will see the lights of some town like a last outpost in a darkness
stretching for hours ahead, and realize that, even if there is no
longer an actual frontier, this is still a continent only partially settled and developed, where human activity seems a tiny thing in
comparison to the magnitude of the earth, and the equality of men
not some dogma of politics or jurisprudence but a self-evident fact.
He will behold a wild nature, compared with which the landscapes
of Salvator Rosa are as cosy as Arcadia and which cannot possibly

be thought of in human or personal terms. If Henry Adams could write:

> When Adams was a boy in Boston, the best chemist in the place had probably never heard of Venus except by way of scandal, or of the Virgin except as idolatry. . . . The force of the Virgin was still felt at Lourdes, and seemed to be as potent as X-rays; but in America neither Venus nor Virgin ever had value as force—at most as sentiment. No American had ever been truly afraid of either.

the reason for this was not simply that the *Mayflower* carried iconophobic dissenters but also that the nature which Americans, even in New England, had every reason to fear could not possibly be imagined as a mother. A white whale whom man can neither understand nor be understood by, whom only a madman like Gabriel can worship, the only relationship with whom is a combat to the death by which a man's courage and skill are tested and judged, or the great buck who answers the poet's prayer for "someone else additional to him" in "The Most of It" are more apt symbols. Thoreau, who certainly tried his best to become intimate with nature, had to confess

> I walk in nature still alone
> And know no one,
> Discern no lineament nor feature
> Of any creature.
> Though all the firmament
> Is o'er me bent,
> Yet still I miss the grace
> Of an intelligent and kindred face.
> I still must seek the friend
> Who does with nature blend,
> Who is the person in her mask,
> He is the man I ask.

Many poets in the Old World have become digusted with human civilization but what the earth would be like if the race became extinct they cannot imagine; an American like Robinson Jeffers can quite easily, for he has seen with his own eyes country as yet untouched by history.

In a land which is fully settled, most men must accept their local environment or try to change it by political means; only the exceptionally gifted or adventurous can leave to seek his fortune elsewhere. In America, on the other hand, to move on and make a fresh start somewhere else is still the normal reaction to dissatisfaction or failure. Such social fluidity has important psychological effects. Since movement involves breaking social and personal ties, the habit creates an attitude towards personal relationships in which impermanence is taken for granted.

One could find no better illustration of the difference between the Old and the New World than the respective conclusions of *Oliver Twist* and *Huckleberry Finn*, both the heroes of which are orphans. When Oliver is at last adopted by Mr. Brownlow, his fondest dream, to have a home, to be surrounded by familiar friendly faces, to receive an education, is realized. Huck is offered adoption too, significantly by a woman not a man, but refuses because he knows she would try to "civilize" him, and announces his intention to light out by himself for the West; Jim, who has been his "buddy" in a friendship far closer than any enjoyed by Oliver, is left behind like an old shoe, just as in *Moby Dick* Ishmael becomes a blood-brother of Queequeg and then forgets all about him. Naturally the daydream of the lifelong comrade in adventure often appears in American literature:

> Camerado, I give you my hand!
> I give you my love more precious than money,
> I give you myself before preaching or law;
> Will you give me yourself? will you come travel with me?
> Shall we stick by each other as long as we live?

> WALT WHITMAN
> ("Song of the Open Road")

but no American seriously expects such a dream to come true.

To be able at any time to break with the past, to move and keep on moving lessens the significance not only of the past but also of the future which is reduced to the immediate future, and minimizes the importance of political action. A European may be a conservative who thinks that the right form of society has been discovered already, or a liberal who believes it is in process of being realized, or a revolutionary who thinks that after long dark ages it can now be realized for the first time, but each of them knows that, by reason or force, he must convince the others that he is right; he may be an optimist about the future or a pessimist. None of these terms applies accurately to an American, for his profoundest feeling towards the

future is not that it will be better or worse but that it is unpredictable, that all things, good and bad, will change. No failure is irre-
deemable, no success a final satisfaction. Democracy is the best form
of government, not because men will necessarily lead better or
happier lives under it, but because it permits constant experiment; a
given experiment may fail but the people have a right to make their
own mistakes. America has always been a country of amateurs
where the professional, that is to say, the man who claims authority
as a member of an elite which knows the law in some field or other,
is an object of distrust and resentment.

> *Amerika, du hast es besser*
> *Als unser Kontinent, der alte,*
> *Hast keine verfallenen Schloesser*
> *Und keine Basalte*

wrote Goethe, by *keine Basalte* meaning, I presume, no violent political revolutions. This is a subject about which, in relation to their
own histories, the English and the Americans cherish opposite fic-
tions. Between 1533 and 1688 the English went through a succession
of revolutions in which a Church was imposed on them by the engines of the State, one king was executed and another deposed, yet
they prefer to forget it and pretend that the social structure of England is the product of organic peaceful growth. The Americans, on
the other hand, like to pretend that what was only a successful war
of secession was a genuine revolution.

If we apply the term revolution to what happened in North
America between 1776 and 1829, it has a special meaning.

Normally, the word describes the process by which man transforms himself from one kind of man, living in one kind of society,
with one way of looking at the world, into another kind of man,
another society, another conception of life. So it is with the Papal,
the Lutheran, the English, and the French revolutions. The American case is different; it is not a question of the Old Man transforming himself into the New, but of the New Man becoming alive to
the fact that he is new, that he has been transformed already without his having realized it.

The War of Independence was the first step, the leaving of the
paternal roof in order to find out who one is; the second and more
important step, the actual discovery, came with Jackson. It was then
that it first became clear that, despite similarities of form, represen-

tative government in America was not to be an imitation of the English parliamentary system, and that, though the vocabulary of the Constitution may be that of the French Enlightenment, its American meaning is quite distinct. There is indeed an American mentality which is new and unique in the world but it is the product less of conscious political action than of nature, of the new and unique environment of the American continent. Even the most revolutionary feature of the Constitution, the separation of Church and State, was a recognition of a condition which had existed since the first settlements were made by various religious denominations whose control of the secular authority could only be local. From the beginning America had been a pluralist state and pluralism is incompatible with an Established Church. The *Basalte* in American history, the Civil War, might indeed be called Counterrevolution, for it was fought primarily on the issue not of slavery but of unity, that is, not for a freedom but for a limitation on freedom, to ensure that the United States should remain pluralist and not disintegrate into an anarchic heap of fragments. Pluralist and experimental: in place of *verfallenen Schloesser,* America has ghost towns and the relics of New Jerusalems which failed.

The American had not intended to become what he was; he had been made so by emigration and the nature of the American continent. An emigrant never knows what he wants, only what he does not want. A man who comes from a land settled for centuries to a virgin wilderness where he faces problems with which none of his traditions and habits was intended to deal cannot foresee the future but must improvise himself from day to day. It is not surprising, therefore, that the first clear realization of the novelty and importance of the United States should have come not from an American but from outsiders, like Crèvecœur and de Tocqueville.

In a society whose dominant task is still that of the pioneer—the physical struggle with nature, and a nature, moreover, particularly recalcitrant and violent—the intellectual is not a figure of much importance. Those with intellectual and artistic tastes, finding themselves a despised or at best an ignored minority, are apt in return to despise the society in which they live as vulgar and think nostalgically of more leisured and refined cultures. The situation of the first important American poets—Emerson, Thoreau, Poe—was therefore doubly difficult. As writers, and therefore intellectuals, they were without status with the majority; and, on the other hand, the cultured minority of which they were members looked to England for its literary standards and did not want to think or read about America.

This dependence on English literature was a hindrance to their development in a way which it would not have been had they lived elsewhere. A poet living in England, for instance, might read nothing but French poetry, or he might move to Italy and know only English, without raising any serious barrier between himself and his experiences. Indeed, in Europe, whenever some journalist raises the patriotic demand for an English or French or Dutch literature free from foreign influences, we know him at once to be a base fellow. The wish for an American literature, on the other hand, has nothing to do really, with politics or national conceit; it is a demand for honesty. All European literature so far has presupposed two things: a nature which is humanized, mythologized, usually friendly, and a human society in which most men stay where they were born and do not move about much. Neither of these presuppositions was valid for America, where nature was virgin, devoid of history, usually hostile; and society was fluid, its groupings always changing as men moved on somewhere else.

The European romantics may praise the charms of wild desert landscape, but they know that for them it is never more than a few hours' walk from a comfortable inn: they may celebrate the joys of solitude but they know that any time they choose they can go back to the family roof or to town and that there their cousins and nephews and nieces and aunts, the club and the salons, will still be going on exactly as they left them. Of real desert, of a loneliness which knows of no enduring relationships to cherish or reject, they have no conception.

The achievement of Emerson and Thoreau was twofold: they wrote of the American kind of nature, and they perceived what qualities were most needed by members of the American kind of society, which was threatened, not by the petrified injustice of any tradition, but by the fluid irresponsibility of crowd opinion. Their work has both the virtues and the vices of the isolated and the protestant: on the one hand it is always genuine and original, it is never superficial; on the other it is a little too cranky, too earnest, too scornful of elegance. Just as in their political thinking Americans are apt to identify the undemocratic with monarchy, so, in their aesthetics, they are apt to identify the falsely conventional with rhyme and meter. The prose of Emerson and Thoreau is superior to their verse, because verse in its formal nature protests against protesting;

it demands that to some degree we accept things as they are, not for any rational or moral reason, but simply because they happen to be that way; it implies an element of frivolity in the creation.

Whatever one may feel about Whitman's poetry, one is bound to admit that he was the first clearly to recognize what the conditions were with which any future American poet would have to come to terms.

> Plenty of songs had been sung—beautiful, matchless songs—adjusted to other lands than these. . . . the Old World has had the poems of myths, fictions, feudalism, conquest, caste, dynastic wars, and splendid exceptional characters, which have been great; but the New World needs the poems of realities and science and of the democratic average and basic equality. . . . As for native American individuality, the distinctive and ideal type of Western character (as consistent with the operative and even money-making features of United States humanity as chosen knights, gentlemen and warriors were the ideals of the centuries of European feudalism) it has not yet appeared. I have allowed the stress of my poems from beginning to end to bear upon American individuality and assist it—not only because that is a great lesson in Nature, amid all her generalizing laws, but as counterpoise to the levelling tendencies of Democracy.

The last sentence makes it quite clear that by the "average" hero who was to replace the "knight," Whitman did not mean the mediocre, but the individual whose "exceptional character" is not derived from birth, education or occupation, and that he is aware of how difficult it is for such an individual to appear without the encouragement which comes from membership in some elite.

What he does not say, and perhaps did not realize, is that, in a democracy, the status of the poet himself is changed. However fantastic, in the light of present-day realities, his notion may be, every European poet, I believe, still instinctively thinks of himself as a "clerk," a member of a professional brotherhood, with a certain social status irrespective of the number of his readers (in his heart of hearts the audience he desires and expects are those who govern the country), and as taking his place in an unbroken historical succession. In the States, poets have never had or imagined they had such a status, and it is up to each individual poet to justify his existence by offering a unique product. It would be grossly unjust to assert that there are fewer lovers of poetry in the New World than in the Old —in how many places in the latter could a poet demand and receive a substantial sum for reading his work aloud?—but there is a tendency, perhaps, in the former, for audiences to be drawn rather by a name than a poem, and for a poet, on his side, to demand approval for his work not simply because it is good but because it is *his*. To some degree every American poet feels that the whole responsibility for contemporary poetry has fallen upon his shoulders, that he is a literary aristocracy of one. "Tradition," wrote Mr. T. S. Eliot in a famous essay, "cannot be inherited, and if you want it you must obtain it by great labour." I do not think that any European critic would have said just this. He would not, of course, deny that every poet must work hard but the suggestion in the first half of the sentence that no sense of tradition is acquired except by conscious effort would seem strange to him.

There are advantages and disadvantages in both attitudes. A British poet can take writing more for granted and so write with a lack of strain and overearnestness. American poetry has many tones, but the tone of a man talking to a group of his peers is rare; for a "serious" poet to write light verse is frowned on in America and if, when he is asked why he writes poetry, he replies, as any European poet would, "For fun," his audience will be shocked. On the other hand, a British poet is in much greater danger of becoming lazy, or academic, or irresponsible. One comes across passages, even in very fine English poets, which make one think: "Yes, very effective but does he believe what he is saying?": in American poetry such passages are extremely rare. The first thing that strikes a reader about the best American poets is how utterly unlike each other they are. Where else in the world, for example, could one find seven poets of approximately the same generation so different as Ezra Pound, W. C. Williams, Vachel Lindsay, Marianne Moore, Wallace Stevens, E. E. Cummings and Laura Riding? The danger for the American poet is not of writing like everybody else but of crankiness and a parody of his own manner.

Plato, following Damon of Athens, said that when the modes of music change, the walls of the city are shaken. It might be truer to say, perhaps, that a change in the modes gives warning of a shaking of the walls in the near future. The social strains which later break out in political action are first experienced by artists as a feeling that the current modes of expression are no longer capable of dealing with their real concerns. Thus, when one thinks of "modern" painting, music, fiction or poetry, the names which immediately come to mind as its leaders and creators are those of persons who were born roughly between 1870 and 1890 and who began producing their "new" work before the outbreak of World War I in 1914, and in poetry and fiction, at least, American names are prominent.

When a revolutionary break with the past is necessary it is an advantage not to be too closely identified with any one particular literature or any particular cultural group. Americans like Eliot and Pound, for example, could be as curious about French or Italian poetry as about English and could hear poetry of the past, like the verse of Webster, freshly in a way that for an Englishman, trammeled by traditional notions of Elizabethan blank verse, would have been difficult.

Further, as Americans, they were already familiar with the dehumanized nature and the social leveling which a technological civilization was about to make universal and with which the European mentality was unprepared to deal. After his visit to America, de Tocqueville made a remarkable prophecy about the kind of poetry which a democratic society would produce.

> I am persuaded that in the end democracy diverts the imagination from all that is external to man and fixes it on man alone. Democratic nations may amuse themselves for a while with considering the productions of nature, but they are excited in reality only by a survey of themselves. . . .
>
> The poets who lived in aristocratic ages have been eminently successful in their delineation of certain incidents in the life of a people or a man; but none of them ever ventured to include within his performances the destinies of mankind, a task which poets writing in democratic ages may attempt. . . .
>
> It may be foreseen in like manner that poets living in democratic times will prefer the delineation of passions and ideas to that of persons and achievements. The language, the dress, and the daily actions of men in democracies are repugnant to conceptions of the ideal. . . . This forces the poet constantly to search below the external surface which is palpable to the senses, in order to read the inner soul; and nothing lends itself more to the delineation of the ideal than the scrutiny of the hidden depths in the immaterial nature of man. . . . The destinies of mankind, man himself taken aloof from his country and his age, and standing in the presence of Nature and of God, with his passions, his doubts, his rare prosperities and inconceivable wretchedness, will become the chief, if not the sole, theme of poetry.

If this be an accurate description of the poetry we call modern, then one might say that America has never known any other kind.

Notes on Music and Opera

Opera consists of significant situations in artificially arranged sequence.

GOETHE

Singing is near miraculous because it is the mastering of what is otherwise a pure instrument of egotism: the human voice.

HUGO VON HOFMANNSTHAL

What is music about? What, as Plato would say, does it imitate? Our experience of Time in its twofold aspect, natural or organic repetition, and historical novelty created by choice. And the full development of music as an art depends upon a recognition that these two aspects are different and that choice, being an experience confined to man, is more significant than repetition. A succession of two musical notes is an act of choice; the first causes the second, not in the scientific sense of making it occur necessarily, but in the historical sense of provoking it, of providing it with a motive for occurring. A successful melody is a self-determined history; it is freely what it intends to be, yet is a meaningful whole, not an arbitrary succession of notes.

Music as an art, i.e., music that has come to a conscious realization of its true nature, is confined to Western civilization alone and only to the last four or five hundred years at that. The music of all other cultures and epochs bears the same relation to Western music that magical verbal formulas bear to the art of poetry. A primitive magic spell may be poetry but it does not know that it is, nor intend to be. So, in all but Western music, history is only implicit; what it thinks it is doing is furnishing verses or movements with a repetitive accompaniment. Only in the West has chant become song.

Lacking a historical consciousness, the Greeks, in their theories of music, tried to relate it to Pure Being, but the becoming implicit in music betrays itself in their theories of harmony in which mathematics becomes numerology and one chord is intrinsically "better" than another.

Western music declared its consciousness of itself when it adopted time signatures, barring and the metronome beat. Without a strictly natural or cyclical time, purified from every trace of historical singularity, as a framework within which to occur, the irreversible historicity of the notes themselves would be impossible.

In primitive proto-music the percussion instruments which best imitate recurrent rhythms and, being incapable of melody, can least imitate novelty, play the greatest role.

The most exciting rhythms seem unexpected and complex, the most beautiful melodies simple and inevitable.

Music cannot imitate nature: a musical storm always sounds like the wrath of Zeus.

A verbal art like poetry is reflective; it stops to think. Music is immediate, it goes on to become. But both are active, both insist on stopping or going on. The medium of passive reflection is painting, of passive immediacy the cinema, for the visual world is an immediately given world where Fate is mistress and it is impossible to tell the difference between a chosen movement and an involuntary reflex. Freedom of choice lies, not in the world we see, but in our freedom to turn our eyes in this direction, or that, or to close them altogether.

Because music expresses the opposite experience of pure volition and subjectivity (the fact that we cannot shut our ears at will allows music to assert that we cannot *not* choose), film music is not music but a technique for preventing us from using our ears to hear extraneous noises and it is bad film music if we become consciously aware of its existence.

Man's musical imagination seems to be derived almost exclusively from his primary experiences—his direct experience of his own body, its tensions and rhythms, and his direct experience of desiring and choosing—and to have very little to do with the experiences of the outside world brought to him through his senses. The possibility of making music, that is, depends primarily, not upon man's possession of an auditory organ, the ear, but upon his possession of a sound-producing instrument, the vocal cords. If the ear were primary, music would have begun as program pastoral symphonies. In the case of the visual arts, on the other hand, it is a visual organ, the eye, which is primary for, without it, the experiences which stimulate the hand into becoming an expressive instrument could not exist.

The difference is demonstrated by the difference in our sensation of motion in musical space and visual space.

An increase in the tension of the vocal cords is conceived in musical space as a going "up," a relaxation as a going "down." But in visual space it is the bottom of the picture (which is also the foreground) which is felt as the region of greatest pressure and, as the eye rises up the picture, it feels an increasing sense of lightness and freedom.

The association of tension in hearing with up and seeing with down seems to correspond to the difference between our experience of the force of gravity in our own bodies and our experience of it in other bodies. The weight of our own bodies is felt as inherent in us, as a personal wish to fall down, so that rising upward is an effort to overcome the desire for rest in ourselves. But the weight (and proximity) of other objects is felt as weighing down on us; they are "on top" of us and rising means getting away from their restrictive pressure.

All of us have learned to talk, most of us, even, could be taught to speak verse tolerably well, but very few have learned or could ever be taught to sing. In any village twenty people could get together and give a performance of *Hamlet* which, however imperfect, would convey enough of the play's greatness to be worth attending, but if they were to attempt a similar performance of *Don Giovanni*, they would soon discover that there was no question of a good or a bad performance because they could not sing the notes at all. Of an actor, even in a poetic drama, when we say that his performance is good, we mean that he simulates by art, that is, consciously, the way in which the character he is playing would, in real life, behave by nature, that is, unconsciously. But for a singer, as for a ballet dancer, there is no question of simulation, of singing the composer's notes "naturally"; his behavior is unabashedly and triumphantly art from beginning to end. The paradox implicit in all drama, namely, that emotions and situations which in real life would be sad or painful are on the stage a source of pleasure becomes, in opera, quite explicit. The singer may be playing the role of a deserted bride who is about to kill herself, but we feel quite certain as we listen that not only we, but also she, is having a wonderful time. In a sense, there can be no tragic opera because whatever errors the characters make and whatever they suffer, they are doing exactly what they wish. Hence the feeling that *opera seria* should not employ a contemporary subject, but confine itself to mythical situations, that is, situations which, as human beings, we are all of us necessarily in and must, therefore, accept, however tragic they may be. A contemporary tragic situation like that in Menotti's *The Consul* is too actual, that is, too clearly a situation some people are in and others, including the audience, are not in, for the latter to forget this and see it as a symbol of, say, man's existential estrangement. Consequently the pleasure we and the singers are obviously enjoying strikes the conscience as frivolous.

On the other hand, its pure artifice renders opera the ideal dramatic medium for a tragic myth. I once went in the same week to a performance of *Tristan und Isolde* and a showing of *L'Eternal Retour*, Jean Cocteau's movie version of the same story. During the former, two souls, weighing over two hundred pounds apiece, were transfigured by a transcendent power; in the latter, a handsome boy met a beautiful girl and they had an affair. This loss of value was due not to any lack of skill on Cocteau's part but to the nature of the cinema as a medium. Had he used a fat middle-aged couple the effect would have been ridiculous because the snatches of language which are all the movie permits have not sufficient power to transcend their physical appearance. Yet if the lovers are young and beautiful, the cause of their love looks "natural," a consequence of their beauty, and the whole meaning of the myth is gone.

> The man who wrote the Eighth Symphony has a right to rebuke the man who put his rapture of elation, tenderness, and nobility into the mouths of a drunken libertine, a silly peasant girl, and a conventional fine lady, instead of confessing them to himself, glorying in them, and uttering them without motley as the universal inheritance.
>
> BERNARD SHAW

Shaw, and Beethoven, are both wrong, I believe, and Mozart right. Feelings of joy, tenderness and nobility are not confined to "noble" characters but are experienced by everybody, by the most conventional, most stupid, most depraved. It is one of the glories of opera that it can demonstrate this and to the shame of the spoken drama that it cannot. Because we use language in everyday life, our style and vocabulary become identified with our social character as others see us, and in a play, even a verse play, there are narrow limits to the range in speech possible for any character beyond which the playwright cannot go without making the character incredible. But precisely because we do not communicate by singing, a song can be out of place but not out of character; it is just as credible that a stupid person should sing beautifully as that a clever person should do so.

If music in general is an imitation of history, opera in particular is an imitation of human willfulness; it is rooted in the fact that we not only have feelings but insist upon having them at whatever cost to ourselves. Opera, therefore, cannot present character in the novelist's sense of the word, namely, people who are potentially good *and* bad, active *and* passive, for music is immediate actuality and neither potentiality nor passivity can live in its presence. This is something a librettist must never forget. Mozart is a greater composer than Rossini but the Figaro of the *Marriage* is less satisfying, to my mind, than the Figaro of the *Barber* and the fault is, I think, Da Ponte's. His Figaro is too interesting a character to be completely translatable into music, so that co-present with the Figaro who is singing, one is conscious of a Figaro who is not singing but thinking to himself. The barber of Seville, on the other hand, who is not a person but a musical busybody, goes into song exactly with nothing over.

Again, I find *La Bohème* inferior to *Tosca*, not because its music is inferior, but because the characters, Mimi in particular, are too passive; there is an awkward gap between the resolution with which they sing and the irresolution with which they act.

The quality common to all the great operatic roles, e.g., Don Giovanni, Norma, Lucia, Tristan, Isolde, Brünnhilde, is that each of them is a passionate and willful state of being. In real life they would all be bores, even Don Giovanni.

In recompense for this lack of psychological complexity, however, music can do what words cannot, present the immediate and simultaneous relation of these states to each other. The crowning glory of opera is the big ensemble.

The chorus can play two roles in opera and two only, that of the mob and that of the faithful, sorrowing or rejoicing community. A little of this goes a long way. Opera is not oratorio.

Drama is based on the Mistake. I think someone is my friend when he really is my enemy, that I am free to marry a woman when in fact she is my mother, that this person is a chambermaid when it is a young nobleman in disguise, that this well-dressed young man is rich when he is really a penniless adventurer, or that if I do this such and such a result will follow when in fact it results in something very different. All good drama has two movements, first the making of the mistake, then the discovery that it was a mistake.

In composing his plot, the librettist has to conform to this law but, in comparison to the dramatist, he is more limited in the kinds of mistake he can use. The dramatist, for instance, procures some of his finest effects from showing how people deceive themselves. Self-deception is impossible in opera because music is immediate, not reflective; whatever is sung is the case. At most, self-deception can be suggested by having the orchestral accompaniment at variance with the singer, e.g., the jolly tripping notes which accompany Germont's approach to Violetta's deathbed in *La Traviata*, but unless employed very sparingly such devices cause confusion rather than insight.

Again, while in the spoken drama the discovery of the mistake can be a slow process and often, indeed, the more gradual it is the greater the dramatic interest, in a libretto the drama of recognition must be tropically abrupt, for music cannot exist in an atmosphere of uncertainty; song cannot walk, it can only jump.

On the other hand, the librettist need never bother his head, as the dramatist must, about probability. A credible situation in opera means a situation in which it is credible that someone should sing. A good libretto plot is a melodrama in both the strict and the conventional sense of the word; it offers as many opportunities as possible for the characters to be swept off their feet by placing them in situations which are too tragic or too fantastic for "words." No good opera plot can be sensible for people do not sing when they are feeling sensible.

The theory of "music-drama" presupposes a libretto in which there is not one sensible moment or one sensible remark: this is not only very difficult to manage, though Wagner managed it, but also extremely exhausting on both singers and the audience, neither of whom may relax for an instant.

In a libretto where there are any sensible passages, i.e., conversation not song, the theory becomes absurd. If, for furthering the action, it becomes necessary for one character to say to another

"Run upstairs and fetch me a handkerchief," then there is nothing in the words, apart from their rhythm, to make one musical setting more apt than another. Wherever the choice of notes is arbitrary, the only solution is a convention, e.g., *recitativo secco*.

In opera the orchestra is addressed to the singers, not to the audience. An opera-lover will put up with and even enjoy an orchestral interlude on condition that he knows the singers cannot sing just now because they are tired or the sceneshifters are at work, but any use of the orchestra by itself which is not filling in time is, for him, wasting it. "Leonora III" is a fine piece to listen to in the concert hall, but in the opera house, when it is played between scenes one and two of the second act of *Fidelio*, it becomes twelve minutes of acute boredom.

If the librettist is a practicing poet, the most difficult problem, the place where he is most likely to go astray, is the composition of the verse. Poetry is in its essence an act of reflection, of refusing to be content with the interjections of immediate emotion in order to understand the nature of what is felt. Since music is in essence immediate, it follows that the words of a song cannot be poetry. Here one should draw a distinction between lyric and song proper. A lyric is a poem intended to be chanted. In a chant the music is subordinate to the words which limit the range and tempo of the notes. In song, the notes must be free to be whatever they choose and the words must be able to do what they are told.

The verses of "Ah non credea" in *La Sonnambula*, though of little interest to read, do exactly what they should: suggest to Bellini one of the most beautiful melodies ever written and then leave him completely free to write it. The verses which the librettist writes are not addressed to the public but are really a private letter to the composer. They have their moment of glory, the moment in which they suggest to him a certain melody; once that is over, they are as expendable as infantry to a Chinese general: they must efface themselves and cease to care what happens to them.

There have been several composers, Campion, Hugo Wolf, Benjamin Britten, for example, whose musical imagination has been stimulated by poetry of a high order. The question remains, however, whether the listener hears the sung words as words in a poem, or, as I am inclined to believe, only as sung syllables. A Cambridge psychologist, P. E. Vernon, once performed the experiment of having a Campion song sung with nonsense verses of equivalent syllabic value substituted for the original; only six per cent of his test audience noticed that something was wrong. It is precisely because I believe that, in listening to song (as distinct from chant), we hear, not words, but syllables, that I am not generally in favor of the performances of operas in translation. Wagner or Strauss in English sounds intolerable, and would still sound so if the poetic merits of the translation were greater than those of the original, because the new syllables have no apt relation to the pitch and tempo of the notes with which they are associated. The poetic value of the words may provoke a composer's imagination, but it is their syllabic values which determine the kind of vocal line he writes. In song, poetry is expendable, syllables are not.

"History," said Stephen Dedalus, "is the nightmare from which I must awake." The rapidity of historical change and the apparent powerlessness of the individual to affect Collective History has led in literature to a retreat from history. Instead of tracing the history of an individual who is born, grows old and dies, many modern novelists and short story writers, beginning with Poe, have devoted their attention to timeless passionate moments in a life, to states of being. It seems to me that, in some modern music, I can detect the same trend, a trend towards composing a static kind of music in which there is no marked difference between its beginning, its middle and its end, a music which sounds remarkably like primitive proto-music. It is not for me to criticize a composer who writes such music. One can say, however, that he will never be able to write an opera. But, probably, he won't want to.

The golden age of opera, from Mozart to Verdi, coincided with the golden age of liberal humanism, of unquestioning belief in freedom and progress. If good operas are rarer today, this may be because, not only have we learned that we are less free than nineteenth-century humanism imagined, but also have become less certain that freedom is an unequivocal blessing, that the free are necessarily the good. To say that operas are more difficult to write does not mean that they are impossible. That would only follow if we should cease to believe in free will and personality altogether. Every high C accurately struck demolishes the theory that we are the irresponsible puppets of fate or chance.

Yonder Peasant, Who Is He?
My Confession
J. D. Salinger's Closed Circuit

MARY MCCARTHY
(b. 1912)

MARY MC CARTHY's novel *The Group* (1963), about
the later adventures of six Vassar classmates of the
early 1930's, has made her the best-known woman
novelist of her generation. But though all her well-
documented fiction is rich in socially sophisticated
observation, many critics have questioned whether
Miss McCarthy has the imaginative sensibility, the
broad human sympathies, and the creativity of the
true novelist. Her penetrating intelligence and
firm judgments seem better suited to the essay, to
interpretations of actual experience.

After graduating a Phi Beta Kappa from Vassar in
1933, Miss McCarthy quickly claimed a place for
herself in leftist liberal journalism, writing book and
theater criticism for *The Nation*, *The New Republic*,
and *Partisan Review*, of which she was briefly an
editor, and engaging zestfully in the literary-political
controversies of the late 1930's. In *The Company She
Keeps* (1942) a young woman, not unlike the author
herself, encounters a series of type-characters of the
period—writers, leftists, businessmen. The story
that attracted most attention, "The Man in the
Brooks Brothers Shirt," describes an amorous night
on a train with a man of intolerably stuffy opinions.
[235] Teaching appointments at Bard and Sarah Lawrence

inspired *The Groves of Academe* (1952), the wittiest
and most knowledgeable of the flood of college novels
appearing in recent decades. In scenes of high comedy,
a faculty failure exploits the sanctimonious public
liberalism of a college president by faking a leftist
past, knowing that this will make him secure against
dismissal.

Miss McCarthy has been married several times, most
notably to the critic Edmund Wilson, by whom she
had a son. In *A Charmed Life* (1955) she describes
the complications that ensue when a woman returns
with a new husband to the Cape Cod village near
which lives, with *his* new wife, her former husband,
a well-known scholar and critic. She had separated
from him under rather sensational circumstances,
fondly remembered by the village gossips. Miss
McCarthy's novels are rich in personal and social
experience, cogently and often wittily described, but
the emotional depth and imaginative identification
we expect of a novelist are found more strongly in
her description of historic places, *Venice Observed*
(1956) and *The Stones of Florence* (1959), sensitive
blendings of personal observation and historical
research.

The autobiography *Memories of a Catholic Girlhood*
(1957) reveals much—and probably not all quite
intentionally—about the personality of the author
and the steps by which she developed. One of the most
significant episodes takes place in a convent school
where, in despair at finding her charms unnoticed
and her talents unrecognized, she stages a carefully
planned loss of faith. Her dramatic doubts win her
the attention, respect, and popularity she craves, but
unexpectedly turn out to be genuine and are not lost
even in the course of acting out her final scene, her
triumphant renewal of faith.

We know from the best-loved fairy tales, like
Cinderella and *Hansel and Gretel*, that a deeply

affecting situation in fiction is that of children whose
parents have been replaced by substitutes who
mistreat them and deny them their social rights.
This is the plight of the young McCarthys in "Yonder
Peasant, Who is He?" But the poignancy of the
situation does not inhibit the author's wit. The father
and mother have died within a few days of each
other from influenza, and the children are made to
feel subtly disgraced by this "as though our mother
had been a pretty secretary with whom he had
wantonly absconded into the irresponsible paradise
of the hereafter." Painful details are included, such
as the adhesive gag removed every morning with
ether, but the emphasis is less on recreating emotion
than explaining adults in terms of character types and
governing concepts. This intellectuality is reflected
in the style, rather eighteenth-century in tone, full
of balance and antithesis, the diction Latinical. As a
schoolgirl, Miss McCarthy fell in love with the prose
of Julius Caesar.

"My Confession" is written more simply and directly,
with less theorizing in proportion to narrative. Self-
centered and somewhat fictionalized though it may
be, it recreates vividly for those of a later generation
the peculiar and irresistible political atmosphere of
the late thirties. As a study of all the elements—
emotional, accidental, and rational—that go into
the taking of a political position, it applies to any
period. She wrote it in 1953, the year that Senator
McCarthy's power was at its height.

"J. D. Salinger's Closed Circuit" is in still a different
style—brisk, brilliant, devastating. Miss McCarthy
could not have picked up Salinger's facts and phrases
and used them against him with such powerful
effect if she had not grasped so clearly the essential
sentimentality of his work.

Yonder Peasant, Who Is He?

Whenever we children came to stay at my grandmother's house, we were put to sleep in the sewing room, a bleak, shabby, utilitarian rectangle, more office than bedroom, more attic than office, that played to the hierarchy of chambers the role of a poor relation. It was a room seldom entered by the other members of the family, seldom swept by the maid, a room without pride; the old sewing machine, some cast-off chairs, a shadeless lamp, rolls of wrapping paper, piles of cardboard boxes that might someday come in handy, papers of pins, and remnants of material united with the iron folding cots put out for our use and the bare floor boards to give an impression of intense and ruthless temporality. Thin white spreads, of the kind used in hospitals and charity institutions, and naked blinds at the windows reminded us of our orphaned condition and of the ephemeral character of our visit; there was nothing here to encourage us to consider this our home.

Poor Roy's children, as commiseration damply styled us, could not afford illusions, in the family opinion. Our father had put us beyond the pale by dying suddenly of influenza and taking our young mother with him, a defection that was remarked on with horror and grief commingled, as though our mother had been a pretty secretary with whom he had wantonly absconded into the irresponsible paradise of the hereafter. Our reputation was clouded by this misfortune. There was a prevailing sense, not only in the family but among storekeepers, servants, streetcar conductors, and other satellites of our circle, that my grandfather, a rich man, had behaved with extraordinary munificence in allotting a sum of money for our support and installing us with some disagreeable middle-aged relations in a dingy house two blocks distant from his own. What alternative he had was not mentioned; presumably he could have sent us to an orphan asylum and no one would have thought the worse of him. At any rate, it was felt, even by those who sympathized with us, that we led a privileged existence, privileged because we had no rights, and the very fact that at the yearly Halloween or Christmas party given at the home of an uncle we appeared so dismal, ill clad, and unhealthy, in contrast to our rosy, exquisite cousins, confirmed the judgment that had been made on us— clearly, it was a generous impulse that kept us in the family at all. Thus, the meaner our circumstances, the greater seemed our grandfather's condescension, a view in which we ourselves shared, looking softly and shyly on this old man—with his rheumatism, his pink face and white hair, set off by the rosebuds in his Pierce-Arrow and in his buttonhole—as the font of goodness and philanthropy, and the nickel he occasionally gave us to drop into the collection plate on Sunday (two cents was our ordinary contribution) filled us not with envy but with simple admiration for his potency; this indeed was princely, *this* was the way to give. It did not occur to us to judge him for the disparity of our styles of living. Whatever bitterness we felt was kept for our actual guardians, who, we believed, must be embezzling the money set aside for us, since the standard of comfort achieved in our grandparents' house—the electric heaters, the gas logs, the lap robes, the shawls wrapped tenderly about the old knees, the white meat of chicken and red meat of beef, the silver, the white tablecloths, the maids, and the solicitous chauffeur—persuaded us that prunes and rice pudding, peeling paint and patched clothes were *hors concours* with these persons and therefore could not have been willed by them. Wealth, in our minds, was equivalent to bounty, and poverty but a sign of penuriousness of spirit.

Yet even if we had been convinced of the honesty of our guardians, we would still have clung to that beneficent image of our grandfather that the family myth proposed to us. We were too poor, spiritually speaking, to question his generosity, to ask why he allowed us to live in oppressed chill and deprivation at a long arm's length from himself and hooded his genial blue eye with a bluff, millionairish gray eyebrow whenever the evidence of our suffering presented itself at his knee. The official answer we knew: our benefactors were too old to put up with four wild young children; our grandfather was preoccupied with business matters and with his rheumatism, to which he devoted himself as though to a pious duty, taking it with him on pilgrimages to Ste. Anne de Beaupré and Miami, offering it with impartial reverence to the miracle of the

Northern Mother and the Southern sun. This rheumatism hallowed my grandfather with the mark of a special vocation; he lived with it in the manner of an artist or a grizzled Galahad; it set him apart from all of us and even from my grandmother, who, lacking such an affliction, led a relatively unjustified existence and showed, in relation to us children, a sharper and more bellicose spirit. She felt, in spite of everything, that she was open to criticism, and, transposing this feeling with a practiced old hand, kept peering into our characters for symptoms of ingratitude.

We, as a matter of fact, were grateful to the point of servility. We made no demands, we had no hopes. We were content if we were permitted to enjoy the refracted rays of that solar prosperity and come sometimes in the summer afternoons to sit on the shady porch or idle through a winter morning on the wicker furniture of the sun parlor, to stare at the player piano in the music room and smell the odor of whisky in the mahogany cabinet in the library, or to climb about the dark living room examining the glassed-in paintings in their huge gilt frames, the fruits of European travel: dusky Italian devotional groupings, heavy and lustrous as grapes, Neapolitan women carrying baskets to market, views of Venetian canals, and Tuscan harvest scenes—secular themes that, to the Irish-American mind, had become tinged with Catholic feelings by a regional infusion from the Pope. We asked no more from this house than the pride of being connected with it, and this was fortunate for us, since my grandmother, a great adherent of the give-them-an-inch-and-they'll-take-a-yard theory of hospitality, never, so far as I can remember, offered any caller the slightest refreshment, regarding her own conversation as sufficiently wholesome and sustaining. An ugly, severe old woman with a monstrous balcony of a bosom, she officiated over certain set topics in a colorless singsong, like a priest intoning a Mass, topics to which repetition had lent a senseless solemnity: her audience with the Holy Father; how my own father had broken with family tradition and voted the Democratic ticket; a visit to Lourdes; the Sacred Stairs in Rome, bloodstained since the first Good Friday, which she had climbed on her knees; my crooked little fingers and how they meant I was a liar; a miracle-working bone; the importance of regular bowel movements; the wickedness of Protestants; the conversion of my mother to Catholicism; and the assertion that my other grandmother must certainly dye her hair. The most trivial reminiscences (my aunt's having hysterics in a haystack) received from her delivery and from the piety of the context a strongly monitory flavor; they inspired fear and guilt, and one searched uncomfortably for the moral in them, as in a dark and riddling fable.

Luckily, I am writing a memoir and not a work of fiction, and therefore I do not have to account for my grandmother's unpleasing character and look for the Oedipal fixation or the traumatic experience which would give her that clinical authenticity that is nowadays so desirable in portraiture. I do not know how my grandmother got the way she was; I assume, from family photographs and from the inflexibility of her habits, that she was always the same, and it seems as idle to inquire into her childhood as to ask what was ailing Iago or look for the error in toilet-training that was responsible for Lady Macbeth. My grandmother's sexual history, bristling with infant mortality in the usual style of her period, was robust and decisive: three tall, handsome sons grew up, and one attentive daughter. Her husband treated her kindly. She had money, many grandchildren, and religion to sustain her. White hair, glasses, soft skin, wrinkles, needlework—all the paraphernalia of motherliness were hers; yet it was a cold, grudging, disputatious old woman who sat all day in her sunroom making tapestries from a pattern, scanning religious periodicals, and setting her iron jaw against any infraction of her ways.

Combativeness was, I suppose, the dominant trait in my grandmother's nature. An aggressive churchgoer, she was quite without Christian feeling; the mercy of the Lord Jesus had never entered her heart. Her piety was an act of war against the Protestant ascendancy. The religious magazines on her table furnished her not with food for meditation but with fresh pretexts for anger; articles attacking birth control, divorce, mixed marriages, Darwin, and secular education were her favorite reading. The teachings of the Church did not interest her, except as they were a rebuke to others; "Honor thy father and thy mother," a commandment she was no longer called upon to practice, was the one most frequently on her lips. The extermination of Protestantism, rather than spiritual perfection, was the boon she prayed for. Her mind was preoccupied with conversion; the capture of a soul for God much diverted her fancy—it made one less Protestant in the world. Foreign missions, with their overtones of good will and social service, appealed to her less strongly; it was not a *harvest* of souls that my grandmother had in mind.

This pugnacity of my grandmother's did not confine itself to sectarian enthusiasm. There was the defense of her furniture and her house against the imagined encroachments of visitors. With her, this was not the gentle and tremulous protectiveness endemic in old ladies, who fear for the safety of their possessions with a truly touching anxiety, inferring the fragility of all things from the brittleness of their old bones and hearing the crash of mortality in the perilous tinkling of a tea cup. My grandmother's sentiment was more autocratic: she hated having her chairs sat in or her lawns stepped on or the water turned on in her basins, for no reason at all except pure officiousness; she even grudged the mailman his daily promenade up her sidewalk. Her home was a center of power, and she would not allow it to be derogated by easy or democratic usage. Under her jealous eye, its social properties had atrophied, and it functioned in the family structure simply as a political headquarters. Family conferences were held there, consultations with the doctor and the clergy; refractory children were brought there for a lecture or an interval of thought-taking; wills were read and loans negotiated and emissaries from the Protestant faction on state occasions received. The family had no friends, and entertaining was held to be a foolish and unnecessary courtesy as between blood relations. Holiday dinners fell, as a duty, on the lesser members of the organization: the daughters and daughters-in-law (converts from the false religion) offered up Baked Alaska on a platter, like the head of John the Baptist, while the old people sat enthroned at the table, and only their digestive processes acknowledged, with rumbling, enigmatic salvos, the festal day.

Yet on one terrible occasion my grandmother had kept open house. She had accommodated us all during those fatal weeks of the influenza epidemic, when no hospital beds were to be had and people went about with masks or stayed shut up in their houses, and the awful fear of contagion paralyzed all services and made each man an enemy to his neighbor. One by one, we had been carried off the train which had brought us from distant Puget Sound to make a new home in Minneapolis. Waving good-by in the Seattle depot, we had not known that we had carried the flu with us into our drawing rooms, along with the presents and the flowers, but, one after another, we had been struck down as the train proceeded eastward.

We children did not understand whether the chattering of our teeth and Mama's lying torpid in the berth were not somehow a part of the trip (until then, serious illness, in our minds, had been associated with innovations—it had always brought home a new baby), and we began to be sure that it was all an adventure when we saw our father draw a revolver on the conductor who was trying to put us off the train at a small wooden station in the middle of the North Dakota prairie. On the platform at Minneapolis, there were stretchers, a wheel chair, redcaps, distraught officials, and, beyond them, in the crowd, my grandfather's rosy face, cigar, and cane, my grandmother's feathered hat, imparting an air of festivity to this strange and confused picture, making us children certain that our illness was the beginning of a delightful holiday.

We awoke to reality in the sewing room several weeks later, to an atmosphere of castor oil, rectal thermometers, cross nurses, and efficiency, and though we were shut out from the knowledge of what had happened so close to us, just out of our hearing—a scandal of the gravest character, a coming and going of priests and undertakers and coffins (Mama and Daddy, they assured us, had gone to get well in the hospital)—we became aware, even as we woke from our fevers, that everything, including ourselves, was different. We had shrunk, as it were, and faded, like the flannel pajamas we wore, which during these few weeks had grown, doubtless from the disinfectant they were washed in, wretchedly thin and shabby. The behavior of the people around us, abrupt, careless, and preoccupied, apprised us without any ceremony of our diminished importance. Our value had paled, and a new image of ourselves—the image, if we had guessed it, of the orphan—was already forming in our minds. We had not known we were spoiled, but now this word, entering our vocabulary for the first time, served to define the change for us and to herald the new order. Before we got sick, we were spoiled; that was what was the matter now, and everything we could not understand, everything unfamiliar and displeasing, took on a certain plausibility when related to this fresh concept. We had not known what it was to have trays dumped summarily on our beds and no sugar and cream for our cereal, to take medicine in a gulp because someone could not be bothered to wait for us, to have our arms jerked into our sleeves and a comb ripped through our hair, to be bathed impatiently, to be told to sit up or lie down quick and no nonsense about it, to find our questions unanswered and our requests unheeded, to lie for hours alone and wait for the doctor's visit, but this, so it seemed, was an oversight in our training, and my grandmother and her household applied themselves with a will to remedying the deficiency.

Their motives were, no doubt, good; it was time indeed that we learned that the world was no longer our oyster. The happy life we had had—the May baskets and the valentines, the picnics in the yard, and the elaborate snowman—was a poor preparation, in truth, for the future that now opened up to us. Our new instructors could hardly be blamed for a certain impatience with our parents, who had been so lacking in foresight. It was to everyone's interest, decidedly, that we should forget the past—the quicker, the better—and a steady disparagement of our habits ("Tea and chocolate, can you imagine, and all those frosted cakes—no wonder poor Tess was always after the doctor") and praise that was rigorously comparative ("You have absolutely no idea of the improvement in those children") flattered the feelings of the speakers and prepared us to accept a loss that was, in any case, irreparable. Like all children, we wished to conform, and the notion that our former ways had been somehow ridiculous and unsuitable made the memory of them falter a little, like a child's recitation to strangers. We no longer demanded our due, and the wish to see our parents insensibly weakened. Soon we ceased to speak of it, and thus, without tears or tantrums, we came to know they were dead.

Why no one, least of all our grandmother, to whose repertory the subject seems so congenial, took the trouble to tell us, it is impossible now to know. It is easy to imagine her "breaking" the news to those of us who were old enough to listen in one of those official interviews in which her nature periodically tumefied, becoming heavy and turgid, like her portentous bosom, like peonies, her favorite flower, or like the dressmaker's dummy, that bombastic image of herself that, half swathed in a sheet for decorum's sake, lent a museumlike solemnity to the sewing room and aroused our first sexual curiosity. The mind's ear frames her sentences, but in reality she did not speak, whether from a hygenic motive (keep the mind ignorant and the bowels open), or from a mistaken kindness, it is difficult to guess. Perhaps really she feared our tears, which might rain on her like reproaches, since the family policy at the time was predicated on the axiom of our virtual insentience, an assumption that allowed

them to proceed with us as if with pieces of furniture. Without explanations or coddling, as soon as they could safely get up, my three
brothers were dispatched to the other house; they were much too
young to "feel" it, I heard the grownups murmur, and would never
know the difference "if Myers and Margaret were careful." In my
case, however, a doubt must have been experienced. I was six—old
enough to "remember"—and this entitled me, in the family's eyes,
to greater consideration, as if this memory of mine were a lawyer
who represented me in court. In deference, therefore, to my age
and my supposed powers of criticism and comparison, I was kept on
for a time, to roam palely about my grandmother's living rooms, a
dangling, transitional creature, a frog becoming a tadpole, while
my brothers, poor little polyps, were already well embedded in the
structure of the new life. I did not wonder what had become of
them. I believe I thought they were dead, but their fate did not
greatly concern me; my heart had grown numb. I considered myself
clever to have guessed the truth about my parents, like a child who
proudly discovers that there is no Santa Claus, but I would not
speak of that knowledge or even react to it privately, for I wished
to have nothing to do with it; I would not co-operate in this loss.
Those weeks in my grandmother's house come back to me very ob-
scurely, surrounded by blackness, like a mourning card: the dark
well of the staircase, where I seem to have been endlessly loitering,
waiting to see Mama when she would come home from the hospital,
and then simply loitering with no purpose whatever; the winter-dim
first-grade classroom of the strange academy I was sent to; the drab
treatment room of the doctor's office, where every Saturday I
screamed and begged on a table while electric shocks were sent
through me, for what purpose I cannot conjecture. But this prefer-
ential treatment could not be accorded me forever; it was time that
I found my niche. "There is someone here to see you"—the maid
met me one afternoon with this announcement and a half-curious,
half-knowledgeable smile. My heart bounded; I felt almost sick
(who else, after all, could it be?), and she had to push me forward.
But the man and woman surveying me in the sun parlor with my
grandmother were strangers, two unprepossessing middle-aged
people—a great-aunt and her husband, so it seemed—to whom I was
now commanded to give a hand and a smile, for, as my grandmother
remarked, Myers and Margaret had come to take me home that very
afternoon to live with them, and I must not make a bad impression.

Once the new household was running, our parents' death was officially conceded and sentiment given its due. Concrete references to the lost ones, to their beauty, gaiety, and good manners, were naturally not welcomed by our guardians, who possessed none of these qualities themselves, but the veneration of our parents' *memory* was considered an admirable exercise. Our evening prayers were lengthened to include one for our parents' souls, and we were thought to make a pretty picture, all four of us in our pajamas with feet in them, kneeling in a neat line, our hands clasped before us, reciting the prayer for the dead. "Eternal rest grant unto them, oh Lord, and let the perpetual light shine upon them," our thin little voices cried, but this remembrancing, so pleasurable to our guardians, was only a chore to us. We connected it with lights out, washing, all the bedtime coercions, and particularly with the adhesive tape that, to prevent mouthbreathing, was clapped upon our lips the moment the prayer was finished, sealing us up for the night, and that was removed, very painfully, with the help of ether, in the morning. It embarrassed us to be reminded of our parents by these persons who had superseded them and who seemed to evoke their wraiths in an almost proprietary manner, as though death, the great leveler, had brought them within their province. In the same spirit, we were taken to the cemetery to view our parents' graves; this, in fact, being free of charge, was a regular Sunday pastime with us, which we grew to hate as we did all recreation enforced by our guardians—department-store demonstrations, band concerts, parades, trips to the Old Soldiers' Home, to the Botanical Gardens, to Minnehaha Park, where we watched other children ride on the ponies, to the Zoo, to the water tower—diversions that cost nothing, involved long streetcar trips or endless walking or waiting, and that had the peculiarly fatigued, dusty, proletarianized character of American municipal entertainment. The two mounds that now were our parents associated themselves in our minds with Civil War cannon balls and monuments to the doughboy dead; we contemplated them stolidly, waiting for a sensation, but these twin grass beds, with their junior-executive headstones, elicited nothing whatever; tired of this interminable staring, we would beg to be allowed to go play in some collateral mausoleum, where the dead at least were buried in drawers and offered some stimulus to fancy.

For my grandmother, the recollection of the dead became a mode of civility that she thought proper to exercise toward us whenever, for any reason, one of us came to stay at her house. The reason was almost always the same. We (that is, my brother Kevin or I) had run away from home. Independently of each other, this oldest of my brothers and I had evolved an identical project—to get ourselves placed in an orphan asylum. We had noticed the heightening of interest that mention of our parentless condition seemed always to produce in strangers, and this led us to interpret the word "asylum" in the old Greek sense and to look on a certain red brick building, seen once from a streetcar near the Mississippi River, as a haven of security. So, from time to time, when our lives became too painful, one of us would set forth, determined to find the red brick building and to press what we imagined was our legal claim to its protection. But sometimes we lost our way, and sometimes our courage, and after spending a day hanging about the streets peering into strange yards, trying to assess the kindheartedness of the owner (for we also thought of adoption), or a cold night hiding in a church confessional box or behind some statuary in the Art Institute, we would be brought by the police, by some well-meaning householder, or simply by fear and hunger, to my grandmother's door. There we would be silently received, and a family conclave would be summoned. We would be put to sleep in the sewing room for a night, or sometimes more, until our feelings had subsided and we could be sent back, grateful, at any rate, for the promise that no reprisals would be taken and that the life we had run away from would go on "as if nothing had happened."

Since we were usually running away to escape some anticipated punishment, these flights at least gained us something, but in spite of the taunts of our guardians, who congratulated us bitterly on our "cleverness," we ourselves could not feel that we came home in triumph as long as we came home at all. The cramps and dreads of those long nights made a harrowing impression on us. Our failure to run away successfully put us, so we thought, at the absolute mercy of our guardians; our last weapon was gone, for it was plain to be seen that they could always bring us back and we never understood why they did not take advantage of this situation to thrash us, as they used to put it, within an inch of our lives. What intervened to save us, we could not guess—a miracle, perhaps; we were not acquainted with any *human* motive that would prompt Omnipotence to desist. We did not suspect that these escapes brought consternation to the family circle, which had acted, so it conceived, only in our best interests, and now saw itself in danger of unmerited obloquy. What would be the Protestant reaction if something still more dreadful were to happen? Child suicides were not unknown, and quiet, asthmatic little Kevin had been caught with matches under the house. The family would not acknowledge error, but it conceded a certain mismanagement on Myers' and Margaret's part. Clearly, we might become altogether intractable if our homecoming on these occasions were not mitigated with leniency. Consequently, my grandmother kept us in a kind of neutral detention. She declined to be aware of our grievance and offered no words of comfort, but the comforts of her household acted upon us soothingly, like an automatic mother's hand. We ate and drank contentedly; with all her harsh views, my grandmother was a practical woman and would not have thought it worthwhile to unsettle her whole schedule, teach her cook to make a lumpy mush and watery boiled potatoes, and market for turnips and parsnips and all the other vegetables we hated, in order to approximate the conditions she considered suitable for our characters. Humble pie could be costly, especially when cooked to order.

Doubtless she did not guess how delightful these visits seemed to us once the fear of punishment had abated. Her knowledge of our own way of living was luxuriously remote. She did not visit our ménage or inquire into its practices, and though hypersensitive to a squint or a dental irregularity (for she was liberal indeed with glasses and braces for the teeth, disfiguring appliances that remained the sole token of our bourgeois origin and set us off from our parochial-school mates like the caste marks of some primitive tribe), she appeared not to notice the darns and patches of our clothing, our raw hands and scarecrow arms, our silence and our elderly faces. She imagined us as surrounded by certain playthings she had once bestowed on us—a sandbox, a wooden swing, a wagon, an ambulance, a toy fire engine. In my grandmother's consciousness, these objects remained always in pristine condition; years after the sand had spilled out of it and the roof had rotted away, she continued to ask tenderly after our lovely sand pile and to manifest displeasure if we declined to join in its praises. Like many egoistic people (I have noticed this trait in myself), she was capable of making a handsome outlay, but the act affected her so powerfully that her generosity was still lively in her memory when its practical effects had long vanished. In the case of a brown beaver hat, which she watched me wear for four years, she was clearly blinded to its matted nap, its shapeless brim, and ragged ribbon by the vision of the price tag it had worn when new. Yet, however her mind embroidered the bare tapestry of our lives, she could not fail to perceive that we felt, during these short stays with her, *some* difference between the two establishments, and to take our wonder and pleasure as a compliment to herself.

She smiled on us quite kindly when we exclaimed over the food and the nice, warm bathrooms, with their rugs and electric heaters. What funny little creatures, to be so impressed by things that were, after all, only the ordinary amenities of life! Seeing us content in her house, her emulative spirit warmed slowly to our admiration: she compared herself to our guardians and though for expedient reasons she could not afford to deprecate them ("You children have been very ungrateful for all Myers and Margaret have done for you"), a sense of her own finer magnanimity disposed her subtly in our favor. In the flush of these emotions, a tenderness sprang up between us. She seemed half reluctant to part with whichever of us she had in her custody, almost as if she were experiencing a genuine pang of conscience. "Try and be good," she would advise us when the moment for leave-taking came, "and don't provoke your aunt and uncle. We might have made different arrangements if there had been only one of you to consider." These manifestations of concern, these tacit admissions of our true situation, did not make us, as one might have thought, bitter against our grandparents, for whom ignorance of the facts might have served as a justification, but, on the contrary, filled us with love for them and even a kind of sympathy —our sufferings were less terrible if someone acknowledged their existence, if someone were suffering for us, for whom we, in our turn, could suffer, and thereby absolve of guilt.

During these respites, the recollection of our parents formed a bond between us and our grandmother that deepened our mutual regard. Unlike our guardians or the whispering ladies who sometimes came to call on us, inspired, it seemed, by a pornographic curiosity as to the exact details of our feelings ("Do you suppose they remember their parents?" "Do they ever *say* anything?"), our grandmother was quite uninterested in arousing an emotion of grief in us. "She doesn't feel it at all," I used to hear her confide, of me, to visitors, but contentedly, without censure, as if I had been a spayed cat that, in her superior foresight, she had had "attended to." For my grandmother, the death of my parents had become, in retrospect, an eventful occasion upon which she looked back with pleasure and a certain self-satisfaction. Whenever we stayed with her, we were allowed, as a special treat, to look into the rooms they had died in, for the fact that, as she phrased it, "they died in separate rooms" had for her a significance both romantic and somehow self-gratulatory, as though the separation in death of two who had loved each other in life were beautiful in itself and also reflected credit on the chatelaine of the house, who had been able to furnish two master bedrooms for the emergency. The housekeeping details of the tragedy, in fact, were to her of paramount interest. "I turned my house into a hospital," she used to say, particularly when visitors were present. "Nurses were as scarce as hen's teeth, and *high* —you can hardly imagine what those girls were charging an hour." The trays and the special cooking, the laundry and the disinfectants recalled themselves fondly to her thoughts, like items on the menu of some long-ago ball-supper, the memory of which recurred to her with a strong, possessive nostalgia.

My parents had, it seemed, by dying on her premises, become in a lively sense her property, and she dispensed them to us now, little by little, with a genuine sense of bounty, just as, later on, when I returned to her a grown-up young lady, she conceded me a diamond lavaliere of my mother's as if the trinket were an inheritance to which she had the prior claim. But her generosity with her memories appeared to us, as children, an act of the greatest indulgence. We begged her for more of these mortuary reminiscences as we might have begged for candy, and since ordinarily we not only had no candy but were permitted no friendships, no movies, and little reading beyond what our teachers prescribed for us, and were kept in quarantine, like carriers of social contagion, among the rhubarb plants of our neglected yard, these memories doled out by our grandmother became our secret treasures; we never spoke of them to each other but hoarded them, each against the rest, in the miserly fastnesses of our hearts. We returned, therefore, from our grandparents' house replenished in all our faculties; these crumbs from the rich man's table were a banquet indeed to us. We did not even mind going back to our guardians, for we now felt superior to them, and besides, as we well knew, we had no choice. It was only by accepting our situation as a just and unalterable arrangement that we could be allowed to transcend it and feel ourselves united to our grandparents in a love that was the more miraculous for breeding no practical results.

In this manner, our household was kept together, and my grandparents were spared the necessity of arriving at a fresh decision about it. Naturally, from time to time a new scandal would break out (for our guardians did not grow kinder in response to being run away from), yet we had come, at bottom, to despair of making any real change in our circumstances, and ran away hopelessly, merely to postpone punishment. And when, after five years, our Protestant grandfather, informed at last of the facts, intervened to save us, his indignation at the family surprised us nearly as much as his action. We thought it only natural that grandparents should know and do nothing, for did not God in the mansions of Heaven look down upon human suffering and allow it to take its course?

There are several dubious points in this memoir.

"*. . . we had not known that we had carried the flu with us into our drawing rooms.*" *Just when we got the flu seems to be arguable. According to the newspaper accounts, we contracted it on the trip. This conflicts with the story that Uncle Harry and Aunt Zula had brought it with them. My present memory supports the idea that someone was sick before we left. But perhaps we did not "know" it was the flu.*

"*. . . we saw our father draw a revolver.*" *If Uncle Harry is right, this is wrong. In any case, we did not "see" it; I heard the story, as I have said, from my other grandmother. When she told me, I had the feeling that I almost remembered it. That is, my mind promptly supplied me with a picture of it, just as it supplied me with a picture of my father standing in the dining room with his arms full of red roses. Actually, I do dimly recall some dispute with the conductor, who wanted to put us off the train.*

"*We awoke to reality in the sewing room several weeks later.*" *We cannot have been sick that long. The newspaper accounts of my parents' death state that "the children are recovering." We must have arrived in Minneapolis on the second or third of November. My parents probably died on the sixth and seventh of November; I say "probably" because the two newspaper stories contradict each other and neither my brothers nor I feel sure. I know I was still sick on the day of the false armistice, for I remember bells ringing and horns and whistles blowing and a nurse standing over my bed and saying that this meant the war was over. I was in a strange room and did not understand how I had got there; I only knew that outside, where the noise was coming from, was Minneapolis. Looking back, putting two and two together, it suddenly strikes me that this must have been the day of my parents' funeral. My brother Kevin agrees. Now that I have established this, or nearly established it, I have the feeling of "remembering," as though I had always known it. In any case, I was in bed for some days after this, having had flu and pneumonia. Kevin says we were still in our grandmother's house at Christmas. He is sure because he was "bad" that day: he punched out the cloth grill on the library phonograph with a drumstick.*

" 'There is someone here to see you'—the maid met me one afternoon with this announcement." I believe this is pure fiction. In reality, I had already seen the people who were going to be my guardians sometime before this, while we were convalescent. We were brought down, in our pajamas, one afternoon to my grandmother's sun parlor, to meet two strangers, a man and a woman, who were sitting there with the rest of the family, like a reception committee. I remember sensing that the occasion had some importance; possibly someone had told us that these people were going to look after us while Mama and Daddy were away, or perhaps stress had merely been laid on "good behavior," Or could it have been just that they were all dressed in black? The man evinced a great deal of paternal good humor, taking my brothers, one by one, on his lap and fondling them while he talked with my grandparents. He paid me no attention at all, and I remember the queer ebb of feeling inside me when I saw I was going to be left out. He did not like me; I noticed this with profound surprise and sorrow. I was not so much jealous as perplexed. After he had played with each of my brothers, we were carried back upstairs to bed. So far as I remember, I did not see him or his wife, following this, for weeks, even months. I cannot recall the circumstances of being moved to the new house at all. But one day I was there, and the next thing I knew, Aunt Margaret was punishing me for having spoiled the wallpaper in my room.

The reader will wonder what made me change this story to something decidedly inferior, even from a literary point of view—Far too sentimental; it even sounds improbable. I forget now, but I think the

*reason must have been that I did not want to "go into" my guard-
ians as individuals here; that was another story, which was to be told
in the next chapter. "Yonder Peasant," unlike the chapters that follow, is not really concerned with individuals. It is, primarily, an
angry indictment of privilege for its treatment of the underprivileged,
a single, breathless, voluble speech on the subject of human indifference. We orphan children were not responsible for being orphans,
but we were treated as if we were and as if being orphans were a
crime we had committed. Read poor for orphan throughout and
you get a kind of allegory or broad social satire on the theme of
wealth and poverty. The anger was a generalized anger, which held
up my grandparents as* specimens *of unfeeling behavior.*

*My Uncle Harry argues that I do not give his mother sufficient
credit: if she had lifted her little finger, he says, she could have had
me cut out of his father's will. He wants me to understand this and
be grateful. (I was fourteen or fifteen when my grandfather died.)
This is typical McCarthy reasoning, as the reader will recognize:
". . . clearly, it was a generous impulse that kept us in the family at
all."*

*Nevertheless, in one sense, I have been unfair to my grand-
mother: I show her, as it were, in retrospect, looking back at her
and judging her as an adult. But as a child, I liked my grandmother;
I thought her a tremendous figure. Many of her faults—her blood-
curdling Catholicism, for example—were not apparent to me as
faults. It gave me a thrill to hear her go on about "the Protestants"
and the outrages of the Ku Klux Klan; I even liked to hear her tell
about my parents' death. In her way, "Aunt Lizzie," as my second
cousins used to call her, was a spellbinder. She spent her winters in
Florida, but in the summer she would let me come in the afternoon,
quite often, and sit on her shaded front porch, watching her sew
and listening to her. Afterward, I was allowed to go out and give
myself a ride on the turntable in her big garage—a sort of merry-go-
round on which the chauffeur turned her cars, so that they never
had to be backed in or out. Besides her Pierce-Arrow, for winter
use, she had a Locomobile, canvas-topped, for summer, which she
sometimes took me driving in, out to Minnetonka or Great Bear Lake
or Winona. Once we visited an Ursuline convent, and once we went
up to St. Joseph to look at St. Benedict's Academy. On these occasions, in her motoring costume, veils, and high-crowned straw hat,
she was an imposing great lady.*

You felt she could be "big" when she wanted to. "My mother was square," says Uncle Harry. She also had a worldly side, fancying herself as a woman of fashion and broad social horizons. One summer, she and my grandfather took me with them to a snappy resort in northern Minnesota called Breezy Point. It was run by a man named Billy Fawcett, the editor of Captain Billy's Whiz Bang; *there I first saw a woman smoke. On the way back, we stopped to visit by grandfather's brother, my uncle John, just outside Duluth, where the grain-elevator company had its main offices. He had a large country house, with formal gardens and walks, set in a deep forest. They showed me phosphorescent wood and fireflies; there were fairies in the garden, they said. Before going to bed, I left a note for the fairies in a rose, fully expecting an answer. But the next morning there was only dew in the rose, and I felt very troubled, for this proved to me that fairies didn't exist.*

There was a spaciousness in my grandmother's personality that made her comfortable to be with, even though you were in awe of her. Marshall Field's, she often related, had offered her a thousand dollars for a tapestried chair she had sewn, but she had promised the chair to Uncle Louis, so, naturally, she had had to turn down the offer. This impressed me mightily, though I wondered why she did not just make another one if she had wanted to sell it to Marshall Field's. Whenever I went shopping with her, I felt that she was about to give me a present, though there was nothing, except her manner, to encourage this notion. On my way east to Vassar, she did propose buying me an electric doughnut-maker for my room. Fortunately, I refused; I later discovered that she was in the habit of deducting the presents she gave my brothers from the trust fund that had been left them. Thus her ample character was strangely touched with meanness.

I have stressed the family's stinginess where we were concerned, the rigid double standard maintained between the two houses. Yet my grandfather, according to Uncle Harry, spent $41,700 for our support between the years 1918 and 1923. During this time, the Preston family contributed $300. This peculiar discrepancy I shall have to deal with later. What interests me now is the question of where the money went. Approximately $8,200 a year was not a small sum, for those days, considering, too, that it was tax free and that nothing had to be put aside for savings or life insurance. Could some *of the money really have been embezzled, as we children used to think?*

With that figure before my eyes, I understand a little more than I did of my grandparents' feelings. In view of his check stubs, my grandfather would have had every reason to assume that we children were being decently taken care of in the house he had bought for us. I do remember his surprise when he found that we were being given only those two pennies to put in the collection plate on Sundays. But he did not see us very often, and when he did, we did not complain. This seems odd, but it is true. I do not think we ever brought our woes to our grandparents. When we finally spoke, it was to our other grandfather, the one we hardly knew. We were afraid of punishment, I suppose. The only form of complaint, from us, that was visible to the family was that silent running away. It was I who spent the night in a confessional and a day hiding behind the statue of Laocoön in the Art Institute. That was as far as I got, for I did not have the carfare that was needed to get me to that red brick orphan asylum. Kevin was hardier. Traveling on a transfer he had somehow acquired, he reached a yellow brick orphan asylum called "The Sheltering Arms" that was run by the Shriners. He did not like it as well, in spite of its name, as the red brick one, and though he peered over the wall for a long time, in the end he was afraid to go in. A householder found him crying, fed him, and eventually the Pierce-Arrow came with Uncle Louis to get him; this made the householder think Kevin a terrible fraud.

The family, I think now, must have been greatly perturbed by our running away. It meant either that we were unhappy or that we were incorrigibly bad. I had stolen a ring from the five-and-ten, and my aunt had had to march me back with it into the manager's office. Kevin had altered his report card when the prize of a dime (no, a nickel) had been offered to the one with the highest marks, and one month I had torn and defaced mine because I was afraid to show a low mark at home. At home, threats of reform school hung over us; yet at school, paradoxically, we, or at least I (I cannot remember about Kevin), stood high in conduct. And when I went to my weekly confession, I seldom got anything but the very lightest penance—those little Our Fathers and Hail Marys were almost a disappointment to me. As my grandmother must have known, I was a favorite with the parish priests.

My present impression is that my grandparents slowly came to *realize the true situation in our household and that they themselves were on the point of acting when my other grandfather intervened. Looking back, I believe my grandmother was planning to enter me in the Ursuline convent we visited; certainly, that was the hope her behavior on the trip gave rise to. No doubt, they blinded themselves as long as possible, for to admit the truth was to face up to the problem of separating us children and either putting us in schools to board (for which we were really too young) or distributing us among the family (which my aunts and uncles would probably have resisted) or letting the Protestants get some of us. That was what it always came back to. . . .*

My Confession

Fall, 1953

Every age has a keyhole to which its eye is pasted. Spicy court-memoirs, the lives of gallant ladies, recollections of an ex-nun, a monk's confession, an atheist's repentance, true-to-life accounts of prostitution and bastardy gave our ancestors a penny peep into the forbidden rom. In our own day, this type of sensational fact-fiction is being produced largely by ex-Communists. Public curiosity shows an almost prurient avidity for the details of political defloration, and the memoirs of ex-Communists have an odd resemblance to the confessions of a white slave. Two shuddering climaxes, two rendezvous with destiny, form the poles between which these narratives vibrate: the first describes the occasion when the subject was seduced by Communism; the second shows him wresting himself from the demon embrace. Variations on the form are possible. Senator McCarthy, for example, in his book, *McCarthyism, the Fight for America,* uses a tense series of flashbacks to dramatize his encounter with Communism: the country lies passive in Communism's clasp; he is given a tryst with destiny in the lonely Arizona hills, where, surrounded by "real Americans without any synthetic sheen," he attains the decision that will send him down the long marble corridors to the Senate Caucus Room to bare the shameful commerce.

MY CONFESSION. Reprinted from *On the Contrary* by Mary McCarthy, by permission of Farrar, Straus & Giroux, Inc. Copyright, 1953 by Mary McCarthy.

The diapason of choice plays, like movie music, round today's apostle to the Gentiles: Whittaker Chambers on a park bench and, in a reprise, awake all night at a dark window, facing the void. These people, unlike ordinary beings, are shown the true course during a lightning storm of revelation, on the road to Damascus. And their decisions are lonely decisions, silhouetted against a background of public incomprehension and hostility.

I object. I have read the reminiscences of Mr. Chambers and Miss Bentley. I too have had a share in the political movements of our day, and my experience cries out against their experience. It is not the facts I balk at—I have never been an espionage agent—but the studio atmosphere of sublimity and purpose that enfolds the facts and the chief actor. When Whittaker Chambers is mounted on his tractor, or Elizabeth Bentley, alone, is meditating her decision in a white New England church, I have the sense that they are on location and that, at any moment, the director will call "Cut." It has never been like that for me; events have never waited, like extras, while I toiled to make up my mind between good and evil. In fact, I have never known these mental convulsions, which appear quite strange to me when I read about them, even when I do not question the author's sincerity.

Is it really so difficult to tell a good action from a bad one? I think one usually knows right away or a moment afterward, in a horrid flash of regret. And when one genuinely hesitates—or at least it is so in my case—it is never about anything of importance, but about perplexing trivial things, such as whether to have fish or meat for dinner, or whether to take the bus or subway to reach a certain destination, or whether to wear the beige or the green. The "great" decisions—those I can look back on pensively and say, "That was a turning-point"—have been made without my awareness. Too late to do anything about it, I discover that I have chosen. And this is particularly striking when the choice has been political or historic. For me, in fact, the mark of the historic is the nonchalance with which it picks up an individual and deposits him in a trend, like a house playfully moved by a tornado. My own experience with Communism prompts me to relate it, just because it had this inadvertence that seems to me lacking in the true confessions of reformed Communists. Like Stendhal's hero, who took part in something confused and disarrayed and insignificant that he later learned was the Battle of Waterloo, I joined the anti-Communist movement without meaning to and only found out afterward, through others, the meaning or "name" assigned to what I had done. This occurred in the late fall of 1936.

Three years before, I had graduated from college—Vassar, the same college Elizabeth Bentley had gone to—without having suffered any fracture of my political beliefs or moral frame. All through college, my official political philosophy was royalism; though I was not much interested in politics, it irritated me to be told that "you could not turn the clock back." But I did not see much prospect for kingship in the United States (unless you imported one, like the Swedes), and, *faute de mieux*, I awarded my sympathies to the Democratic Party, which I tried to look on as the party of the Southern patriciate. At the same time, I had an aversion to Republicans—an instinctive feeling that had been with me since I was a child of eight pedaling my wagon up and down our cement driveway and howling "Hurray for Cox" at the Republican neighbors who passed by. I disliked businessmen and business attitudes partly, I think, because I came from a professional (though Republican) family and had picked up a disdain for businessmen as being beneath us, in education and general culture. And the anti-Catholic prejudice against Al Smith during the 1928 election, the tinkling amusement at Mrs. Smith's vulgarity, democratized me a little in spite of myself: I was won by Smith's plebeian charm, the big coarse nose, and rubbery politician's smile.

But this same distrust of uniformity made me shrink, in 1932, from the sloppily dressed Socialist girls at college who paraded for Norman Thomas and tirelessly argued over "Cokes"; their eager fellowship and scrawled placards and heavy personalities bored me —there was something, to my mind, deeply athletic about this socialism. It was a kind of political hockey played by big, gaunt, dyspeptic girls in pants. It startled me a little, therefore, to learn that in an election poll taken of the faculty, several of my favorite teachers had voted for Thomas; in them, the socialist faith appeared rather charming, I decided—a gracious and attractive oddity, like the English Ovals they gave you when you came for tea. That was the winter Hitler was coming to power and, hearing of the anti-Jewish atrocities, I had a flurry of political indignation. I wrote a prose-poem that dealt, in a mixed-up way, with the Polish Corridor and the Jews. This poem was so unlike me that I did not know whether to be proud of it or ashamed of it when I saw it in a college magazine. At this period, we were interested in surrealism and automatic writing, and the poem had a certain renown because it had come out of my interior without much sense or order, just the way automatic writing was supposed to do. But there my political development stopped.

The depression was closer to home; in New York I used to see apple-sellers on the street corners, and, now and then, a bread line, but I had a very thin awareness of mass poverty. The depression was too close to home to awaken anything but curiosity and wonder— the feelings of a child confronted with a death in the family. I was conscious of the suicides of stockbrokers and businessmen, and of the fact that some of my friends had to go on scholarships and had their dress allowances curtailed, while their mothers gaily turned to doing their own cooking. To most of us at Vassar, I think, the depression was chiefly an upper-class phenomenon.

My real interests were literary. In a paper for my English Renaissance seminar, I noted a resemblance between the Elizabethan puritan pundits and the school of Marxist criticism that was beginning to pontificate about proletarian literature in the *New Masses*. I disliked the modern fanatics, cold, envious little clerics, equally with the insufferable and ridiculous Gabriel Harvey—Cambridge pedant and friend of Spenser—who tried to introduce the rules of Latin quantity into English verse and vilified a true poet who had died young, in squalor and misery. I really hated absolutism and officiousness of any kind (I preferred my kings martyred) and was pleased to be able to recognize a Zeal-of-the-Land-Busy in proletarian dress. And it was through a novel that I first learned, in my senior year, about the Sacco-Vanzetti case. The discovery that two innocent men had been executed only a few years back while I, oblivious, was in boarding school, gave me a disturbing shock. The case was still so near that I was tantalized by a feeling that it was not too late to do something—try still another avenue, if Governor Fuller and the Supreme Court obdurately would not be moved. An unrectified case of injustice has a terrible way of lingering, restlessly, in the social atmosphere like an unfinished equation. I went on to the Mooney case, which vexed not only my sense of equity but my sense of plausibility—how was it possible for the prosecution to lie so, in broad daylight, with the whole world watching? When in May, 1933, however, before graduation, I went down to apply for a job at the old *New Republic* offices, I was not drawn there by the magazine's editorial policy—I hardly knew what it was—but because the book-review section seemed to me to possess a certain elegance and independence of thought that would be hospitable to a critical spirit like me. And I was badly taken aback when the book-review editor, to whom I had been shunted—there was no job—puffed his pipe and remarked that he would give me a review if I could show him that I was either a genius or starving. "I'm not starving," I said quickly; I knew I was not a genius and I was not pleased by the suggestion that I would be taking bread from other people's mouths. I did not think this a fair criterion and in a moment I said so. In reply, he put down his pipe, shrugged, reached out for the material I had brought with me, and half-promised, after an assaying glance, to send me a book. My notice finally appeared; it was not very good, but I did not know that and was elated. Soon I was reviewing novels and biographies for both the *New Republic* and the *Nation* and preening myself on the connection. Yet, whenever I entered the *New Republic's* waiting room, I was seized with a feeling of nervous guilt toward the shirtsleeved editors upstairs and their busy social conscience, and, above all, toward the shabby young men who were waiting too and who had, my bones told me, a better claim than I to the book I hoped to take away with me. They looked poor, pinched, scholarly, and supercilious, and I did not know which of these qualities made me, with my clicking high heels and fall "ensemble," seem more out of place.

I cannot remember the moment when I ceased to air my old royalist convictions and stuffed them away in an inner closet as you do a dress or an ornament that you perceive strikes the wrong note. It was probably at the time when I first became aware of Communists as a distinct entity. I had known about them, certainly, in college, but it was not until I came to New York that I began to have certain people, celebrities, pointed out to me as Communists and to turn my head to look at them, wonderingly. I had no wish to be one of them, but the fact that they were there—an unreckoned factor —made my own political opinions take on a protective coloration. This process was accelerated by my marriage—a week after graduation—to an actor and playwright who was in some ways very much like me. He was the son of a Minnesota normal school administrator who had been the scapegoat in an academic scandal that had turned him out of his job and reduced him, for a time, when my husband was nine or ten, to selling artificial limbs and encyclopedia sets from door to door. My husband still brooded over his father's misfortune, like Hamlet or a character in Ibsen, and this had given his nature a sardonic twist that inclined him to behave like a paradox —to follow the mode and despise it, live in a Beekman Place apartment while lacking the money to buy groceries, play bridge with society couples and poker with the stage electricians, dress in the English style and carry a walking stick while wearing a red necktie.

He was an odd-looking man, prematurely bald, with a tense, arresting figure, a broken nose, a Standard English accent, and wry, circumflexed eyebrows. There was something about him both baleful and quizzical; whenever he stepped on the stage he had the ironic air of a symbol. This curious appearance of his disqualified him for most Broadway roles; he was too young for character parts and too bald for juveniles. Yet just this disturbing ambiguity—a Communist painter friend did a drawing of him that brought out a resemblance to Lenin—suited the portentous and equivocal atmosphere of left-wing drama. He smiled dryly at Marxist terminology, but there was social anger in him. During the years we were married, the only work he found was in productions of "social" significance. He played for the Theatre Union in *The Sailors of Cattaro*, about a mutiny in the Austrian fleet, and in *Black Pit*, about coal miners; the following year, he was in *Winterset* and Archibald MacLeish's *Panic*—the part of a blind man in both cases. He wrote revue sketches and unproduced plays, in a mocking, despairing, but none the less radical vein; he directed the book of a musical called *Americana* that featured the song, "Brother, Can You Spare a Dime?" I suppose there was something in him of both the victim and the leader, an undertone of totalitarianism; he was very much interested in the mythic qualities of leadership and talked briskly about a Farmer-Labor party in his stage English accent. Notions of the superman and the genius flickered across his thoughts. But this led him, as it happened, away from politics, into sheer personal vitalism, and it was only in plays that he entered "at the head of the mob." In personal life he was very winning, but that is beside the point here.

The point is that we both, through our professional connections, began to take part in a left-wing life, to which we felt superior, which we laughed at, but which nevertheless was influencing us without our being aware of it. If the composition of the body changes every seven years, the composition of our minds during the seven years changed, so that though our thoughts looked the same to us, inside we had been altered, like an old car which has had part after part replaced in it under the hood.

We wore our rue with a difference; we should never have considered joining the Communist Party. We were not even fellow-travelers; we did not sign petitions or join "front" groups. We were not fools, after all, and were no more deceived by the League against War and Fascism, say, than by a Chinatown bus with a car-load of shills aboard. It was part of our metropolitan sophistication to know the truth about Communist fronts. We accepted the need for social reform, but we declined to draw the "logical" inference that the Communists wanted us to draw from this. We argued with the comrades backstage in the dressing rooms and at literary cock-tail parties; I was attacked by a writer in the *New Masses*. We knew about Lovestoneites and Trotskyites, even while we were ignorant of the labor theory of value, the law of uneven development, the theory of permanent revolution *vs.* socialism in one country, and so on. "Lovestone is a Lovestoneite!" John wrote in wax on his dress-ing-room mirror, and on his door in the old Civic Repertory he put up a sign: "Through these portals pass some of the most beautiful tractors in the Ukraine."

The comrades shrugged and laughed, a little unwillingly. They knew we were not hostile but merely unserious, politically. The comrades who knew us best used to assure us that our sophistication was just an armor; underneath, we must care for the same things they did. They were mistaken, I am afraid. Speaking for myself, I cannot remember a single broad altruistic emotion visiting me dur-ing that period—the kind of emotion the simpler comrades, with their shining eyes and exalted faces, seemed to have in copious secre-tion. And yet it was true: we were not hostile. We marched in May Day parades, just for the fun of it, and sang, "Hold the Fort, for We Are Coming," and "*Bandiera Rossa*," and "The Interna-tionale," though we always bellowed "The *Socialist* International shall be the human race," instead of "The International Soviet," to pique the Communists in our squad. We took part in evening clothes in a consumers' walkout at the Waldorf to support a waiters' strike—the Communists had nothing to do with this—and we grew very excited (we did have negative feelings) when another young literary independent was arrested and booked. During a strike at a department store, John joined the sympathetic picketing and saw two of his fellow actors carried off in the Black Maria; they missed a matinee and set off a controversy about what was the *first* responsibility of a Communist playing in a proletarian drama. We went once or twice to a class for actors in Marxism, just to see what was up; we went to a debate on Freud and/or Marx, to a debate on the execution of the hundred and four White Guards following Kirov's assassination.

Most ex-Communists nowadays, when they write their autobiographies or testify before Congressional committees, are at pains to point out that their actions were very, very bad and their motives very, very good. I would say the reverse of myself, though without the intensives. I see no reason to disavow my actions, which were perfectly all right, but my motives give me a little embarrassment, and just because I cannot disavow them: that fevered, contentious, trivial show-off in the May Day parade is still recognizably me.

We went to dances at Webster Hall and took our uptown friends. We went to parties to raise money for the sharecroppers, for the Theatre Union, for the *New Masses*. These parties generally took place in a borrowed apartment, often a sculptor's or commercial artist's studio; you paid for your drinks, which were dispensed at a long, wet table; the liquor was dreadful; the glasses were small, and there was never enough ice. Long-haired men in turtle-necked sweaters marched into the room in processions and threw their overcoats on the floor, against the wall, and sat on them; they were only artists and bit-actors, but they gave these affairs a look of gangsterish menace, as if the room were guarded by the goons of the future. On couches with wrinkled slipcovers, little spiky-haired girls, like spiders, dressed in peasant blouses and carapaced with Mexican jewelry, made voracious passes at baby-faced juveniles; it was said that they "did it for the Party," as a recruiting effort. Vague, soft-faced old women with dust mops of whitish hair wandered benevolently about seeking a listener; on a sofa against a wall, like a deity, sat a bearded scion of an old Boston family, stiff as a post. All of us, generally, became very drunk; the atmosphere was horribly sordid, with cigarette burns on tables, spilled drinks, ashes everywhere, people passed out on the bed with the coats or necking, you could not be sure which. Nobody cared what happened because there was no host or hostess. The fact that a moneyed person had been simple enough to lend the apartment seemed to make the guests want to desecrate it, to show that they were exercising not a privilege but a right.

Obviously, I must have hated these parties, but I went to them, partly because I was ashamed of my own squeamishness, and partly because I had a curiosity about the Communist men I used to see there, not the actors or writers, but the higher-ups, impresarios and theoreticians—dark, smooth-haired owls with large white lugubrious faces and glasses. These were the spiritual directors of the Communist cultural celebrities and they moved about at these parties like so many monks or abbés in a worldly salon. I had always liked to argue with the clergy, and I used to argue with these men, who had the air, as they stood with folded arms, of listening not to a disagreement but to a confession. Whenever I became tight, I would bring up (oh, *vino veritas*) the Czar and his family. I did not see why they all had had to be killed—the Czar himself, yes, perhaps, and the Czarina, but not the young girls and the children. I knew the answer, of course (the young Czarevitch or one of his sisters might have served as a rallying point for the counter-revolutionary forces), but still I gazed hopefully into these docents' faces, seeking a trace of scruple or compassion. But I saw only a marmoreal astuteness. The question was of bourgeois origin, they said with finality.

The next morning I was always bitterly ashamed. I had let these omniscient men see the real me underneath, and the other me squirmed and gritted her teeth and muttered, Never, never, *never* again. And yet they had not convinced me—there was the paradox. The superiority I felt to the Communists I knew had, for me at any rate, good grounding; it was based on their lack of humor, their fanaticism, and the slow drip of cant that thickened their utterance like a nasal catarrh. *And yet* I was tremendously impressed by them. They made me feel petty and shallow; they had, shall I say, a daily ugliness in their life that made my pretty life tawdry. I think all of us who moved in that ambience must have felt something of the kind, even while we laughed at them. When John and I, for instance, would say of a certain actor, "He is a Party member," our voices always contained a note of respect. This respect might be mixed with pity, as when we saw some blue-eyed young profile, fresh from his fraternity and his C average, join up because a sleazy girl had persuaded him. The literary Communists I sincerely despised because I was able to judge the quality of the work they published and see their dishonesty and contradictions; even so, when I beheld them in person, at a Webster Hall dance, I was troubled and felt perhaps I had wronged them—perhaps there was something in them that my vision could not perceive, as some eyes cannot perceive color.

People sometimes say that they envied the Communists because they were so "sure." In my case, this was not exactly it; I was sure, too, intellectually speaking, as far as I went. That is, I had a clear mind and was reasonably honest, while many of the Communists I knew were pathetically fogged up. In any case, my soul was not particularly hot for certainties.

And yet in another way I did envy the Communists, or, to be more accurate, wonder whether I ought to envy them. I could not, I saw, be a Communist because I was not "made that way." Hence, to be a Communist was to possess a sort of privilege. And this privilege, like all privileges, appeared to be a source of power. Any form of idiocy or aberration can confer this distinction on its owner, at least in our age, which aspires to a "total" experience; in the thirties it was the Communists who seemed fearsomely to be the happy few, not because they had peace or certitude but because they were a mutation—a mutation that threatened, in the words of their own anthem, to become the human race.

There was something arcane in every Communist, and the larger this area was the more we respected him. That was why the literary Communists, who operated in the open, doing the hatchet work on artists' reputations, were held in such relatively low esteem. An underground worker rated highest with us; next were the theoreticians and oracles; next were the activists, who mostly worked, we heard, on the waterfront. Last came the rank and file, whose work consisted of making speeches, distributing leaflets, attending Party and faction meetings, joining front organizations, marching in parades and demonstrations. These people we dismissed as uninteresting not so much because their work was routine but because the greater part of it was visible. In the same way, among individual comrades, we looked up to those who were close-lipped and stern about their beliefs and we disparaged the more voluble members—the forensic little actors who tried to harangue us in the dressing rooms. The idea of a double life was what impressed us: the more talkative

comrades seemed to have only one life, like us; but even they, we
had to remind ourselves, had a secret annex to their personality,
which was signified by their Party name. It is hard not to respect
somebody who has an alias.

Of fellow-travelers, we had a very low opinion. People who were
not willing to "go the whole way" filled us with impatient disdain. The only fellow-travelers who merited our notice were those
of whom it was said: the Party prefers that they remain on the outside. I think some fellow-travelers circulated such stories about themselves deliberately, in order to appear more interesting. There was
another type of fellow-traveler who let it be known that they
stayed out of the Party because of some tiny doctrinal difference
with Marxism. This tiny difference magnified them enormously in
their own eyes and allowed them to bear gladly the accusation of
cowardice. I knew one such person very well—a spruce, ingratiating
swain, the heir to a large fortune—and I think it was not cowardice
but a kind of pietistic vanity. He felt he cut more of a figure if he
seemed to be doing the Party's dirty work gratuitously, without
compulsion, like an oblate.

In making these distinctions (which were the very distinctions
the Party made), I had no idea, of course, that I was allowing myself to be influenced by the Party in the field where I was most open
to suasion—the field of social snobbery. Yet in fact I was being de-
terred from forming any political opinions of my own, lest I find I
was that despised article, a "mere" socialist or watery liberal, in the
same way that a young snob coming to college and seeing who the
"right" people are will strive to make no friends rather than be
caught with the wrong ones.

For me, the Communist Party was *the* party, and even though I
did not join it, I prided myself on knowing that it was the pinnacle.
It is only now that I see the social component in my attitude. At the
time I simply supposed that I was being clear-sighted and logical.
I used to do research and typing for a disgruntled middle-aged man
who was a freak for that day—an anti-Communist Marxist—and I
was bewildered by his anti-Party bias. While we were drinking
hot tea, Russian style, from glasses during the intervals of our work,
I would try to show him his mistake. "Don't you think it's rather
futile," I expostulated, "to criticize the Party the way you do, from
the outside? After all, it's the *only* working-class Party, and if *I*
were a Marxist I would join it and try to reform it." Snorting, he

would raise his small deep-set blue eyes and stare at me and then try patiently to show me that there was no democracy in the Party. I listened disbelievingly. It seemed to me that it would just be a question of converting first one comrade and then another to your point of view till gradually you had achieved a majority. And when my employer assured me that they would throw you out if you tried that, my twenty-three-year-old wisdom cocked an eyebrow. I thought I knew what was the trouble: he was a pathologically lazy man and his growling criticisms of the Party were simply a form of malingering, like the aches and pains he used to manufacture to avoid working on an article. A real revolutionary who was not afraid of exertion would get into the Party and fight.

The curious idea that being critical of the Party was a compelling reason for joining it must have been in the air, for the same argument was brought to bear on me in the summer of 1936—the summer my husband and I separated and that I came close to the gravitational pull of the Communist world. Just before I went off to Reno, there was a week in June when I stayed in Southampton with the young man I was planning to marry and a little Communist organizer in an old summer house furnished with rattan and wicker and Chinese matting and mother-of-pearl and paper fans. We had come there for a purpose. The little organizer had just been assigned a car—a battered old Ford roadster that had been turned over to the Party for the use of some poor organizer; it may have been the very car that figured in the Hiss case. My fiancé, who had known him for years, perhaps from the peace movement, was going to teach him to drive. We were all at a pause in our lives. The following week our friend was supposed to take the car to California and do propaganda work among the migrant fruit-pickers; I was to go to Reno; my fiancé, a vivacious young bachelor, was to conquer his habits of idleness and buckle down to a serious job. Those seven days, therefore, had a special, still quality, like the days of a novena you make in your childhood; a part of each of them was set aside for the Party's task. It was early in June; the musty house that belonged to my fiancé's parents still had the winter-smell of mice and old wood and rust and mildew. The summer colony had not yet arrived; the red flag, meaning that it was dangerous to swim, flew daily on the beach; the roads were nearly empty. Every afternoon we would take the old car, canvas flapping, to a deserted stretch of straight road in the dunes, where the neophyte could take the wheel.

He was a large-browed, dwarfish man in his late thirties, with a deep widow's peak, a bristly short mustache, and a furry western accent—rather simple, open-natured, and cheerful, the sort of person who might have been a small-town salesman or itinerant news-paperman. There was an energetic, hopeful innocence about him that was not confined to his political convictions—he could *not* learn to drive. Every day the same thing happened; he would settle his frail yet stocky figure trustingly in the driver's seat, grip the wheel, step on the starter, and lose control of the car, which would shoot ahead in first or backward in reverse for a few perilous feet till my fiancé turned off the ignition; Ansel always mistook the gas for the brake and forgot to steer while he was shifting gears.

It was clear that he would never be able to pass the driver's test at the county seat. In the evenings, to make up to him for his oncom-ing disappointment (we smiled when he said he could start with-out a license), we encouraged him to talk about the Party and tried to take an intelligent interest. We would sit by the lamp and drink and ask questions, while he smoked his short pipe and from time to time took a long draught from his highball, like a man alone musing in a chair.

And finally one night, in the semi-dark, he knocked out his pipe and said to me: "You're very critical of the Party. Why don't you join it?" A thrill went through me, but I laughed, as when some-body has proposed to you and you are not sure whether they are serious. "I don't think I'd make very good material." "You're wrong," he said gravely. "You're just the kind of person the Party needs. You're young and idealistic and independent." I broke in: "I thought independence was just what the Party didn't want." "The Party needs criticism," he said. "But it needs it from the inside. If people like you who agree with its main objectives would come in and criticize, we wouldn't be so narrow and sectarian." "You admit the Party is narrow?" exclaimed my fiancé. "Sure, I admit it," said Ansel, grinning. "But it's partly the fault of people like Mary who won't come in and broaden us." And he confided that he himself made many of the same criticisms I did, but he made them from within the Party, and so could get himself listened to. "The big problem of the American Party," said Ansel, puffing at his pipe, "is the smallness of the membership. People say we're ruled from Moscow; I've never seen any sign of it. But let's suppose it's true, for the sake of argument. This just means that the American Party isn't big enough yet to stand on its own feet. A big, indigenous party couldn't be ruled from Moscow. The will of the members would have to rule it, just as their dues and contributions would support it." "That's where I come in, I suppose?" I said, teasing. "That's where you come in," he calmly agreed. He turned to my fiancé. "Not you," he said. "You won't have the time to give to it. But for Mary I think it would be an interesting experiment."

An interesting experiment . . . I let the thought wander through my mind. The subject recurred several times, by the lamplight, though with no particular urgency. Ansel, I thought (and still think), was speaking sincerely and partly in my own interest, almost as a spectator, as if he would be diverted to see how I worked out in the Party. All this gave me quite a new sense of Communism and of myself too; I had never looked upon my character in such a favorable light. And as a beneficiary of Ansel's charity, I felt somewhat ashamed of the very doubt it raised: the suspicion that he might be blind to the real facts of inner Party life. I could admire where I could not follow, and, studying Ansel, I decided that I admired the Communists and would probably be one, if I were the person he thought me. Which I was afraid I was not. For me, such a wry conclusion is always uplifting, and I had the feeling that I mounted in understanding when Sunday morning came and I watched Ansel pack his sturdy suitcase and his briefcase full of leaflets into the old roadster. He had never yet driven more than a few yards by himself, and we stood on the front steps to await what was going to happen: he would not be able to get out of the driveway, and we would have to put him on the train and return the car to the Party when we came back to New York. As we watched, the car began to move; it picked up speed and grated into second, holding to the middle of the road as it turned out of the driveway. It hesitated and went into third: Ansel was driving! Through the back window we saw his figure hunched over the wheel; the road dipped and he vanished. We had witnessed a miracle, and we turned back into the house, frightened. All day we sat waiting for the call that would tell us there had been an accident, but the day passed without a sound, and by nightfall we accepted the phenomenon and pictured the little car on the highway, traveling steadily west in one indefatigable thrust, not daring to stop for gas or refreshment, lest the will of the driver falter.

This parting glimpse of Ansel through the car's back window was, as it turned out, ultimate. Politically speaking, we reached a watershed that summer. The first Moscow trial took place in August. I knew nothing of this event because I was in Reno and did not see the New York papers. Nor did I know that the Party line had veered to the right and that all the fellow-travelers would be voting, not for Browder as I was now prepared to do (if only I remembered to register), but for Roosevelt. Isolated from these developments in the mountain altitudes, I was blossoming, like a lone winter rose overlooked by the frost, into a revolutionary thinker of the pure, uncompromising strain. The detached particles of the past three years' experience suddenly "made sense," and I saw myself as a radical.

"Book Bites Mary," wrote back a surprised literary editor when I sent him, from Reno, a radiant review of a novel about the Paris Commune that ended with the heroine sitting down to read the *Communist Manifesto*. In Seattle, when I came to stay with my grandparents, I found a strike on and instantly wired the *Nation* to ask if I could cover it. Every night I was off to the Labor Temple or a longshoreman's hall while my grandparents took comfort from the fact that I seemed to be against Roosevelt, the Democrats, and the Czars of the A. F. of L.—they did not quite grasp my explanation, that I was criticizing "from the left."

Right here, I come up against a puzzle: why didn't I take the *next step*? But it is only a puzzle if one thinks of me not as a concrete entity but as a term in a logical operation: you agree with the Communist Party; *ergo*, you join it. I reasoned that way but I did not behave so. There was something in me that capriciously resisted being a term in logic, and the very fact that I cannot elicit any specific reason why I did not join the Party shows that I was never really contemplating it, though I can still hear my own voice, raised very authoritatively at a cafeteria table at the Central Park Zoo, pointing out to a group of young intellectuals that if we were serious we would join the Communists.

This was in September and I was back in New York. The Spanish Civil War had begun. The pay-as-you-go parties were now all for the Loyalists, and young men were volunteering to go and fight in

Spain. I read the paper every morning with tears of exaltation in my eyes, and my sympathies rained equally on Communists, Socialists, Anarchists, and the brave Catholic Basques. My heart was tense and swollen with popular-front solidarity. I applauded the Lincoln Battalion, protested non-intervention, hurried into Wanamaker's to look for cotton-lace stockings: I was boycotting silk on account of Japan in China. I was careful to smoke only union-made cigarettes; the white package with Sir Walter Raleigh's portrait came proudly out of my pocketbook to rebuke Chesterfields and Luckies.

It was a period of intense happiness; the news from the battlefront was often encouraging and the practice of virtue was surprisingly easy. I moved into a one-room apartment on a crooked street in Greenwich Village and exulted in being poor and alone. I had a part-time job and read manuscripts for a publisher; the very riskness of my situation was zestful—I had decided not to get married. The first month or so was scarifyingly lonely, but I survived this, and, starting early in November, I began to feel the first stirrings of popularity. A new set of people, rather smart and moneyed, young Communists with a little "name," progressive hosts and modernist hostesses, had discovered me. The fact that I was poor and lived in such a funny little apartment increased the interest felt: I was passed from hand to hand, as a novelty, like Gulliver among the Brobdingnagians. During those first days in November, I was chiefly conscious of what a wonderful time I was starting to have. All this while, I had remained ignorant of the fissure that was opening. Nobody, I think, had told me of the trial of Zinoviev and Kamenev—the trial of the sixteen—or of the new trial that was being prepared in Moscow, the trial of Pyatakov and Radek.

Then, one afternoon in November, I was taken to a cocktail party, in honor of Art Young, the old *Masses* cartoonist, whose book, *The Best of Art Young*, was being published that day. It was the first publisher's party I had ever been to, and my immediate sensation was one of disappointment: nearly all these people were strangers and, to me, quite unattractive. Art Young, a white-haired little kewpie, sitting in a corner, was pointed out to me, and I turned a respectful gaze on him, though I had no clear idea who he was or how he had distinguished himself. I presumed he was a veteran Communist, like a number of the stalwarts in the room, survivors of the old *Masses* and the *Liberator*. Their names were whispered to me and I nodded; this seemed to be a commemorative occasion, and the young men hovered in groups around the old men, as if to catch a word for posterity. On the outskirts of certain groups I noticed a few poorly dressed young men, bolder spirits, nervously flexing their lips, framing sentences that would propel them into the conversational center, like actors with a single line to speak.

The solemnity of these proceedings made me feel terribly ill at ease. It was some time before I became aware that it was not just me who was nervous: the whole room was under a constraint. Some groups were avoiding other groups, and now and then an arrow of sarcasm would wing like a sniper's bullet from one conversation to another.

I was standing, rather bleakly, by the refreshment table, when a question was thrust at me: did I think Trotsky was entitled to a hearing? It was a novelist friend of mine, dimple-faced, shaggy-headed, earnest, with a whole train of people, like a deputation, behind him. Trotsky? I glanced for help at a sour little man I had been talking with, but he merely shrugged. My friend made a beckoning gesture and a circle closed in. What had Trotsky done? Alas, I had to ask. A tumult of voices proffered explanations. My friend raised a hand for silence. Leaning on the table, he supplied the background, speaking very slowly, in his dragging, disconsolate voice, like a schoolteacher wearied of his subject. Trotsky, it appeared, had been accused of fostering a counter-revolutionary plot in the Soviet Union—organizing terrorist centers and conspiring with the Gestapo to murder the Soviet leaders. Sixteen old Bolsheviks had confessed and implicated him. It had been in the press since August.

I blushed; everybody seemed to be looking at me strangely. I made a violent effort to take in what had been said. The enormity of the charge dazed me, and I supposed that some sort of poll was being taken and that I was being asked to pronounce on whether Trotsky was guilty or innocent. I could tell from my friend's low, even, melancholy tone that he regarded the charges as derisory. "What do you want me to say?" I protested. "I don't know anything about it." "Trotsky denies the charges," patiently intoned my friend. "He declares it's a GPU fabrication. Do you think he's entitled to a hearing?" My mind cleared. "Why, of course." I laughed—were there people who would say that Trotsky was *not* entitled to a hearing? But my friend's voice tolled a rebuke to this levity. "She says Trotsky is entitled to his day in court."

The sour little man beside me made a peculiar, sucking noise. "You disagree?" I demanded, wonderingly. "I'm smart," he retorted. "I don't let anybody ask me. You notice, he doesn't ask me?" "Shut up, George," said my novelist friend impatiently. "I'm asking *her*. One thing more, Mary," he continued gravely. "Do you believe that Trotsky should have the right of asylum?" The right of asylum! I looked for someone to share my amusement—were we in ancient Greece or the Middle Ages? I was sure the U.S. government would be delighted to harbor such a distinguished foreigner. But nobody smiled back. Everybody watched dispassionately, as for form's sake I assented to the phrasing: yes, Trotsky, in my opinion, was entitled to the right of asylum.

I went home with the serene feeling that all these people were slightly crazy. *Right of asylum, his day in court!*—in a few hours I had forgotten the whole thing.

Four days later I tore open an envelope addressed to me by something that called itself "Committee for the Defense of Leon Trotsky," and idly scanned the contents. "We demand for Leon Trotsky the right of a fair hearing and the right of asylum." Who were these demanders, I wondered, and, glancing down the letterhead, I discovered my own name. I sat down on my unmade studio couch, shaking. How dared they help themselves to my signature? This was the kind of thing the Communists were always being accused of pulling; apparently, Trotsky's admirers had gone to the same school. I had paid so little heed to the incident at the party that a connection was slow to establish itself. Reading over the list of signers, I recognized "names" that had been present there and remembered my novelist-friend going from person to person, methodically polling. . . .

How were they feeling, I wondered, when they opened their mail this morning? My own feelings were crisp. In two minutes I had decided to withdraw my name and write a note of protest. Trotsky had a right to a hearing, but I had a right to my signature. For even if there had been a legitimate misunderstanding (it occurred to me that perhaps I had been the only person there not to see the import of my answers), nothing I had said committed me to Trotsky's *defense*.

The "decision" was made, but according to my habit I procrastinated. The severe letter I proposed to write got put off till the next day and then the next. Probably I was not eager to offend somebody who had been a good friend to me. Nevertheless, the letter would undoubtedly have been written, had I been left to myself. But within the next forty-eight hours the phone calls began. People whom I had not seen for months or whom I knew very slightly telephoned to advise me to get off the newly formed Committee. These calls were not precisely threatening. Indeed, the caller often sounded terribly weak and awkward, as if he did not like the mission he had been assigned. But they were peculiar. For one thing, they usually came after nightfall and sometimes quite late, when I was already in bed. Another thing, there was no real effort at persuasion: the caller stated his purpose in standardized phrases, usually plaintive in tone (the Committee was the tool of reaction, and all liberal people should dissociate themselves from its activities, which were an unwarranted intervention in the domestic affairs of the Soviet Union), and then hung up, almost immediately, before I had a proper chance to answer. Odd too—the voices were not those of my Communist friends but of the merest acquaintances. These people who admonished me to "think about it" were not people whose individual opinions could have had any weight with me. And when I did think about it, this very fact took on an ominous and yet to me absurd character: I was not being appealed to personally but impersonally warned.

Behind these phone calls there was a sense of the Party wheeling its forces into would-be disciplined formations, like a fleet or an army maneuvering. This, I later found, was true: a systematic telephone campaign was going on to dislodge members from the Committee. The phone calls generally came after dark and sometimes (especially when the recipient was elderly) in the small hours of the morning. The more prominent signers got anonymous messages and threats.

And in the morning papers and the columns of the liberal magazines I saw the results. During the first week, name after name fell off the Committee's letterhead. Prominent liberals and literary figures issued statements deploring their mistake. And a number of people protested that their names had been used without permission. . . .

There, but for the grace of God, went I, I whispered, awestruck, to myself, hugging my guilty knowledge. Only Heaven—I plainly saw—by making me dilatory had preserved me from joining this sorry band. Here was the occasion when I should have been wrestling with my conscience or standing, floodlit, at the crossroads of choice. But in fact I was only aware that I had had a providential escape. I had been saved from having to decide about the Committee; *I* did not decide it—the Communists with their pressure tactics took the matter out of my hands. We all have an instinct that makes us side with the weak, if we do not stop to reason about it, the instinct that makes a householder shield a wounded fugitive without first conducting an inquiry into the rights and wrongs of his case. Such "decisions" are simple reflexes; they do not require courage; if they did, there would be fewer of them. When I saw what was happening, I rebounded to the defense of the Committee without a single hesitation—it was nobody's business, I felt, how I happened to be on it, and if anybody had asked me, I should have lied without a scruple.

Of course, I did not foresee the far-reaching consequences of my act—how it would change my life. I had no notion that I was now an anti-Communist, where before I had been either indifferent or pro-Communist. I did, however, soon recognize that I was in a rather awkward predicament—not a moral quandary but a social one. I knew nothing about the cause I had espoused; I had never read a word of Lenin or Trotsky, nothing of Marx but the *Communist Manifesto*, nothing of Soviet history; the very names of the old Bolsheviks who had confessed were strange and almost barbarous in my ears. As for Trotsky, the only thing that made me think that he might be innocent was the odd behavior of the Communists and the fellow-traveling liberals, who seemed to be infuriated at the idea of a free inquiry. All around me, in the fashionable Stalinist circles I was now frequenting, I began to meet with suppressed excitement and just-withheld disapproval. Jeweled lady-authors turned white and shook their bracelets angrily when I came into a soirée; rising young men in publishing or advertising tightened their neckties dubiously when I urged them to examine the case for themselves; out dancing in a night club, tall, collegiate young Party members would press me to their shirt-bosoms and tell me not to be silly, honey.

And since I seemed to meet more Stalinists every day, I saw that I was going to have to get some arguments with which to defend myself. It was not enough, apparently, to say you were for a fair hearing; you had to rebut the entire case of the prosecution to get anybody to incline an ear in your direction. I began to read, headlong, the literature on the case—the pamphlets issued by Trotsky's adherents, the verbatim report of the second trial published by the Soviet Union, the "bourgeois" press, the Communist press, the radical press. To my astonishment (for I had scarcely dared think it), the trials did indeed seem to be a monstrous frame-up. The defendant, Pyatakov, flew to Oslo to "conspire" with Trotsky during a winter when, according to the authorities, no planes landed at the Oslo airfield; the defendant, Holtzmann, met Trotsky's son, Sedov, in 1936, at the Hotel Bristol in Copenhagen, which had burned down in 1912; the witness, Romm, met Trotsky in Paris at a time when numerous depositions testified that he had been in Royan, among clouds of witnesses, or on the way there from the south of France.

These were only the most glaring discrepancies—the ones that got in the newspapers. Everywhere you touched the case something crumbled. The carelessness of the case's manufacture was to me its most terrifying aspect; the slovenly disregard for credibility defied credence, in its turn. How did they dare? I think I was more shaken by finding that I was on the right side than I would have been the other way round. And yet, except for a very few people, nobody seemed to mind whether the Hotel Bristol had burned down or not, whether a real plane had landed, whether Trotsky's life and writings were congruent with the picture given of him in the trials. When confronted with the facts of the case, people's minds sheered off from it like jelly from a spoon.

Anybody who has ever tried to rectify an injustice or set a record straight comes to feel that he is going mad. And from a social point of view, he *is* crazy, for he is trying to undo something that is finished, to unravel the social fabric. That is why my liberal friends looked so grave and solemn when I would press them to come to a meeting and listen to a presentation of the facts—for them this was a Decision, too awful to be considered lightly. The Moscow trials were a historical fact and those of us who tried to undo them were uneasily felt to be crackpots, who were trying to turn the clock back. And of course the less we were listened to, the more insistent and earnest we became, even while we realized we were doing our cause harm. It is impossible to take a moderate tone under such conditions. If I admitted, though, to being a little bit hipped on the subject of Trotsky, I could sometimes gain an indulgent if flickering attention—the kind of attention that stipulates, "She's a bit off but let's hear her story." And now and then, by sheer chance, one of my hearers would be arrested by some stray point in my narrative; the disparaging smile would slowly fade from his features, leaving a look of blank consternation. He would go off and investigate for himself, and in a few days, when we met again, he would be a crackpot too.

Most of us who became anti-Communists at the time of the trials were drawn in, like me, by accident and almost unwillingly. Looking back, as on a love affair, a man could say that if he had not had lunch in a certain restaurant on a certain day, he might not have been led to ponder the facts of the Moscow trials. Or not then at any rate. And had he pondered them at a later date, other considerations would have entered and his conversion would have had a different style. On the whole, those of us who became anti-Communists during that year, 1936–37, have remained liberals—a thing that is less true of people of our generation who were converted earlier or later. A certain doubt of orthodoxy and independence of mass opinion was riveted into our anti-Communism by the heat of that period. As soon as I make this statement, exceptions leap into my mind, but I think as a generalization it will stand. Those who became anti-Communist earlier fell into two classes: the experts and those to whom any socialist ideal was repugnant. Those whose eyes were opened later, by the Nazi-Soviet pact, or still later, by God knows what, were left bruised and full of self-hatred or self-commiseration, because they had palliated so much and truckled to a power-center; to them, Communism's chief sin seems to be that it deceived *them*, and their public atonement takes on both a vindicating and a vindictive character.

We were luckier. Our anti-Communism came to us neither as the fruit of a special wisdom nor as a humiliating awakening from a prolonged deception, but as a natural event, the product of chance and propinquity. One thing followed another, and the will had little to say about it. For my part, during that year, I realized, with a certain wistfulnes, that it was too late for me to become any kind of Marxist. Marxism, I saw, from the learned young men I listened to at Committee meetings, was something you had to take up young, like ballet dancing.

So, I did not try to be a Marxist or a Trotskyite, though for the first time I read a little in the Marxist canon. But I got the name of being a Trotskyite, which meant, in the end, that I saw less of the conventional Stalinists I had been mingling with and less of conventional people generally. (My definition of a conventional person was quite broad: it included anyone who could hear of the Moscow trials and maintain an unruffled serenity.) This, then, was a break or a rupture, not very noticeable at first, that gradually widened and widened, without any conscious effort on my part, sometimes to my regret. This estrangement was not marked by any definite stages; it was a matter of tiny choices. Shortly after the Moscow trials, for instance, I changed from the *Herald Tribune* to the *Times;* soon I had stopped doing crossword puzzles, playing bridge, reading detective stories and popular novels. I did not "give up" these things; they departed from me, as it were, on tiptoe, seeing that my thoughts were elsewhere.

To change from the *Herald Tribune* to the *Times*, is not, I am aware, as serious a step as breaking with international Communism when you have been its agent; and it occurs to me that Mr. Chambers and Miss Bentley might well protest the comparison, pointing out that they were profoundly dedicated people, while I was a mere trifler, that their decisions partook of the sublime, where mine descended to the ridiculous—as Mr. Chambers says, he was ready to give his life for his beliefs. Fortunately (though I could argue the point, for we all give our lives for our beliefs, piecemeal or whole), I have a surprise witness to call for my side, who did literally die for his political views.

I am referring to Trotsky, the small, frail, pertinacious old man who wore whiskers, wrinkles, glasses, shock of grizzled hair, like a gleeful disguise for the erect young student, the dangerous revolutionary within him. Nothing could be more alien to the convulsed and tormented moonscapes of the true confessions of ex-Communists than Trotsky's populous, matter-of-fact recollections set out in *My Life*. I have just been rereading this volume, and though I no longer subscribe to its views, which have certainly an authoritarian and doctrinaire cast that troubles me today, nevertheless I experience a sense of recognition here that I cannot find in the pages of our own repentant "revolutionaries." The old man remained unregenerate; he never admitted that he had sinned. That is probably why nobody seems to care for, or feel apologetic to, his memory. It is an interesting point—and relevant, I think, to my story—that many people today actually have the impression that Trotsky died a natural death.

In a certain sense, this is perfectly true. I do not mean that he lived by violence and therefore might reasonably be expected to die by violence. He was a man of words primarily, a pamphleteer and orator. He was armed, as he said, with a pen and peppered his enemies with a fusillade of articles. Hear the concluding passages of his autobiography: "Since my exile, I have more than once read musings in the newspapers on the subject of the 'tragedy' that has befallen me. I know no *personal* tragedy. I know the change of two chapters of revolution. One American paper which published an article of mine accompanied it with a profound note to the effect that in spite of the blows the author had suffered, he had, as evidenced by his article, preserved his clarity of reason. I can only express my astonishment at the Philistine attempt to establish a connection between the power of reasoning and a government post, between mental balance and the present situation. I do not know, and never have known, of any such connection. In prison, with a book or pen in my hand, I experienced the same sense of deep satisfaction that I did at mass-meetings of the revolution. I felt the mechanics of power as an inescapable burden, rather than as a spiritual satisfaction."

This was not a man of violence. Nevertheless, one can say that he died a natural death—a death that was in keeping with the open manner of his life. There was nothing arcane in Trotsky; that was his charm. Like an ordinary person he was hospitably open to hazard and accident. In his autobiography, he cannot date the moment when he became a socialist.

One factor in his losing out in the power-struggle at the time of Lenin's death was his delay in getting the telegram that should have called him home from the Caucasus, where he was convalescent, to appear at Lenin's funeral—*had* he got the telegram, the outcome perhaps would have been different. Or again, perhaps not. It may be that the whims of chance are really the importunities of design. But if there is a Design, it aims, in real lives, like the reader's or mine or Trotsky's, to look natural and fortuitous; that is how it gets us into its web.

Trotsky himself, looking at his life in retrospect, was struck, as most of us are on such occasions, by the role chance had played in it. He tells how one day, during Lenin's last illness, he went duck-shooting with an old hunter in a canoe on the River Dubna, walked through a bog in felt boots—only a hundred steps—and contracted influenza. This was the reason he was ordered to Sukhu for the cure, missed Lenin's funeral, and had to stay in bed during the struggle for primacy that raged that autumn and winter. "I cannot help noting," he says, "how obligingly the accidental helps the historical law. Broadly speaking, the entire historical process is a refraction of historical law through the accidental. In the language of biology, one might say that the historical law is realized through the natural selection of accidents." And with a touch of quizzical gaiety he sums up the problem as a Marxian: "One can foresee the consequences of a revolution or a war, but it is impossible to foresee the consequences of an autumn shooting-trip for wild ducks." This shrug before the unforeseen implies an acceptance of consequences that is a far cry from penance and prophecy. Such, it concedes, is life. *Bravo,* old sport, I say, even though the hall is empty.

J. D. Salinger's Closed Circuit

Who is to inherit the mantle of Papa Hemingway? Who if not J. D. Salinger? Holden Caulfield in *The Catcher in the Rye* has a brother in Hollywood who thinks *A Farewell to Arms* is terrific. Holden does not see how his brother, who is *his* favorite writer, can like a phony book like that. But the very image of the hero as pitiless phony-detector comes from Hemingway. In *Across the River and Into the Trees,* the colonel gets a message on his private radar that a pock-marked writer he darkly spies across the room at Harry's Bar in Venice has "outlived his talents"—apparently some sort of crime. "I think he has the same pits on his heart and in his soul," confides the heroine, in her careful foreign English. That was Sinclair Lewis.

Like Hemingway, Salinger sees the world in terms of allies and enemies. He has a good deal of natural style, a cruel ear, a dislike of ideas (the enemy's intelligence system), a toilsome simplicity, and a ventriloquist's knack of disguising his voice. The artless dialect writ-

J. D. SALINGER'S CLOSED CIRCUIT. From *Harper's,* October, 1962. By Mary McCarthy. Reprinted by permission of Miss McCarthy.

ten by Holden is an artful ventriloquial trick of Salinger's, like the deliberate, halting English of Hemingway's waiters, fishermen, and peasants—anyone who speaks it is a good guy, a friend of the author's, to be trusted.

The Catcher in the Rye, like Hemingway's books, is based on a scheme of exclusiveness. The characters are divided into those who belong to the club and those who don't—the clean marlin, on the one hand, and the scavenger sharks on the other. Those who don't belong are "born that way"—headmasters, philanthropists, roommates, teachers of history and English, football coaches, girls who like the Lunts. They cannot help the way they are, the way they talk; they are obeying a law of species—even the pimping elevator operator, the greedy prostitute, the bisexual teacher of English who makes an approach to Holden in the dark.

It is not anybody's fault if just about everybody is excluded from the club in the long run—everybody but Ring Lardner, Thomas Hardy, Gatsby, Isak Dinesen, and Holden's little sister Phoebe. In fact it is a pretty sad situation, and there is a real adolescent sadness and lonely desperation in The Catcher in the Rye; the passages where Holden, drunk and wild with grief, wanders like an errant pinball through New York at night are very good.

But did Salinger sympathize with Holden or vice versa? That remained dubious. Stephen Dedalus in a similar situation met Mr. Bloom, but the only "good" person Holden meets is his little sister —himself in miniature or in apotheosis, riding a big brown horse on a carousel and reaching for the gold ring. There is something false and sentimental here. Holden is supposed to be an outsider in his school, in the middle-class world, but he is really an insider with the track all to himself.

And now, ten years after The Catcher in the Rye we have Franny and Zooey.[1] The event was commemorated by a cover story in Time; the book has been a best-seller since before publication.

Again the theme is the good people against the stupid phonies, and the good is still all in the family, like a family-owned "closed" corporation. The heroes are or were seven children (two are dead), the wonderful Glass kids of a radio quiz show called "It's a Wise Child," half-Jewish, half-Irish, the progeny of a team of vaudevillians. These prodigies, nationally known and the subjects of many psychological studies, are now grown up: one is a writer-in-

[1] By J. D. Salinger. Boston, Little, Brown, $4.

residence in a girls' junior college; one is a Jesuit priest; one is a housewife; one is a television actor (Zooey); and one is a student (Franny). They are all geniuses, but the greatest genius of them all was Seymour, who committed suicide on vacation in an early story of Salinger's called "A Perfect Day for Bananafish." Unlike the average genius, the Glass kids are good guys; they love each other and their parents and their cat and their goldfish, and they are expert phony-detectors. The dead sage Seymour has initiated them into Zen and other mystical cults.

During the course of the story, Franny has a little nervous breakdown, brought on by reading a small green religious book titled *The Way of a Pilgrim*, relating the quest for prayer of a simple Russian peasant. She is cured by her brother Zooey in two short séances between his professional television appointments; he recognizes the book (it was in Seymour's library, of course) and, on his own inspiration, without help from their older brother Buddy or from the Jesuit, teaches her that Jesus, whom she has been sweating to find via the Jesus Prayer, is not some fishy *guru* but just the Fat Lady in the audience, the average ordinary humanity with varicose veins, the you and me the performer has to reach if the show is going to click.

THE ADMISSIONS POLICY

This democratic commercial is "sincere" in the style of an advertising man's necktie. The Jesus Zooey sells his sister is the old Bruce Barton Jesus—the word made flesh, Madison Avenue's motto. The Fat Lady is not quite everybody, despite Zooey's fast sales patter. She is the kind of everybody the wonderful Glass kids tolerantly approve of. Jesus may be a television sponsor or a housewife or a television playwright or your Mother and Dad, but He (he?) cannot be an intellectual like Franny's horrible boyfriend, Lane, who has written a paper on Flaubert and talks about Flaubert's "testicularity," or like his friend Wally, who, as Franny says plaintively, "looks like somebody who spent the summer in Italy or someplace."

These fakes and phonies are the outsiders who ruin everything. Zooey feels the same way. "I hate any kind of so-called creative type who gets on any kind of ship. I don't give a goddam what his reasons are." Zooey likes it here. He likes people, as he says, who wear horrible neckties and funny, padded suits, but he does not mind a man who dresses well and owns a two-cabin cruiser so long as he belongs to the real, native, video-viewing America. The wonderful Glass family have three radios, four portable phonographs, and a TV in their wonderful living-room, and their wonderful, awesome medicine cabinet in the bathroom is full of sponsored products all of which have been loved by someone in the family.

The world of insiders, it would appear, has grown infinitely larger and more accommodating as Salinger has "matured." Where Holden Caulfield's club excluded just about everybody but his kid sister, Zooey's and Franny's secret society includes just about everybody but creative types and students and professors. Here exception is made, obviously, for the Glass family: Seymour, the poet and thinker, Buddy, the writer, and so on. They all have college degrees; the family bookshelves indicate a wide, democratic culture:

> *Dracula* now stood next to *Elementary Pali, The Boy Allies at the Somme* stood next to *Bolts of Melody, The Scarab Murder Case* and *The Idiot* were together, *Nancy Drew and the Hidden Staircase* lay on top of *Fear and Trembling.*

The Glass family librarian does not discriminate, in keeping with the times, and books are encouraged to "mix." In Seymour's old bedroom, however, which is kept as a sort of temple to his memory, quotations, hand-lettered, from a select group of authors are displayed on the door: Marcus Aurelius, Issa, Tolstoy, Ring Lardner, Kafka, St. Francis de Sales, Mu Mon Kwan, etc. This honor roll is extremely institutional.

The broadening of the admissions policy—which is the text of Zooey's sermon—is more a propaganda aim, though, than an accomplishment. No doubt the author and his mouthpiece (who is smoking a panatela) would like to spread a message of charity. "Indiscrimination," as Seymour says in another Salinger story, ". . . leads to health and a kind of very real, enviable happiness." But this remark itself exhales an ineffable breath of gentle superiority. The club, for all its pep talks, remains a closed corporation, since the function of the Fat Lady, when you come down to it, is to be what? —an audience for the Glass kids, while the function of the Great Teachers is to act as their coaches and prompters. And who are these wonder kids but Salinger himself, splitting and multiplying like the original amoeba?

BATHROOM WORSHIP

In Hemingway's work there was never anybody but Hemingway in a series of disguises, but at least there was only one Papa per book. To be confronted with the seven faces of Salinger, all wise and lovable and simple, is to gaze into a terrifying narcissus pool. Salinger's world contains nothing but Salinger, his teachers, and his tolerantly cherished audience—humanity; outside are the phonies, vainly signaling to be let in, like the kids' Irish mother, Bessie, a home version of the Fat Lady, who keeps invading the bathroom while her handsome son Zooey is in the tub or shaving.

The use of the bathroom as stage set—sixty-eight pages of "Zooey" are laid there—is all too revealing as a metaphor. The bathroom is the holy-of-holies of family life, the seat of privacy, the center of the cult of self-worship. What methodical attention Salinger pays to Zooey's routines of shaving and bathing and nail cleaning, as though these were rituals performed by a god on himself, priest and deity at the same time! The scene in the bathroom, with the mother seated on the toilet, smoking and talking, while her son behind the figured shower curtain reads, smokes, bathes, answers, is of a peculiar snickering indecency; it is worth noting, too, that this scene matches a shorter one in a public toilet in the story "Franny," a scene that by its strange suggestiveness misled many *New Yorker* readers into thinking that Franny was pregnant—that was why, they presumed, such significance was attached to her shutting herself up in a toilet in the ladies' room, hanging her head and feeling sick.

These readers were not "in" on the fact that Franny was having a mystical experience. Sex is unimportant for Salinger; not the bed but the bathroom is the erotic center of the narcissus ego, and Zooey behind the shower curtain is taboo, even to the mother who bore him—behind the veil. The reader, however, is allowed an extended look.

A great deal of attention is paid, too, to the rituals of cigarette lighting and to the rites of drinking from a glass, as though these oral acts were sacred—epiphanies. In the same way, the family writings are treated by Salinger as sacred scriptures or the droppings of holy birds, to be studied with care by the augurs: letters from Seymour, citations from his diary, a letter from Buddy, a letter from Franny, a letter from Boo Boo, a note written by Boo Boo in soap on a bathroom mirror (the last two are from another story, "Raise High the Roof Beam, Carpenters").

These imprints of the Glass collective personality are preserved as though they were Veronica's veil in a relic case of well-wrought prose. And the eerie thing is, spaking of Veronica's veil, a popular subject for those paintings in which Christ's eyes are supposed to follow the spectator with a doubtless reproachful gaze, the reader has the sensation in this latest work of Salinger that the author is sadly watching him or listening to him read. That is, the ordinary relation is reversed, and instead of the reader reading Salinger, Salinger, that Man of Sorrows, is reading the reader.

At the same time, this quasi-religious volume is full of a kind of Broadway humor. The Glass family is like a Jewish family in a radio serial. Everyone is a "character." Mr. Glass with his tangerine is a character; Mrs. Glass in her hairnet and commodious wrapper with her cups of chicken broth is a character. The shower curtain, scarlet nylon with a design of canary-yellow sharps, clefs, and flats, is a character; the teeming medicine cabinet is a character. Every phonograph, every chair is a character. The family relationship, rough, genial, insulting, is a character.

In short, every single object possessed by the Glass communal ego is bent on lovably expressing the Glass personality—eccentric, homey, good-hearted. Not unlike "Abie's Irish Rose." And the family is its own best audience. Like Hemingway stooges, they have the disturbing faculty of laughing delightedly or smiling discreetly at each other's jokes. Again a closed circuit: the Glass family is the Fat Lady, who is Jesus. The Glass medicine cabinet is Jesus, and Seymour is his prophet.

Yet below this self-loving barbershop harmony a chord of terror is struck from time to time, like a judgment. Seymour's suicide suggests that Salinger guesses intermittently or fears intermittently that there may be something wrong somewhere. Why did he kill himself? Because he had married a phony, whom he worshiped for her "simplicity, her terrible honesty"? Or because he was so happy and the Fat Lady's world was so wonderful?

Or because he had been lying, his author had been lying, and it was all terrible, and he was a fake?

Notes of a Native Son
Equal in Paris
The Male Prison

JAMES BALDWIN
(*b. 1924*)

THE SHAPING pressures which James Baldwin describes
with such terrible clarity and concentration in the
title essay of *Notes of a Native Son* (1955) had
already been embodied poetically and fictionally
in his first novel, *Go Tell It on the Mountain* (1953).
The original version of this had won a prize in 1945,
when Baldwin was only twenty-one, and still remains
by far his best novel. With amazing artistic control
of violent emotional memories, it tells the story of a
boy preacher who tries to escape through religion
from the three concentric hells in which he is trapped:
his home, with its damaged and damaging father;
the Harlem ghetto, with its brutal sin and poverty;
the malevolent, rejecting white community outside.

A second novel, *Giovanni's Room* (1956), reports
another attempt at escape. Baldwin had left the
frustrations of Negro life in America and sought
in what seemed the freer climate of Europe the
acceptance which his talents deserved and his temperament required. But this attempt failed. The nerveless,
directionless writing of *Giovanni's Room*, a story
of rootless homosexuals in Paris, showed what
happened creatively when the pressure was removed
or displaced. A second collection of essays, *Nobody
Knows My Name* (1961), reflects wisely and frankly
on these same European experiences.

[287]

An elaborate design of whites and blacks, male and female, forced into all possible combinations, shows that the novel *Another Country* (1962) is Baldwin's ambitious attempt to deal totally with the fate of being an American, a writer, a homosexual, and a Negro. Implicit in the novel is the conviction, opposed to many of Baldwin's explicit statements in his essays, that a white can never be a true friend to a black, that his deep mysterious hate and guilt must poison the most selfless and even sacrificial act of love and render it worthless. Implicit also is a curious denial of the universality of human suffering. *Another Country* may represent, in part at least and perhaps unconsciously, still one more attempt to escape—this time, paradoxically, *from* the general human condition back *into* the specific Negro condition where there need be no personal guilt or responsibility since that burden is exclusively the whites'. This may explain the weakness of the book, which, for all its sensational events, is written in a style that is dogged and perfunctory. The speeches in the equally violent drama, *Blues for Mr. Charlie,* were more eloquent, but reviewers were dismayed by the stereotyped scenes and characters.

Baldwin's creative passion has shown at its best in the polemics which he has been pouring out with such brilliant effect for several years, especially in *The Fire Next Time* (1963). Appearing first in *The New Yorker,* this magnificently sustained appeal to conscience is the best piece of writing done by anyone on any subject during the last decade. It aroused national concern and made Baldwin the principal voice of his race. His commentary for *Nothing Personal* (1964), a collection of spitefully realistic photographs by Richard Avedon, is closer in spirit to the later novels.

In its nightmarish subjectivity and dramatic shifts of focus, "Notes of a Native Son" may be contrasted with Mary McCarthy's more detached but equally penetrating study of the psychic shocks of childhood.

Prison experience has been one of the great subjects of literature in all periods. "Equal in Paris" is the work of a superb raconteur recreating, with sardonic humor, the misadventures of the stolen bedsheet. But its real theme, and here it can be related to "Marrakech" and Chesterton's "Twelve Men," is the horror of institutionalized indifference.

"The Male Prison" shows Baldwin's supreme qualities of compassion and understanding. He is able to define the precise nature of André Gide's problem, and to use it to suggest what is really needed if we are to surmount the cultural crisis expressed in all-pervasive images of sexual violence and perversion.

Notes of a Native Son

On the 29th of July, in 1943, my father died. On the same day, a few hours later, his last child was born. Over a month before this, while all our energies were concentrated in waiting for these events, there had been, in Detroit, one of the bloodiest race riots of the century. A few hours after my father's funeral, while he lay in state in the undertaker's chapel, a race riot broke out in Harlem. On the morning of the 3rd of August, we drove my father to the graveyard through a wilderness of smashed plate glass.

The day of my father's funeral had also been my nineteenth birthday. As we drove him to the graveyard, the spoils of injustice, anarchy, discontent, and hatred were all around us. It seemed to me that God himself had devised, to mark my father's end, the most sustained and brutally dissonant of codas. And it seemed to me, too, that the violence which rose all about us as my father left the world had been devised as a corrective for the pride of his eldest son. I had declined to believe in that apocalypse which had been central to my father's vision; very well, life seemed to be saying, here is something

NOTES OF A NATIVE SON. From *Notes of a Native Son* by James Baldwin. Reprinted by permission of the Beacon Press, copyright © 1955 by James Baldwin.

that will certainly pass for an apocalypse until the real thing comes along. I had inclined to be contemptuous of my father for the conditions of his life, for the conditions of our lives. When his life had ended I began to wonder about that life and also, in a new way, to be apprehensive about my own.

I had not known my father very well. We had got on badly, partly because we shared, in our different fashions, the vice of stubborn pride. When he was dead I realized that I had hardly ever spoken to him. When he had been dead a long time I began to wish I had. It seems to be typical of life in America, where opportunities, real and fancied, are thicker than anywhere else on the globe, that the second generation has no time to talk to the first. No one, including my father, seems to have known exactly how old he was, but his mother had been born during slavery. He was of the first generation of free men. He, along with thousands of other Negroes, came North after 1919 and I was part of that generation which had never seen the landscape of what Negroes sometimes call the Old Country.

He had been born in New Orleans and had been a quiet young man there during the time that Louis Armstrong, a boy, was running errands for the dives and honky-tonks of what was always presented to me as one of the most wicked of cities—to this day, whenever I think of New Orleans, I also helplessly think of Sodom and Gomorrah. My father never mentioned Louis Armstrong, except to forbid us to play his records; but there was a picture of him on our wall for a long time. One of my father's strong-willed female relatives had placed it there and forbade my father to take it down. He never did, but he eventually maneuvered her out of the house and when, some years later, she was in trouble and near death, he refused to do anything to help her.

He was, I think, very handsome. I gather this from photographs and from my own memories of him, dressed in his Sunday best and on his way to preach a sermon somewhere, when I was little. Handsome, proud, and ingrown, "like a toe-nail," somebody said. But he looked to me, as I grew older, like pictures I had seen of African tribal chieftains: he really should have been naked, with war-paint on and barbaric mementos, standing among spears. He could be chilling in the pulpit and indescribably cruel in his personal life and he was certainly the most bitter man I have ever met; yet it must be said that there was something else in him, buried in him, which lent him his tremendous power and, even, a rather crushing charm. It had something to do with his blackness, I think—he was very black—with his blackness and his beauty, and with the fact that he knew that he was black but did not know that he was beautiful. He claimed to be proud of his blackness but it had also been the cause of much humiliation and it had fixed bleak boundaries to his life. He was not a young man when we were growing up and he had already suffered many kinds of ruin; in his outrageously demanding and protective way he loved his children, who were black like him and menaced, like him; and all these things sometimes showed in his face when he tried, never to my knowledge with any success, to establish contact with any of us. When he took one of his children on his knee to play, the child always became fretful and began to cry; when he tried to help one of us with our homework the absolutely unabating tension which emanated from him caused our minds and our tongues to become paralyzed, so that he, scarcely knowing why, flew into a rage and the child, not knowing why, was punished. If it ever entered his head to bring a surprise home for his children, it was, almost unfailingly, the wrong surprise and even the big watermelons he often brought home on his back in the summertime led to the most appalling scenes. I do not remember, in all those years, that one of his children was ever glad to see him come home. From what I was able to gather of his early life, it seemed that this inability to establish contact with other people had always marked him and had been one of the things which had driven him out of New Orleans. There was something in him, therefore, groping and tentative, which was never expressed and which was buried with him. One saw it most clearly when he was facing new people and hoping to impress them. But he never did, not for long. We went from church to smaller and more improbable church, he found himself in less and less demand as a minister, and by the time he died none of his friends had come to see him for a long time. He had lived and died in an intolerable bitterness of spirit and it frightened me, as we drove him to the graveyard through those unquiet, ruined streets, to see how powerful and overflowing this bitterness could be and to realize that this bitterness now was mine.

When he died I had been away from home for a little over a year. In that year I had had time to become aware of the meaning of all my father's bitter warnings, had discovered the secret of his proudly pursed lips and rigid carriage: I had discovered the weight of white people in the world. I saw that this had been for my ancestors and now would be for me an awful thing to live with and that the bitterness which had helped to kill my father could also kill me.

He had been ill a long time—in the mind, as we now realized, reliving instances of his fantastic intransigence in the new light of his affliction and endeavoring to feel a sorrow for him which never, quite, came true. We had not known that he was being eaten up by paranoia, and the discovery that his cruelty, to our bodies and our minds, had been one of the symptoms of his illness was not, then, enough to enable us to forgive him. The younger children felt, quite simply, relief that he would not be coming home anymore. My mother's observation that it was he, after all, who had kept them alive all these years meant nothing because the problems of keeping children alive are not real for children. The older children felt, with my father gone, that they could invite their friends to the house without fear that their friends would be insulted or, as had sometimes happened with me, being told that their friends were in league with the devil and intended to rob our family of everything we owned. (I didn't fail to wonder, and it made me hate him, what on earth we owned that anybody else would want.)

His illness was beyond all hope of healing before anyone realized that he was ill. He had always been so strange and had lived, like a prophet, in such unimaginably close communion with the Lord that his long silences which were punctuated by moans and hallelujahs and snatches of old songs while he sat at the living-room window never seemed odd to us. It was not until he refused to eat because, he said, his family was trying to poison him that my mother was forced to accept as a fact what had, until then, been only an unwilling suspicion. When he was committed, it was discovered that he had tuberculosis and, as it turned out, the disease of his mind allowed the disease of his body to destroy him. For the doctors could not force him to eat, either, and, though he was fed intravenously, it was clear from the beginning that there was no hope for him.

In my mind's eye I could see him, sitting at the window, locked up in his terrors; hating and fearing every living soul including his children who had betrayed him, too, by reaching towards the world which had despised him. There were nine of us. I began to wonder what it could have felt like for such a man to have had nine children whom he could barely feed. He used to make little jokes about our poverty, which never, of course, seemed very funny to us; they could not have seemed very funny to him, either, or else our all to feeble response to them would never have caused such rages. He spent great energy and achieved, to our chagrin, no small amount of success in keeping us away from the people who surrounded us, people who had all-night rent parties to which we listened when we should have been sleeping, people who cursed and drank and flashed razor blades on Lenox Avenue. He could not understand why, if they had so much energy to spare, they could not use it to make their lives better. He treated almost everybody on our block with a most uncharitable asperity and neither they, nor, of course, their children were slow to reciprocate.

The only white people who came to our house were welfare workers and bill collectors. It was almost always my mother who dealt with them, for my father's temper, which was at the mercy of his pride, was never to be trusted. It was clear that he felt their very presence in his home to be a violation: this was conveyed by his carriage, almost ludicrously stiff, and by his voice, harsh and vindictively polite. When I was around nine or ten I wrote a play which was directed by a young, white schoolteacher, a woman, who then took an interest in me, and gave me books to read and, in order to corroborate my theatrical bent, decided to take me to see what she somewhat tactlessly referred to as "real" plays. Theater-going was forbidden in our house, but, with the really cruel intuitiveness of a child, I suspected that the color of this woman's skin would carry the day for me. When, at school, she suggested taking me to the theater, I did not, as I might have done if she had been a Negro, find a way of discouraging her, but agreed that she should pick me up at my house one evening. I then, very cleverly, left all the rest to my mother, who suggested to my father, as I knew she would, that it would not be very nice to let such a kind woman make the trip for nothing. Also, since it was a schoolteacher, I imagine that my mother countered the idea of sin with the idea of "education," which word, even with my father, carried a kind of bitter weight.

Before the teacher came my father took me aside to ask *why* she was coming, what *interest* she could possibly have in our house, in a boy like me. I said I didn't know but I, too, suggested that it had something to do with education. And I understood that my father was waiting for me to say something—I didn't quite know what; perhaps that I wanted his protection against this teacher and her "education." I said none of these things and the teacher came and we went out. It was clear, during the brief interview in our living room, that my father was agreeing very much against his will and that he would have refused permission if he had dared. The fact that he did not dare caused me to despise him: I had no way of knowing that he was facing in that living room a wholly unprecedented and frightening situation.

Later, when my father had been laid off from his job, this woman became very important to us. She was really a very sweet and generous woman and went to a great deal of trouble to be of help to us, particularly during one awful winter. My mother called her by the highest name she knew: she said she was a "christian." My father could scarcely disagree but during the four or five years of our relatively close association he never trusted her and was always trying to surprise in her open, Midwestern face the genuine, cunningly hidden, and hideous motivation. In later years, particularly when it began to be clear that this "education" of mine was going to lead me to perdition, he became more explicit and warned me that my white friends in high school were not really my friends and that I would see, when I was older, how white people would do anything to keep a Negro down. Some of them could be nice, he admitted, but none of them were to be trusted and most of them were not even nice. The best thing was to have as little to do with them as possible. I did not feel this way and I was certain, in my innocence, that I never would.

But the year which preceded my father's death had made a great change in my life. I had been living in New Jersey, working in defense plants, working and living among southerners, white and black. I knew about the south, of course, and about how southerners treated Negroes and how they expected them to behave, but it had never entered my mind that anyone would look at me and expect *me* to behave that way. I learned in New Jersey that to be a Negro meant, precisely, that one was never looked at but was simply at the mercy of the reflexes the color of one's skin caused in other people. I acted in New Jersey as I had always acted, that is as though I thought a great deal of myself—I had to *act* that way—with results that were, simply, unbelievable. I had scarcely arrived before I had earned the enmity, which was extraordinarily ingenious, of all my superiors and nearly all my co-workers. In the beginning, to make matters worse, I simply did not know what was happening. I did not know what I had done, and I shortly began to wonder what *anyone* could possibly do, to bring about such unanimous, active, and un-bearably vocal hostility. I knew about jim-crow but I had never ex-perienced it. I went to the same self-service restaurant three times and stood with all the Princeton boys before the counter, waiting for a hamburger and coffee; it was always an extraordinarily long time before anything was set before me; but it was not until the fourth visit that I learned that, in fact, nothing had ever been set before me: I had simply picked something up. Negroes were not served there, I was told, and they had been waiting for me to realize that I was always the only Negro present. Once I was told this, I determined to go there all the time. But now they were ready for me and, though some dreadful scenes were subsequently enacted in that restaurant, I never ate there again.

It was the same story all over New Jersey, in bars, bowling alleys, diners, places to live. I was always being forced to leave, silently, or with mutual imprecations. I very shortly became notorious and chil-dren giggled behind me when I passed and their elders whispered or shouted—they really believed that I was mad. And it did begin to work on my mind, of course; I began to be afraid to go anywhere and to compensate for this I went places to which I really should not have gone and where, God knows, I had no desire to be. My reputation in town naturally enhanced my reputation at work and my working day became one long series of acrobatics designed to keep me out of trouble. I cannot say that these acrobatics succeeded. It began to seem that the machinery of the organization I worked for was turning over, day and night, with but one aim: to eject me. I was fired once, and contrived, with the aid of a friend from New York, to get back on the payroll; was fired again, and bounced back again. It took a while to fire me for the third time, but the third time took. There were no loopholes anywhere. There was not even any way of getting back inside the gates.

That year in New Jersey lives in my mind as though it were the year during which, having an unsuspected predilection for it, I first contracted some dread, chronic disease, the unfailing symptom of which is a kind of blind fever, a pounding in the skull and fire in the bowels. Once this disease is contracted, one can never be really carefree again, for the fever, without an instant's warning, can recur at any moment. It can wreck more important things than race rela-tions. There is not a Negro alive who does not have this rage in his blood—one has the choice, merely, of living with it consciously or surrendering to it. As for me, this fever has recurred in me, and does, and will until the day I die.

My last night in New Jersey, a white friend from New York took me to the nearest big town, Trenton, to go to the movies and have a few drinks. As it turned out, he also saved me from, at the very least, a violent whipping. Almost every detail of that night stands out very clearly in my memory. I even remember the name of the movie we saw because its title impressed me as being so patly ironical. It was a movie about the German occupation of France, starring Maureen O'Hara and Charles Laughton and called *This Land Is Mine*. I remember the name of the diner we walked into when the movie ended: it was the "American Diner." When we walked in the counterman asked what we wanted and I remember answering with the casual sharpness which had become my habit: "We want a hamburger and a cup of coffee, what do you think we want?" I do not know why, after a year of such rebuffs, I so completely failed to anticipate his answer, which was, of course, "We don't serve Negroes here." This reply failed to discompose me, at least for the moment. I made some sardonic comment about the name of the diner and we walked out into the streets.

This was the time of what was called the "brownout," when the lights in all American cities were very dim. When we re-entered the streets something happened to me which had the force of an optical illusion, or a nightmare. The streets were very crowded and I was facing north. People were moving in every direction but it seemed to me, in that instant, that all of the people I could see, and many more than that, were moving toward me, against me, and that everyone was white. I remember how their faces gleamed. And I felt, like a physical sensation, a *click* at the nape of my neck as though some interior string connecting my head to my body had been cut. I began to walk. I heard my friend call after me, but I ignored him. Heaven only knows what was going on in his mind, but he had the good sense not to touch me—I don't know what would have happened if he had—and to keep me in sight. I don't know what was going on in my mind, either; I certainly had no conscious plan. I wanted to do something to crush these white faces, which were crushing me. I walked for perhaps a block or two until I came to an enormous, glittering, and fashionable restaurant in which I knew not even the intercession of the Virgin would cause me to be served.

I pushed through the doors and took the first vacant seat I saw, at a table for two, and waited.

I do not know how long I waited and I rather wonder, until today, what I could possibly have looked like. Whatever I looked like, I frightened the waitress who shortly appeared, and the moment she appeared all of my fury flowed towards her. I hated her for her white face, and for her great, astounded, frightened eyes. I felt that if she found a black man so frightening I would make her fright worth-while.

She did not ask me what I wanted, but repeated, as though she had learned it somewhere, "We don't serve Negroes here." She did not say it with the blunt, derisive hostility to which I had grown so accustomed, but, rather, with a note of apology in her voice, and fear. This made me colder and more murderous than ever. I felt I had to do something with my hands. I wanted her to come close enough for me to get her neck between my hands.

So I pretended not to have understood her, hoping to draw her closer. And she did step a very short step closer, and with her pencil poised incongruously over her pad, and repeated the formula: ". . . don't serve Negroes here."

Somehow, with the repetition of that phrase, which was already ringing in my head like a thousand bells of a nightmare, I realized that she would never come any closer and that I would have to strike from a distance. There was nothing on the table but an ordinary water-mug half full of water, and I picked this up and hurled it with all my strength at her. She ducked and it missed her and shattered against the mirror behind the bar. And, with that sound, my frozen blood abruptly thawed, I returned from wherever I had been, I *saw*, for the first time, the restaurant, the people with their mouths open, already, as it seemd to me, rising as one man, and I realized what I had done, and where I was, and I was frightened. I rose and began running for the door. A round, potbellied man grabbed me by the nape of the neck just as I reached the doors and began to beat me about the face. I kicked him and got loose and ran into the streets. My friend whispered, "*Run!*" and I ran.

My friend stayed outside the restaurant long enough to misdirect my pursuers and the police, who arrived, he told me, at once. I do not know what I said to him when he came to my room that night. I could not have said much. I felt, in the oddest, most awful way, that I had somehow betrayed him. I lived it over and over and over again, the way one relives an automobile accident after it has happened and one finds oneself alone and safe. I could not get over two facts, both equally difficult for the imagination to grasp, and one was that I could have been murdered. But the other was that I had been ready to commit murder. I saw nothing very clearly but I did see this: that my life, my *real* life, was in danger, and not from anything other people might do but from the hatred I carried in my own heart.

II

I had returned home around the second week in June—in great haste because it seemed that my father's death and my mother's confinement were both but a matter of hours. In the case of my mother, it soon became clear that she had simply made a miscalculation. This had always been her tendency and I don't believe that a single one of us arrived in the world, or has since arrived anywhere else, on time. But none of us dawdled so intolerably about the business of being born as did my baby sister. We sometimes amused ourselves, during those endless, stifling weeks, by picturing the baby sitting within in the safe, warm dark, bitterly regretting the necessity of becoming a part of our chaos and stubbornly putting it off as long as possible. I understood her perfectly and congratulated her on showing such good sense so soon. Death, however, sat as purposefully at my father's bedside as life stirred within my mother's womb and it was harder to understand why he so lingered in that long shadow. It seemed that he had bent, and for a long time, too, all of his energies towards dying. Now death was ready for him but my father held back.

All of Harlem, indeed, seemed to be infected by waiting. I had never before known it to be so violently still. Racial tensions throughout this country were exacerbated during the early years of the war, partly because the labor market brought together hundreds of thousands of ill-prepared people and partly because Negro soldiers, regardless of where they were born, received their military training in the south. What happened in defense plants and army camps had repercussions, naturally, in every Negro ghetto. The situation in Harlem had grown bad enough for clergymen, policemen, educators, politicians, and social workers to assert in one breath that there was no "crime wave" and to offer, in the very next breath, suggestions as to how to combat it. These suggestions always

seemed to involve playgrounds, despite the fact that racial skir-
mishes were occurring in the playgrounds, too. Playground or not,
crime wave or not, the Harlem police force had been augmented in
March, and the unrest grew—perhaps, in fact, partly as a result of
the ghetto's instinctive hatred of policemen. Perhaps the most revealing news item, out of the steady parade of reports of muggings,
stabbings, shootings, assaults, gang wars, and accusations of police
brutality, is the item concerning six Negro girls who set upon a
white girl in the subway because, as they all too accurately put it,
she was stepping on their toes. Indeed she was, all over the nation.

I had never before been so aware of policemen, on foot, on horse-
back, on corners, everywhere, always two by two. Nor had I ever
been so aware of small knots of people. They were on stoops and on
corners and in doorways, and what was striking about them, I think,
was that they did not seem to be talking. Never, when I passed these
groups, did the usual sound of a curse or a laugh ring out and neither
did there seem to be any hum of gossip. There was certainly, on the
other hand, occurring between them communication extraordinarily
intense. Another thing that was striking was the unexpected diversity of the people who made up these groups. Usually, for example,
one would see a group of sharpies standing on the street corner, jiv-
ing the passing chicks; or a group of older men, usually, for some
reason, in the vicinity of a barber shop, discussing baseball scores, or
the numbers, or making rather chilling observations about women
they had known. Women, in a general way, tended to be seen less
often together—unless they were church women, or very young
girls, or prostitutes met together for an unprofessional instant. But
that summer I saw the strangest combinations: large, respectable,
churchly matrons standing on the stoops or the corners with their
hair tied up, together with a girl in sleazy satin whose face bore the
marks of gin and the razor, or heavy-set, abrupt, no-nonsense older
men, in company with the most disreputable and fanatical "race"
men, or these same "race" men with the sharpies, or these sharpies
with the churchly women. Seventh Day Adventists and Methodists
and Spiritualists seemed to be hobnobbing with Holyrollers and
they were all, alike, entangled with the most flagrant disbelievers;
something heavy in their stance seemed to indicate that they had all,
incredibly, seen a common vision, and on each face there seemed to
be the same strange, bitter shadow.

The churchly women and the matter-of-fact, no-nonsense men

had children in the Army. The sleazy girls they talked to had lovers there, the sharpies and the "race" men had friends and brothers there. It would have demanded an unquestioning patriotism, happily as uncommon in this country at it is undesirable, for these people not to have been disturbed by the bitter letters they received, by the newspaper stories they read, not to have been enraged by the posters, then to be found all over New York, which described the Japanese as "yellow-bellied Japs." It was only the "race" men, to be sure, who spoke ceaselessly of being revenged—how this vengence was to be exacted was not clear—for the indignities and dangers suffered by Negro boys in uniform; but everybody felt a direction-less, hopeless bitterness, as well as that panic which can scarcely be suppressed when one knows that a human being one loves is beyond one's reach, and in danger. This helplessness and this gnawing un-easiness does something, at length, to even the toughest mind. Per-haps the best way to sum all this up is to say that the people I knew felt, mainly, a peculiar kind of relief when they knew that their boys were being shipped out of the south, to do battle overseas. It was, perhaps, like feeling that the most dangerous part of a dangerous journey had been passed and that now, even if death should come, it would come with honor and without the complicity of their coun-trymen. Such a death would be, in short, a fact with which one could hope to live.

It was on the 28th of July, which I believe was a Wednesday, that I visited my father for the first time during his illness and for the last time in his life. The moment I saw him I knew why I had put off this visit so long. I had told my mother that I did not want to see him because I hated him. But this was not true. It was only that I *had* hated him and I wanted to hold on to this hatred. I did not want to look on him as a ruin: it was not a ruin I had hated. I imagine that one of the reasons people cling to their hates so stubbornly is be-cause they sense, once hate is gone, that they will be forced to deal with pain.

We traveled out to him, his older sister and myself, to what seemed to be the very end of a very Long Island. It was hot and dusty and we wrangled, my aunt and I, all the way out, over the fact that I had recently begun to smoke and, as she said, to give myself airs. But I knew that she wrangled with me because she could not bear to face the fact of her brother's dying. Neither could I endure the reality of her despair, her unstated bafflement as to what had happened to her brother's life, and her own. So we wrangled and I smoked and from time to time she fell into a heavy reverie. Covertly, I watched her face, which was the face of an old woman; it had fallen in, the eyes were sunken and lightless; soon she would be dying, too.

In my childhood—it had not been so long ago—I had thought her beautiful. She had been quick-witted and quick-moving and very generous with all the children and each of her visits had been an event. At one time one of my brothers and myself had thought of running away to live with her. Now she could no longer produce out of her handbag some unexpected and yet familiar delight. She made me feel pity and revulsion and fear. It was awful to realize that she no longer caused me to feel affection. The closer we came to the hospital the more querulous she became and at the same time, naturally, grew more dependent on me. Between pity and guilt and fear I began to feel that there was another me trapped in my skull like a jack-in-the-box who might escape my control at any moment and fill the air with screaming.

She began to cry the moment we entered the room and she saw him lying there, all shriveled and still, like a little black monkey. The great, gleaming apparatus which fed him and would have compelled him to be still even if he had been able to move brought to mind, not beneficence, but torture; the tubes entering his arm made me think of pictures I had seen when a child, of Gulliver, tied down by the pigmies on that island. My aunt wept and wept, there was a whistling sound in my father's throat; nothing was said; he could not speak. I wanted to take his hand, to say something. But I do not know what I could have said, even if he could have heard me. He was not really in that room with us, he had at last really embarked on his journey; and though my aunt told me that he said he was going to meet Jesus, I did not hear anything except that whistling in his throat. The doctor came back and we left, into that unbearable train again, and home. In the morning came the telegram saying that he was dead. Then the house was suddenly full of relatives, friends, hysteria, and confusion and I quickly left my mother and the children to the care of those impressive women, who, in Negro communities at least, automatically appear at times of bereavement armed with lotions, proverbs, and patience, and an ability to cook. I went downtown. By the time I returned, later the same day, my mother had been carried to the hospital and the baby had been born.

III

For my father's funeral I had nothing black to wear and this posed a nagging problem all day long. It was one of those problems, simple, or impossible of solution, to which the mind insanely clings in order to avoid the mind's real trouble. I spent most of that day at the downtown apartment of a girl I knew, celebrating my birthday with whiskey and wondering what to wear that night. When planning a birthday celebration one naturally does not expect that it will be up against competition from a funeral and this girl had anticipated taking me out that night, for a big dinner and a night club afterwards. Sometime during the course of that long day we decided that we would go out anyway, when my father's funeral service was over. I imagine *I* decided it, since, as the funeral hour approached, it became clearer and clearer to me that I would not know what to do with myself when it was over. The girl, stifling her very lively concern as to the possible effects of the whiskey on one of my father's chief mourners, concentrated on being conciliatory and practically helpful. She found a black shirt for me somewhere and ironed it and, dressed in the darkest pants and jacket I owned, and slightly drunk, I made my way to my father's funeral.

The chapel was full, but not packed, and very quiet. There were, mainly, my father's relatives, and his children, and here and there I saw faces I had not seen since childhood, the faces of my father's one-time friends. They were very dark and solemn now, seeming somehow to suggest that they had known all along that something like this would happen. Chief among the mourners was my aunt, who had quarreled with my father all his life; by which I do not mean to suggest that her mourning was insincere or that she had not loved him. I suppose that she was one of the few people in the world who had, and their incessant quarreling proved precisely the strength of the tie that bound them. The only other person in the world, as far as I knew, whose relationship to my father rivaled my aunt's in depth was my mother, who was not there.

It seemed to me, of course, that it was a very long funeral. But it was, if anything, a rather shorter funeral than most, nor, since there were no overwhelming, uncontrollable expressions of grief, could it be called—if I dare to use the word—successful. The minister who preached my father's funeral sermon was one of the few my father had still been seeing as he neared his end. He presented to us in his sermon a man whom none of us had ever seen—a man thoughtful, patient, and forbearing, a Christian inspiration to all who knew him, and a model for his children. And no doubt the children, in their disturbed and guilty state, were almost ready to believe this; he had been remote enough to be anything and, anyway, the shock of the incontrovertible, that it was really our father lying up there in that casket, prepared the mind for anything. His sister moaned and this grief-stricken moaning was taken as corroboration. The other faces held a dark, non-committal thoughtfulness. This was not the man they had known, but they had scarcely expected to be confronted with *him;* this was, in a sense deeper than questions of fact, the man they had not known, and the man they had not known may have been the real one. The real man, whoever he had been, had suffered and now he was dead: this was all that was sure and all that mattered now. Every man in the chapel hoped that when his hour came he, too, would be eulogized, which is to say forgiven, and that all of his lapses, greeds, errors, and strayings from the truth would be invested with coherence and looked upon with charity. This was perhaps the last thing human beings could give each other and it was what they demanded, after all, of the Lord. Only the Lord saw the midnight tears, only He was present when one of His children, moaning and wringing hands, paced up and down the room. When one slapped one's child in anger the recoil in the heart reverberated through heaven and became part of the pain of the universe. And when the children were hungry and sullen and distrustful and one watched them, daily, growing wilder, and further away, and running headlong into danger, it was the Lord who knew what the charged heart endured as the strap was laid to the backside; the Lord alone who knew what one *would* have said if one had had, like the Lord, the gift of the living word. It was the Lord who knew of the impossibility every parent in that room faced: how to prepare the child for the day when the child would be despised and how to *create* in the child—by what means?—a stronger antidote to this poison than one had found for oneself. The avenues, side streets, bars, billiard halls, hospitals, police stations, and even the playgrounds of Harlem—not to mention the houses of correction, the jails, and the morgue—testified to the potency of the poison while remaining silent as to the efficacy of whatever antidote, irresistibly raising the question of whether or not such an antidote existed; raising, which was worse, the question of whether or not an antidote was desirable; perhaps poison should be fought with poison. With these several schisms in the mind and with more terrors in the heart than could be named, it was better not to judge the man who had gone down under an impossible burden. It was better to remember: *Thou knowest this man's fall; but thou knowest not his wrassling.*

While the preacher talked and I watched the children—years of changing their diapers, scrubbing them, slapping them, taking them to school, and scolding them had had the perhaps inevitable result of making me love them, though I am not sure I knew this then—my mind was busily breaking out with a rash of disconnected impressions. Snatches of popular songs, indecent jokes, bits of books I had read, movie sequences, faces, voices, political issues—I thought I was going mad; all these impressions suspended, as it were, in the solution of the faint nausea produced in me by the heat and liquor. For a moment I had the impression that my alcoholic breath, inefficiently disguised with chewing gum, filled the entire chapel. Then someone began singing one of my father's favorite songs and, abruptly, I was with him, sitting on his knee, in the hot, enormous, crowded church which was the first church we attended. It was the Abyssinia Baptist Church on 138th Street. We had not gone there long. With this image, a host of others came. I had forgotten, in the rage of my growing up, how proud my father had been of me when I was little. Apparently, I had had a voice and my father had liked to show me off before the members of the church. I had forgotten what he had looked like when he was pleased but now I remembered that he had always been grinning with pleasure when my solos ended. I even remembered certain expressions on his face when he teased my mother—had he loved her? I would never know. And when had it all begun to change? For now it seemed that he had not always been cruel. I remembered being taken for a haircut and scraping my knee on the footrest of the barber's chair and I remembered my father's face as he soothed my crying and applied the stinging iodine. Then I remembered our fights, fights which had been of the worst possible kind because my technique had been silence.

I remembered the one time in all our life together when we had really spoken to each other.

It was on a Sunday and it must have been shortly before I left home. We were walking, just the two of us, in our usual silence, to or from church. I was in high school and had been doing a lot of writing and I was, at about this time, the editor of the high school

magazine. But I had also been a Young Minister and had been preaching from the pulpit. Lately, I had been taking fewer engagements
and preached as rarely as possible. It was said in the church, quite
truthfully, that I was "cooling off."

My father asked me abruptly, "You'd rather write than preach,
wouldn't you?"

I was astonished at his question—because it was a real question. I
answered, "Yes."

That was all we said. It was awful to remember that that was all
we had *ever* said.

The casket now was opened and the mourners were being led up
the aisle to look for the last time on the deceased. The assumption
was that the family was too overcome with grief to be allowed to
make this journey alone and I watched while my aunt was led to the
casket and, muffled in black, and shaking, led back to her seat. I disapproved of forcing the children to look on their dead father, considering that the shock of his death, or, more truthfully, the shock
of death as a reality, was already a little more than a child could
bear, but my judgment in this matter had been overruled and there
they were, bewildered and frightened and very small, being led, one
by one, to the casket. But there is also something very gallant about
children at such moments. It has something to do with their silence
and gravity and with the fact that one cannot help them. Their legs,
somehow, seem *exposed*, so that it is at once incredible and terribly
clear that their legs are all they have to hold them up.

I had not wanted to go to the casket myself and I certainly had
not wished to be led there, but there was no way of avoiding either
of these forms. One of the deacons led me up and I looked on my
father's face. I cannot say that it looked like him at all. His blackness
had been equivocated by powder and there was no suggestion in
that casket of what his power had or could have been. He was simply an old man dead, and it was hard to believe that he had ever given
anyone either joy or pain. Yet, his life filled that room. Further up
the avenue his wife was holding his newborn child. Life and death
so close together, and love and hatred, and right and wrong, said
something to me which I did not want to hear concerning man, concerning the life of man.

After the funeral, while I was downtown desperately celebrating
my birthday, a Negro soldier, in the lobby of the Hotel Braddock,
got into a fight with a white policeman over a Negro girl. Negro

girls, white policemen, in or out of uniform, and Negro males—in or out of uniform—were part of the furniture of the lobby of the Hotel Braddock and this was certainly not the first time such an incident had occurred. It was destined, however, to receive an unprecedented publicity, for the fight between the policeman and the soldier ended with the shooting of the soldier. Rumor, flowing immediately to the streets outside, stated that the soldier had been shot in the back, an instantaneous and revealing invention, and that the soldier had died protecting a Negro woman. The facts were somewhat different—for example, the soldier had not been shot in the back, and was not dead, and the girl seems to have been as dubious a symbol of womanhood as her white counterpart in Georgia usually is, but no one was interested in the facts. They preferred the invention because this invention expressed and corroborated their hates and fears so perfectly. It is just as well to remember that people are always doing this. Perhaps many of those legends, including Christianity, to which the world clings began their conquest of the world with just some such concerted surrender to distortion. The effect, in Harlem, of this particular legend was like the effect of a lit match in a tin of gasoline. The mob gathered before the doors of the Hotel Braddock simply began to swell and to spread in every direction, and Harlem exploded.

The mob did not cross the ghetto lines. It would have been easy, for example, to have gone over Morningside Park on the west side or to have crossed the Grand Central railroad tracks at 125th Street on the east side, to wreak havoc in white neighborhoods. The mob seems to have been mainly interested in something more potent and real than the white face, that is, in white power, and the principal damage done during the riot of the summer of 1943 was to white business establishments in Harlem. It might have been a far bloodier story, of course, if, at the hour the riot began, these establishments had still been open. From the Hotel Braddock the mob fanned out, east and west along 125th Street, and for the entire length of Lenox, Seventh, and Eighth avenues. Along each of these avenues, and along each major side street—116th, 125th, 135th, and so on—bars, stores, pawnshops, restaurants, even little luncheonettes had been smashed open and entered and looted—looted, it might be added, with more haste than efficiency. The shelves really looked as though a bomb had struck them. Cans of beans and soup and dog food, along with toilet paper, corn flakes, sardines and milk tumbled every which way, and abandoned cash registers and cases of beer leaned crazily out of the splintered windows and were strewn along the avenues. Sheets, blankets, and clothing of every description formed a kind of path, as though people had dropped them while running. I truly had not realized that Harlem *had* so many stores until I saw them all smashed open; the first time the word *wealth* ever entered my mind in relation to Harlem was when I saw it scattered in the streets. But one's first, incongruous impression of plenty was countered immediately by an impression of waste. None of this was doing anybody any good. It would have been better to have left the plate glass as it had been and the goods lying in the stores.

It would have been better, but it would also have been intolerable, for Harlem had needed something to smash. To smash something is the ghetto's chronic need. Most of the time it is the members of the ghetto who smash each other, and themselves. But as long as the ghetto walls are standing there will always come a moment when these outlets do not work. That summer, for example, it was not enough to get into a fight on Lenox Avenue, or curse out one's cronies in the barber shops. If ever, indeed, the violence which fills Harlem's churches, pool halls, and bars erupts outward in a more direct fashion, Harlem and its citizens are likely to vanish in an apocalyptic flood. That this is not likely to happen is due to a great many reasons, most hidden and powerful among them the Negro's real relation to the white American. This relation prohibits, simply, anything as uncomplicated and satisfactory as pure hatred. In order really to hate white people, one has to blot so much out of the mind —and the heart—that this hatred itself becomes an exhausting and self-destructive pose. But this does not mean, on the other hand, that love comes easily: the white world is too powerful, too complacent, too ready with gratuitous humiliation, and, above all, too ignorant and too innocent for that. One is absolutely forced to make perpetual qualifications and one's own reactions are always canceling each other out. It is this, really, which has driven so many people mad, both white and black. One is always in the position of having to decide between amputation and gangrene. Amputation is swift but time may prove that the amputation was not necessary—or one may delay the amputation too long. Gangrene is slow, but it is impossible to be sure that one is reading one's symptoms right. The idea of going through life as a cripple is more than one can bear, and equally unbearable is the risk of swelling up slowly, in agony, with poison. And the trouble, finally, is that the risks are real even if the choices do not exist.

"But as for me and my house," my father had said, "we will serve the Lord." I wondered, as we drove him to his resting place, what this line had meant for him. I had heard him preach it many times. I had preached it once myself, proudly giving it an interpretation different from my father's. Now the whole thing came back to me, as though my father and I were on our way to Sunday school and I were memorizing the golden text: *And if it seem evil unto you to serve the Lord, choose you this day whom you will serve; whether the gods which your fathers served that were on the other side of the flood, or the gods of the Amorites, in whose land ye dwell: but as for me and my house, we will serve the Lord.* I suspected in these familiar lines a meaning which had never been there for me before. All of my father's texts and songs, which I had decided were meaningless, were arranged before me at his death like empty bottles, waiting to hold the meaning which life would give them for me. This was his legacy: nothing is ever escaped. That bleakly memorable morning I hated the unbelievable streets and the Negroes and whites who had, equally, made them that way. But I knew that it was folly, as my father would have said, this bitterness was folly. It was necessary to hold on to the things that mattered. The dead man mattered, the new life mattered; blackness and whiteness did not matter; to believe that they did was to acquiesce in one's own destruction. Hatred, which could destroy so much, never failed to destroy the man who hated and this was an immutable law.

It began to seem that one would have to hold in the mind forever two ideas which seemed to be in opposition. The first idea was acceptance, the acceptance, totally without rancor, of life as it is, and men as they are: in the light of this idea, it goes without saying that injustice is a commonplace. But this did not mean that one could be complacent, for the second idea was of equal power: that one must never, in one's own life, accept these injustices as commonplace but must fight them with all one's strength. This fight begins, however, in the heart and it now had been laid to my charge to keep my own heart free of hatred and despair. This intimation made my heart heavy and, now that my father was irrecoverable, I wished that he had been beside me so that I could have searched his face for the answers which only the future would give me now.

Equal in Paris

On the 19th of December, in 1949, when I had been living in Paris for a little over a year, I was arrested as a receiver of stolen goods and spent eight days in prison. My arrest came about through an American tourist whom I had met twice in New York, who had been given my name and address and told to look me up. I was then living on the top floor of a ludicrously grim hotel on the rue du Bac, one of those enormous dark, cold, and hideous establishments in which Paris abounds that seem to breathe forth, in their airless, humid, stone-cold halls, the weak light, scurrying chambermaids, and creaking stairs, an odor of gentility long long dead. The place was run by an ancient Frenchman dressed in an elegant black suit which was green with age, who cannot properly be described as bewildered or even as being in a state of shock, since he had really stopped breathing around 1910. There he sat at his desk in the weirdly lit, fantastically furnished lobby, day in and day out, greeting each one of his extremely impoverished and *louche* lodgers with a stately inclination of the head that he had no doubt been taught in some impossibly remote time was the proper way for a *propriétaire* to greet his guests. If it had not been for his daughter, an extremely hardheaded *tricoteuse*—the inclination of *her* head was chilling and abrupt, like the downbeat of an ax—the hotel would certainly have gone bankrupt long before. It was said that this old man had not gone farther than the door of his hotel for thirty years, which was not at all difficult to believe. He looked as though the daylight would have killed him.

I did not, of course, spend much of my time in this palace. The moment I began living in French hotels I understood the necessity of French cafés. This made it rather difficult to look me up, for as soon as I was out of bed I hopefully took notebook and fountain pen off to the upstairs room of the Flore, where I consumed rather a lot of coffee and, as evening approached, rather a lot of alcohol, but did not get much writing done. But one night, in one of the cafés of St.

EQUAL IN PARIS. From *Notes of a Native Son* by James Baldwin. Reprinted by permission of the Beacon Press, copyright © 1955 by James Baldwin.

Germain des Près, I was discovered by this New Yorker and only because we found ourselves in Paris we immediately established the illusion that we had been fast friends back in the good old U.S.A. This illusion proved itself too thin to support an evening's drinking, but by that time it was too late. I had committed myself to getting him a room in my hotel the next day, for he was living in one of the nest of hotels near the Gare St. Lazare, where, he said, the *propriétaire* was a thief, his wife a repressed nymphomaniac, the chambermaids "pigs," and the rent a crime. Americans are always talking this way about the French and so it did not occur to me that he meant what he said or that he would take into his own hands the means of avenging himself on the French Republic. It did not occur to me, either, that the means which he *did* take could possibly have brought about such dire results, results which were not less dire for being also comic-opera.

It came as the last of a series of disasters which had perhaps been made inevitable by the fact that I had come to Paris originally with a little over forty dollars in my pockets, nothing in the bank, and no grasp whatever of the French language. It developed, shortly, that I had no grasp of the French character either. I considered the French an ancient, intelligent, and cultured race, which indeed they are. I did not know, however, that ancient glories imply, at least in the middle of the present century, present fatigue and, quite probably, paranoia; that there is a limit to the role of the intelligence in human affairs; and that no people come into possession of a culture without having paid a heavy price for it. This price they cannot, of course, assess, but it is revealed in their personalities and in their institutions. The very word "institutions," from my side of the ocean, where, it seemed to me, we suffered so cruelly from the lack of them, had a pleasant ring, as of safety and order and common sense; one had to come into contact with these institutions in order to understand that they were also outmoded, exasperating, completely impersonal, and very often cruel. Similarly, the personality which had seemed from a distance to be so large and free had to be dealt with before one could see that, if it was large, it was also inflexible and, for the foreigner, full of strange, high, dusty rooms which could not be inhabited. One had, in short, to come into contact with an alien culture in order to understand that a culture was not a community basket-weaving project, nor yet an act of God; was something neither desirable nor undesirable in itself, being inevitable, being nothing more

or less than the recorded and visible effects on a body of people of
the vicissitudes with which they had been forced to deal. And their
great men are revealed as simply another of these vicissitudes, even
if, quite against their will, the brief battle of their great men with
them has left them richer.

When my American friend left his hotel to move to mine, he
took with him, out of pique, a bedsheet belonging to the hotel and
put it in his suitcase. When he arrived at my hotel I borrowed the
sheet, since my own were filthy and the chambermaid showed no
sign of bringing me any clean ones, and put it on my bed. The
sheets belonging to *my* hotel I put out in the hall, congratulating
myself on having thus forced on the attention of the Grand Hôtel du
Bac the unpleasant state of its linen. Thereafter, since, as it turned
out, we kept very different hours—I got up at noon, when, as I
gathered by meeting him on the stairs one day, he was only just getting in—my new-found friend and I saw very little of each other.

On the evening of the 19th I was sitting thinking melancholy
thoughts about Christmas and staring at the walls of my room. I imagine that I had sold something or that someone had sent me a
Christmas present, for I remember that I had a little money. In those
days in Paris, though I floated, so to speak, on a sea of acquaintances,
I knew almost no one. Many people were eliminated from my orbit
by virtue of the fact that they had more money than I did, which
placed me, in my own eyes, in the humiliating role of a free-loader;
and other people were eliminated by virtue of the fact that they enjoyed their poverty, shrilly insisting that this wretched round of
hotel rooms, bad food, humiliating concierges, and unpaid bills was
the Great Adventure. It couldn't, however, for me, end soon
enough, this Great Adventure; there was a real question in my mind
as to which would end soonest, the Great Adventure or me. This
meant, however, that there were many evenings when I sat in my
room, knowing that I couldn't work there, and not knowing what
to do, or whom to see. On this particular evening I went down and
knocked on the American's door.

There were two Frenchmen standing in the room, who immediately introduced themselves to me as policemen; which did not
worry me. I had got used to policemen in Paris bobbing up at the
most improbable times and places, asking to see one's *carte d'iden-
tité*. These policemen, however, showed very little interest in my
papers. They were looking for something else. I could not imagine

what this would be and, since I knew I certainly didn't have it, I scarcely followed the conversation they were having with my friend. I gathered that they were looking for some kind of gangster and since I wasn't a gangster and knew that gangsterism was not, insofar as he had one, my friend's style, I was sure that the two policemen would presently bow and say *Merci, messieurs,* and leave. For by this time, I remember very clearly, I was dying to have a drink and go to dinner.

I did not have a drink or go to dinner for many days after this, and when I did my outraged stomach promptly heaved everything up again. For now one of the policemen began to exhibit the most vivid interest in me and asked, very politely, if he might see my room. To which we mounted, making, I remember, the most civilized small talk on the way and even continuing it for some moments after we were in the room in which there was certainly nothing to be seen but the familiar poverty and disorder of that precarious group of people of whatever age, race, country, calling, or intention which Paris recognizes as *les étudiants* and sometimes, more ironically and precisely, as *les nonconformistes.* Then he moved to my bed, and in a terrible flash, not quite an instant before he lifted the bedspread, I understood what he was looking for. We looked at the sheet, on which I read, for the first time, lettered in the most brilliant scarlet I have ever seen, the name of the hotel from which it had been stolen. It was the first time the word *stolen* entered my mind. I had certainly seen the hotel monogram the day I put the sheet on the bed. It had simply meant nothing to me. In New York I had seen hotel monograms on everything from silver to soap and towels. Taking things from New York hotels was practically a custom, though, I suddenly realized, I had never known anyone to take a *sheet.* Sadly, and without a word to me, the inspector took the sheet from the bed, folded it under his arm, and we started back downstairs. I understood that I was under arrest.

And so we passed through the lobby, four of us, two of us very clearly criminal, under the eyes of the old man and his daughter, neither of whom said a word, into the streets where a light rain was falling. And I asked, in French, "But is this very serious?"

For I was thinking, it is, after all, only a sheet, not even new.

"No," said one of them. "It's not serious."

"It's nothing at all," said the other.

I took this to mean that we would receive a reprimand at the police station and be allowed to go to dinner. Later on I concluded that they were not being hypocritical or even trying to comfort us. They meant exactly what they said. It was only that they spoke another language.

In Paris everything is very slow. Also, when dealing with the bureaucracy, the man you are talking to is never the man you have to see. The man you have to see has just gone off to Belgium, or is busy with his family, or has just discovered that he is a cuckold; he will be in next Tuesday at three o'clock, or sometime in the course of the afternoon, or possibly tomorrow, or, possibly, in the next five minutes. But if he is coming in the next five minutes he will be far too busy to be able to see you today. So that I suppose I was not really astonished to learn at the commissariat that nothing could possibly be done about us before The Man arrived in the morning. But no, we could not go off and have dinner and come back in the morning. Of course he knew that we *would* come back—that was not the question. Indeed, there was no question: we would simply have to stay there for the night. We were placed in a cell which rather resembled a chicken coop. It was now about seven in the evening and I relinquished the thought of dinner and began to think of lunch.

I discouraged the chatter of my New York friend and this left me alone with my thoughts. I was beginning to be frightened and I bent all my energies, therefore, to keeping my panic under control. I began to realize that I was in a country I knew nothing about, in the hands of a people I did not understand at all. In a similar situation in New York I would have had some idea of what to do because I would have had some idea of what to expect. I am not speaking now of legality which, like most of the poor, I had never for an instant trusted, but of the temperament of the people with whom I had to deal. I had become very accomplished in New York at guessing and, therefore, to a limited extent manipulating to my advantage the reactions of the white world. But this was not New York. None of my old weapons could serve me here. I did not know what they saw when they looked at me. I knew very well what Americans saw when they looked at me and this allowed me to play endless and sinister variations on the role which they had assigned me; since I knew that it was, for them, of the utmost importance that they never be confronted with what, in their own personalities, made this role so necessary and gratifying to them, I knew that they could never call my hand or, indeed, afford to know what I was doing; so that I moved into every crucial situation with the deadly and rather desperate advantages of bitterly accumulated perception, of pride and contempt. This is an awful sword and shield to carry through the world, and the discovery that, in the game I was playing, I did myself a violence of which the world, at its most ferocious, would scarcely have been capable, was what had driven me out of New York. It was a strange feeling, in this situation, after a year in Paris, to discover that my weapons would never again serve me as they had.

It was quite clear to me that the Frenchmen in whose hands I found myself were no better or worse than their American counterparts. Certainly their uniforms frightened me quite as much, and their impersonality, and the threat, always very keenly felt by the poor, of violence, was as present in that commissariat as it had ever been for me in any police station. And I had seen, for example, what Paris policemen could do to Arab peanut vendors. The only difference here was that I did not understand these people, did not know what techniques their cruelty took, did not know enough about their personalities to see danger coming, to ward it off, did not know on what ground to meet it. That evening in the commissariat I was not a despised black man. They would simply have laughed at me if I had behaved like one. For them, I was an American. And here it was they who had the advantage, for that word, *Américain*, gave them some idea, far from inaccurate, of what to expect from me. In order to corroborate none of their ironical expectations I said nothing and did nothing—which was not the way any Frenchman, white or black, would have reacted. The question thrusting up from the bottom of my mind was not *what* I was, but *who*. And this question, since a *what* can get by with skill but a *who* demands resources, was my first real intimation of what humility must mean.

In the morning it was still raining. Between nine and ten o'clock a black Citroën took us off to the Ile de la Cité, to the great, gray Préfecture. I realize now that the questions I put to the various policemen who escorted us were always answered in such a way as to corroborate what I wished to hear. This was not out of politeness, but simply out of indifference—or, possibly, an ironical pity—since each of the policemen knew very well that nothing would speed or halt the machine in which I had become entangled. They knew I did not know this and there was certainly no point in their telling me.

In one way or another I would certainly come out at the other side
—for they also knew that being found with a stolen bedsheet in
one's possession was not a crime punishable by the guillotine. (They
had the advantage over me there, too, for there were certainly moments later on when I was not so sure.) If I did *not* come out at the
other side—well, that was just too bad. So, to my question, put
while we were in the Citroën—"Will it be over today?"—I received
a *"Oui, bien sûr."* He was not lying. As it turned out, the *procès-
verbal* was over that day. Trying to be realistic, I dismissed, in the
Citroën, all thoughts of lunch and pushed my mind ahead to dinner.

At the Préfecture we were first placed in a tiny cell, in which it
was almost impossible either to sit or to lie down. After a couple of
hours of this we were taken down to an office, where, for the first
time, I encountered the owner of the bedsheet and where the
procès-verbal took place. This was simply an interrogation, quite
chillingly clipped and efficient (so that there was, shortly, no doubt
in one's own mind that one *should* be treated as a criminal), which
was recorded by a secretary. When it was over, this report was
given to us to sign. One had, of course, no choice but to sign it, even
though my mastery of written French was very far from certain.
We were being held, according to the law in France, incommu-
nicado, and all my angry demands to be allowed to speak to my em-
bassy or to see a lawyer met with a stony *"Oui, oui. Plus tard."* The
procès-verbal over, we were taken back to the cell, before which,
shortly, passed the owner of the bedsheet. He said he hoped we had
slept well, gave a vindictive wink, and disappeared.

By this time there was only one thing clear: that we had no way
of controlling the sequence of events and could not possibly guess
what this sequence would be. It seemed to me, since what I regarded
as the high point—the *procès-verbal*—had been passed and since
the hotel-keeper was once again in possession of his sheet, that we
might reasonably expect to be released from police custody in a
matter of hours. We had been detained now for what would soon
be twenty-four hours, during which time I had learned only that
the official charge against me was *receleur*. My mental shifting, between lunch and dinner, to say nothing of the physical lack of either
of these delights, was beginning to make me dizzy. The steady chatter of my friend from New York, who was determined to keep my
spirits up, made me feel murderous; I was praying that some power
would release us from this freezing pile of stone before the impulse

became the act. And I was beginning to wonder what was happening in that beautiful city, Paris, which lived outside these walls. I wondered how long it would take before anyone casually asked, "But where's Jimmy? He hasn't been around"—and realized, knowing the people I knew, that it would take several days.

Quite late in the afternoon we were taken from our cells; handcuffed, each to a separate officer; led through a maze of steps and corridors to the top of the building; fingerprinted; photographed. As in movies I had seen, I was placed against a wall, facing an old-fashioned camera, behind which stood one of the most completely cruel and indifferent faces I had ever seen, while someone next to me and, therefore, just outside my line of vision, read off in a voice from which all human feeling, even feeling of the most base description, had long since fled, what must be called my public characteristics—which, at that time and in that place, seemed anything but that. He might have been roaring to the hostile world secrets which I could barely, in the privacy of midnight, utter to myself. But he was only reading off my height, my features, my approximate weight, my color—that color which, in the United States, had often, odd as it may sound, been my salvation—the color of my hair, my age, my nationality. A light then flashed, the photographer and I staring at each other as though there was murder in our hearts, and then it was over. Handcuffed again, I was led downstairs to the bottom of the building, into a great enclosed shed in which had been gathered the very scrapings off the Paris streets. Old, old men, so ruined and old that life in them seemed really to prove the miracle of the quickening power of the Holy Ghost—for clearly their life was no longer their affair, it was no longer even their burden, they were simply the clay which had once been touched. And men not so old, with faces the color of lead and the consistency of oatmeal, eyes that made me think of stale *café-au-lait* spiked with arsenic, bodies which could take in food and water—any food and water—and pass it out, but which could not do anything more, except possibly, at midnight, along the riverbank where rats scurried, rape. And young men, harder and crueler than the Paris stones, older by far than I, their chronological senior by some five to seven years. And North Africans, old and young, who seemed the only living people in this place because they yet retained the grace to be bewildered. But they were not bewildered by being in this shed: they were simply bewildered because they were no longer in North Africa. There was a great hole in the center of this shed which was the common toilet. Near it, though it was impossible to get very far from it, stood an old man with white hair, eating a piece of camembert. It was at this point, probably, that thought, for me, stopped, that physiology, if one may say so, took over. I found myself incapable of saying a word, not because I was afraid I would cry but because I was afraid I would vomit. And I did not think any longer of the city of Paris but my mind flew back to that home from which I had fled. I was sure that I would never see it any more. And it must have seemed to me that my flight from home was the cruelest trick I had ever played on myself, since it had led me here, down to a lower point than any I could ever in my life have imagined—lower, far, than anything I had seen in that Harlem which I had so hated and so loved, the escape from which had soon become the greatest direction of my life. After we had been here an hour or so a functionary came and opened the door and called out our names. And I was sure that *this* was my release. But I was handcuffed again and led out of the Préfecture into the streets—it was dark now, it was still raining —and before the steps of the Préfecture stood the great police wagon, doors facing me, wide open. The handcuffs were taken off, I entered the wagon, which was peculiarly constructed. It was divided by a narrow aisle, and on each side of the aisle was a series of narrow doors. These doors opened on a narrow cubicle, beyond which was a door which opened onto another narrow cubicle: three or four cubicles, each private, with a locking door. I was placed in one of them; I remember there was a small vent just above my head which let in a little light. The door of my cubicle was locked from the outside. I had no idea where this wagon was taking me and, as it began to move, I began to cry. I suppose I cried all the way to prison, the prison called Fresnes, which is twelve kilometers outside of Paris.

For reasons I have no way at all of understanding, prisoners whose last initial is A, B, or C are always sent to Fresnes; everybody else is sent to a prison called, rather cynically it seems to me, La Santé. I will, obviously, never be allowed to enter La Santé, but I was told by people who certainly seemed to know that it was infinitely more unbearable than Fresnes. This arouses in me, until today, a positive storm of curiosity concerning what I promptly began to think of as The Other Prison. My colleague in crime, occurring lower in the alphabet, had been sent there and I confess that the minute he was gone I missed him. I missed him because he was not French and because he was the only person in the world who knew that the story I told was true.

For, once locked in, divested of shoelaces, belt, watch, money, papers, nailfile, in a freezing cell in which both the window and the toilet were broken, with six other adventurers, the story I told of *l'affaire du drap de lit* elicited only the wildest amusement or the most suspicious disbelief. Among the people who shared my cell the first three days no one, it is true, had been arrested for anything much more serious—or, at least, not serious in my eyes. I remember that there was a boy who had stolen a knitted sweater from a *monoprix*, who would probably, it was agreed, receive a six-month sentence. There was an older man there who had been arrested for some kind of petty larceny. There were two North Africans, vivid, brutish, and beautiful, who alternated between gaiety and fury, not at the fact of their arrest but at the state of the cell. None poured as much emotional energy into the fact of their arrest as I did; they took it, as I would have liked to take it, as simply another unlucky happening in a very dirty world. For, though I had grown accustomed to thinking of myself as looking upon the world with a hard, penetrating eye, the truth was that they were far more realistic about the world than I, and more nearly right about it. The gap between us, which only a gesture I made could have bridged, grew steadily, during thirty-six hours, wider. I could not make any gesture simply because they frightened me. I was unable to accept my imprisonment as a fact, even as a temporary fact. I could not, even for a moment, accept my present companions as *my* companions. And they, of course, felt this and put it down, with perfect justice, to the fact that I was an American.

There was nothing to do all day long. It appeared that we would one day come to trial but no one knew when. We were awakened at seven-thirty by a rapping on what I believe is called the Judas, that small opening in the door of the cell which allows the guards to survey the prisoners. At this rapping we rose from the floor—we slept on straw pallets and each of us was covered with one thin blanket—and moved to the door of the cell. We peered through the opening into the center of the prison, which was, as I remember, three tiers high, all gray stone and gunmetal steel, precisely that prison I had seen in movies, except that, in the movies, I had not known that it was cold in prison. I had not known that when one's shoelaces and belt have been removed one is, in the strangest way, demoralized. The necessity of shuffling and the necessity of holding up one's trousers with one hand turn one into a rag doll. And the movies fail, of course, to give one any idea of what prison food is like. Along the corridor, at seven-thirty, came three men, each pushing before him a great garbage can, mounted on wheels. In the garbage can of the first was the bread—this was passed to one through the small opening in the door. In the can of the second was the coffee. In the can of the third was what was always called *la soupe*, a pallid paste of potatoes which had certainly been bubbling on the back of the prison stove long before that first, so momentous revolution. Naturally, it was cold by this time and, starving as I was, I could not eat it. I drank the coffee—which was not coffee—because it was hot, and spent the rest of the day, huddled in my blanket, munching on the bread. It was not the French bread one bought in bakeries. In the evening the same procession returned. At ten-thirty the lights went out. I had a recurring dream, each night, a nightmare which always involved my mother's fried chicken. At the moment I was about to eat it came the rapping at the door. Silence is really all I remember of those first three days, silence and the color gray.

I am not sure now whether it was on the third or the fourth day that I was taken to trial for the first time. The days had nothing, obviously, to distinguish them from one another. I remember that I was very much aware that Christmas Day was approaching and I wondered if I was really going to spend Christmas Day in prison. And I remember that the first trial came the day before Christmas Eve.

On the morning of the first trial I was awakened by hearing my name called. I was told, hanging in a kind of void between my mother's fried chicken and the cold prison floor, "*Vous préparez. Vous êtes extrait*"—which simply terrified me, since I did not know what interpretation to put on the word "*extrait*," and since my cellmates had been amusing themselves with me by telling terrible stories about the inefficiency of French prisons, an inefficiency so extreme that it had often happened that someone who was supposed to be taken out and tried found himself on the wrong line and was guillotined instead. The best way of putting my reaction to this is to say that, though I knew they were teasing me, it was simply not possible for me to totally *dis*believe them. As far as I was concerned, once in the hands of the law of France, anything could happen. I shuffled along with the others who were *extrait* to the center of the prison, trying, rather, to linger in the office, which seemed the only warm spot in the whole world, and found myself again in that dreadful wagon, and was carried again to the Ile de la Cité, this time to the Palais de Justice. The entire day, except for ten minutes, was spent in one of the cells, first waiting to be tried, then waiting to be taken back to prison.

For I was *not* tried that day. By and by I was handcuffed and led through the halls, upstairs to the courtroom where I found my New York friend. We were placed together, both stage-whisperingly certain that this was the end of our ordeal. Nevertheless, while I waited for our case to be called, my eyes searched the courtroom, looking for a face I knew, hoping, anyway, that there was someone there who knew *me*, who would carry to someone outside the news that I was in trouble. But there was no one I knew there and I had had time to realize that there was probably only one man in Paris who could help me, an American patent attorney for whom I had worked as an office boy. He could have helped me because he had a quite solid position and some prestige and would have testified that, while working for him, I had handled large sums of money regularly, which made it rather unlikely that I would stoop to trafficking in bedsheets. However, he was somewhere in Paris, probably at this very moment enjoying a snack and a glass of wine and as far as the possibility of reaching him was concerned, he might as well have been on Mars. I tried to watch the proceedings and to make my mind a blank. But the proceedings were not reassuring. The boy, for example, who had stolen the sweater *did* receive a six-month sentence. It seemed to me that all the sentences meted out that day were excessive; though, again, it seemed that all the people who were sentenced that day had made, or clearly were going to make, crime their career. This seemed to be the opinion of the judge, who scarcely looked at the prisoners or listened to them; it seemed to be the opinion of the prisoners, who scarcely bothered to speak in their own behalf; it seemed to be the opinion of the lawyers, state lawyers for the most part, who were defending them. The great impulse of the courtroom seemed to be to put these people where they could not be seen—and not because they were offended at the crimes unless, indeed, they were offended that the crimes were so petty, but because they did not wish to know that their society could be counted on to produce, probably in greater and greater numbers, a whole body of people for whom crime was the only possible career. Any society inevitably produces its criminals, but a society at once rigid and unstable can do nothing whatever to alleviate the poverty of its lowest members, cannot present to the hypothetical young man at the crucial moment that so-well-advertised right path. And the fact, perhaps, that the French are the earth's least sentimental people and must also be numbered among the most proud aggravates the plight of their lowest, youngest, and unluckiest members, for it means that the idea of rehabilitation is scarcely real to them. I confess that this attitude on their part raises in me sentiments of exasperation, admiration, and despair, revealing as it does, in both the best and the worst sense, their renowned and spectacular hardheadedness.

Finally our case was called and we rose. We gave our names. At the point that it developed that we were American the proceedings ceased, a hurried consultation took place between the judge and what I took to be several lawyers. Someone called out for an interpreter. The arresting officer had forgotten to mention our nationalities and there was, therefore, no interpreter in the court. Even if our French had been better than it was we would not have been allowed to stand trial without an interpreter. Before I clearly understood what was happening, I was handcuffed again and let out of the courtroom. The trial had been set back for the 27th of December.

I have sometimes wondered if I would *ever* have got out of prison if it had not been for the older man who had been arrested for the mysterious petty larceny. He was acquitted that day and when he returned to the cell—for he could not be released until morning—he found me sitting numbly on the floor, having just been prevented, by the sight of a man, all blood, being carried back to *his* cell on a stretcher, from seizing the bars and screaming until they let me out. The sight of the man on the stretcher proved, however, that screaming would not do much for me. The petty-larceny man went around asking if he could do anything in the world outside for those he was leaving behind. When he came to me I, at first, responded, "No, nothing"—for I suppose I had by now retreated into the attitude, the earliest I remember, that of my father, which was simply (since I had lost his God) that nothing could help me. And I suppose I will remember with gratitude until I die the fact that the man now insisted: *"Mais, êtes-vous sûr?"* Then it swept over me that he was going *outside* and he instantly became my first contact since the

Lord alone knew how long with the outside world. At the same time, I remember, I did not really believe that he would help me. There was no reason why he should. But I gave him the phone number of my attorney friend and my own name.

So, in the middle of the next day, Christmas Eve, I shuffled downstairs again, to meet my visitor. He looked extremely well fed and sane and clean. He told me I had nothing to worry about any more. Only not even he could do anything to make the mill of justice grind any faster. He would, however, send me a lawyer of his acquaintance who would defend me on the 27th, and he would himself, along with several other people, appear as a character witness. He gave me a package of Lucky Strikes (which the turnkey took from me on the way upstairs) and said that, though it was doubtful that there would be any celebration in the prison, he would see to it that I got a fine Christmas dinner when I got out. And this, somehow, seemed very funny. I remember being astonished at the discovery that I was actually laughing. I was, too, I imagine, also rather disappointed that my hair had not turned white, that my face was clearly not going to bear any marks of tragedy, disappointed at bottom, no doubt, to realize, facing him in that room, that far worse things had happened to most people and that, indeed, to paraphrase my mother, if this was the worst thing that ever happened to me I could consider myself among the luckiest people ever to be born. He injected—my visitor—into my solitary nightmare common sense, the world, and the hint of blacker things to come.

The next day, Christmas, unable to endure my cell, and feeling that, after all, the day demanded a gesture, I asked to be allowed to go to Mass, hoping to hear some music. But I found myself, for a freezing hour and a half, locked in exactly the same kind of cubicle as in the wagon which had first brought me to prison, peering through a slot placed at the level of the eye at an old Frenchman, hatted, overcoated, muffled, and gloved, preaching in this language which I did not understand, to this row of wooden boxes, the story of Jesus Christ's love for men.

The next day, the 26th, I spent learning a peculiar kind of game, played with match-sticks, with my cellmates. For, since I no longer felt that I would stay in this cell forever, I was beginning to be able to make peace with it for a time. On the 27th I went again to trial and, as had been predicted, the case against us was dismissed. The story of the *drap de lit*, finally told, caused great merriment in the courtroom, whereupon my friend decided that the French were "great." I was chilled by their merriment, even though it was meant to warm me. It could only remind me of the laughter I had often heard at home, laughter which I had sometimes deliberately elicited. This laughter is the laughter of those who consider themselves to be at a safe remove from all the wretched, for whom the pain of the living is not real. I had heard it so often in my native land that I had resolved to find a place where I would never hear it any more. In some deep, black, stony, and liberating way, my life, in my own eyes, began during that first year in Paris, when it was borne in on me that this laughter is universal and never can be stilled.

The Male Prison

There is something immensely humbling in this last document [*Madeleine* by André Gide] from the hand of a writer whose elaborately graceful fiction very often impressed me as simply cold, solemn and irritatingly pious, and whose precise memoirs made me accuse him of the most exasperating egocentricity. He does not, to be sure, emerge in *Madeleine* as being less egocentric; but one is compelled to see this egocentricity as one of the conditions of his life and one of the elements of his pain. Nor can I claim that reading *Madeleine* has caused me to reevaluate his fiction (though I care more now for *The Immoralist* than I did when I read it several years ago); it has only made me feel that such a reevaluation must be made. For, whatever Gide's shortcomings may have been, few writers of our time can equal his devotion to a very high ideal.

It seems to me now that the two things which contributed most heavily to my dislike of Gide—or, rather, to the discomfort he caused me to feel—were his Protestantism and his homosexuality. It was clear to me that he had not got over his Protestantism and that he had not come to terms with his nature. (For I believed at one time—rather oddly, considering the examples by which I was surrounded, to say nothing of the spectacle I myself presented—that

THE MALE PRISON. Reprinted from *Nobody Knows My Name* by James Baldwin. Copyright © 1954, 1961 by James Baldwin, and used with the permission of the publishers, The Dial Press, Inc.

people *did* "get over" their earliest impressions and that "coming to terms" with oneself simply demanded a slightly more protracted stiffening of the will.) It was his Protestantism, I felt, which made him so pious, which invested all of his work with the air of an endless winter, and which made it so difficult for me to care what happened to any of his people.

And his homosexuality, I felt, was his own affair which he ought to have kept hidden from us, or, if he needed to be so explicit, he ought at least to have managed to be a little more scientific—whatever, in the domain of morals, that word may mean—less illogical, less romantic. He ought to have leaned less heavily on the examples of dead, great men, of vanished cultures, and he ought certainly to have known that the examples provided by natural history do not go far toward illuminating the physical, psychological and moral complexities faced by men. It he were going to talk about homosexuality at all, he ought, in a word, to have sounded a little less *disturbed*.

This is not the place and I am certainly not the man to assess the work of André Gide. Moreover, I confess that a great deal of what I felt concerning his work I still feel. And that argument, for example, as to whether or not homosexuality is natural seems to me completely pointless—pointless because I really do not see what difference the answer makes. It seems clear, in any case, at least in the world we know, that no matter what encyclopedias of physiological and scientific knowledge are brought to bear the answer never can be Yes. And one of the reasons for this is that it would rob the normal—who are simply the many—of their very necessary sense of security and order, of their sense, perhaps, that the race is and should be devoted to outwitting oblivion—and will surely manage to do so.

But there are a great many ways of outwitting oblivion, and to ask whether or not homosexuality is natural is really like asking whether or not it was natural for Socrates to swallow hemlock, whether or not it was natural for St. Paul to suffer for the Gospel, whether or not it was natural for the Germans to send upwards of six million people to an extremely twentieth-century death. It does not seem to me that nature helps us very much when we need illumination in human affairs. I am certainly convinced that it is one of the greatest impulses of mankind to arrive at something higher than a natural state. How to be natural does not seem to me to be a problem—quite the contrary. The great problem is how to be—in the best sense of that kaleidoscopic word—a man.

This problem was at the heart of all Gide's anguish, and it proved itself, like most real problems, to be insoluble. He died, as it were, with the teeth of this problem still buried in his throat. What one learns from *Madeleine* is what it cost him, in terms of unceasing agony, to live with this problem at all. Of what it cost her, his wife, it is scarcely possible to conjecture. But she was not so much a victim of Gide's sexual nature—homosexuals do not choose women for their victims, nor is the difficulty of becoming a victim so great for a woman that she is compelled to turn to homosexuals for this—as she was a victim of his overwhelming guilt, which connected, it would seem, and most unluckily, with her own guilt and shame.

If this meant, as Gide says, that "the spiritual force of my love [for Madeleine] inhibited all carnal desire," it also meant that some corresponding inhibition in her prevented her from seeking carnal satisfaction elsewhere. And if there is scarcely any suggestion throughout this appalling letter that Gide ever really understood that he had married a woman or that he had any apprehension of what a woman was, neither is there any suggestion that she ever, in any way, insisted on or was able to believe in her womanhood and its right to flower.

Her most definite and also most desperate act is the burning of his letters—and the anguish this cost her, and the fact that in this burning she expressed what surely must have seemed to her life's monumental failure and waste—Gide characteristically (indeed, one may say, necessarily) cannot enter into and cannot understand. "They were my most precious belongings," she tells him, and perhaps he cannot be blamed for protecting himself against the knife of this dreadful conjugal confession. But: "It is the best of me that disappears," he tells us, *"and it will no longer counterbalance the worst."* (Italics mine.) He had entrusted, as it were, to her his purity, that part of him that was not carnal; and it is quite clear that, though he suspected it, he could not face the fact that it was only when her purity ended that her life could begin, that the key to her liberation was in his hands.

But if he had ever turned that key madness and despair would have followed for him, his world would have turned completely dark, the string connecting him to heaven would have been cut. And this is because then he could no longer have loved Madeleine as an ideal, as Emanuele, God-with-us, but would have been compelled to love her as a woman, which he could not have done except physically. And then he would have had to hate her, and at that moment those gates which, as it seemed to him, held him back from utter corruption would have been opened. He loved her as a woman, indeed, only in the sense that no man could have held the place in Gide's dark sky which was held by Madeleine. She was his Heaven who would forgive him for his Hell and help him to endure it. As indeed she was and, in the strangest way possible, did—by allowing him to feel guilty about *her* instead of boys on the *Piazza d'Espagne*—with the result that, in Gide's work, both his Heaven and his Hell suffer from a certain lack of urgency.

Gide's relations with Madeleine place his relations with men in rather a bleak light. Since he clearly could not forgive himself for his anomaly, he must certainly have despised them—which almost certainly explains the fascination felt by Gide and so many of his heroes for countries like North Africa. It is not necessary to despise people who are one's inferiors—whose inferiority, by the way, is amply demonstrated by the fact that they appear to relish, without guilt, their sensuality.

It is possible, as it were, to have one's pleasure without paying for it. But to have one's pleasure without paying for it is precisely the way to find oneself reduced to a search for pleasure which grows steadily more desperate and more grotesque. It does not take long, after all, to discover that sex is only sex, that there are few things on earth more futile or more deadening than a meaningless round of conquests. The really horrible thing about the phenomenon of present-day homosexuality, the horrible thing which lies curled like a worm at the heart of Gide's trouble and his work and the reason that he so clung to Madeleine, is that today's unlucky deviate can only save himself by the most tremendous exertion of all his forces from falling into an underworld in which he never meets either men or women, where it is impossible to have either a lover or a friend, where the possibility of genuine human involvement has altogether ceased. When this possibility has ceased, so has the possibility of growth.

And, again: It is one of the facts of life that there are two sexes, which fact has given the world most of its beauty, cost it not a little of its anguish, and contains the hope and glory of the world. And it is with this fact, which might better perhaps be called a mystery,

that every human being born must find some way to live. For, no
matter what demons drive them, men cannot live without women
and women cannot live without men. And this is what is most
clearly conveyed in the agony of Gide's last journal. However little
he was able to understand it, or, more important perhaps, take upon
himself the responsibility for it, Madeleine kept open for him a kind
of door of hope, of possibility, the possibility of entering into communion with another sex. This door, which is the door to life and
air and freedom from the tyranny of one's own personality, *must* be
kept open, and none feel this more keenly than those on whom the
door is perpetually threatening or has already seemed to close.

Gide's dilemma, his wrestling, his peculiar, notable and extremely
valuable failure testify—which should not seem odd—to a powerful
masculinity and also to the fact that he found no way to escape the
prison of that masculinity. And the fact that he endured this prison
with such dignity is precisely what ought to humble us all, living as
we do in a time and country where communion between the sexes
has become so sorely threatened that we depend more and more on
the strident exploitation of externals, as, for example, the breasts of
Hollywood glamour girls and the mindless grunting and swaggering
of Hollywood he-men.

It is important to remember that the prison in which Gide strug-
gled is not really so unique as it would certainly comfort us to believe, is not very different from the prison inhabited by, say, the
heroes of Mickey Spillane. Neither can they get through to women,
which is the only reason their muscles, their fists and their tommy
guns have acquired such fantastic importance. It is worth observing,
too, that when men can no longer love women they also cease to love
or respect or trust each other, which makes their isolation complete.
Nothing is more dangerous than this isolation, for men will commit
any crimes whatever rather than endure it. We ought, for our own
sakes, to be humbled by Gide's confession as he was humbled by his
pain and make the generous effort to understand that his sorrow was
not different from the sorrow of all men born. For, if we do not
learn this humility, we may very well be strangled by a most petu-
lant and unmasculine pride.

The Bachelor's Dilemma
The Age of Happy Problems
The American as Hipster

HERBERT GOLD
(b. 1924)

HERBERT GOLD has an intimate, amused knowledge of
the overlapping worlds of avant-garde Bohemia,
Madison Avenue, professional sports, and popular
entertainment. He loves to talk their language, parody
it, or transform it. Though the phrases he has picked
up as a carnival worker and in Harlem and in the
beatnik coffee houses of San Francisco are racier and
more outlandish than any to be found in the essays
of E. B. White or E. M. Forster, he has the same
flair for mingling the literary and the colloquial. He
is quoting, with one intrusive addition, Keats' "Ode
on a Grecian Urn" when he speaks of the "still
unravished bride of bop quietness," and playing on
Eliot's "Prufrock" with "He has time for everything,
visions and decisions and revisions." The conjunction
of "stars" and "closet" in his sentence, "That ladder
to the stars lies folded in a closet somewhere" reminds
us of Thoreau's coupling of Uranus and the shutter,
though to a very different effect. "Strictly from
nadaville" recalls the way "nada," the Spanish word
for "nothing," was used by Goya in his "Miseries
of War" and by Hemingway in the famous prayer
of his story, "A Clean Well-lighted Place." Like
most successful parodists, Gold can beat the Hip
[329]   speakers—or nonspeakers—at their own game.

Because Gold is well read in the literature of other
periods and in other disciplines than literature, he
can view our culture in perspective, if not under
the aspect of Uranus. See his reference to binary
fission in "The Bachelor's Dilemma." Born in Cleveland, Ohio, he took his B.A. and M.A. at Columbia
University, studied at the Sorbonne in Paris on a
Fulbright grant, and spent several later periods abroad.
He has taught writing and literature at Brandeis, the
University of Iowa, and Western Reserve. As editor
of the two influential anthologies, *Fiction of the
Fifties* (1959) and *First Person Singular: Essays for
the Sixties* (1963), he helped to define a literary
period whose character had been less clear than that
of the twenties and thirties. Along with Saul Bellow
he edited the review *The Noble Savage*. A selection of
his own essays appeared as *The Age of Happy
Problems* (1962).

Along with all these other activities, Gold has published
six novels. The first, *Birth of a Hero* (1951), is
about professional baseball players. His third, and
probably most satisfying, *The Man Who Was Not
with It* (1956), tells the picaresque adventures of a
boy fleeing his relationship with his father into the
jungle world of carnivals. With his great talent for
combining comedy and compassion Gold describe the
boy's struggle, especially in the course of his relationship with a drug addict, to comprehend the depth of
man's stubborn resistance to love and salvation. Gold
shows the same gifts, appealingly though less intensely,
in *Therefore Be Bold*, a tale of growing up in a suburb
near Cleveland. *Love and Like* (1960) is a collection
of short fiction.

Many of Gold's later stories and articles have been
written for *Playboy Magazine*. In these and in his
novel *Salt* (1963), he shows some unfortunate effects
of too complete imaginative immersion in the scene
of sex and money obsession that he writes about.

Though Gold stoutly maintains that he intends to

show the sickness of his age through the adventures of this novel's lonely divorced hero, and though page after page is full of comic observation expressed with his inexhaustible phrasal fecundity, the plot does seem contrived, the material—some of it devoted to the making of pornographic movies—seems calculatedly provocative, and the happy ending sentimental and untrue. Like Baldwin, Gold apparently has difficulty finding adequate symbols in fiction for the strong positive values upon which the judgments in his essays are based.

"The Bachelor's Dilemma" begins with the interesting technique of multiple perspective and ends with a biological-moral definition of health close to that of Baldwin in "The Male Prison."

"The Age of Happy Problems" is a richly complete survey of the debilitating effect with which Madison Avenue, popular culture, and popular psychologizing have taken over or pervaded our lives. The question here, as in *Salt*, is whether Gold, so skilled in using or parodying the techniques of our corruptors, is really untouched by them; whether the recourse to inner life which he offers as a solution is more than a pious or conventional gesture.

"The American as Hipster," on the other hand, is a thoroughly tough, witty, sociologically informed denunciation of the decadent faddism which has settled like a blight on avant-garde art and behavior and spread into popular culture. He liberates us from false liberation by seeing so clearly, as Mary McCarthy did in her piece on Salinger, what is false and sentimental and life-denying at its roots.

The Bachelor's Dilemma

The confirmed bachelor can be defined as the man who has the courage of his lack of convictions. Once he hasn't made his mind up, he really sticks to it. Swinging more and more wildly from his loosening trapeze, he is another reeling acrobat in the disorganized circus of American love and marriage.

Let us look at him with magical omnipresence from a privileged station in the air above a big-city party. It could be anywhere in America—New York, Cleveland, Chicago, St. Louis, Houston, Denver, San Francisco. There is a crowd—busy, talkative, curious, and anxious—of human creatures hoping for amusement. Chink of glasses, gaggle of laughter, roll of eye. The bachelor enters alone.

What does the wife see? Sometimes she sees him as a bad example for her own husband, but more often she has tender feelings for him. She sees forbidden possibility: a handsome, perfect cavalier, perhaps, mysterious and challenging—unlike her all-too-real, all-too-known, heavy, snoring husband. (The bachelor never snores in the fancy of this lady.) Or she knows he is lonely and she sees a sweet lost lad to be comforted. Or she sees a combination of challenge and need. She wants to feed him, ease him of sorrow, perhaps—she tucks a tooth into her thoughtful lip—perhaps find him someone. Or, in some cases, if she and he are crowded into a corner with their drinks in their hands, she finds herself whispering those strange, hasty words in that bizarre language of invitation: "Call me. Call me. Hang up if a man answers."

What does the husband see? He may see a lucky man who has avoided the tender trap (a trap baited only with hope and desire) or a man who has been able to undo the clamps by brute force. He claps him on the back and says, "Still got your pick of things, eh Jack?" Or he sees a poor fellow who hasn't yet tasted the joys of children, hearth, steady conjugal affection. Or a paltry jokester, still trying to make out of an evening, like a fraternity boy or a conven-

THE BACHELOR'S DILEMMA. Reprinted from *The Age of Happy Problems* by Herbert Gold. Copyright © 1962, 1959, 1958, 1957 by Herbert Gold, and reprinted with the permission of the publishers, The Dial Press, Inc.

tioneer. Or perhaps he sees a challenge and a rival. ("Funny thing keeps happening. I answer the phone and the party on the other end hangs up.")

What does the girl see? Ah, she scents rather than sees. She recognizes a possible catch. But if he carries the reputation of a confirmed bachelor, the girlish mind boggles before vague threats from Sunday supplements and ancient movies—weekends at ski lodges, abrupt petulance and shortness of mood, flowers and candy, and then echoing silence heaped up about her while she shrivels into scorned spinsterhood. . . . She blinks. He approaches. He has nice teeth. He's a pleasant chap—no spats, cane, or waxed mustache. Still, she has been told that he has run through a dozen like her, and that his gray temples may bespeak merely an ironic heart. But I am different, she decides bravely. Let's see, if I spread my net in front of the canapé table, and bait it with dimples, promises of home cooking, and—"What kind of work do you do?"

What does another bachelor see? A comrade, a rival, a friend with one button missing from his shirt, who is likely to bore him with complaints and then steal his girl.

The hostess sees the available extra man. The food table—little bits of things placed upon little bits of things—sees a gobbling mouth which has skipped dinner. And perhaps the psychiatrist sees a patient. Our individual confirmed bachelor in his J. Press suit turns out to have about as many identities as there are people in the room.

And what does *he* see when he looks into the bathroom mirror in his studio apartment while dressing for this party? Perhaps he sees a healthy young man with plenty of time, money (as much as the Bureau of Internal Revenue allows him to keep), opportunity, willingness for adventure. He is all set and the lights are winking on and the evening is before him. No wife will make demands; no child will wake him later; he can eat, drink, and wander where, when, and how he pleases; he has the initiative. He can look over the world and take his pick and accept the challenge of fighting for her, or *her*, or HER. He dwells in realms of liberal choice. He has time for everything, visions and decisions and revisions. Showered, shaved, brushed, he finds himself the freest man on earth, if only he be willing to define the world narrowly and shrewdly enough.

Or he may discover somebody else in that mirror.

He stares and sees the frazzled face of the undecided man who slides down the razor blade of time—lonely, bored, lonely, lonely, and lonely. Asked why he finally married, one ex-bachelor said, "I got sick of that same old face in the bathroom mirror." He is tormented by a twisting loneliness which, oddly enough, feels to the belly very much like the pain of jealousy. But here we find just one person involved, a straight line any way you turn him, not three people, a triangle, as in the socialized pain of jealousy. He has less to contemplate; he has only his solitary, retracted state. The bachelor often suffers from indigestion and incipient ulcers. Too much restaurant food? Pans not clean enough? Or was the restaurant good but the interior monologue accompanying dinner stewed in unfriendly juices? He knows that all the statistics give him a shorter life expectancy—practical thought—than that of married men. Despite his naps, his self-indulgence, his cheerful acceptance of the haphazard, he dies young.

There is a law that a battery must be charged or it will be exhausted. It cannot generate from itself. The bachelor is a battery trying to charge itself.

In nature there is another parallel. A certain primitive variety of one-celled creature reproduces by what is called "binary fission"—by simply splitting in two. It requires no other, no mate. There appears to be nothing like sex needed. However, scientists notice under the microscope that a culture of these paramecia soon becomes "tired," "sluggish," and inactive, reproducing more and more slowly. Unless . . . and here is the curious detail. If the creature does not occasionally swim up to another like it, move alongside and exchange nuclei for a reason which has no normal mechanical explanation, it will finally slow down absolutely, disintegrate, die. But if it *does* perform this mysteriously friendly act, it will regain strength, move and feed with healthy vigor, and renew its process of reproduction by binary fission with elegant enthusiasm.

Which leads us back to the confirmed bachelor and a delicate matter. He is not a boy. He is not a child. It is no secret: one of his major problems is sex, and this fact fills a large part of his life and has obvious repercussions on the lives of all the people around him. If he is a confirmed bachelor, the genuine article, he has no guarantees in this area. Sex produces two kinds of trouble, and accordingly two kinds of bachelor. One bachelor is the shrewd Don Juan, attractive, capable, efficient, going off into the evening of his life to do battle with little black address book in hand and perhaps a list of historical, used-up girls in a secret drawer in his heart. He gets what he wants; but the trouble is: *he doesn't want what he gets.* He is often courted by women—as in that boyish dream where the responsibilities of manhood are taken over by clairvoyant girls—and he finds himself fought for as a commodity. Especially in large cities, where there tend to be more girls than men, he has an easy time of it. Everything works in his favor, even statistics. One confirmed bachelor says, "When I want to move or furnish a new apartment for myself, I just pick a girl who knows my taste. I tell her what I want, give her as much money as I want to spend, and tell her—*go.* I don't have time. She finds me what I want."

Smug? Hard-hearted?

Perhaps, but he can point out that the girl enjoys what she is doing. She wants to oblige; she wants to be needed, even if only as an unpaid interior decorator. Unmarried, without children, she is chafing to take hold. Far from feeling exploited, she is likely to harbor a tender indulgence for the man who trusts her so. She enjoys a brief glow of maternal and wifely joy. Later he can move her out of his life—or inform her that she has never moved in. "I didn't make her do anything she didn't want to do," he says. "She could have said no. Elaine or Barbara would have been glad to do it if she hadn't."

His friend pounds him on the shoulder. "You old manipulator! Playing with fire! Just you wait!"

"Of course, she really didn't have to sew all those curtains by hand. . . ."

And then there is the meeker, milder bachelor who, in his secret reverie, imagines himself a conqueror of dames, a hero in the lists of love, a brave commissioner of apartments to be decorated. He has girls who sew curtains for him in his dreams, but not during the long waking day. What about him? He is that man who sits on the automatic washer in the basement of his apartment house, waiting for his clothes to be done—a rumble in the machine and a rumble in his heart—and trying to figure out how to pass the evening after his TV dinner and his little stint of ironing. Later, wandering, he is one of the ghost ships that cruise the great cities, watching, discouraged, gray. (If he has a sun lamp, he can cruise discouraged and tanned.) He may be lucky. Some equally saddened, equally hopeful girl may take pity. He may even find himself buying love in that most paltry way—spending a few dollars for an imitation of feeling that no paramecium would envy. More likely, he takes a couple of drinks, numbs himself, sighs, hopes for better luck another time, and tumbles into bed.

Are these two men so different—the sleek Don Juan in quest of his ideal, the meek Don Mitty unable to find anything? No, they are blood brothers under the thick or thin skin; they are both deprived. Neither can attain a state of rest; neither has been able to settle for the possible. Both are forever looking, forever disappointed. The earth spins and they spin. They may buy themselves all sorts of pleasure—hi-fi, foreign travel, sports cars, the paraphernalia of elegant consumption. They are likely to have time and money for these things—one can live cheaper than two. They pamper themselves because they have no one else to love. In the first weeks after birth, infants think of the rest of the world as extensions of their own bodies; they don't understand that mother's breast and father's arms belong to separate, other persons. Like the infant, the bachelor is in primitive contact with the world of love, knowing only his craving, and so he remains infantile—extending his solitary body with the balm of luxury and indulgence. He follows the rule of constant enticement, seduction, dissatisfaction, another girl, wandering to another town, another girl, another job, another car, another girl. And again another.

Because no one reassures him very deeply his vanity is inflexible —it is the savage vanity of the child. In his search for "true love," he is eternally deceived and mocked. After the thrill of easy conquest, he asks himself once more, "Was it really conquest? She was, after all, so much like the others."

What does this do for the bachelor's masculine pride? It does not help it very much, any more than scratching an insect bite makes it stop itching. He itches more fiercely and knows no remedy. There are few things sadder than the success of the man who achieves all he craves, but then discovers his inmost thought: And now what? And now? And now?

The bachelor enacts an immense joke in which the leg he pulls may be his own. He searches for the "true meaning" of love, whose true meaning is that it has no single true meaning. He may finally, like the male models in certain advertisements, seem to be held together by little more than his clothes and his vanity; and if they were to let go, he would tinkle to earth in a little heap of discrete parts. His arms enfold air, his mouth kisses glass. His present is without a future or a past: it is only a place to store his tubes, drops, and pills (he grows hypochondriacal with age); with mysterious hope he takes vitamin E, which is said to be for fertility. Unless he explodes, protests, cries *No! no to all that!*—and thus joins the harried legions of newly-weds, forgetting his vitamins, and afterwards troubled in other ways.

Most of the time we see only the glamour of the bachelor's freedom. We find him dressed, preened, rested, at his social best. He may simply age peacefully in our sight, growing gracefully into the permanent "extra man" for hostesses. Or he may finally be more fortunate than most men and find the girl of his dreams, the girl out of whose kisses he builds—as a poet wrote—"a ladder to the stars." Equipped with experience and age, patience and determination, he wins exactly what he wants. He is then much to be envied. The prince has wandered the enchanted forest and found his heart's perfect desire—not merely fallen out of bed and awakened groping on the cold floor. What a lucky man! He lifts the wand and She speaks to him. . . .

We see him during his best moments, on the verge of that discovery, with new girls, trying.

Usually he does not find the girl of his dreams. That ladder to the stars lies folded in a closet somewhere. Another evening has been spilled away with a swell kid whose name he will soon forget.

We do not see him during those moments when he is alone in his apartment, wondering why. *Alone.* Back home alone to his cold bed, his vacant hopes, and his Dacron shirt drying in the bathroom.

The Age of Happy Problems

Recently I have had occasion to live again near my old college campus. I went into a hole-in-the-wall bakery where the proprietor recognized me after ten years. "You haven't changed a bit, son," he said, "but can you still digest my pumpernickel? The stomach gets older, no? Maybe you want something softer now—a nice little loaf I got here."

He had worn slightly. But for me the change was from twenty-two to thirty-two, and it is this ten-year time that I want to think about—the generation which came back from the war to finish college on the GI Bill and is now deep into its career. We are the generation which knew the Depression only through the exhilaration of the burgeoning New Deal and the stunned passion of war. I remember the bank crash because my mother wept and I said, "If we're poor now, can I wear corduroy pants?" For the most part, we were taken care of and never hopelessly hunted jobs. Now some of us say we are cool, say we are beat; but most of us are allrightniks—doing okay. We are successful. In the late forties and the fifties, it was hard to know economic struggle and want—and for the most part we didn't experience these traditional elements of youth—and it was hard for the skilled and the trained not to know success. We did not doubt overmuch. We have done well. How well?

"Money money money," as Theodore Roethke says.

> I have married my hands to perpetual agitation,
> I run, I run to the whistle of money.
>
> Money money money
> Water water water

I should like to take a look at some of the college idealists. The lawyer, fascinated by "the philosophy of law," now uses his study to put a smooth surface on his cleverness. Cardozo and Holmes? Very interesting, but let's find that loophole. The doctor who sent flowers to the first mother whose baby he delivered now specializes in "real-estate medicine"—his practice gives him capital for buying apartment houses. The architect who sat up all night haranguing his friends about Lewis Mumford and Frank Lloyd Wright now works for a mass builder who uses bulldozers to level trees and slopes, then puts up tri-level, semi-detached, twenty-year-mortgaged, fundamentally identical dormitories for commuters. He admits that his designs make no decent sense, but they do have that trivial, all-important meaning: "It's what the market wants, man. You'd rather I taught city planning for six thousand a year?"

The actor becomes a disc jockey, the composer an arranger, the painter a designer; the writer does TV scripts in that new classic formula, "happy stories about happy people with happy problems." How hard it is to be used at our best! One of the moral issues of every age has been that of finding a way for men and women to test, reach, and overreach their best energies. Society has always worked to level us. Socrates has always made it hot for the citizens in the market place. But there was usually room for the heroic—hemlock not a serious deterrent—and perhaps rarely so much room on all levels as in the frontier turbulence of the nineteenth and early twentieth century in America. Hands reached out like the squirming, grasping, struggling railroad networks; the open society existed; freedom had a desperate allure for the strongly ambitious, and men stepped up to take their chances—Abraham Lincoln and William James, Mark Twain and Melville, Edison and Rockefeller and Bet-a-Million Gates.

Allowing for a glitter of nostalgia on what we imagine about the past, still something has happened to change the old, movemented, free, open American society to something persuasive, plausible, comfortable, and much less open. We are prosperous, we get what we think we want, we have a relatively stable economy without totalitarian rule. "I'm not selling out," my friend the architect says, "I'm buying in." Without attempting a simple explanation of the causes of this age of happy problems, let us look at its consequences for the new postwar young people who should be in full action toward their ambitions and the surest, sturdiest signs of a civilization's health.

What are these personal symptoms? How is the vital individual human creature doing in his staff meetings, at his family's table, over the baby's bassinet, and with that distant secret self that he may sometimes meet at the water cooler? Well, for this man it is very hard to be exceptional. Talent apart, he has too much to do, too much on his mind, to give himself over to his best energies. Think, for example, of the writers in the advertising agencies, on TV, or in the colleges. They all wanted to write great books; they tend now to prefer "competence" as an ideal to greatness. Some of them are trying, but they risk the situation of the girl in the short-story writing class: "I can't be a creative writer, I can't, because I'm still a stupid virgin." She will take up going steady, she will take up marriage; she will be mildly disappointed; she will remain as she was, but aging—"adjusted," "integrated," virgin to danger, struggle, and the main chance of love and work.

In composite, in our thirties, we of this prosperous and successful generation are still in good health and rather fast at tennis (but practicing place shots which will eliminate the need to rush the net);

hair receding but still attractive to college girls, or at least recent graduates; a slight heaviness at the middle which makes us fit our jackets with especial care (sullen jowls beginning, too) or, if not that, a skinniness of anxiety (etching around the mouth, dryness of lips). We go to an athletic club. We play handball in heavy shirts "to sweat it off."

The girls we marry are beautiful in wondrous ways. Savant make-up is no longer sufficient. Blemishes are scraped until the skin is pink and new; scars are grown away by cortisone injections—what reason to be marked in this world?; noses are remade, the same for mother and daughter, just like heredity. Money is spent much more gracefully than in those fantastic times when silver coins were put in ears and jewels in navels.

The old truth—"we must all come from someplace"—is amended in 1956. We can create ourselves in our own image. And what is our own image? The buttery face in the Pond's advertisement, the epicene face in the Marlboro publicity.

The matters that we are told to worry about—and perhaps we think we worry about them—do not really trouble us. The prospect of war is like a vague headache, no worse. The memory of war is even dimmer. A depression is something which will reduce the value of our shares in the mutual fund, make us keep the old car another year. Radioactive fallout and the slow destruction of the human species through cancerous mutation—well, what is so much bother to imagine cannot really come to pass. Who lets the newspaper interfere with a good meal?

II

Still, we are not blithe spirits; birds we are not. This generation is particularly distinguished by its worry about making its wives happy, about doing right by its kids (title of a hugely popular paperbound book: *How to Play with Your Child*), about acquiring enough leisure and symbols of leisure, which it hopes to cash in for moral comfort. *Fortune* reports a method used by salesmen to get the second room air conditioner to the couple which already has one in its bedroom. "The machine operates as expected? Fine! You sleep better with it? So do I, that's just dandy. But, friends, let me tell you how I sleep so much better now that I know my kiddies are cool and comfy, too."

This capitalizes on the child-oriented anxiety which the class known commercially as Young Marrieds has been taught to feel by modern psychiatry. Advertisements for *McCall's*, "The Magazine of Togetherness," demonstrate Togetherness in a brilliant summer scene. The man, wearing a white skirtlike apron and a proud simper, is bending to serve a steak to his wife (summer frock, spike heels), who will season it for them and for their happy gamboling children. The little boy and girl are peeking and smiling. The wife is lying in a garden chair. Togetherness consists in the husband's delighting his wife and kids by doing the cooking.

Actually, of course, most American women don't want to go this far. They are already equal with men. Women are usually too wise to define "equal" as "better than." It is not momism or any such simple psychological gimmick that tells this sad tale. The consumer culture—in which leisure is a menace to be met by anxious continual consuming—devours both the masculinity of men and the femininity of women. The life of consuming requires a neuter anxiety, and the pressure to conform, to watch for our cues, to consume, makes us all the same—we are customers—only with slightly different gadgets. Women have long bought men's shirts; men are buying colognes with "that exciting musky masculine tang."

Togetherness represents a curious effort by a woman's magazine to bring men back into the American family. Togetherness does not restore to the man a part of his old-time independence. It does not even indicate that he may be the provider with an independent role defined partly by ambitions outside his family. Instead, it suggests the joys of being a helpmate, a part of the woman's full life, and battens greedily on the contemporary male's anxiety about pleasing his wife. The Togetherness theme has been a great commercial success. A full-page advertisement by that canny old American institution, the New York Stock Exchange, shows a photograph of a harried young man pleading with a young woman on a parlor couch. She remains unconvinced, pouting, hands gloved and folded together, as brutal as the shocked beauties in the classical halitosis or B.O. tragedies. The caption reads: "Is the girl you want to marry reluctant to say Yes? Do you need to build character with your wife? Then just use the magic words: I'LL START A MONTHLY INVESTMENT PLAN."

It used to be thought that answering economic needs was the main purpose of man's economic efforts. Now, however, an appeal to emotional insecurity about money—without crass financial trouble—can do good work for an advertiser. "Do you need to build character with your wife?" This is whimsey with a whammy in it. Money works symbolically to stimulate, then assuage male doubts.

> SHE: What can the stock do for our marriage?
> HE: It can help keep it sweet and jolly because when we own stock we are part-owners of the company.

In the image projected by this advertisement, the wife prosecutor, judge, and jury. She may fall into a less exalted role, however, while her husband is downtown making the money which will go for food, clothing, shelter, and sound common stocks. That she too frets about keeping her marriage sweet and jolly is obvious. The popular media again point to trouble while pitching a new solution to her problems. One of the former radio soap operas is now sponsored by Sleep-eze. Apparently almost everyone uses soap these days, but not everyone has caught on to the virtues of non-habit-forming sedatives. Want your husband to love you? This pill will help or your money back. "Ladies! Fall asleep without that unsightly twisting and turning."

It's time to mention Barbara. A tough wise creature of a girl, Barbara comes to this observation out of her marriage and love life: "Men worry too much about making the girl happy. We seem to scare them out of themselves. Let them really be pleased—that's what we want most of all—and then we'll be happy. Delighted. But really."

In other words, long live primary narcissism! And secondary. And tertiary. But let us call it by an older, better name—respect for the possibilities of the self. This includes the possibility of meaningful relationships with meaningful others.

III

Our wounds as a people in this time and place are not unique in kind, but the quality of difference makes this a marvelously disturbing period. The economic problem, no longer rooted in hunger for essential goods, food, housing, clothing, is an illustration of the difference. Sure, we are still busy over food—but packaged foods, luxury foods, goodies in small cans; housing—but the right house in the right neighborhood with the right furnishings and the right mortgage; clothing—but the cap with the strap in the back, Ivy

League pants, charcoal gray last year and narrow lapels this year, and male fashions changing as fast as female.

It used to be thought that, given money, relative job security, and the short work week, culture would then bloom like the gardens in the suburbs and the individual spirit would roar with the driving power of a Thunderbird getting away after a red light.

Who could have predicted that we would have to keep pace with a cultural assembly line in the leisure-time sweatshop? At least in the older sweatshop, you sighed, packed, and left the plant at last. Now we are forever harassed to give more, more, more. We no longer have to keep up with the Joneses; we must keep up with Clifton Fadiman. He is watching *you*. The steady pressure to consume, absorb, participate, receive, by eye, ear, mouth, and mail, involves a cruelty to intestines, blood pressure, and psyche unparalleled in history. The frontiersmen could build a stockade against the Indians, but what home is safe from Gilbert Highet? We are being killed with kindness. We are being stifled with cultural and material joys. Our wardrobes are full. What we really need is a new fabric that we don't have to wrinkle, spot, wash, iron, or wear. At a beautiful moment in *Walden*, Thoreau tells how he saw a beggar walking along with all his belongings in a single sack on his back. He wanted to weep for the poor man—because he still had that sack to carry.

The old-style sweatshop crippled mainly the working people. Now there are no workers left in America; we are almost all middle class as to income and expectations. Even the cultural elite labors among the latest in hi-fi equipment, trips to Acapulco and Paris, the right books in the sewn paper editions (Elizabeth Bowen, Arnold Toynbee, Jacques Barzun—these are the cultivated ones, remember), *Fortune* and the *Reporter*, art movies and the barbecue pit and the Salzburg music festival. It is too easy to keep up with the Joneses about cars and houses, but the Robert Shaw Chorale is a *challenge*. In the meantime, the man in the sweatshop is divorced or psychoanalyzed (these are perhaps remedies in a few cases); he raises adjusted children, or kills them trying; he practices Togetherness in a home with a wife who is frantic to be a woman and a non-woman at the same time; he broods about a job which does not ask the best that he can give. But it does give security; it is a good job. (In college this same man learned about the extreme, tragic instances of desire. Great men, great books. Now he reads Evelyn Waugh.)

In his later, philosophical transmogrification, David Riesman consoles the radar-flaunting other-directeds by holding out the reward of someday being "autonomous" if they are very, very good. Same thing, brother, same thing. When he describes the autonomous personality's "intelligent" distinctions among consumer products, exercising his creative imagination by figuring out why *High Noon* is a better western than a Gene Autry, well, then, in the words of Elvis Presley:

> Ah feel so lonely,
> Ah feel so lo-oh-oh-lonely.

We're in Heartbreak Hotel where, as another singer, Yeats, put it:

> The ceremony of innocence is drowned;
> The best lack all conviction, while the worst
> Are filled with a passionate intensity.

Refusal to share to the fullest degree in the close amity of the leisure-time sweatshop is—for Mr. Riesman—a kind of ethical bohemianism. His autonomous consumer, sociable, trained, and in the know, is a critic of the distinctions between the Book-of-the-Month Club and the Reader's Subscription, Inc., marks the really good shows in his TV guide, buys educational comic books for his children, tastes the difference in fine after-dinner coffee, knows that the novel is a dead form and why. Bumper to bumper in the traffic home from work, or jammed into the commuter train, he has plenty of time to think. And he does think (thinking means worrying) while the radio blares "The House with the Stained Glass Window" or "The Magic of Believing," a little rock-and-roll philosophical number.

Does he have a moral problem, let's say, about leaving a changing neighborhood "for the sake of the children"? He is a liberal, of course, but after all, the Negroes who are moving in come from a different world, and he should not inflict his principles on his children. Still, there is a certain discomfort. He discusses it with his analyst. *Why* does he suffer from this moral qualm? Does it have some link with the ever-ambiguous relationship with parents? *What* moral problem? They are all psychological. Anxiety can be consumed like any product. And from his new, split-level, sapling-planted housing development he speeds into the city now ten miles further out.

We are a disappointed generation. We are a discontented people. Our manner of life says it aloud even if discreetly our public faces smile. The age of happy problems has brought us confusion and anxiety amid the greatest material comfort the world has ever seen. Culture has become a consolation for the sense of individual powerlessness in politics, work, and love. With gigantic organizations determining our movements, manipulating the dominion over self which alone makes meaningful communion with others possible, we ask leisure, culture, and recreation to return to us a sense of ease and authority. But work, love, and culture need to be connected. Otherwise we carry our powerlessness with us onto the aluminum garden furniture in the back yard. Power lawn mowers we can buy, of course.

The solution in our age of happy problems is not to install (on time) a central air-conditioning system and a color TV this year because the room air conditioner and the black-and-white TV last year did not change our lives in any important respect. The solution is not in stylish religious conversions or a new political party. The answer is not even that Panglossian fantasy about "the autonomous personality" which will naturally emerge out of the fatal meeting of the other-directed consumer with a subscription to the *Saturday Review*.

The ache of unfulfilled experience throbs within us. Our eyes hurt. Vicarious pleasures buzz in our heads. Isn't there something more, something more?

There is still awareness; there is still effort. "It should be every man's ambition to be his own doctor." This doesn't mean that he should not see a dentist when his tooth hurts, perhaps a psychoanalyst when his psyche hurts; but he must hold in mind the ideal maximum of humanity—the exercise of intelligence and desire within a context of active health. The Stoic philosophers had a great, although impossible, idea for these crowding times: cultivate your own garden. We cannot retreat from the world any more—we never really could—but we can look for our best gardens within the world's trouble. There we must give ourselves silence and space; we can see what the will wants; we can make decisions. Only then—having come to terms with our own particularities—can we give the world more than a graceless, prefabricated commodity.

Hope? Some sweet Barbara is hope. And a work we love. And the strength, O Lord, not to accept the easy pleasures (easy anxieties) which have pleased us (made us anxious) so far. And the strength, O Lord, you who reign undefined above the psychoanalysts and the sociologists, the market researchers and the advertising agencies, the vice-presidents and the book clubs, to refuse the easy solutions which have becalmed us so far.

Then with good belly luck we will be able to digest strong, irregular, yeasty, black bread.

The American as Hipster

In Greenwich Village a dreamy young beggar in a tattered Ivy League summer suit and a buttondown collar with both buttons missing turns on an uptown couple to ask, "Gimme a quarter for a Cadillac, hey?"

In New Orleans a pretty little department store model approaches a man at a party, takes off her sweater, then her bra, and says, "Let's ball, dig"—by which she means, Let's try a new far-out sound on the hi-fi. If he reaches out to touch anything but the tone arm, she will say, "You're through, frantic boy. You are sawed off." He disappears from future guest lists.

In Denver a gaggle of young lads, not knowing what to do on a warm spring evening, steal a car each, drive them to the other side of town, park, steal a few more, drive back to the starting point, park, and then settle down to giggle about the confusion of the owners and the police. Silence. Return of boredom. Yawn. Finally one says softly, "Pops, why didn't we think of picking up on some chicks?"

In St. Louis a girl and her friend, who used to be a drummer with a well-known quintet, both of them suffering withdrawal symptoms —he has been working to support their habits by pimping for the girl—beg an old pal to put them up with bed and fridge for a few days. While the friend is away at work, they telephone a friend in San Francisco, give him the bit, and after gassing awhile, suggest that they both just keep the connection and leave the telephones off the hook. Their friend won't get the bill until they are gone, far gone. Why do this to him? "He's square, *so* square, man."

In Detroit a hi-fi engineer clucks sympathetically at the plight of a young couple in college. It's true love, but they have no place to go. The back seat of a car is for puppy love and sprained backs. OK, they can use his apartment. What they don't know is that there is a microphone concealed in the mattress. Their friend invites them to a party where he plays the tape before strangers.

In San Francisco a group of young poets announces Religious Poetry Night, attracting a hall full of the plump, mournful ladies (purple hats, veils, heaving freckled bosoms) who adore such things. The first poet gets up to read. "C— S——!" he shrieks at the audience.

On State Street in Chicago a frozen-faced grifter stops a passer-by, pushing out his hand and murmuring, "What you say, pop? Give me a piece of skin."

"I'm sorry, I don't know you."

"I don't know you either, man, but you like to have a party?" He slides off and away with a passive dreamy girlish look which has nothing sweet about it: it plots impossible meanness, anything to make him feel something. He doesn't know anybody, and says "man" to everybody because he can't be bothered remembering names.

In midtown Manhattan a writer, Jack Kerouac, prepares for his interview on TV. "We're beat, man," he says. "Beat means beatific, it means you get the beat, it means something. I invented it." For the television audience he announces, "We love everything, Billy Graham, the Big Ten, rock and roll, Zen, apple pie, Eisenhower— we dig it all. We're in the vanguard of the new religion." Jack Kerouac likes to write of Charlie Parker as God and himself as the Prophet.

These are hipsters.

Who is the hipster, what is it? The pure beast is as hard to track as the pure "student" or "midwesterner," but let us follow the spoor of history and symptoms. We will probably find that "pure hipster" is a phrase like "100% American"—an unstable compound with an indefinite content.

Hipsterism began in a complex effort of the Negro to escape his imposed role of happy-go-lucky animal. A few highly self-conscious urban Negro men sought to imitate "white" diffidence, or coolness, or beatness. They developed a style which was both a criticism of their Bible-shouting and jazz-loving parents and a parody of the detached, uninvolved city ofays. They improvised on an unstated theme—like bop—and if you weren't with it, with it and for it, you heard nothing but jangle. The horn rims of the intellectual came to be known as bop glasses. They blew fine abstractions. The joke was a good one.

Then their white friends took up the fashion, complicating the joke by parodying a parody of themselves. Cool music was the artistic expression of this hypertensive chill. However, in order to keep from dancing, keep from shouting, keep from feeling, a further help was needed and it was found in heroin. Some of the earlier hot musicians had used marijuana, many drank; these were springs toward jumping high in a group. There was a strong prejudice against the cats who went on junk, expressed in the superstition that you might mainline a fatal bubble of air into your veins. Uh-uh, no baby, they said: and in practice they found that the junkie blew lousy drum or horn, no matter what he thought he was blowing.

The new generation preferred supercelestial private music, however. Heroin dissolves the group and each man flies alone all the way to Barbados. And without flapping his arms.

Many other young Americans felt beat, wanted to keep cool, and so into the arms of the first hipster society, that still unravished bride of bop quietness, ran three angry herds: (1) Main-street thugs with their sideburns, their cycles, and their jeans; (2) college kids and a few literary chappies, finding in the addict's cool stance an expression of the frustration of fluid-drive lives in which the juicebox had gone dry; and (3) Upper Bohemia, tired of Van Gogh, Italian movies, charades, and sex, and so ready to try anti-art, anti-sex, anti-frantic nonmovement. These latter comprise the Madison Avenue hippies, models who strip merely to express their hatred of fashion magazines, admen and lawyers who marry call girls, a host of Ivy League symbol-manipulators, bloated with money and debt, pink with General Electric sun tans and shame, who express their benzedrine blues by wigging at night near a blasting rig. "Well, you know . . . Albert Schweitzer doesn't make me climb the wall. . . . Is it true he eloped with Kim Novak?"

"Everyone says," remarks the pretty girl who seeks to please, "that I'm exceptionally fastidious, but would you like me to do something nasty for you? I really wouldn't mind. My name is Grape-Nuts, what's yours?"

Let us now move in closer to the hipster's harried heart. When the hipster makes it with a girl, he avoids admitting that he likes her. He keeps cool. He asks her to do the work, and his ambition is to think about nothing, zero, strictly from nadaville, while she plays bouncy-bouncy on him. When the hipster makes it with boys, it's not because he's a homosexual and cares for it—it's for money, a ride home, pass the time of night while waiting for the band to come back on. When the hipster steals a car, he doesn't keep it or sell it; he hides it where the squares will have trouble finding it, and writes "Mort à Louis A" in soap on the windshield. When the hipster digs music, Proust, or religion, it's to talk over, it's to carry around in his jeans, it's to hit his buddies with; it makes no sense or feeling, and the weirder it is, the cooler the kick.

In other words, the hipster is a spectacular instance of the flight from emotion. He is like a sick refrigerator, laboring with tremendous violence, noise and heat, and all for one purpose—to keep cool. This refrigerator is powered by crime without economic need; an editor to one of the hipster writers complains, "Jeez, when I slept on park benches and boosted from the A and P, I did it because I had to. My kick was that I needed sleep and food. I didn't do it to tell people about." The refrigerator is powered by sex without passion; the sole passion is for the murder of feeling, the extinguishing of the jitters. The refrigerator is powered by religion without faith; the hipster teases himself toward the black battiness of oblivion, and all the vital refreshment which religion has given the mystics of the past is a distraction from the lovely stupor he craves. Unlike Onan, who spilled his seed upon the ground, the hipster spills his brains and calls it piety. He also wears music, art, and religion as a kind of badge for identification. Instead of the secret handshake which got him into Uncle Don's Boys' Club or the Orphan Annie Secret Society, he now says, "You dig the Bird? Proust? Zen?"

"I'm hip," says his friend. This phrase means: No need to talk. No more discussion. I'm with you. I got you. Cool. In. Bye-bye.

The language of hipsterism is a means toward noncommunication, a signal for silence. The truest lingo is narcotics, because this more than anything gives Little Boy Beat what he wants—release from imagination and the body—an illusion not of omnipotence, as we are sometimes told, but of a timeless browsing in eternity. In other words, a cool simulation of death. The sentimental and sensational talk about drugs producing sex maniacs is nonsense. The man on a habit needs nothing more than his fix. Quiet, quiet. He may perform terrible violence to get the drug, but not sex: pleasure has nothing to do with the dreamy high of heroin. The pale soft face of the addict, with his smudged passive eyes and his drooping mouth, is almost ladylike in his sweetness. It has no fight or love in it.

Heroin enables the hipster to stand guard over his soul, dreaming of cool nothing, beautiful beat nothing, while his feet go ratatat and he strokes a switchblade, a hand, or a copy of *Swann's Way*. Needless to say, the proto- and quasi-hipsters do not usually go all the way to the perfection of heroin.

The current fad for the hipster—his language, manners and attitudes—indicates that he is, as that fearful phrase goes, "no isolated phenomenon." Jack Kerouac proclaimed, "Even the Ivy League is going hip." Emerging out of bop, narcotics, and the subtle rebellion of the Negro against the charge of being "happy, excitable, emotional," the hipster takes one of his chief public models from that most authentic American source, the movies. He ignores the injunction of the pious thirteenth-century moralist, John of Garland, who wrote: "Be not a fornicator, O Student! Stand and sit upright, do not scratch thyself!" The Stanislavsky hipsters scratch as if their soul's unease were actually juicy fleas, slouch as if leaning to catch Marlon's word from earth or Jimmy's from vaulted heaven. The movie shadow of Dean or the Brando of *The Wild One* is a part of the image of the hipster, whether he be the smooth pink Ivy League metahipster, staring at himself in the mirror of one of those shops where they apparently do operations to remove the bones from men's shoulders, or the long-chinned hairy protohipster with a girl jiggling on the behind seat of his Harley-Davidson "74." In many theaters where *The Wild One* played, there was a lineup afterwards in the men's room, the cyclists in their nail-studded black jackets scowling with adoration into the mirror as they rehearsed their public roles. Each man was Brando, distant and violent. Each man was Marlon, cool and beat. They stood in a row without shame, almost without vanity (so pure it was), like neophytes for sacrifice in their penitential leather, silver trim, sideburns, and duckass haircuts. Scratch not, O Hipster!

And so the hipster's lines of communication spread from a four-bit movie-house in a small town of the Midwest to the chic saloons of New York and the Coast. He reminds us of the Teddy Boys of England, the breaking-loose wild brats of defeated Japan, the existentialist *zazous* of Paris, tootling the petrified dixie they learned from old Beiderbecke records. His apologists, particularly the literary hipsters of San Francisco and New York are fond of reaching back into history to invoke the criminal gods of French poetry— Rimbaud, who mysteriously vanished into Africa, Villon, who ended up dancing on the gallows, Genet, who is now a poet and playwright hero of Paris after a career of thievery, blackmail, and male prostitution. The very important difference between the American literary hipster and his foreign models is that the great artist-criminals were true outcasts from society: they did not pick themselves up by the seat of their own pants and toss themselves out. They were driven by class differences and economic pressure. A few of the Americans have performed spectacularly—mostly in the loony bin; one even played William Tell with his wife and blew her head off—but these are individual troubles, not the product of any vast and windy guilt of society. Who ain't got personal troubles? I dig yours, man; but I got mine too.

In any case, the 1958 hipster is not the bold medieval troubadour prince of song and con, nor the romantic adventurer poet of later times, nor the angry driven Depression stiff: he is the true rebel without a cause. No, of course, he has a cause—his charred self, but a self without connection or need. He is a reticent boyo with a yen for thuggery, a reluctant visitor to the affairs of men, a faintly girlish loiterer near the scenes of violence. If he can't be a big boom-boom hero in a war, like Gary Cooper, at least he can take the muffler off his rod, like Marlon. Mainly he is afflicted with the great triumvirate disease of the American male—Passivity, Anxiety, Boredom. Individualists without individuality, a sleepy brawl of knowing nonthinkers, the lonely crowd at its grumbling loneliest, the hipsters fall naturally to the absolute submission of a marriage to heroin. Like the submission to boredom in television and all the other substitutes for personal creativeness in American life, narcotics involve an abdication of good sense by men deprived of the will to make their own ways.

"I dig everything, man."

"What do you want to do now?"

"I don't know, man. Get some kicks somehow."

If the description of the hipster as "passive" strikes you as harsh, look up the dictionary definition of the word: "*Med.* Pertaining to certain morbid conditions characterized by deficient vitality and reaction."

The word hipster came in with bop, which is a way of keeping cool musically, at the same time that narcotics addiction burgeoned —a way of keeping cool sexually. The drug-taking hipster is not a sexual anarchist; he is a sexual zero, and heroin is his mama, papa, and someone in bed. (The pusher in *A Hatful of Rain* is called "Mother.") Not every quasi-hipster mainlines into the tattoo on his arm, of course, but the style of life is set by those who do. The coolest boys call each other "daddy-o," as if their passivity extends to thinking of every man as a potential guardian father. Of course, the traveling musician also cannot be bothered to remember names, so everyone is "man," "pops," "daddy-o." They worship the purple fantasy of torn–tee-shirted masculinity created by Tennessee Williams, William Inge, and others who have invented a new theatrical type—the male impersonator. Adorably brutal, stripped of the prime attributes of manliness—intelligence, purpose, control—they are the curvaceous Mae Wests of popular melodrama. Having died, James Dean and Charlie Parker are defined as immortal. Living and growing up a bit, Marlon Brando is a traitor to this myth of saintly suicide by sports car or heroin. They might have forgiven his giving up the bongos, but his receding hairline is a disgrace to the cause. The strong silent hero must also be weak and pretty.

One of the curious bypaths of hipsterism leads to their far-out religious camp. Jack Kerouac says, "We're in the vanguard of the new religion," which is a little like the monk in the story who claimed that he was the world champion for humility. They picked up on St. John of the Cross for a time, Catholic ritual, St. Francis of Assisi (they were St. Frantics); then they moved on toward Byzantine, Greek, and Orthodox fantasies, with ikons and incense; they made the Dostoevski scene. In recent years some have taken to calling themselves Zen Hipsters, and Zen Buddhism has spread like the Asian flu, so that now you can open your fortune cookie in one of the real cool Chinese restaurants of San Francisco and find a slip of paper with the straight poop: "Dig that crazy Zen sukiyaki. Only a square eats Chinese food." Promiscuity in religion stands, like heroin, for despair, a feverish embracing of despair, a passive sinking into irrationality. Zen and other religions surely have their beauties, but the hipster dives through them like a sideshow acrobat through a paper hoop—into the same old icy water of self-distrust below. The religious activities of the hipsters cure their unease in the world the way dancing cheek to cheek cures halitosis.

No wonder the hipster says, "Nada, I'm beat—I'm right in there, see—I'm the most religious, the most humble—I'm swinging, man." He stammers because something is missing, a vital part, the central works. His soul, sense of meaning, individual dignity (call it how you like) has been excised as unnecessary by a civilization very often producing without good purpose. He feels that love is not love, work is not work, even protest is not protest any more. On the consumer's assembly line, in the leisure-time sweatshop, he piece-works that worst of all products of anxiety—boredom. This is the response of retreat from the cold inanities of his time payments, luxurious discomfort, dread of the successful future. Boredom is a corollary to anxiety. As the middle-class man now buys a brick for the new church (Does God need that basement bowling alley?), so the hipster tries to find himself in intuitions of meaning through the Anchor edition of Zen tales, or through some other fashionable interior decoration. Naturally he stammers, "Cool, mon, real cool." He wants to stop moving, jittering, flittering. He displays himself as exemplary because he has no wife, children, responsibilities, politics, work. The middle-class man both has and does not have these things. Who can call moving bits of paper a job? Most Americans are paper-movers. How is love of wife and children more than a social habit when a man feels *qua* man (not as husband or father) that he has no authority except in his own home?

When a man's house is his only castle, then he has no castle.

Both smugness and ambition are characteristics of human beings, not of animals, though rats and rabbits can be taught despair by repeated electric shocks. Faced by the threat of absolute manipulation, the hipster mobilizes himself for a last stand—and hops about the cage, twitching his tail, bumping the charged wires.

The cliché which tells us that Americans love Things, Possessions, does not go far enough. Americans also demand experiences of power, one way or the other, in person or out of the picture tube. This seems normal enough to be a condition of life, but not when the starved mirage of power crowds out the quietness which gives experience meaning and organizes a man to face his private issues of working, loving, having children, dying. Certain experiences lead *away from* rather than *toward*, and faster and faster we go: the experience does not help; we try wilder experience; this does not help; still more wild, wilder. The extreme of a flatulent submission to the mass media eventually stops all experience in its tracks, in the guise of giving perfect experiences which make it possible to carry on. Television as a medium of entertainment is not the villain any more than good whiskey is a villain; they can both be good friends. It is the bleared submission by depleted souls which destroys. Relaxation is one thing—sharing experience vicariously is a great experience to which the imagination entitles us. To be stunned is another matter entirely. Despair by electronic shock.

Sensitive to all this, the hipster has decided to quit—resign—have no more of it. Instead of being part of a mass audience before the picture tubes, he becomes an audience of one before the hypo. He gives up on the issue of being human in society. He decides that the problem does not exist for him. He disaffiliates. The man who cares is now derided for being "frantic."

But of course the hipster is still a part of a bewildered America in which Tab Hunter confides to an interviewer that he can only sleep with his Teddy bear in bed with him. The hipster is victim of the most hopeless condition of slavery—the slave who does not know that he is a slave and is proud of his slavery, calling it "freedom." Incurable? Nearly. The posture of negation and passivity thinks it is religion and rebellion; instead it is a mob phenomenon. These nihilists sail dreamy down the Nile of throughway America, spending many a sleepless day figuring out something real cool to do at night, and end up trying to convince themselves, as Jack Kerouac does, that Charlie Parker is God. Kerouac's birdmen in his novel, *On the Road*, search for coolness within their beatness, hipness within their jeans-and-dirty-hair dream of quickies with marvelous girls (who also wear dirty hair and jeans). Occasionally, as in the Kerouac variety of superfrantic subhipster, sex takes the place of dope. This is a kind of sex which also takes the place of sex. The way some men gloat over possessions, he keeps score of his hero's erotic blitzes, forgetting that—if you are the trooper who uses sex as a weapon—every notch in a weapon weakens the weapon.

The hipster is a street-corner, bar, and partying phenomenon, a creature of mobs. One Rimbaud may be a genius; a crowd of them is a fad. An earlier fad for psychoanalysis has this in favor of it: Freud believed in the prime value of emotions, but in a necessary control by the intelligence. In other words, he valued society despite the discontents of civilization. The hipster gives up society, gives up intelligence, and thinks he is doing this in favor of the emotions; but he has already, without making a decision about them, let his feelings seep away through a leaky personality. What is left is a spasmodic jerk, though some of the individual spokesmen also have vivacious talent. No wonder that the madhouse is seen as the refuge of their "best minds." Catatonia, here we come.

These shrill moonbirds turn out to be rigid earth satellites, rocketed by bureaucrats beyond their ken into the air of reality, where they circle in a pattern determined without choice, give out a diminishing signal, draw to earth and burn, crumble, vanish.

When Yeats looked into the future to find a terrible savior, an evolution up from animality into something strange and wonderful:

> What rough beast, its hour come round at last,
> Slouches toward Bethlehem to be born?

—he did not mean James Dean. Perhaps, as they claim, the tunneling hipster's avoidance of feeling can lead to a new honesty of emotion. Perhaps a groundhog might some day learn to fly, but man O man, that will be one strange bird.

APPENDIX

THE SELECTIONS which follow are by some of the best or most amusing essayists of the past four centuries, arranged in the order of their authors' birth dates. They were chosen, first, because what they say is still relevant and interesting; second, because their subjects are discussed in contrasted or complementary ways by other contributors to this volume; and, third, because they are sufficiently characteristic of their period in style, diction, and attitude, to give us a sense of historical change and continuity.

Francis Bacon's "Of Death" is composed of terse, pregnant sentences imitated from the Latin authors whom he too abundantly quotes. His attitude toward personal death is, for his epoch, surprisingly psychological and nontheological. Compare it with Hamlet's "To be or not to be" soliloquy, and the selections from Lamb and Emerson.

Swift's "Modest Proposal" is the most famous short satire in English. Its technical virtuosity consists of working out so monstrous and impossible a project at such length—perhaps too great length—in ostensibly practical terms. The real shock comes from feelings, rooted very deep in infantile anxiety, about eating and being eaten. Is there a certain perversity, a sadistic satisfaction, in dwelling, and forcing others to dwell, on this particularly upsetting form of cannibalism? Still, this macabre proposal for population control grows out of a social concern as serious as Huxley's in "The Double Crisis."

Addison's "Will Wimble," already discussed in the Introduction, combines a type character sketch with sociological observation. In the light of what Gold, Baldwin, Lawrence, and others say about

357

psychological satisfactions and cultural health, we may ask whether Wimble's life really was so wasted.

Johnson's "Letter from Euphelia" is also an inquiry into what makes life worth living, to be compared with the responses to nature or rural residence found in essays by Forster, Hazlitt, and White. It is amusing to see Johnson writing as a fashionable young lady without much modification of his famous style. Is he as condescendingly ironic about her tastes as might at first appear? Johnson, himself, was a thoroughly urban type who dined out constantly and blossomed in the company of cultivated ladies.

Charles Lamb has always been held up as the very model of the familiar essayist. "Witches, and Other Night-Fears," however, is more than merely charming or fanciful in the manner of "A Dissertation on Roast Pig." Written with his usual brilliance, it is a searching study of how emotional imagination is stimulated in childhood, and anticipates many of the insights of depth psychology. He even uses the Jungian word "archetype" in exactly the Jungian sense.

Hazlitt is usually named immediately after Lamb in lists of the classic familiar essayists in English. But Hazlitt had also a serious concern with philosophy and aesthetics. Here such thinking leads to the discovery of a very fruitful distinction between the general and the specific, which "On the Love of the Country" develops lucidly and with fine use of illustration.

Thomas De Quincey, the "English opium-eater," anticipated both the psychoanalysts and the surrealists in his preoccupation with dreams and hallucinations. Although some of its alliterations and patterned recurrences may seem excessive, "Levana and Our Ladies of Sorrow" is one of the most famous stylistic displays in the whole history of English prose. In a period when teachers on the whole discourage "fine writing" or experimentation with formal rhetoric by their students, it is well to be reminded that writing, like music and cookery, has many modes, and that the wider our appreciation the greater our enjoyment. The three goddesses who appear here can be compared with those discussed by Freud in an essay called "The Theme of the Three Caskets."

Ralph Waldo Emerson was a popular lecturer without making any concessions to popularity in spiritual exaltation and vision. But like a number of the essayists included, he combined startling rhetorical effects with homely allusions and language. Emersonian optimism and his sense of being at one with the world have often been criticized for ignoring pain and ineradicable conflict. In this essay, written for the transcendentalist magazine *The Dial*, Emerson starts with an apparently full acknowledgment of suffering and tragedy. Then he moves step by step toward the Emersonian position, but by what may seem questionable arguments or even a callous "explaining away" of others' suffering, especially in the references to the slave trade.

Max Beerbohm's "A Relic," a beautifully controlled piece of writing, was discussed fully in the Introduction.

G. K. Chesterton, one of the most prolific producers of essays in the early twentieth century, begins "The Twelve Men" playfully but almost immediately makes use of the jury experience as occasion for an indictment of official indifference, professional narrowness, and the general human failure really to "see" what is before us. From a background of very different religious and political views he is attacking the same problem of man's inhumanity that later preoccupied Orwell, Baldwin, Forster, and Lawrence.

"Poe's Helen," a book review by Virginia Woolf, shows how a critic can cull some of the more diverting details from a book so as to make us want to read the whole, and at the same time develop coherently a theme suggested by the work. As a character sketch and study of the poetic temperament, it may be compared with "Trooper Silas Tomkyn Comberbacke" written by her friend E. M. Forster. Mrs. Woolf was a brilliant stylist whose deep artistic sympathies developed out of a life of psychic suffering that ended with suicide.

Though Thurber's "Here Lies Miss Groby" seems a slight and light-hearted essay, it gives us a much sharper sense of metonymy and metaphor, of the relation between the literal and figurative, at the same time that it pokes friendly fun at those who are happy with literary analysis only when it can be forced into the Procrustean bed of the quantitative and definitive, as if it were a physical science.

Edmund Wilson's "Mr. More and the Mithraic Bull," already discussed in the Introduction, gives us in narrative form a glimpse of all the elements that go into the forming and limiting of literary attitudes, as Mary McCarthy's "My Confession" did for political positions.

Robert Benchley's essay illustrates the kind of wish-fufillment daydreaming in which everyone indulges, especially where conflicts with authority are concerned, and from which much popular literature is derived. At the same time, by showing that after violent mental effort even his imaginary conversations come out wrong, he makes comic capital of his own ineptness and misadventures. This ability is typical of *The New Yorker* writer of the period.

Frank Sullivan's "The Night the Old Nostalgia Burned Down" is a kind of surrealist synthesis of all narratives of personal reminiscence, which have filled publishers' lists for decades. His humour is directed, obviously, not at reminiscence itself, but at its clichés and egotism and sentimentality.

Books loved in childhood provide a kind of absorbed delight that never can be quite duplicated in adult experience. No subject of conversation causes such an animated sharing of recollections as the comparison of childhood tastes in books, comics, television series, and moving pictures. Early encounters with literature, of course, are really decisive experiences for those who become authors. Many authors have discussed this, but Greene's essay is one of the best, and makes us understand, as we could not have understood before, what gave his own fiction its distinctive character.

Of Death

FRANCIS BACON

Men fear death, as children fear to go in the dark; and as that natural fear in children is increased with tales, so is the other. Certainly, the contemplation of death, as the *wages of sin*, and passage to another world, is holy and religious; but the fear of it, as a tribute due unto nature, is weak. Yet in religious meditations there is sometimes mixture of vanity and of superstition. You shall read in some of the friars' books of mortification, that a man should think with himself what the pain is if he have but his finger's end pressed or tortured, and thereby imagine what the pains of death are, when the whole body is corrupted and dissolved: when many times death passeth with less pain than the torture of a limb; for the most vital parts are not the quickest of sense. And by him, that spake only as a philosopher and natural man, it was well said, *Pompa mortis magis terret quam mors ipsa.*[1] Groans and convulsions, and a discoloured face, and friends weeping, and blacks, and obsequies, and the like, shew death terrible. It is worthy the observing, that there is no passion in the mind of man so weak, but it mates and masters the fear of death; and therefore death is no such terrible enemy, when a man hath so many attendants about him that can win the combat of him. Revenge triumphs over death; love slights it; honour aspireth to it; grief flieth to it; fear pre-occupateth it; nay, we read, after Otho the emperor had slain himself, pity (which is the tenderest of affections) provoked many to die, out of mere compassion to their sovereign, and as the truest sort of followers. Nay, Seneca adds niceness and satiety: *Cogita quam diu eadem feceris; mori velle, non tantum fortis, aut miser, sed etiam fastidiosus potest.*[2] A man would die, though he were neither valiant nor miserable, only upon a weariness to do the same thing so oft over and over. It is no less worthy to observe, how little alteration, in good spirits, the approaches of death make; for they appear to be the same men till the last instant.

---

[1] The trappings of death terrify more than death itself.
[2] Think how long you have been doing the same thing; death may be desired not only by the valiant or the miserable, but also by the bored.

Augustus Cæsar died in a compliment: *Livia, conjugii nostri memor, vive et vale.*[3] Tiberius in dissimulation, as Tacitus saith of him: *Jam Tiberium vires et corpus, non dissimulatio, deserebant.*[4] Vespasian in a jest, sitting upon the stool: *Ut puto Deus fio.*[5] Galba with a sentence, *Feri, si ex re sit populi Romani,*[6] holding forth his neck. Septimius Severus in dispatch: *Adeste si quid mihi restat agendum.*[7] And the like. Certainly the Stoics bestowed too much cost upon death, and by their great preparations made it appear more fearful. Better saith he, *Qui finem vitae extremum inter munera ponat Naturae.*[8] It is as natural to die as to be born; and to a little infant, perhaps, the one is as painful as the other. He that dies in an earnest pursuit is like one that is wounded in hot blood; who, for the time, scarce feels the hurt; and therefore a mind fixed and bent upon somewhat that is good doth avert the dolours of death. But above all, believe it, the sweetest canticle is *Nunc dimittis;*[9] when a man hath obtained worthy ends and expectations. Death hath this also, that it openeth the gate to good fame, and extinguisheth envy.— *Extinctus amabitur idem.*[10]

(*A Modest Proposal*) for Preventing the Children of Ireland from being a Burden to their Parents or Country and for making them beneficial to the Publick (*1729*)

JONATHAN SWIFT

It is a melancholly Object to those, who walk through this great Town or travel in the Country, when they see the *Streets*, the *Roads* and *Cabbin-doors* crowded with *Beggars* of the Female Sex, followed by three, four, or six Children, *all in Rags,* and importun-

---

[3] Remembering our marriage, Livia, live and fare well.
[4] Tiberius was now losing his bodily strength, but not his powers of dissimulation.
[5] I think I am becoming a god.
[6] Strike if it be for the sake of the Roman people.
[7] Be ready if anything remains for me to do.
[8] Who considers the end of life one of the blessings of nature.
[9] Now lettest thou thy servant depart. (Luke 2:29)
[10] The same man (who was envied) will be loved when dead.

ing every Passenger for an Alms. These *Mothers* instead of being able to work for their honest Livelyhood, are forced to employ all their Time in stroling to beg Sustenance for their *helpless Infants,* who, as they grow up, either turn *Thieves* for want of Work; or leave *their dear Native Country, to fight for the Pretender in Spain;* or sell themselves to the *Barbadoes.*

I think it is agreed by all Parties, that this prodigious number of Children in the Arms, or on the Backs, or at the *Heels* of their *Mothers,* and frequently of their *Fathers,* is *in the present deplorable state of the Kingdom,* a very great additional Grievance; and therefore, whoever could find out a fair, cheap and easy Method of making these Children sound and useful Members of the Commonwealth, would deserve so well of the Publick, as to have his Statue set up for a Preserver of the Nation.

But my Intention is very far from being confined to provide only for the Children of *professed Beggars:* it is of a much greater Extent, and shall take in the whole Number of Infants at a certain Age, who are born of Parents in effect as little able to support them, as those who demand our Charity in the Streets.

As to my own Part, having turned my Thoughts, for many Years, upon this important Subject, and maturely weighed the several *Schemes of other Projectors,* I have always found them grosly mistaken in their *computation.* It is true a Child, *just dropt from its Dam,* may be supported by her Milk, for a Solar Year with little other Nourishment at most not above the Value of two Shillings, which the Mother may certainly get, or the Value in *Scraps,* by *her lawful Occupation of Begging;* and it is exactly at one Year Old that I propose to provide for them in such a Manner, as, instead of being a *Charge* upon their *Parents,* or the *Parish,* or *wanting Food and Raiment* for the rest of their Lives, they shall, on the Contrary, contribute to the *Feeding* and partly to the *Cloathing* of many Thousands.

There is likewise another great Advantage in my Scheme, that it will prevent those *voluntary Abortions,* and that horrid Practice of *Women murdering their Bastard Children,* alas! too frequent among us; sacrificing the *poor innocent Babes,* I doubt, more to avoid the expence than the Shame, which would move Tears and Pity in the most Savage and inhuman Breast.

The number of Souls in *Ireland* being usually reckoned one Million and a half; of these I calculate there may be about two hundred thousand Couple whose Wives are Breeders; from which number I substract thirty Thousand Couples, who are able to maintain their own Children; although I apprehend there cannot be so many, under *the present Distresses of the Kingdom;* but this being granted, there will remain an hundred and seventy thousand Breeders. I again Substract fifty Thousand, for those Women who miscarry, or whose Children die by accident, or disease within the Year. There only remain an hundred and twenty thousand Children of poor Parents annually born: The question therefore is, How this number shall be reared, and provided for? which, as I have already said, under the present Situation of Affairs, is utterly impossible by all the Methods hitherto proposed: For we can *neither employ them in Handicraft* or *Agriculture;* we neither build Houses, (I mean in the Country) nor cultivate Land: They can very seldom pick up a Livelyhood *by Stealing* until they arrive at six years Old; except where they are of towardly parts; although, I confess, they learn the Rudiments much earlier; during which time they can however be properly looked upon only as *Probationers;* as I have been informed by a principal Gentleman in the County of Cavan, who protested to me, that he never knew above one or two Instances under the Age of six, even in a part of the Kingdom *so renowned for the quickest Proficiency in that Art.*

I am assured by our Merchants, that a Boy or a Girl before twelve years Old, is no saleable Commodity; and even when they come to this Age, they will not yield above three Pounds, or three Pounds and a half a Crown at most, on the Exchange; which cannot turn to Account either to the Parents or Kingdom, the Charge of Nutriment and Rags having been at least four times that Value.

I shall now therefore humbly propose my own Thoughts, which I hope will not be liable to the least Objection.

I have been assured by a very knowing *American* of my acquaintance in *London,* that a young healthy Child well Nursed is, at a year Old, a most delicious nourishing and wholesome Food, whether *Stewed, Roasted, Baked,* or *Boiled;* and I make no doubt that it will equally serve in a *Fricasie,* or a *Ragoust.*

I do therefore humbly offer it to *publick consideration,* that of the Hundred and twenty thousand Children, already computed, twenty thousand may be reserved for Breed, whereof only one fourth part to be Males; which is more than we allow to *Sheep, black Cattle,* or *Swine;* and my Reason is, that these Children are seldom the Fruits of Marriage, *a Circumstance not much regarded by our Savages;* therefore, *one Male* will be sufficient to serve *four Females.* That the remaining Hundred thousand may, at a year Old, be offered in Sale to the *Persons of Quality* and *Fortune,* through the Kingdom; always advising the Mother to let them suck plentifully in the last Month, so as to render them Plump, and Fat, for a good Table. A Child will make two Dishes at an Entertainment for Friends; and when the Family dines alone, the fore or hind Quarter will make a reasonable Dish; and seasoned with a little Pepper or Salt will be very good Boiled on the fourth Day, especially in *Winter.*

I have reckoned upon a Medium, that a Child just born will weigh twelve pounds; and in a solar Year, if tolerably nursed, encreaseth to twenty eight Pounds.

I grant this Food will be somewhat dear, and therefore very *proper for Landlords;* who, as they have already devoured most of the Parents seem to have the best Title to the Children.

Infant's Flesh will be in Season throughout the Year; but more plentiful in *March,* and a little before and after; for we are told by a grave *Author an eminent *French* Physician, that *Fish being a prolifick Dyet,* there are more Children born in *Roman Catholick Countries* about Nine Months after *Lent,* than at any other Season: Therefore reckoning a Year after *Lent,* the Markets will be more glutted than usual; because the Number of *Popish Infants,* is, at least, three to one in this Kingdom; and therefore it will have one other Collateral advantage; by lessening the Number of *Papists* among us.

I have already computed the Charge of nursing a Beggar's Child (in which List I reckon all *Cottagers, Labourers,* and Four fifths of the *Farmers*) to be about two Shillings *per Annum,* Rags included; and I believe no Gentleman would repine to give Ten Shillings for the *Carcase of a good fat Child;* which, as I have said, will make four Dishes of excellent nutritive meat, when he hath only some particular Friend, or his own Family, to dine with him. Thus the Squire will learn to be a good Landlord, and grow popular among his Tenants; the Mother will have Eight Shillings net Profit, and be fit for Work till she produceth another Child.

Those who are more thrifty (as *I must confess the Times require*) may flay the Carcase; the Skin of which, artificially dressed, will make admirable *Gloves for Ladies,* and *Summer Boots for fine Gentlemen.*

As to our City of *Dublin;* Shambles may be appointed for this Purpose, in the most convenient Parts of it, and Butchers we may be assured will not be wanting; although I rather recommend buying the Children alive, and dressing them hot from the Knife, as we do *roasting Pigs*.

A very worthy Person, a *true Lover of his Country*, and whose Virtues I highly esteem, was lately pleased, in discoursing on this Matter, to offer a Refinement upon my Scheme. He said, that many Gentlemen of this Kingdom, having of late destroyed their Deer; he conceived that the Want of Venison might be well supplied by the Bodies of young Lads and Maidens, not exceeding fourteen Years of Age, nor under twelve; so great a Number of both Sexes in every County being ready to Starve, for want of Work and Service: And these to be disposed of by their Parents, if alive, or otherwise by their nearest Relations. But with due Deference to so excellent a Friend, and so deserving a Patriot, I cannot be altogether in his Sentiments. For as to the Males, my *American* Acquaintance assured me from frequent Experience, that their Flesh was generally tough and lean, like that of our School-boys, by continual Exercise, and their Taste disagreeable; and to fatten them would not answer the Charge. Then, as to the Females, it would, I think, with humble Submission, *be a Loss to the Publick*, because they soon would become Breeders themselves: And besides it is not improbable, that some scrupulous People might be apt to censure such a Practice, (although indeed very unjustly) as a little bordering upon Cruelty; which, I confess, hath always been with me the strongest Objection against any Project, how well soever intended.

But in order to justify my Friend; he confessed, that this Expedient was put into his Head by the famous *Salmanaazor*, a Native of the Island *Formosa*, who came thence to *London*, above twenty Years ago, and in Conversation told my Friend, that in his Country, when any young Person happened to be put to Death, the Executioner sold the Carcase to *Persons of Quality*, as a prime Dainty, and that, in his Time, the Body of a plump Girl of fifteen, who was crucified for an Attempt to poison the Emperor, was sold to his Imperial *Majesty's prime Minister of State*, and other great *Mandarins* of the Court, *in Joints from the Gibbet*, at Four hundred Crowns. Neither indeed can I deny, that if the same Use were made of several plump young girls in this Town, who, without one single Groat to their Fortunes, cannot stir Abroad without a Chair, and appear at the *Play-house*, and *Assemblies* in foreign fineries, which they never will pay for; the Kingdom would not be the worse.

Some Persons of a desponding Spirit are in great Concern about that vast Number of poor People, who are Aged, Diseased, or Maimed; and I have been desired to imploy my Thoughts what Course may be taken, to ease the Nation of so grievous an Incumbrance. But I am not in the least Pain upon that Matter; because it is very well known, that they are every Day *dying*, and *rotting*, by *Cold* and *Famine*, and *Filth*, and *Vermin*, as fast as can be reasonably expected. And as to the younger Labourers, they are now in almost as hopeful a Condition: They cannot get Work, and consequently pine away for Want of Nourishment, to a Degree, that if at any Time they are accidentally hired to common Labour, they have not Strength to perform it; and thus the Country, and themselves, are in a fair Way of being delivered from the Evils to come.

I have too long digressed; and therefore shall return to my Subject. I think the Advantages by the Proposal which I have made are obvious, and many, as well as of the highest Importance.

For *First*, as I have already observed, it would greatly lessen the *Number of Papists*, with whom we are yearly over-run; being the principal Breeders of the Nation, as well as our most dangerous Enemies; and who stay at home on purpose with a Design *to deliver the Kingdom to the Pretender;* hoping to take their Advantage by the Absence of *so many good Protestants*, who have chosen rather to leave their Country, than stay at home, and pay Tithes against their Conscience, to an idolatrous *Episcopal Curate*.

Secondly, The poorer Tenants will have something valuable of their own, which by Law may be made lyable to Distress, and help to pay their Landlord's Rent; their Corn and Cattle being already seized, and *Money a Thing unknown*.

Thirdly, Whereas the Maintenance of an hundred thousand Children, from two Years old, and upwards, cannot be computed at less than Ten Shillings a Piece *per Annum*, the Nation's Stock will be thereby increased fifty thousand Pounds *per Annum;* besides the Profit of a new Dish, introduced to the Tables of all *Gentlemen of Fortune* in the Kingdom, who have any Refinement in Taste; and the Money will circulate among our Selves, the Goods being entirely of our own Growth and Manufacture.

Fourthly, The constant Breeders, besides the Gain of eight Shillings *Sterling per Annum*, by the Sale of their Children, will be rid of the Charge of maintaining them after the first Year.

Fifthly, This Food would likewise bring great *Custom to Taverns,* where the Vintners will certainly be so prudent as to procure the best Receipts for dressing it to Perfection; and consequently have their Houses frequented by all the *fine Gentlemen,* who justly value themselves upon their Knowledge in good Eating; and a skilful Cook, who understands how to oblige his Guests, will contrive to make it as expensive as they please.

Sixthly, This would be a great Inducement to Marriage, which all wise Nations have either encouraged by Rewards, or enforced by Laws and Penalties. It would encrease the Care and Tenderness of Mothers towards their Children, when they were sure of a Settlement for Life, to the poor Babes, provided in some Sort by the Publick, to their annual Profit instead of Expence. We should soon see an honest Emulation among the married Women, *which of them could bring the fattest Child to the Market.* Men would become as *fond* of their Wives, during the Time of their Pregnancy, as they are now of their *Mares* in Foal, their *Cows* in Calf, or *Sows* when they are ready to farrow; nor offer to beat or kick them (as is too *frequent* a Practice) for fear of a Miscarriage.

Many other Advantages might be enumerated. For Instance, the addition of some thousand Carcasses in our Exportation of Barreled Beef: The Propagation of *Swine's Flesh,* and Improvement in the Art of making good *Bacon,* so much wanted among us by the great Destruction of Pigs, too frequent at our Tables, which are no way comparable in Taste, or Magnificence to a well grown, fat yearling Child; which roasted whole will make a considerable Figure at a *Lord Mayor's Feast,* or any other Publick Entertainment. But this, and many others, I omit, being studious of Brevity.

Supposing that one thousand Families in this City, would be constant Customers for Infant's Flesh; besides others who might have it at *merry Meetings,* particularly at *Weddings* and *Christenings;* I compute that *Dublin* would take off Annually about twenty thousand Carcasses; and the rest of the Kingdom (where probably they will be sold somewhat cheaper) the remaining eighty Thousand.

I can think of no one Objection, that will possibly be raised against this Proposal; unless it should be urged, that the Number of People will be thereby much lessened in the Kingdom. This I freely own, and it was indeed one principal Design in offering it to the World. I desire the Reader will observe, that I calculate my Remedy *for this one individual Kingdom of* IRELAND, *and for no*

other that ever was, is, or, I think, ever can be upon Earth. Therefore let no man talk to me of other Expedients: *Of taxing our Ab-
sentees at five Shillings a Pound: Of using neither Cloaths, nor
Household Furniture, except what is of our own Growth and Manufacture: Of utterly rejecting the Materials and Instruments that
promote Foreign Luxury: Of curing the Expensiveness of Pride,
Vanity, Idleness, and Gaming in our Women: Of introducing a
Vein of Parsimony, Prudence, and Temperance: Of learning to love
our Country, wherein we differ even from* LAPLANDERS, *and the Inhabitants of* TOPINAMBOO: *Of quitting our Animosities, and Fac-
tions, nor act any longer like the Jews, who were murdering one
another at the very Moment their City was taken: Of being a little
cautious not to sell our Country and Consciences for nothing: Of
teaching Landlords to have at least one Degree of Mercy towards
their Tenants.* Lastly, *of putting a Spirit of Honesty, Industry, and
Skill into our Shopkeepers; who, if a Resolution could now be taken
to buy only our Native Goods, would immediately unite to cheat
and exact upon us in the Price, the Measure, and the Goodness; nor
could ever yet be brought to make one fair Proposal of just Dealing,
though often and earnestly invited to it.*

Therefore I repeat, let no Man talk to me of these and the like
expedients; till he hath at least some Glimspe of Hope, that there
will ever be some hearty and sincere Attempt to put *them in Practice.*

But as to my self; having been wearied out for many Years with
offering vain, idle, visionary Thoughts, and at length utterly
despairing of Success, I fortunately fell upon this Proposal; which as
it is wholly new, so it hath something *Solid* and *Real*, of no Expence
and little Trouble, full in our own Power; and whereby we can in-
cur no Danger in *disobliging* ENGLAND. For this kind of Commodity
will not bear Exportation; the Flesh being of too tender a Consist-
ence to admit a long Continuance in Salt; *although perhaps I could
name a Country, which would be glad to eat up our whole Nation
without it.*

After all, I am not so violently bent upon my own Opinion, as to
reject any Offer proposed by wise Men, which shall be found
equally Innocent, Cheap, Easy, and Effectual. But before something
of that kind shall be advanced, in Contradiction to my Scheme, and
offering a better; I desire the Author, or Authors, will be pleased
maturely to consider two Points. *First,* As Things now stand, how

they will be able to find Food and Raiment for a hundred Thousand useless Mouths and Backs. And *Secondly*, There being a round Million of Creatures in Human Figure, throughout this Kingdom; whose whole Subsistence put into a common Stock, would leave them in Debt two Millions of Pounds *Sterling;* adding those, who are Beggars by Profession, to the Bulk of Farmers, Cottagers and Labourers, with their Wives and Children, who are Beggars in Effect; I desire those Politicians, who dislike my Overture, and may perhaps be so bold to attempt an Answer, that they will first ask the Parents of these Mortals, Whether they would not, at this Day, think it a great Happiness to have been sold for Food at a Year Old, in the manner I prescribe; and thereby have avoided such a perpetual Scene of Misfortunes, as they have since gone through; by the *Oppression of Landlords;* the Impossibility of paying Rent without Money or Trade; the Want of common Sustenance, with neither House nor Cloaths to cover them from the Inclemencies of the Weather; and the most inevitable Prospect of intailing the like, or greater Miseries, upon their Breed for ever.

I profess, in the Sincerity of my Heart, that I have not the least Personal Interest in endeavouring to promote this necessary Work; having no other Motive than the *Publick Good of my Country, by advancing our Trade, providing for Infants, relieving the Poor, and giving some Pleasure to the Rich.* I have no Children, by which I can propose to get a single Penny; the youngest being nine Years old, and my Wife past Child-bearing.

Will Wimble (Spectator 108)

JOSEPH ADDISON

Wednesday, July 4
Gratis anhelans, multa agendo nihil agens.
Phaed.

As I was Yesterday Morning walking with Sir ROGER before his House, a Country-Fellow brought him a huge Fish, which, he told him, Mr. *William Wimble* had caught that very Morning; and that he presented it, with his Service, to him, and intended to come and dine with him. At the same Time he delivered a Letter, which my Friend read to me as soon as the Messenger left him.

SIR ROGER,

I Desire you to accept of a Jack, which is the best I have caught this Season. I intend to come and stay with you a Week, and see how the Perch bite in the *Black River*. I observed, with some Concern, the last Time I saw you upon the Bowling-Green, that your Whip wanted a Lash to it: I will bring half a Dozen with me that I twisted last Week, which I hope will serve you all the Time you are in the Country. I have not been out of the Saddle for six Days last past, having been at *Eaton* with Sir *John's* eldest Son. He takes to his Learning hugely.

I am, Sir,

Your humble Servant,

WILL WIMBLE

This extraordinary Letter, and Message that accompanied it, made me very curious to know the Character and Quality of the Gentleman who sent them; which I found to be as follows: *Will. Wimble* is younger Brother to a Baronet, and descended of the ancient Family of the *Wimbles.* He is now between Forty and Fifty; but being bred to no Business and born to no Estate, he generally lives with his elder Brother as Superintendant of his Game. He hunts a Pack of Dogs better than any Man in the Country, and is very famous for finding out a Hare. He is extremely well versed in all the little Handicrafts of an idle Man: He makes a *May*-fly to a Miracle; and furnishes the whole Country with Angle-Rods. As he is a good-natur'd officious Fellow, and very much esteemed upon Account of his Family, he is a welcome Guest at every House, and keeps up a good Correspondence among all the Gentlemen about him. He carries a Tulip-Root in his Pocket from one to another, or exchanges a Puppy between a couple of Friends that live perhaps in the opposite Sides of the County. *Will.* is a particular Favourite of all the young Heirs, whom he frequently obliges with a Net that he has weaved, or a Setting-dog that he has *made* himself: He now and then presents a Pair of Garters of his own knitting to their Mothers or Sisters; and raises a great deal of Mirth among them, by enquiring as often as he meets them *how they wear?* These Gentleman-like Manufactures and obliging little Humours, make *Will.* the Darling of the Country.

Sir ROGER was proceeding in the Character of him, when we saw

him make up to us, with two or three Hazle-twigs in his Hand that
he had cut in Sir ROGER's Woods, as he came through them, in his
Way to the House. I was very much pleased to observe on one Side
the hearty and sincere Welcome with which Sir ROGER received
him, and on the other the secret Joy which his Guest discovered at
Sight of the good old Knight. After the first Salutes were over,
Will. desired Sir ROGER to lend him one of his Servants to carry a
Set of Shuttlecocks he had with him in a little Box to a Lady that
liv'd about a Mile off, to whom it seems he had promised such a
Present for above this half Year. Sir ROGER's Back was no sooner
turn'd, but honest *Will.* began to tell me of a large Cock-Pheasant
that he had sprung in one of the neighbouring Woods, with two or
three other Adventures of the same Nature. Odd and uncommon
Characters are the Game that I look for, and most delight in; for
which Reason I was as much pleased with the Novelty of the Person
that talked to me, as he could be for his Life with the springing of a
Pheasant, and therefore listened to him with more than ordinary Attention.

In the Midst of his Discourse the Bell rung to Dinner, where the
Gentleman I have been speaking of had the Pleasure of seeing the
huge Jack, he had caught, served up for the first Dish in a most
sumptuous Manner. Upon our sitting down to it he gave us a long
Account how he had hooked it, played with it, foiled it, and at
length drew it out upon the Bank, with several other Particulars that
lasted all the first Course. A Dish of Wild-fowl that came afterwards furnished Conversation for the rest of the Dinner, which
concluded with a late Invention of *Will's* for improving the Quail
Pipe.

Upon withdrawing into my Room after Dinner, I was secretly
touched with Compassion towards the honest Gentleman that had
dined with us; and could not but consider with a great deal of Concern, how so good an Heart and such busy Hands were wholly
employed in such Trifles; that so much Humanity should be so little
beneficial to others, and so much Industry so little advantageous to
himself. The same Temper of Mind and Application to Affairs
might have recommended him to the publick Esteem, and have
raised his Fortune in another Station of Life. What Good to his
Country or himself might not a Trader or Merchant have done with
such useful tho' ordinary Qualifications?

Will Wimble's is the Case of many a younger Brother of a great

Family, who had rather see their Children starve like Gentlemen, than thrive in a Trade or Profession that is beneath their Quality. This Humour fills several Parts of *Europe* with Pride and Beggary. It is the Happiness of a trading Nation, like ours, that the younger Sons, tho' uncapable of any liberal Art or Profession, may be placed in such a Way of Life, as may perhaps enable them to vie with the best of their Family: Accordingly we find several Citizens that were launched into the World with narrow Fortunes, rising by an honest Industry to greater Estates than those of their elder Brothers. It is not improbable but *Will.* was formerly tried at Divinity, Law, or Physick; and that finding his Genius did not lie that Way, his Parents gave him up at length to his own Inventions: But certainly, however improper he might have been for Studies of a higher Nature, he was perfectly well turned for the Occupations of Trade and Commerce. As I think this is a Point which cannot be too much inculcated, I shall desire my Reader to compare what I have here written with what I have said in my Twenty first Speculation.

Letter from Euphelia (Rambler 42)

SAMUEL JOHNSON

Saturday, August 11, 1750

Mihi tarda fluunt ingrataque tempora.
—HOR. EPIST. i. 1. 23.
How heavily my time revolves along. —ELPHINSTON.
TO THE RAMBLER.

MR. RAMBLER,

I am no great admirer of grave writings, and, therefore, very frequently lay your papers aside before I have read them through; yet I cannot but confess that, by slow degrees, you have raised my opinion of your understanding, and that, though I believe it will be long before I can be prevailed upon to regard you with much kindness, you have, however, more of my esteem than those whom I sometimes make happy with opportunities to fill my teapot, or pick up my fan. I shall, therefore, choose you for the confidant of my distresses, and ask your counsel with regard to the means of conquering or escaping them, though I never expect from you any of that softness and pliancy, which constitutes the perfection of a companion for the ladies; as, in the place where I now am, I have recourse to the mastiff for protection, though I have no intention of making him a lapdog.

My mamma is a very fine lady, who has more numerous and more frequent assemblies at our house, than any other person in the same quarter of the town. I was bred from my earliest infancy in a perpetual tumult of pleasure, and remember to have heard of little else than messages, visits, play-houses, and balls; of the awkwardness of one woman, and the coquetry of another; the charming convenience of some rising fashion, the difficulty of playing a new game, the incidents of a masquerade, and the dresses of a court-night. I knew before I was ten years old all the rules of paying and receiving visits, and to how much civility every one of my acquaintance was entitled: and was able to return, with the proper degree of reserve, or of vivacity, the stated and established answer to every compliment; so that I was very soon celebrated as a wit and a beauty, and had heard before I was thirteen all that is ever said to a young lady. My mother was generous to so uncommon a degree as to be pleased with my advance into life, and allowed me, without envy or reproof, to enjoy the same happiness with herself; though most women about her own age were very angry to see young girls so forward, and many fine gentlemen told her how cruel it was to throw new chains upon mankind, and to tyrannize over them at the same time with her own charms, and those of her daughter.

I have now lived two and twenty years, and have passed of each year nine months in town, and three at Richmond; so that my time has been spent uniformly in the same company, and the same amusements, except as fashion has introduced new diversions, or the revolutions of the gay world have afforded new successions of wits and beaus. However, my mother is so good an economist of pleasure, that I have no spare hours upon my hands; for every morning brings some new appointment, and every night is hurried away by the necessity of making our appearance at different places, and of being with one lady at the opera, and with another at the card-table.

When the time came of settling our scheme of felicity for the summer, it was determined that I should pay a visit to a rich aunt in a remote country. As you know the chief conversation of all tea-tables, in the spring, arises from a communication of the manner in which time is to be passed till winter, it was a great relief to the barrenness of our topics, to relate the pleasures that were in store for me, to describe my uncle's seat, with the park and gardens, the charming walks and beautiful waterfalls; and every one told me how much she envied me, and what satisfaction she had once enjoyed in a situation of the same kind.

As we are all credulous in our own favour, and willing to imagine some latent satisfaction in any thing which we have not experienced, I will confess to you, without restraint, that I had suffered my head to be filled with expectations of some nameless pleasure in a rural life, and that I hoped for the happy hour that should set me free from noise, and flutter, and ceremony, dismiss me to the peaceful shade, and lull me in content and tranquillity. To solace myself under the misery of delay, I sometimes heard a studious lady of my acquaintance read pastorals, I was delighted with scarce any talk but of leaving the town, and never went to bed without dreaming of groves, and meadows, and frisking lambs.

At length I had all my clothes in a trunk, and saw the coach at the door; I sprung in with ecstasy, quarrelled with my maid for being too long in taking leave of the other servants, and rejoiced as the ground grew less which lay between me and the completion of my wishes. A few days brought me to a large old house, encompassed on three sides with woody hills, and looking from the front on a gentle river, the sight of which renewed all my expectations of pleasure, and gave me some regret for having lived so long without the enjoyment which these delightful scenes were now to afford me. My aunt came out to receive me, but in a dress so far removed from the present fashion, that I could scarcely look upon her without laughter, which would have been no kind requital for the trouble which she had taken to make herself fine against my arrival. The night and the next morning were driven along with inquiries about our family; my aunt then explained our pedigree, and told me stories of my great-grandfather's bravery in the civil wars; nor was it less than three days before I could persuade her to leave me to myself.

At last, economy prevailed; she went in the usual manner about her own affairs, and I was at liberty to range in the wilderness, and sit by the cascade. The novelty of the objects about me pleased me for a while, but after a few days they were new no longer, and I soon began to perceive that the country was not my element; that shades, and flowers, and lawns, and waters, had very soon exhausted all their power of pleasing, and that I had not in myself any fund of satisfaction with which I could supply the loss of my customary amusements.

I unhappily told my aunt, in the first warmth of our embraces, that I had leave to stay with her ten weeks. Six only are yet gone, and how shall I live through the remaining four? I go out and return; I pluck a flower, and throw it away; I catch an insect, and when I have examined its colours, set it at liberty; I fling a pebble into the water, and see one circle spread after another. When it chances to rain, I walk in the great hall, and watch the minute-hand upon the dial, or play with a litter of kittens, which the cat happens to have brought in a lucky time.

My aunt is afraid I shall grow melancholy, and therefore encourages the neighbouring gentry to visit us. They came at first with great eagerness to see the fine lady from London, but when we met, we had no common topic on which we could converse; they had no curiosity after plays, operas, or music; and I find as little satisfaction from their accounts of the quarrels or alliances of families, whose names, when once I can escape, I shall never hear. The women have now seen me, know how my gown is made, and are satisfied; the men are generally afraid of me, and say little, because they think themselves not at liberty to talk rudely.

Thus I am condemned to solitude; the day moves slowly forward, and I see the dawn with uneasiness, because I consider that night is at a great distance. I have tried to sleep by a brook, but find its murmurs ineffectual; so that I am forced to be awake at least twelve hours, without visits, without cards, without laughter, and without flattery. I walk because I am disgusted with sitting still, and sit down because I am weary with walking. I have no motive to action, nor any object of love, or hate, or fear, or inclination. I cannot dress with spirit, for I have neither rival nor admirer. I cannot dance without a partner, nor be kind, nor cruel, without a lover.

Such is the life of Euphelia, and such it is likely to continue for a month to come. I have not yet declared against existence, nor called upon the Destinies to cut my thread; but I have sincerely resolved not to condemn myself to such another summer, nor too hastily to flatter myself with happiness. Yet I have heard, Mr. Rambler, of those who never thought themselves so much at ease as in solitude, and cannot but suspect it to be some way or other my own fault, that, without great pain, either of mind or body, I am thus weary of myself: that the current of youth stagnates, and that I am languishing in a dead calm, for want of some external impulse. I shall therefore think you a benefactor to our sex, if you will teach me the art of living alone; for I am confident that a thousand and a thousand and a thousand ladies, who affect to talk with ecstasies of the pleasures of the country, are in reality, like me, longing for the winter, and wishing to be delivered from themselves by company and diversion.

I am, Sir, Yours,
EUPHELIA

Witches, and Other Night-Fears

CHARLES LAMB

We are too hasty when we set down our ancestors in the gross for fools, for the monstrous inconsistencies (as they seem to us) involved in their creed of witchcraft. In the relations of this visible world we find them to have been as rational, and shrewd to detect an historic anomaly, as ourselves. But when once the invisible world was supposed to be opened, and the lawless agency of bad spirits assumed, what measures of probability, of decency, of fitness, or proportion—of that which distinguishes the likely from the palpable absurd—could they have to guide them in the rejection or admission of any particular testimony?—That maidens pined away, wasting inwardly as their waxen images consumed before a fire—that corn was lodged, and cattle lamed—that whirlwinds uptore in diabolic revelry the oaks of the forest—or that spits and kettles only danced a fearful-innocent vagary about some rustic's kitchen when no wind was stirring—were all equally probable where no law of agency was understood. That the prince of the powers of darkness, passing by the flower and pomp of the earth, should lay preposterous siege to the weak fantasy of indigent eld—has neither likelihood nor unlikelihood *à priori* to us, who have no measure to guess at his policy, or standard to estimate what rate those anile souls may fetch in the devil's market. Nor, when the wicked are expressly symbolized by a goat, was it to be wondered at so much, that *he* should come sometimes in that body, and assert his metaphor.—That the intercourse was opened at all between both worlds was perhaps the mistake—but that once assumed, I see no reason for disbelieving one attested story of this nature more than another on the score of absurdity. There is no law to judge of the lawless, or canon by which a dream may be criticised.

I have sometimes thought that I could not have existed in the days of received witchcraft; that I could not have slept in a village where one of those reputed hags dwelt. Our ancestors were bolder or more obtuse. Amidst the universal belief that these wretches were in league with the author of all evil, holding hell tributary to their muttering, no simple Justice of the Peace seems to have scrupled issuing, or silly Headborough serving, a warrant upon them—as if they should subpœna Satan!—Prospero in his boat, with his books and wand about him, suffers himself to be conveyed away at the mercy of his enemies to an unknown island. He might have raised a storm or two, we think, on the passage. His acquiescence is in exact analogy to the non-resistance of witches to the constituted powers. —What stops the Fiend in Spenser from tearing Guyon to pieces —or who had made it a condition of his prey, that Guyon must take assay of the glorious bait—we have no guess. We do not know the laws of that country.

From my childhood I was extremely inquisitive about witches and witch-stories. My maid, and more legendary aunt, supplied me with good store. But I shall mention the accident which directed my curiosity originally into this channel. In my father's book-closet, the History of the Bible, by Stackhouse, occupied a distinguished station. The pictures with which it abounds—one of the ark, in particular, and another of Solomon's temple, delineated with all the fidelity of ocular admeasurement, as if the artist had been upon the spot —attracted my childish attention. There was a picture, too, of the Witch raising up Samuel, which I wish that I had never seen. We shall come to that hereafter. Stackhouse is in two huge tomes—and there was a pleasure in removing folios of that magnitude, which, with infinite straining, was as much as I could manage, from the situation which they occupied upon an upper shelf. I have not met with the work from that time to this, but I remember it consisted of Old Testament stories, orderly set down, with the *objection* appended to each story, and the *solution* of the objection regularly tacked to that. The *objection* was a summary of whatever difficulties had been opposed to the credibility of the history, by the shrewdness of ancient or modern infidelity, drawn up with an almost complimentary excess of candour. The *solution* was brief, modest, and satisfactory. The bane and antidote were both before you. To doubts so put, and so quashed, there seemed to be an end for ever. The dragon lay dead, for the foot of the veriest babe to trample on. But—like as was rather feared than realised from that slain monster in Spenser—from the womb of those crushed errors young dragonets would creep, exceeding the prowess of so tender a Saint George as myself to vanquish. The habit of expecting objections to every passage, set me upon starting more objections; for the glory of finding a solution of my own for them. I became staggered and perplexed, a sceptic in long coats. The pretty Bible stories which I had read, or heard read in church, lost their purity and sincerity of impression, and were turned into so many historic or chronologic theses to be defended against whatever impugners. I was not to disbelieve them, but—the next thing to that—I was to be quite sure that some one or other would or had disbelieved them. Next to making a child an infidel, is the letting him know that there are infidels at all. Credulity is the man's weakness, but the child's strength. O, how ugly sound scriptural doubts from the mouth of a babe and a suckling!—I should have lost myself in these mazes, and have pined away, I think, with such unfit sustenance as these husks afforded, but for a fortunate piece of ill-fortune, which about this time befel me. Turning over the picture of the ark with too much haste, I unhappily made a breach in its ingenious fabric—driving my inconsiderate fingers right through the two larger quadrupeds—the elephant, and the camel—that stare (as well they might) out of the two last windows next the steerage in that unique piece of naval architecture. Stackhouse was henceforth locked up, and became an interdicted treasure. With the book, the *objections* and *solutions* gradually cleared out of my head, and have seldom returned since in any force to trouble me.—But there was one impression which I had imbibed from Stackhouse, which no lock or bar could shut out, and which was destined to try my childish nerves rather more seriously.—That detestable picture!

I was dreadfully alive to nervous terrors. The night-time solitude, and the dark, were my hell. The sufferings I endured in this nature would justify the expression. I never laid my head on my pillow, I suppose, from the fourth to the seventh or eighth year of my life—

so far as memory serves in things so long ago—without an assurance, which realized its own prophecy, of seeing some frightful spectre. Be old Stackhouse then acquitted in part, if I say, that to his picture of the Witch raising up Samuel—(O that old man covered with a mantle!) I owe—not my midnight terrors, the hell of my infancy—but the shape and manner of their visitation. It was he who dressed up for me a hag that nightly sate upon my pillow—a sure bed-fellow, when my aunt or my maid was far from me. All day long, while the book was permitted me, I dreamed waking over his delineation, and at night (if I may use so bold an expression) awoke into sleep, and found the vision true. I durst not, even in the day-light, once enter the chamber where I slept, without my face turned to the window, aversely from the bed where my witch-ridden pillow was.—Parents do not know what they do when they leave tender babes alone to go to sleep in the dark. The feeling about for a friendly arm—the hoping for a familiar voice—when they wake screaming—and find none to soothe them—what a terrible shaking it is to their poor nerves! The keeping them up till midnight, through candle-light and the unwholesome hours, as they are called,—would, I am satisfied, in a medical point of view, prove the better caution.—That detestable picture, as I have said, gave the fashion to my dreams—if dreams they were—for the scene of them was invariably the room in which I lay. Had I never met with the picture, the fears would have come self-pictured in some shape or other—

Headless bear, black man, or ape—

but, as it was, my imaginations took that form.—It is not book, or picture, or the stories of foolish servants, which create these terrors in children. They can at most but give them a direction. Dear little T.H. who of all children has been brought up with the most scrupulous exclusion of every taint of superstition—who was never allowed to hear of goblin or apparition, or scarcely to be told of bad men, or to read or hear of any distressing story—finds all this world of fear, from which he has been so rigidly excluded *ab extra,* in his own "thick-coming fancies;" and from his little midnight pillow, this nurse-child of optimism will start at shapes, unborrowed of tradition, in sweats to which the reveries of the cell-damned murderer are tranquillity.

Gorgons, and Hydras, and Chimæras—dire stories of Celæno

and the Harpies—may reproduce themselves in the brain of superstition—but they were there before. They are transcripts, types—
the archetypes are in us, and eternal. How else should the recital of
that, which we know in a waking sense to be false, come to affect us
at all?—or

> ——Names, whose sense we see not,
> Fray us with things that be not?

Is it that we naturally conceive terror from such objects, considered
in their capacity of being able to inflict upon us bodily injury?—O,
least of all! These terrors are of older standing. They date beyond
body—or, without the body, they would have been the same. All
the cruel, tormenting, defined devils in Dante—tearing, mangling,
choking, stifling, scorching demons—are they one half so fearful to
the spirit of a man, as the simple idea of a spirit unembodied following him—

> Like one that on a lonesome road
> Doth walk in fear and dread,
> And having once turn'd round, walks on,
> And turns no more his head;
> Because he knows a frightful fiend
> Doth close behind him tread.[1]

That the kind of fear here treated of is purely spiritual—that it is
strong in proportion as it is objectless upon earth—that it predomi-
nates in the period of sinless infancy—are difficulties, the solution of
which might afford some probable insight into our antemundane
condition, and a peep at least into the shadow-land of pre-existence.

My night-fancies have long ceased to be afflictive. I confess an occasional night-mare; but I do not, as in early youth, keep a stud of
them. Fiendish faces, with the extinguished taper, will come and
look at me; but I know them for mockeries, even while I cannot
elude their presence, and I fight and grapple with them. For the
credit of my imagination, I am almost ashamed to say how tame and
prosaic my dreams are grown. They are never romantic, seldom
even rural. They are of architecture and of buildings—cities abroad,
which I have never seen, and hardly have hope to see. I have trav-
ersed, for the seeming length of a natural day, Rome, Amsterdam,
Paris, Lisbon—their churches, palaces, squares, marketplaces, shops,

[1] Mr. Coleridge's *Ancient Mariner.*

suburbs, ruins, with an inexpressible sense of delight—a map-like distinctness of trace—and a day-light vividness of vision, that was all but being awake.—I have formerly travelled among the Westmoreland fells—my highest Alps,—but they are objects too mighty for the grasp of my dreaming recognition; and I have again and again awoke with ineffectual struggles of the inner eye, to make out a shape in any way whatever, of Helvellyn. Methought I was in that country, but the mountains were gone. The poverty of my dreams mortifies me. There is Coleridge, at his will can conjure up icy domes, and pleasure-houses for Kubla Khan, and Abyssinian maids, and songs of Abara, and caverns,

Where Alph, the sacred river, runs,

to solace his night solitudes—when I cannot muster a fiddle. Barry Cornwall has his tritons and his nereids gamboling before him in nocturnal visions, and proclaiming sons born to Neptune—when my stretch of imaginative activity can hardly, in the night season, raise up the ghost of a fish-wife. To set my failures in somewhat a mortifying light—it was after reading the noble Dream of this poet, that my fancy ran strong upon these marine spectra; and the poor plastic power, such as it is, within me set to work, to humor my folly in a sort of dream that very night. Methought I was upon the ocean billows at some sea nuptials, riding and mounted high, with the customary train sounding their conchs before me, (I myself, you may be sure, the *leading god*,) and jollily we went careering over the main, till just where Ino Leucothea should have greeted me (I think it was Ino) with a white embrace, the billows gradually subsiding, fell from a sea-roughness to a sea-calm, and thence to a river-motion, and that river (as happens in the familiarization of dreams) was no other than the gentle Thames, which landed me, in the wafture of a placid wave or two, alone, safe and inglorious, somewhere at the foot of Lambeth palace.

The degree of the soul's creativeness in sleep might furnish no whimsical criterion of the quantum of poetical faculty resident in the same soul waking. An old gentleman, a friend of mine, and a humorist, used to carry this notion so far, that when he saw any stripling of his acquaintance ambitious of becoming a poet, his first question would be,—"Young man, what sort of dreams have you?" I have so much faith in my old friend's theory, that when I feel that idle vein returning upon me, I presently subside into my proper element of prose, remembering those eluding nereids, and that inauspicious inland landing.

On the Love of the Country

WILLIAM HAZLITT

To the Editor of 'THE ROUND TABLE'

SIR,

I do not know that any one has ever explained satisfactorily the true source of our attachment to natural objects, or of that soothing emotion which the sight of the country hardly ever fails to infuse into the mind. Some persons have ascribed this feeling to the natural beauty of the objects themselves; others to the freedom from care, the silence and tranquillity, which scenes of retirement afford; others to the healthy and innocent employments of a country life; others to the simplicity of country manners, and others to different causes; but none to the right one. All these causes may, I believe, have a share in producing this feeling; but there is another more general principle, which has been left untouched, and which I shall here explain, endeavouring to be as little sentimental as the subject will admit.

Rousseau, in his 'Confessions'—the most valuable of all his works —relates that, when he took possession of his room at Annecy, at the house of his beloved mistress and friend, he found that he could see "a little spot of green" from his window, which endeared his situation the more to him, because, he says, it was the first time he had had this object constantly before him since he left Boissy, the place where he was at school when a child.[1] Some such feeling as that here described will be found lurking at the bottom of all our attachments of this sort. Were it not for the recollections habitually associated with them, natural objects could not interest the mind in the manner they do. No doubt the sky is beautiful; the clouds sail majestically along its bosom; the sun is cheering; there is something

[1] Pope also declares that he had a particular regard for an old post which stood in the courtyard before the house where he was brought up.

exquisitely graceful in the manner in which a plant or tree puts
forth its branches; the motion with which they bend and tremble in
the evening breeze is soft and lovely; there is music in the babbling
of a brook; the view from the top of a mountain is full of grandeur;
nor can we behold the ocean with indifference. Or, as the minstrel
sweetly sings—

> Oh, how can'st thou renounce the boundless store
> Of charms which Nature to her vot'ry yields?
> The warbling woodland, the resounding shore,
> The pomp of groves, and garniture of fields;
> All that the genial ray of morning gilds,
> And all that echoes to the song of even;
> All that the mountain's sheltering bosom shields,
> And all the dread magnificence of heaven—
> Oh, how can'st thou renounce, and hope to be forgiven!

It is not, however, the beautiful and magnificent alone that we
admire in Nature; the most insignificant and the rudest objects are
often found connected with the strongest emotions; we become attached to the most common and familiar images, as to the face of a
friend whom we have long known, and from whom we have received many benefits. It is because natural objects have been associated with the sports of our childhood, with air and exercise, with
our feelings in solitude, when the mind takes the strongest hold of
things, and clings with the fondest interest to whatever strikes its
attention; with change of place, the pursuit of new scenes, and
thoughts of distant friends: it is because they have surrounded us in
almost all situations, in joy and in sorrow, in pleasure and in pain—
because they have been one chief source and nourishment of our
feelings, and a part of our being, that we love them as we do ourselves.

There is, generally speaking, the same foundation for our love of
Nature as for all our habitual attachments, namely, association of
ideas. But this is not all. That which distinguishes this attachment
from others is the transferable nature of our feelings with respect to
physical objects, the associations connected with any one object extending to the whole class. My having been attached to any particular person does not make me feel the same attachment to the next
person I may chance to meet; but if I have once associated strong
feelings of delight with the objects of natural scenery, the tie becomes indissoluble, and I shall ever after feel the same attachment to

other objects of the same sort. I remember, when I was abroad, the trees and grass and wet leaves rustling in the walks of the Tuileries seemed to be as much English, to be as much the same trees and grass that I had always been used to, as the sun shining over my head was the same sun which I saw in England; the faces only were foreign to me. Whence comes this difference? It arises from our always imperceptibly connecting the idea of the individual with man, and only the idea of the class with natural objects. In the one case, the external appearance or physical structure is the least thing to be attended to; in the other, it is everything. The springs that move the human form, and make it friendly or adverse to me, lie hid within it. There is an infinity of motives, passions, and ideas contained in that narrow compass, of which I know nothing, and in which I have no share. Each individual is a world to himself, governed by a thousand contradictory and wayward impulses. I can, therefore, make no inference from one individual to another; nor can my habitual sentiments, with respect to any individual, extend beyond himself to others. But it is otherwise with respect to Nature. There is neither hypocrisy, caprice, nor mental reservation in her favours. Our intercourse with her is not liable to accident or change, interruption or disappointment. She smiles on us still the same. Thus, to give an obvious instance, if I have once enjoyed the cool shade of a tree, and been lulled into a deep repose by the sound of a brook running at its feet, I am sure that wherever I can find a tree and a brook I can enjoy the pleasure again. Hence, when I imagine these objects, I can easily form a mystic personification of the friendly power that inhabits them, dryad or naiad, offering its cool fountain or its tempting shade. Hence the origin of the Grecian mythology. All objects of the same kind being the same, not only in their appearance but in their practical uses, we habitually confound them together under the same general idea; and whatever fondness we may have conceived for one is immediately placed to the common account. The most opposite kinds and remote trains of feeling gradually go to enrich the same sentiment; and in our love of Nature there is all the force of individual attachment combined with the most airy abstraction. It is this circumstance which gives that refinement, expansion, and wild interest to feelings of this sort, when strongly excited, which every one must have experienced who is a true lover of Nature. The sight of the setting sun does not affect me so much from the beauty of the object itself, from the glory kindled through the glowing skies, the rich broken columns of light, or the dying streaks of day, as that it indistinctly recalls to me numberless thoughts and feelings with which, through many a year and season, I have watched his bright descent in the warm summer evenings, or beheld him struggling to cast a "farewell sweet" through the thick clouds of winter. I love to see the trees first covered with leaves in the spring, the primroses peeping out from some sheltered bank, and the innocent lambs running races on the soft green turf; because at that birth-time of Nature I have always felt sweet hopes and happy wishes—which have not been fulfilled! The dry reeds rustling on the side of a stream—the woods swept by the loud blast—the dark massy foliage of autumn—the gray trunks and naked branches of the trees in winter—the sequestered copse and wide extended heath —the warm sunny showers and December snows—have all charms for me; there is no object, however trifling or rude, that has not, in some mood or other, found the way to my heart; and I might say, in the words of the poet:

> To me the meanest flower that blows can give
> Thoughts that do often lie too deep for tears.

Thus Nature is a kind of universal home, and every object it presents to us an old acquaintance with unaltered looks:

> ———Nature did ne'er betray
> The heart that lov'd her, but through all the years
> Of this our life, it is her privilege
> To lead from joy to joy.

For there is that consent and mutual harmony among all her works —one undivided spirit pervading them throughout—that, if we have once knit ourselves in hearty fellowship to any of them, they will never afterwards appear as strangers to us, but, whichever way we turn, we shall find a secret power to have gone out before us, moulding them into shapes such as fancy loves, informing them with life and sympathy, bidding them put on their festive looks and gayest attire at our approach, and to pour all their sweets and choicest treasures at our feet. For him, then, who has well acquainted himself with Nature's works, she wears always one face, and speaks the same well-known language, striking on the heart, amidst unquiet thoughts and the tumult of the world, like the music of one's native tongue heard in some far-off country.

We do not connect the same feelings with the works of Art as with those of Nature, because we refer them to man, and associate with them the separate interests and passions which we know belong to those who are the authors or possessors of them. Nevertheless, there are some such objects, as a cottage or a village church, which excite in us the same sensations as the sight of Nature, and which are, indeed, almost always included in descriptions of natural scenery.

> Or from the mountain's sides
> View wilds and swelling floods,
> And hamlets brown, and dim-discover'd spires,
> And hear their simple bell.

Which is in part, no doubt, because they are surrounded with natural objects, and, in a populous country, inseparable from them; and also because the human interest they excite relates to manners and feelings which are simple, common, such as all can enter into, and which, therefore, always produce a pleasing effect upon the mind.

Levana and Our Ladies of Sorrow [1]

THOMAS DE QUINCEY

Oftentimes at Oxford I saw Levana in my dreams. I knew her by her Roman symbols. Who is Levana? Reader, that do not pretend to have leisure for very much scholarship, you will not be angry with me for telling you. Levana was the Roman goddess that performed for the new-born infant the earliest office of ennobling kindness—

[1] To "Levana and Our Ladies of Sorrow" as printed in *Blackwood's*, De Quincey added this note: The reader who wishes at all to understand the course of these Confessions ought not to pass over this dream-legend. There is no great wonder that a vision which occupied my waking thoughts in those years should reappear in my dreams. It was, in fact, a legend recurring in sleep, most of which I had myself silently written or sculptured in my daylight reveries. But its importance to the present *Confessions* is this—that it rehearses or prefigures their course. This FIRST Part belongs to Madonna. The THIRD belongs to the "Mater Suspiriorum," and will be entitled *The Pariah Worlds*. The FOURTH, which terminates the work, belongs to the "Mater Tenebrarum," and will be entitled *The Kingdom of Darkness*. As to the SECOND, it is an interpolation requisite to the effect of the others, and will be explained in its proper place.

typical, by its mode, of that grandeur which belongs to man every-where, and of that benignity in powers invisible which even in Pagan worlds sometimes descends to sustain it. At the very moment of birth, just as the infant tasted for the first time the atmosphere of our troubled planet, it was laid on the ground. *That* might bear different interpretations. But immediately, lest so grand a creature should grovel there for more than one instant, either the paternal hand, as proxy for the goddess Levana, or some near kinsman, as proxy for the father, raised it upright, bade it look erect as the king of all this world, and presented its forehead to the stars, saying, perhaps, in his heart, "Behold what is greater than yourselves!" This symbolic act represented the function of Levana. And that mysterious lady, who never revealed her face (except to me in dreams), but always acted by delegation, had her name from the Latin verb (as still it is the Italian verb) *levare*, to raise aloft.

This is the explanation of Levana. And hence it has arisen that some people have understood by Levana the tutelary power that controls the education of the nursery. She, that would not suffer at his birth even a prefigurative or mimic degradation for her awful ward, far less could be supposed to suffer the real degradation attaching to the non-development of his powers. She therefore watches over human education. Now, the word *edŭco*, with the penultimate short, was derived (by a process often exemplified in the crystallization of languages) from the word *edūco*, with the penultimate long. Whatsoever *educes*, or develops, *educates*. By the education of Levana, therefore, is meant, not the poor machinery that moves by spelling-books and grammars, but by that mighty system of central forces hidden in the deep bosom of human life, which by passion, by strife, by temptation, by the energies of resistance, works for ever upon children, resting not day or night, any more than the mighty wheel of day and night themselves, whose moments, like restless spokes, are glimmering [2] for ever as they revolve.

[2] As I have never allowed myself to covet any man's ox nor his ass, nor anything that is his, still less would it become a philosopher to covet other people's images or metaphors. Here, therefore, I restore to Mr. Wordsworth this fine image of the revolving wheel and the glimmering spokes, as applied by him to the flying successions of day and night. I borrowed it for one moment in order to point my own sentence; which being done, the reader is witness that I now pay it back instantly by a note made for that sole purpose. On the same principle I often borrow their seals from young ladies, when closing my letters, because

If, then, *these* are the ministries by which Levana works, how profoundly must she reverence the agencies of grief! But you, reader, think that children generally are not liable to grief such as mine. There are two senses in the word *generally*—the sense of Euclid, where it means *universally* (or in the whole extent of the *genus*), and a foolish sense of this world, where it means *usually*. Now, I am far from saying that children universally are capable of grief like mine. But there are more than you ever heard of who die of grief in this island of ours. I will tell you a common case. The rules of Eton require that a boy on the *foundation* should be there twelve years: he is superannuated at eighteen; consequently he must come at six. Children torn away from mothers and sisters at that age not unfrequently die. I speak of what I know. The complaint is not entered by the registrar as grief; but *that* it is. Grief of that sort, and at that age, has killed more than ever have been counted amongst its martyrs.

Therefore it is that Levana often communes with the powers that shake man's heart; therefore it is that she dotes upon grief. "These ladies," said I softly to myself, on seeing the ministers with whom Levana was conversing, "these are the Sorrows; and they are three in number: as the *Graces* are three, who dress man's life with beauty; the *Parcae* are three, who weave the dark arras of man's life in their mysterious loom always with colours sad in part, sometimes angry with tragic crimson and black; the *Furies* are three, who visit with retributions called from the other side of the grave offences that walk upon this; and once even the *Muses* were but three, who fit the harp, the trumpet, or the lute, to the great burdens of man's impassioned creations. These are the Sorrows; all three of whom I know." The last words I say now; but in Oxford I said, "one of whom I know, and the others too surely I *shall* know." For already, in my fervent youth, I saw (dimly relieved upon the dark background of my dreams) the imperfect lineaments of the awful Sisters.

These Sisters—by what name shall we call them? If I say simply "The Sorrows," there will be a chance of mistaking the term; it might be understood of individual sorrow—separate cases of sorrow

---

there is sure to be some tender sentiment upon them about "memory," or "hope," or "roses," or "reunion," and my correspondent must be a sad brute who is not touched by the eloquence of the seal, even if his taste is so bad that he remains deaf to mine.

—whereas I want a term expressing the mighty abstractions that incarnate themselves in all individual sufferings of man's heart, and I wish to have these abstractions presented as impersonations, that is, as clothed with human attributes of life, and with functions pointing to flesh. Let us call them, therefore, *Our Ladies of Sorrow.*

I know them thoroughly, and have walked in all their kingdoms. Three sisters they are, of one mysterious household; and their paths are wide apart; but of their dominion there is no end. Them I saw often conversing with Levana, and sometimes about myself. Do they talk, then? O no! Mighty phantoms like these disdain the infirmities of language. They may utter voices through the organs of man when they dwell in human hearts, but amongst themselves is no voice nor sound; eternal silence reigns in *their* kingdoms. They spoke not as they talked with Levana; they whispered not; they sang not; though oftentimes methought they *might* have sung: for I upon earth had heard their mysteries oftentimes deciphered by harp and timbrel, by dulcimer and organ. Like God, whose servants they are, they utter their pleasure not by sounds that perish, or by words that go astray, but by signs in heaven, by changes on earth, by pulses in secret rivers, heraldries painted on darkness, and hieroglyphics written on the tablets of the brain. *They* wheeled in mazes; *I* spelled the steps. *They* telegraphed from afar; *I* read the signals. *They* conspired together; and on the mirrors of darkness *my* eye traced the plots. *Theirs* were the symbols; *mine* are the words.

What is it the Sisters are? What is it that they do? Let me describe their form and their presence, if form it were that still fluctuated in its outline, or presence it were that for ever advanced to the front or for ever receded amongst shades.

The eldest of the three is named *Mater Lachrymarum,* Our Lady of Tears. She it is that night and day raves and moans, calling for vanished faces. She stood in Rama, where a voice was heard of lamentation—Rachel weeping for her children, and refusing to be comforted. She it was that stood in Bethlehem on the night when Herod's sword swept its nurseries of Innocents, and the little feet were stiffened for ever which, heard at times as they trotted along floors overhead, woke pulses of love in household hearts that were not unmarked in heaven. Her eyes are sweet and subtle, wild and sleepy, by turns; oftentimes rising to the clouds, oftentimes challenging the heavens. She wears a diadem round her head. And I knew by childish memories that she could go abroad upon the winds, when she heard the sobbing of litanies, or the thundering of organs, and when she beheld the mustering of summer clouds. This Sister, the elder, it is that carries keys more than papal at her girdle, which open every cottage and every palace. She, to my knowledge, sat all last summer by the bedside of the blind beggar, him that so often and so gladly I talked with, whose pious daughter, eight years old, with the sunny countenance, resisted the temptations of play and village mirth, to travel all day long on dusty roads with her afflicted father. For this did God send her a great reward. In the spring time of the year, and whilst yet her own spring was budding, He recalled her to himself. But her blind father mourns for ever over *her:* still he dreams at midnight that the little guiding hand is locked within his own; and still he wakens to a darkness that is *now* within a second and a deeper darkness. This *Mater Lachrymarum* also has been sitting all this winter of 1844-5 within the bedchamber of the Czar, bringing before his eyes a daughter (not less pious) that vanished to God not less suddenly, and left behind her a darkness not less profound. By the power of the keys it is that Our Lady of Tears glides, a ghostly intruder, into the chambers of sleepless men, sleepless women, sleepless children, from Ganges to the Nile, from Nile to Mississippi. And her, because she is the first-born of her house, and has the widest empire, let us honour with the title of "Madonna."

The second Sister is called *Mater Suspiriorum,* Our Lady of Sighs. She never scales the clouds, nor walks abroad upon the winds. She wears no diadem. And her eyes, if they were ever seen, would be neither sweet nor subtle; no man could read their story; they would be found filled with perishing dreams, and with wrecks of forgotten delirium. But she raises not her eyes; her head, on which sits a dilapidated turban, droops for ever, for ever fastens on the dust. She weeps not. She groans not. But she sighs inaudibly at intervals. Her sister, Madonna, is oftentimes stormy and frantic, raging in the highest against heaven, and demanding back her darlings. But Our Lady of Sighs never clamours, never defies, dreams not of rebellious aspirations. She is humble to abjectness. Hers is the meekness that belongs to the hopeless. Murmur she may, but it is in her sleep. Whisper she may, but it is to herself in the twilight. Mutter she does at times, but it is in solitary places that are desolate as she is desolate, in ruined cities, and when the sun has gone down to his rest. This Sister is the visitor of the Pariah, of the Jew, of the bondsman to the oar in the Mediterranean galleys; of the English criminal in Norfolk Island, blotted out from the books of remembrance in sweet far-off England; of the baffled penitent reverting his eyes for ever upon a solitary grave, which to him seems the altar overthrown of some past and bloody sacrifice, on which altar no oblations can now be availing, whether towards pardon that he might implore, or towards reparation that he might attempt. Every slave that at noon-day looks up to the tropical sun with timid reproach, as he points with one hand to the earth, our general mother, but for *him* a step-mother, as he points with the other hand to the Bible, our general teacher, but against *him* sealed and sequestered; [3] every woman sitting in darkness, without love to shelter her head, or hope to illumine her solitude, because the heaven-born instincts kindling in her nature germs of holy affections, which God implanted in her womanly bosom, having been stifled by social necessities, now burn sullenly to waste, like sepulchral lamps amongst the ancients; every nun defrauded of her unreturning May-time by wicked kinsman, whom God will judge; every captive in every dungeon; all that are betrayed, and all that are rejected; outcasts by traditionary law, and children of *hereditary* disgrace: all these walk with Our Lady of Sighs. She also carries a key; but she needs it little. For her kingdom is chiefly amongst the tents of Shem, and the houseless vagrant of every clime. Yet in the very highest ranks of man she finds chapels of her own; and even in glorious England there are some that, to the world, carry their heads as proudly as the reindeer, who yet secretly have received her mark upon their foreheads.

But the third Sister, who is also the youngest——! Hush! whisper whilst we talk of *her!* Her kingdom is not large, or else no flesh should live; but within that kingdom all power is hers. Her head, turreted like that of Cybele, rises almost beyond the reach of sight. She droops not; and her eyes, rising so high, *might* be hidden by distance. But, being what they are, they cannot be hidden: through the treble veil of crape which she wears the fierce light of a blazing misery, that rests not for matins or for vespers, for noon of day or noon of night, for ebbing or for flowing tide, may be read from the very ground. She is the defier of God. She also is the mother of lunacies,

[3] This, the reader will be aware, applies chiefly to the cotton and tobacco States of North America; but not to them only: on which account I have not scrupled to figure the sun which looks down upon slavery as *tropical*—no matter if strictly within the tropics, or simply so near to them as to produce a similar climate.

and the suggestress of suicides. Deep lie the roots of her power; but narrow is the nation that she rules. For she can approach only those in whom a profound nature has been upheaved by central convulsions; in whom the heart trembles and the brain rocks under conspiracies of tempest from without and tempest from within. Madonna moves with uncertain steps, fast or slow, but still with tragic grace. Our Lady of Sighs creeps timidly and stealthily. But this youngest Sister moves with incalculable motions, bounding, and with tiger's leaps. She carries no key; for, though coming rarely amongst men, she storms all doors at which she is permitted to enter at all. And *her* name is *Mater Tenebrarum*—Our Lady of Darkness.

These were the *Semnai Theai* or Sublime Goddesses,[4] these were the *Eumenides* or Gracious Ladies (so called by antiquity in shuddering propitiation), of my Oxford dreams. Madonna spoke. She spoke by her mysterious hand. Touching my head, she beckoned to Our Lady of Sighs; and *what* she spoke, translated out of the signs which (except in dreams) no man reads, was this:

"Lo! here is he whom in childhood I dedicated to my altars. This is he that once I made my darling. Him I led astray, him I beguiled; and from heaven I stole away his young heart to mine. Through me did he become idolatrous; and through me it was, by languishing desires, that he worshipped the worm, and prayed to the wormy grave. Holy was the grave to him; lovely was its darkness; saintly its corruption. Him, this young idolater, I have seasoned for thee, dear gentle Sister of Sighs! Do thou take him now to *thy* heart, and season him for our dreadful sister. And thou," turning to the *Mater Tenebrarum*, she said, "wicked sister, that temptest and hatest, do thou take him from *her*. See that thy sceptre lie heavy on his head. Suffer not woman and her tenderness to sit near him in his darkness. Banish the frailties of hope; wither the relenting of love; scorch the fountains of tears; curse him as only *thou* canst curse. So shall he be accomplished in the furnace; so shall he see the things that ought *not* to be seen, sights that are abominable, and secrets that are unutterable. So shall he read elder truths, sad truths, grand truths, fearful truths. So shall he rise again *before* he dies. And so shall our commission be accomplished which from God we had—to plague his heart until we had unfolded the capacities of his spirit."

[4] *"Sublime Goddesses"*: The word σεμνος is really rendered *venerable* in dictionaries—not a very flattering epithet for females. But I am disposed to think that it comes nearest to our idea of the *sublime*—as near as a Greek word *could* come.

The Tragic

RALPH WALDO EMERSON

He has seen but half the universe who never has been shown the house of Pain. As the salt sea covers more than two thirds of the surface of the globe, so sorrow encroaches in man on felicity. The conversation of men is a mixture of regrets and apprehensions. I do not know but the prevalent hue of things to the eye of leisure is melancholy. In the dark hours, our existence seems to be a defensive war, a struggle against the encroaching All, which threatens surely to engulf us soon, and is impatient of our short reprieve. How slender the possession that yet remains to us; how faint the animation! how the spirit seems already to contract its domain, retiring within narrower walls by the loss of memory, leaving its planted fields to erasure and annihilation. Already our thoughts and words have an alien sound. There is a simultaneous diminution of memory and hope. Projects that once we laughed and leapt to execute find us now sleepy and preparing to lie down in the snow. And in the serene hours we have no courage to spare. We cannot afford to let go any advantages. The riches of body or of mind which we do not need to-day are the reserved fund against the calamity that may arrive to-morrow. It is usually agreed that some nations have a more sombre temperament, and one would say that history gave no record of any society in which despondency came so readily to heart as we see it and feel it in ours. Melancholy cleaves to the English mind in both hemispheres as closely as to the strings of an Æolian harp. Men and women at thirty years, and even earlier, have lost all spring and vivacity, and if they fail in their first enterprises, they throw up the game. But whether we and those who are next to us are more or less vulnerable, no theory of life can have any right which leaves out of account the values of vice, pain, disease, poverty, insecurity, disunion, fear and death.

What are the conspicuous tragic elements in human nature? The bitterest tragic element in life to be derived from an intellectual source is the belief in a brute Fate or Destiny; the belief that the order of Nature and events is controlled by a law not adapted to man, nor man to that, but which holds on its way to the end, serving him if his wishes chance to lie in the same course, crushing him if his wishes lie contrary to it, and heedless whether it serves or crushes him. This is the terrible meaning that lies at the foundation of the old Greek tragedy, and makes the Œdipus and Antigone and Orestes objects of such hopeless commiseration. They must perish, and there is no overgod to stop or to mollify this hideous enginery that grinds or thunders, and snatches them up into its terrific system. The same idea makes the paralyzing terror with which the East Indian mythology haunts the imagination. The same thought is the predestination of the Turk. And universally, in uneducated and unreflecting persons on whom too the religious sentiment exerts little force, we discover traits of the same superstition: "If you balk water you will be drowned the next time;" "if you count ten stars you will fall down dead;" "if you spill the salt;" "if your fork sticks upright in the floor;" "if you say the Lord's prayer backwards;" —and so on, a several penalty, nowise grounded in the nature of the thing, but on an arbitrary will. But this terror of contravening an unascertained and unascertainable will cannot co-exist with reflection: it disappears with civilization, and can no more be reproduced than the fear of ghosts after childhood. It is discriminated from the doctrine of Philosophical Necessity herein: that the last is an Optimism, and therefore the suffering individual finds his good consulted in the good of all, of which he is a part. But in destiny, it is not the good of the whole or the *best will* that is enacted, but only *one particular will*. Destiny properly is not a will at all, but an immense whim; and this the only ground of terror and despair in the rational mind, and of tragedy in literature. Hence the antique tragedy, which was founded on this faith, can never be reproduced.

After reason and faith have introduced a better public and private tradition, the tragic element is somewhat circumscribed. There must always remain, however, the hindrance of our private satisfaction by the laws of the world. The law which establishes nature and the human race, continually thwarts the will of ignorant individuals, and this in the particulars of disease, want, insecurity and disunion.

But the essence of tragedy does not seem to me to lie in any list of particular evils. After we have enumerated famine, fever, inaptitude, mutilation, rack, madness and loss of friends, we have not yet included the proper tragic element, which is Terror, and which does not respect definite evils but indefinite; an ominous spirit which haunts the afternoon and the night, idleness and solitude.

A low, haggard sprite sits by our side, "casting the fashion of uncertain evils"—a sinister presentiment, a power of the imagination to dislocate things orderly and cheerful and show them in startling array. Hark! what sounds on the night wind, the cry of Murder in that friendly house; see these marks of stamping feet, of hidden riot. The whisper overheard, the detected glance, the glare of malignity, ungrounded fears, suspicions, half-knowledge and mistakes, darken the brow and chill the heart of men. And accordingly it is natures not clear, not of quick and steady perceptions, but imperfect characters from which somewhat is hidden that all others see, who suffer most from these causes. In those persons who move the profoundest pity, tragedy seems to consist in temperament, not in events. There are people who have an appetite for grief, pleasure is not strong enough and they crave pain, mithridatic stomachs which must be fed on poisoned bread, natures so doomed that no prosperity can soothe their ragged and dishevelled desolation. They mis-hear and mis-behold, they suspect and dread. They handle every nettle and ivy in the hedge, and tread on every snake in the meadow.

> Come bad chance,
> And we add it to our strength,
> And we teach it art and length,
> Itself o'er us to advance.

Frankly, then, it is necessary to say that all sorrow dwells in a low region. It is superficial; for the most part fantastic, or in the appearance and not in things. Tragedy is in the eye of the observer, and not in the heart of the sufferer. It looks like an insupportable load under which earth moans aloud. But analyze it; it is not I, it is not you, it is always another person who is tormented. If a man says, Lo! I suffer—it is apparent that he suffers not, for grief is dumb. It is so distributed as not to destroy. That which would rend you falls on tougher textures. That which seems intolerable reproach or bereavement does not take from the accused or bereaved man or woman appetite or sleep. Some men are above grief, and some below it. Few are capable of love. In phlegmatic natures calamity is unaffecting, in shallow natures it is rhetorical. Tragedy must be somewhat which I can respect. A querulous habit is not tragedy. A panic such as frequently in ancient or savage nations put a troop or an army to flight without an enemy; a fear of ghosts; a terror of freezing to death that seizes a man in a winter midnight on the moors; a fright at uncertain sounds heard by a family at night in the cellar or on the stairs,—are terrors that make the knees knock and the teeth clatter, but are no tragedy, any more than seasickness, which may also destroy life. It is full of illusion. As it comes, it has its support. The most exposed classes, soldiers, sailors, paupers, are nowise destitute of animal spirits. The spirit is true to itself, and finds its own support in any condition, learns to live in what is called calamity as easily as in what is called felicity; as the frailest glass bell will support a weight of a thousand pounds of water at the bottom of a river or sea, if filled with the same.

A man should not commit his tranquillity to things, but should keep as much as possible the reins in his own hands, rarely giving way to extreme emotion of joy or grief. It is observed that the earliest works of the art of sculpture are countenances of sublime tranquillity. The Egyptian sphinxes, which sit to-day as they sat when the Greek came and saw them and departed, and when the Roman came and saw them and departed, and as they will still sit when the Turk, the Frenchman and the Englishman, who visit them now, shall have passed by,—"with their stony eyes fixed on the East and on the Nile," have countenances expressive of complacency and repose, an expression of health, deserving their longevity, and verifying the primeval sentence of history on the permanency of that people, "Their strength is to sit still." To this architectural stability of the human form, the Greek genius added an ideal beauty, without disturbing the seals of serenity; permitting no violence of mirth, or wrath, or suffering. This was true to human nature. For in life, actions are few, opinions even few, prayers few; loves, hatreds, or any emissions of the soul. All that life demands of us through the greater part of the day is an equilibrium, a readiness, open eyes and ears, and free hands. Society asks this, and truth, and love, and the genius of our life. There is a fire in some men which demands an outlet in some rude action; they betray their impatience of quiet by an irregular Catilinarian gait; by irregular, faltering, disturbed speech, too emphatic for the occasion. They treat trifles with a tragic air. This is not beautiful. Could they not lay a rod or two of stone wall, and work off this superabundant irritability? When two strangers meet in the highway, what each demands of the other is that the aspect should show a firm mind, ready for any event of good or ill, prepared alike to give death or to give life, as the emergency of the next moment may require. We must walk as guests in Nature; not impassioned, but cool and disengaged. A man should try Time, and his face should wear the expression of a just judge, who has nowise made up his opinion, who fears nothing, and even hopes nothing, but who puts Nature and fortune on their merits: he will hear the case out, and then decide. For all melancholy, as all passion, belongs to the exterior life. Whilst a man is not grounded in the divine life by his proper roots, he clings by some tendrils of affection to society—mayhap to what is best and greatest in it, and in calm times it will not appear that he is adrift and not moored; but let any shock take place in society, any revolution of custom, of law, of opinion, and at once his type of permanence is shaken. The disorder of his neighbors appears to him universal disorder; chaos is come again. But in truth he was already a driving wreck before the wind arose, which only revealed to him his vagabond state. If a man is centred men and events appear to him a fair image or reflection of that which he knoweth beforehand in himself. If any perversity or profligacy break out in society, he will join with others to avert the mischief, but it will not arouse resentment or fear, because he discerns its impassable limits. He sees already in the ebullition of sin the simultaneous redress.

Particular reliefs, also, fit themselves to human calamities; for the world will be in equilibrium, and hates all manner of exaggeration.

Time the consoler, Time the rich carrier of all changes, dries the freshest tears by obtruding new figures, new costumes, new roads, on our eye, new voices on our ear. As the west wind lifts up again the heads of the wheat which were bent down and lodged in the storm, and combs out the matted and dishevelled grass as it lay in night-locks on the ground, so we let in Time as a drying wind into the seed-field of thoughts which are dark and wet and low bent. Time restores to them temper and elasticity. How fast we forget the blow that threatened to cripple us. Nature will not sit still; the faculties will do somewhat; new hopes spring, new affections twine, and the broken is whole again.

Time consoles, but Temperament resists the impression of pain. Nature proportions her defence to the assault. Our human being is wonderfully plastic; if it cannot win this satisfaction here, it makes itself amends by running out there and winning that. It is like a stream of water, which, if dammed up on one bank, overruns the other, and flows equally at its own convenience over sand, or mud, or marble. Most suffering is only apparent. We fancy it is torture; the patient has his own compensations. A tender American girl doubts of Divine Providence whilst she reads the horrors of "the middle passage;" and they are bad enough at the mildest; but to such as she these crucifixions do not come; they come to the obtuse and barbarous, to whom they are not horrid, but only a little worse than the old sufferings. They exchange a cannibal war for the stench of the hold. They have gratifications which would be none to the civilized girl. The market-man never damned the lady because she had not paid her bill, but the stout Irishwoman has to take that once a month. She, however, never feels weakness in her back because of the slave-trade. This self-adapting strength is especially seen in disease. "It is my duty," says Sir Charles Bell, "to visit certain wards of the hospital where there is no patient admitted but with that complaint which most fills the imagination with the idea of insupportable pain and certain death. Yet these wards are not the least remarkable for the composure and cheerfulness of their inmates. The individual who suffers has a mysterious counterbalance to that condition, which, to us who look upon her, appears to be attended with no alleviating circumstance." Analogous supplies are made to those individuals whose character leads them to vast exertions of body and mind. Napoleon said to one of his friends at St. Helena, "Nature seems to have calculated that I should have great reverses to endure, for she has given me a temperament like a block of marble. Thunder cannot move it; the shaft merely glides along. The great events of my life have slipped over me without making any demand on my moral or physical nature."

The intellect is a consoler, which delights in detaching or putting an interval between a man and his fortune, and so converts the sufferer into a spectator and his pain into poetry. It yields the joys of conversation, of letters and of science. Hence also the torments of life become tuneful tragedy, solemn and soft with music, and garnished with rich dark pictures. But higher still than the activities of art, the intellect in its purity and the moral sense in its purity are not distinguished from each other, and both ravish us into a region whereunto these passionate clouds of sorrow cannot rise.

A Relic

MAX BEERBOHM

1918

Yesterday I found in a cupboard an old, small, battered portmanteau which, by the initials on it, I recognised as my own property. The lock appeared to have been forced. I dimly remembered having forced it myself, with a poker, in my hot youth, after some journey in which I had lost the key; and this act of violence was probably the reason why the trunk had so long ago ceased to travel. I unstrapped it, not without dust; it exhaled the faint scent of its long closure; it contained a tweed suit of Late Victorian pattern, some bills, some letters, a collar-stud, and—something which, after I had wondered for a moment or two what on earth it was, caused me suddenly to murmur, 'Down below, the sea rustled to and fro over the shingle.'

Strange that these words had, year after long year, been existing in some obscure cell at the back of my brain!—forgotten but all the while existing, like the trunk in that cupboard. What released them, what threw open the cell door, was nothing but the fragment of a fan; just the butt-end of an inexpensive fan. The sticks are of white bone, clipped together with a semicircular ring that is not silver. They are neatly oval at the base, but variously jagged at the other end. The longest of them measures perhaps two inches. Ring and all, they have no market value; for a farthing is the least coin in our currency. And yet, though I had so long forgotten them, for me they are not worthless. They touch a chord . . . Lest this confession raise false hopes in the reader, I add that I did not know their owner.

I did once see her, and in Normandy, and by moonlight, and her name was Angélique. She was graceful, she was even beautiful. I was but nineteen years old. Yet even so I cannot say that she impressed me favourably. I was seated at a table of a café on the ter-

---

A RELIC. From the book *And Even Now* by Max Beerbohm. Copyright, 1921 by E. P. Dutton & Co., Inc. Renewal, 1949 by Max Beerbohm. Reprinted by permission of E. P. Dutton & Co., Inc., and William Heinemann Ltd., Publishers, London.

race of a casino. I sat facing the sea, with my back to the casino. I
sat listening to the quiet sea, which I had crossed that morning. The
hour was late, there were few people about. I heard the swing-door
behind me flap open, and was aware of a sharp snapping and crackling sound as a lady in white passed quickly by me. I stared at her
erect thin back and her agitated elbows. A short fat man passed in
pursuit of her—an elderly man in a black alpaca jacket that bil-
lowed. I saw that she had left a trail of little white things on the
asphalt. I watched the efforts of the agonised short fat man to over-
take her as she swept wraithlike away to the distant end of the terrace. What was the matter? What had made her so spectacularly
angry with him? The three or four waiters of the café were exchanging cynical smiles and shrugs, as waiters will. I tried to feel
cynical, but was thrilled with excitement, with wonder and curiosity. The woman out yonder had doubled on her tracks. She had not
slackened her furious speed, but the man waddlingly contrived to
keep pace with her now. With every moment they became more
distinct, and the prospect that they would presently pass by me,
back into the casino, gave me that physical tension which one feels
on a wayside platform at the imminent passing of an express. In the
rushingly enlarged vision I had of them, the wrath on the woman's
face was even more saliently the main thing than I had supposed it
would be. That very hard Parisian face must have been white as
the powder that coated it. 'Écoute, Angélique,' gasped the perspiring bourgeois, 'écoute, je te supplie—' The swing-door received
them and was left swinging to and fro. I wanted to follow, but had
not paid for my bock. I beckoned my waiter. On his way to me he
stooped down and picked up something which, with a smile and a
shrug, he laid on my table: 'Il semble que Mademoiselle ne s'en
servira plus.' This is the thing I now write of, and at sight of it I
understood why there had been that snapping and crackling, and
what the white fragments on the ground were.

I hurried through the rooms, hoping to see a continuation of that
drama—a scene of appeasement, perhaps, or of fury still implacable.
But the two oddly-assorted players were not performing there. My
waiter had told me he had not seen either of them before. I suppose
they had arrived that day. But I was not destined to see either of
them again. They went away, I suppose, next morning; jointly or
singly; singly, I imagine.

They made, however, a prolonged stay in my young memory,

and would have done so even had I not had that tangible memento
of them. Who were they, those two of whom that one strange
glimpse had befallen me? What, I wondered, was the previous history of each? What, in particular, had all that tragic pother been
about? Mlle. Angélique I guessed to be thirty years old, her friend
perhaps fifty-five. Each of their faces was as clear to me as in the
moment of actual vision—the man's fat shiny bewildered face; the
taut white face of the woman, the hard red line of her mouth, the
eyes that were not flashing, but positively dull, with rage. I presumed that the fan had been a present from him, and a recent
present—bought perhaps that very day, after their arrival in the
town. But what, *what* had he done that she should break it between
her hands, scattering the splinters as who should sow dragon's teeth?
I could not believe he had done anything much amiss. I imagined
her grievance a trivial one. But this did not make the case less en-
grossing. Again and again I would take the fan-stump from my
pocket, examining it on the palm of my hand, or between finger and
thumb, hoping to read the mystery it had been mixed up in, so that I
might reveal that mystery to the world. To the world, yes; nothing
less than that. I was determined to make a story of what I had seen
—a *conte* in the manner of great Guy de Maupassant. Now and
again, in the course of the past year or so, it had occurred to me that
I might be a writer. But I had not felt the impulse to sit down and
write something. I did feel that impulse now. It would indeed have
been an irresistible impulse if I had known just what to write.

I felt I might know at any moment, and had but to give my mind
to it. Maupassant was an impeccable artist, but I think the secret of
the hold he had on the young men of my day was not so much that
we discerned his cunning as that we delighted in the simplicity
which his cunning achieved. I had read a great number of his short
stories, but none that had made me feel as though I, if I were a
writer, mightn't have written it myself. Maupassant had an European reputation. It was pleasing, it was soothing and gratifying, to
feel that one could at any time win an equal fame if one chose to set
pen to paper. And now, suddenly, the spring had been touched in
me, the time was come. I was grateful for the fluke by which I had
witnessed on the terrace that evocative scene. I looked forward to
reading the MS. of 'The Fan'—to-morrow, at latest. I was not
wildly ambitious. I was not inordinately vain. I knew I couldn't

ever, with the best will in the world, write like Mr. George Mere-
dith. Those wondrous works of his, seething with wit, with poetry
and philosophy and what not, never had beguiled me with the sense
that I might do something similar. I had full consciousness of not
being a philosopher, of not being a poet, and of not being a wit.
Well, Maupassant was none of these things. He was just an observer
like me. Of course he was a good deal older than I, and had observed
a good deal more. But it seemed to me that he was not my superior
in knowledge of life. I knew all about life through *him*.

Dimly, the initial paragraph of my tale floated in my mind. I—not
exactly I myself, but rather that impersonal *je* familiar to me
through Maupassant—was to be sitting at that table, with a bock before me, just as I *had* sat. Four or five short sentences would give
the whole scene. One of these I had quite definitely composed. You
have already heard it. 'Down below, the sea rustled to and fro over
the shingle.'

These words, which pleased me much, were to do double duty.
They were to recur. They were to be, by a fine stroke, the very last
words of my tale, their tranquillity striking a sharp ironic contrast
with the stress of what had just been narrated. I had, you see, advanced further in the form of my tale than in the substance. But
even the form was as yet vague. What, exactly, was to happen after
Mlle. Angélique and M. Joumand (as I provisionally called him)
had rushed back past me into the casino? It was clear that I must
hear the whole inner history from the lips of one or the other of
them. Which? Should M. Joumand stagger out on to the terrace, sit
down heavily at the table next to mine, bury his head in his hands,
and presently, in broken words, blurt out to me all that might be of
interest? . . .

' "And I tell you I gave up everything for her—everything." He
stared at me with his old hopeless eyes. "She is more than the fiend I
have described to you. Yet I swear to you, monsieur, that if I had
anything left to give, it should be hers."

'Down below, the sea rustled to and fro over the shingle.'

Or should the lady herself be my informant? For a while, I rather
leaned to this alternative. It was more exciting, it seemed to make the
writer more signally a man of the world. On the other hand, it was
less simple to manage. Wronged persons might be ever so communi-
cative, but I surmised that persons in the wrong were reticent. Mlle.

Angélique, therefore, would have to be modified by me in appearance and behaviour, toned down, touched up; and poor M. Joumand must look like a man of whom one could believe anything. . . .

'She ceased speaking. She gazed down at the fragments of her fan, and then, as though finding in them an image of her own life, whispered, "To think what I once was, monsieur!—what, but for him, I might be, even now!" She buried her face in her hands, then stared out into the night. Suddenly she uttered a short, harsh laugh.

'Down below, the sea rustled to and fro over the shingle.'

I decided that I must choose the first of these two ways. It was the less chivalrous as well as the less lurid way, but clearly it was the more artistic as well as the easier. The 'chose vue,' the 'tranche de la vie'—this was the thing to aim at. Honesty was the best policy. I must be nothing if not merciless. Maupassant was nothing if not merciless. He would not have spared Mlle. Angélique. Besides, why should I libel M. Joumand? Poor—no, not *poor* M. Joumand! I warned myself against pitying him. One touch of 'sentimentality,' and I should be lost. M. Joumand was ridiculous. I must keep him so. But—what was his position in life? Was he a lawyer perhaps?— or the proprietor of a shop in the Rue de Rivoli? I toyed with the possibility that he kept a fan shop—that the business had once been a prosperous one, but had gone down, down, because of his infatuation for this woman to whom he was always giving fans—which she *always* smashed. . . . ' "Ah monsieur, cruel and ungrateful to me though she is, I swear to you that if I had anything left to give, it should be hers; but," he stared at me with his old hopeless eyes, "the fan she broke tonight was the last—the last, monsieur—of my stock." Down below,'—but I pulled myself together, and asked pardon of my Muse.

It may be that I had offended her by my fooling. Or it may be that she had a sisterly desire to shield Mlle. Angélique from my mordant art. Or it may be that she was bent on saving M. de Maupassant from a dangerous rivalry. Anyway, she withheld from me the inspiration I had so confidently solicited. I *could not* think what had led up to that scene on the terrace. I tried hard and soberly. I turned the 'chose vue' over and over in my mind, day by day, and the fan-stump over and over in my hand. But the 'chose à figurer' —what, oh what, was that? Nightly I revisited the café, and sat there with an open mind—a mind wide-open to catch the idea that should drop into it like a ripe golden plum. The plum did not ripen.

The mind remained wide-open for a week or more, but nothing except that phrase about the sea rustled to and fro in it.

A full quarter of a century has gone by. M. Joumand's death, so far too fat was he all those years ago, may be presumed. A temper so violent as Mlle. Angélique's must surely have brought its owner to the grave, long since. But here, all unchanged, the stump of her fan is; and once more I turn it over and over in my hand, not learning its secret—no, nor even trying to, now. The chord this relic strikes in me is not one of curiosity as to that old quarrel, but (if you will forgive me) one of tenderness for my first effort to write, and for my first hopes of excellence.

The Twelve Men

G. K. CHESTERTON

The other day, while I was meditating on morality and Mr. H. Pitt, I was, so to speak, snatched up and put into a jury box to try people. The snatching took some weeks, but to me it seemed something sudden and arbitrary. I was put into this box because I lived in Battersea, and my name began with a C. Looking round me, I saw that there were also summoned and in attendance in the court whole crowds and processions of men, all of whom lived in Battersea, and all of whose names began with a C.

It seems that they always summon jurymen in this sweeping alphabetical way. At one official blow, so to speak, Battersea is denuded of all its C's, and left to get on as best it can with the rest of the alphabet. A Cumberpatch is missing from one street—a Chizzolpop from another—three Chucksterfields from Chucksterfield House; the children are crying out for an absent Cadgerboy; the woman at the street corner is weeping for her Coffintop, and will not be comforted. We settle down with a rollicking ease into our seats (for we are a bold, devil-may-care race, the C's of Battersea), and an oath is administered to us in a totally inaudible manner by an individual resembling an army surgeon in his second childhood. We

THE TWELVE MEN. From *Tremendous Trifles* by G. K. Chesterton, copyright, 1909, published by Sheed & Ward Inc., New York. Reprinted by permission of Miss Dorothy Collins and the publishers.

understand, however, that we are to well and truly try the case between our sovereign lord the King and the prisoner at the bar, neither of whom has put in an appearance as yet.

* * * * *

Just when I was wondering whether the King and the prisoner were, perhaps, coming to an amicable understanding in some adjoining public-house, the prisoner's head appears above the barrier of the dock; he is accused of stealing bicycles, and he is the living image of a great friend of mine. We go into the matter of the stealing of the bicycles. We do well and truly try the case between the King and the prisoner in the affair of the bicycles. And we come to the conclusion, after a brief but reasonable discussion, that the King is not in any way implicated. Then we pass on to a woman who neglected her children, and who looks as if somebody or something had neglected her. And I am one of those who fancy that something had.

All the time that the eye took in these light appearances and the brain passed these light criticisms, there was in the heart a barbaric pity and fear which men have never been able to utter from the beginning, but which is the power behind half the poems of the world. The mood cannot even inadequately be suggested, except faintly by this statement that tragedy is the highest expression of the infinite value of human life. Never had I stood so close to pain; and never so far away from pessimism. Ordinarily, I should not have spoken of these dark emotions at all, for speech about them is too difficult; but I mention them now for a specific and particular reason to the statement of which I will proceed at once. I speak of these feelings because out of the furnace of them there came a curious realisation of a political or social truth. I saw with a queer and indescribable kind of clearness what a jury really is, and why we must never let it go.

The trend of our epoch up to this time has been consistently towards socialism and professionalism. We tend to have trained soldiers because they fight better, trained singers because they sing better, trained dancers because they dance better, specially instructed laughers because they laugh better, and so on and so on. The principle has been applied to law and politics by innumerable modern writers. Many Fabians have insisted that a greater part of our political work should be performed by experts. Many legalists have declared that the untrained jury should be altogether supplanted by the trained Judge.

Now, if this world of ours were really what is called reasonable, I do not know that there would be any fault to find with this. But the true result of all experience and the true foundation of all religion is this. That the four or five things that it is most practically essential that a man should know, are all of them what people call paradoxes. That is to say, that though we all find them in life to be mere plain truths, yet we cannot easily state them in words without being guilty of seeming verbal contradictions. One of them, for instance, is the unimpeachable platitude that the man who finds most pleasure for himself is often the man who least hunts for it. Another is a paradox of courage; the fact that the way to avoid death is not to have too much aversion to it. Whoever is careless enough of his bones to climb some hopeless cliff above the tide may save his bones by that carelessness. Whoever will lose his life, the same shall save it; an entirely practical and prosaic statement.

Now, one of these four or five paradoxes which should be taught to every infant prattling at his mother's knee is the following: That the more a man looks at a thing, the less he can see it, and the more a man learns a thing the less he knows it. The Fabian argument of the expert, that the man who is trained should be the man who is trusted, would be absolutely unanswerable if it were really true that a man who studied a thing and practiced it every day went on seeing more and more of its significance. But he does not. He goes on seeing less and less of its significance. In the same way, alas! we all go on every day, unless we are continually goading ourselves into gratitude and humility, seeing less and less of the significance of the sky or the stones.

Now, it is a terrible business to mark a man out for the vengeance of men. But it is a thing to which a man can grow accustomed, as he can to other terrible things; he can even grow accustomed to the sun. And the horrible thing about all legal officials, even the best, about all judges, magistrates, barristers, detectives, and policemen, is not that they are wicked (some of them are good), not that they are stupid (several of them are quite intelligent), it is simply that they have got used to it.

Strictly they do not see the prisoner in the dock; all they see is the usual man in the usual place. They do not see the awful court of judgment; they only see their own workshop. Therefore, the instinct of Christian civilisation has most wisely declared that into their judgments there shall upon every occasion be infused fresh blood and fresh thoughts from the streets. Men shall come in who can see the court and the crowd, and coarse faces of the policemen and the professional criminals, the wasted faces of the wastrels, the unreal faces of the gesticulating counsel, and see it all as one sees a new picture or a ballet hitherto unvisited.

Our civilisation has decided, and very justly decided, that determining the guilt or innocence of men is a thing too important to be trusted to trained men. It wishes for light upon that awful matter, it asks men who know no more law than I know, but who can feel the things that I felt in the jury box. When it wants a library catalogued, or the solar system discovered, or any trifle of that kind, it uses up its specialists. But when it wishes anything done which is really serious, it collects twelve of the ordinary men standing round. The same thing was done, if I remember right, by the Founder of Christianity.

Poe's Helen

VIRGINIA WOOLF

The real interest of Miss Ticknor's volume [1] lies in the figure of Mrs. Whitman, and not in the love letters from Poe, which have already been published. It is true that if it had not been for her connexion with Poe we should never have heard of Helen Whitman; but it is also true that Poe's connexion with Mrs. Whitman was neither much to his credit nor a matter of moment to the world at large. If it were our object to enhance the charm of 'the only true romantic figure in our literature', as Miss Ticknor calls him, we

[1] *Poe's Helen*, by Caroline Ticknor.

POE'S HELEN. From *Granite and Rainbow* by Virginia Woolf, © 1958 by Leonard Woolf. Appeared in *Times Literary Supplement*, April 5, 1917. Reprinted by permission of Harcourt, Brace & World, Inc., Leonard Woolf, and the Hogarth Press Ltd., London.

should have suppressed his love letters altogether. Mrs. Whitman, on the other hand, comes very well out of the ordeal, and was evidently, apart from Poe, a curious and interesting person.

She wrote poetry from her childhood, and when in early youth she was left a widow she settled down to lead a literary life in earnest. In those days and in America this was not so simple a proceeding as it has since become. If you wrote an essay upon Shelley, for example, the most influential family in Providence considered that you had fallen from grace. If, like Mr. Ellery Channing, you went to Europe and left your wife behind, this was sufficient proof that you were not a 'great perfect man', as the true poet is bound to be. Mrs. Whitman took her stand against such crudities, and, indeed, rather went out of her way to invite attack. Whatever the fashion and whatever the season she wore her 'floating veils' and her thin slippers, and carried a fan in her hand. By means of 'inverting her lampshades' and hanging up bits of drapery her sitting-room was kept in a perpetual twilight. It was the age of the Transcendentalists, and the fans and the veils and the twilight were, no doubt, intended to mitigate the solidity of matter, and entice the soul out of the body with as little friction as possible. Nature too had been kind in endowing her with a pale, eager face, a spiritual expression, and deep-set eyes that gazed 'beyond but never at you'.

Her house became a centre for the poets of the district, for she was witty and charming as well as enthusiastic. John Hay, G. W. Curtis, and the Hon. Wilkins Updike used to send her their works to criticize, or in very long and abstruse letters tried to define what they meant by poetry. The mark of that particular set, which was more or less connected with Emerson and Margaret Fuller, was an enthusiastic championship of the rights of the soul. They ventured into a sphere where words naturally were unable to support them. 'Poetry', as Mr. Curtis said, 'is the adaption of music to an intellectual sphere. But it must therefore be revealed through souls too fine to be measured by the intellect. . . . Music . . . is a womanly accomplishment, because it is sentiment, and the instinct declares its nature', etc. This exalted mood never quite deserted them when they were writing about matters of fact. When Mrs. Whitman forgot to answer a letter Mr. Curtis inquired whether she was ill 'or has the autumn which lies round the horizon like a beautifully hued serpent crushing the flower of summer fascinated you to silence with its soft, calm eyes?' Mrs. Whitman, it is clear, was the person who kept them all up to this very high standard. Thus things went on until Mrs. Whitman had reached the age of forty-two. One July night, in 1845, she happened to be wandering in her garden in the moonlight when Edgar Allan Poe passed by and saw her. 'From that hour I loved you', he wrote later. '. . . your unknown heart seemed to pass into my bosom—there to dwell for ever.' The immediate result was that he wrote the verses *To Helen* which he sent her. Three years later, when he was the famous poet of *The Raven*, Mrs. Whitman replied with a valentine, of which the last stanza runs—

> Then, oh grim and ghastly Raven
> Wilt thou to my heart and ear
> Be a Raven true as ever
> Flapped his wings and croaked 'Despair'?
> Not a bird that roams the forest
> Shall our lofty eyrie share.

For some time their meeting was postponed, and no word of prose passed between them. It might have been postponed for ever had it not been for another copy of verses which Mrs. Whitman ended with the line

> I dwell with 'Beauty which is Hope'.

Upon receipt of these verses Poe immediately procured a letter of introduction and set off to Providence. His declaration of love took place in the course of the next fortnight during a walk in the cemetery. Mrs. Whitman would not consent to an engagement, but she agreed to write to him, and thus the famous correspondence began.

Professor Harrison can only compare Poe's letters to the letters of Abelard and Eloise or to the *Sonnets from the Portuguese;* Miss Ticknor says that they have won themselves a niche among the world's classic love letters. Professor Woodberry, on the other hand, thinks that they should never have been published. We agree with Professor Woodberry, not because they do damage to Poe's reputation, but because we find them very tedious compositions. Whether you are writing a review or a love letter the great thing is to be confronted with a very vivid idea of your subject. When Poe wrote to Mrs. Whitman he might have been addressing a fashion plate in a ladies' newspaper—a fashion plate which walks the cemetery by moonlight, for the atmosphere is one of withered roses and moonshine. The fact that he had buried Virginia a short time before, that he denied his love for her, that he was writing to Annie at the same time and in the same style, that he was about to propose to a widow for the sake of her money—all his perfidies and meannesses do not by themselves make it impossible that he loved Mrs. Whitman genuinely. Were it not for the letters we might accept the charitable view that this was his last effort at redemption. But when we read the letters we feel that the man who wrote them had no emotion left about anything; his world was a world of phantoms and fashion plates; his phrases are the cast-off phrases that were not quite good enough for a story. He could see neither himself nor others save through a mist of opium and alcohol. The engagement, which had been made conditional upon his reform, was broken off; Mrs. Whitman sank on to a sofa holding a handkerchief 'drenched in ether' to her face, and her old mother rather pointedly observed to Poe that the train was about to leave for New York.

Cynical though it sounds, we doubt whether Mrs. Whitman lost as much as she gained by the unfortunate end of her love affair. Her feeling for Poe was probably more that of a benefactress than of a lover; for she was one of those people who 'devoutly believe that serpents may be reclaimed. This is only effected by patience and prayer—but the results are wonderful.' This particular serpent was irreclaimable; he was picked up unconscious in the street and died a year later. But he left behind him a crop of reptiles who taxed Mrs. Whitman's patience and needed her prayers for the rest of her life. She became the recognized authority upon Poe, and whenever a biographer was in need of facts or old Mrs. Clemm was in need of money they applied to her. She had to decide the disputes of the different ladies as to which had been loved the most, and to keep the peace between the rival historians, for whether a woman is more vain of her love or an author of his work has yet to be decided. But the opportunities which such a position gave her of endless charity and literary discussion evidently suited her and the good sense and wit of the bird-like little woman, who was extremely poor and had an eccentric sister to provide for, seem to justify her statement that 'the results are wonderful'.

Here Lies Miss Groby

JAMES THURBER

Miss Groby taught me English composition thirty years ago. It wasn't what prose said that interested Miss Groby; it was the way prose said it. The shape of a sentence crucified on a blackboard (parsed, she called it) brought a light to her eye. She hunted for Topic Sentences and Transitional Sentences the way little girls hunt for white violets in springtime. What she loved most of all were Figures of Speech. You remember her. You must have had her, too. Her influence will never die out of the land. A small schoolgirl asked me the other day if I could give her an example of metonymy. (There are several kinds of metonymies, you may recall, but the one that will come to mind most easily, I think, is Container for the Thing Contained.) The vision of Miss Groby came clearly before me when the little girl mentioned the old, familiar word. I saw her sitting at her desk, taking the rubber band off the roll-call cards, running it back upon the fingers of her right hand, and surveying us all separately with quick little henlike turns of her head.

Here lies Miss Groby, not dead, I think, but put away on a shelf with the other T squares and rulers whose edges had lost their certainty. The fierce light that Miss Groby brought to English literature was the light of Identification. Perhaps, at the end, she could no longer retain the dates of the birth and death of one of the Lake poets. That would have sent her to the principal of the school with her resignation. Or perhaps she could not remember, finally, exactly how many Cornishmen there were who had sworn that Trelawny should not die, or precisely how many springs were left to Housman's lad in which to go about the woodlands to see the cherry hung with snow.

Verse was one of Miss Groby's delights because there was so much in both its form and content that could be counted. I believe she would have got an enormous thrill out of Wordsworth's famous lines about Lucy if they had been written this way:

> A violet by a mossy stone
> Half hidden from the eye,
> Fair as a star when ninety-eight
> Are shining in the sky.

It is hard for me to believe that Miss Groby ever saw any famous work of literature from far enough away to know what it meant. She was forever climbing up the margins of books and crawling between their lines, hunting for the little gold of phrase, making marks with a pencil. As Palamides hunted the Questing Beast, she hunted the Figure of Speech. She hunted it through the clangorous halls of Shakespeare and through the green forests of Scott.

Night after night, for homework, Miss Groby set us to searching in "Ivanhoe" and "Julius Caesar" for metaphors, similes, metonymies, apostrophes, personifications, and all the rest. It got so that figures of speech jumped out of the pages at you, obscuring the sense and pattern of the novel or play you were trying to read. "Friends, Romans, countrymen, lend me your ears." Take that, for instance. There is an unusual but perfect example of Container for the Thing Contained. If you read the funeral oration unwarily—that is to say, for its meaning—you might easily miss the C.F.T.T.C. Antony is, of course, not asking for their ears in the sense that he wants them cut off and handed over; he is asking for the function of those ears, for their power to hear, for, in a word, the thing they contain.

At first I began to fear that all the characters in Shakespeare and Scott were crazy. They confused cause with effect, the sign for the thing signified, the thing held for the thing holding it. But after a while I began to suspect that it was I myself who was crazy. I would find myself lying awake at night saying over and over, "The thinger for the thing contained." In a great but probably misguided attempt to keep my mind on its hinges, I would stare at the ceiling and try to think of an example of the Thing Contained for the Container. It struck me as odd that Miss Groby had never thought of that inversion. I finally hit on one, which I still remember. If a woman were to grab up a bottle of Grade A and say to her husband, "Get away from me or I'll hit you with the milk," that would be a Thing Contained for the Container. The next day in class I raised my hand and brought my curious discovery straight out before Miss Groby and my astonished schoolmates. I was eager and serious about it and it never occurred to me that the other children would laugh. They laughed loudly and long. When Miss Groby had quieted them she said to me rather coldly, "That was not really amusing, James." That's the mixed-up kind of thing that happened to me in my teens.

In later years I came across another excellent example of this figure of speech in a joke long since familiar to people who know vaudeville or burlesque (or radio, for that matter). It goes something like this:

> A: What's your head all bandaged up for?
> B: I got hit with some tomatoes.
> A: How could that bruise you up so bad?
> B: These tomatoes were in a can.

I wonder what Miss Groby would have thought of that one.

I dream of my old English teacher occasionally. It seems that we are always in Sherwood Forest and that from far away I can hear Robin Hood winding his silver horn.

"Drat that man for making such a racket on his cornet!" cries Miss Groby. "He scared away a perfectly darling Container for the Thing Contained, a great, big, beautiful one. It leaped right back into its context when that man blew that cornet. It was the most wonderful Container for the Thing Contained I ever saw here in the Forest of Arden."

"This is Sherwood Forest," I say to her.

"That doesn't make any difference at all that I can see," she says to me.

Then I wake up, tossing and moaning.

Mr. More and the Mithraic Bull [1]

EDMUND WILSON

I met Mr. Paul Elmer More several times, but had an extended conversation with him only once. I wrote down a record of it at the time and give it here, as I wrote it then, embedded in a Princeton weekend.

[1] Written on the occasion of Paul Elmer More's death, March 9, 1937.

MR. MORE AND THE MITHRAIC BULL. From *The Triple Thinkers* (Oxford University Press, 1948) by Edmund Wilson. Reprinted by permission of Edmund Wilson.

I was taken to Mr. More's house by Dean Gauss, who was one of his closest friends at Princeton. Dean Gauss, on this Saturday afternoon, had a special reason for wanting to consult him.

At that time—this visit took place in the December of 1929—compulsory chapel had been partially abolished at Princeton, but it had been found desirable to make the students attend half the chapel services on Sundays in order to keep them in town over the weekends. Those students who professed unorthodox views—and who were often, as it turned out, the same ones that wanted to spend Saturday nights in Philadelphia or New York—were obliged to attend non-sectarian religious discussions which took place on Sunday evenings and were conducted by members of the faculty in rotation. That month it had been Dean Gauss's turn, and he had begun on his first evening by attempting to find out how much the students knew about or were interested in religion. It had turned out that, though several boys believed in Heaven, nobody believed in the Devil; and when he had chalked up a list of theological words beginning with *infralapsarian* and *supralapsarian* and ending with *theism* and *deism*, it had been obvious that nobody knew anything about any of them. In dismissing the class, he had invited them to hand in questions which might stimulate discussion; and the sole response to this had been a letter written in Latin by a freshman and expressing a desire to learn something about Mithraism. Dean Gauss had decided to brush up on the subject by calling on Mr. More, who had the history of religions at his fingertips.

Mr. More had at that time just built himself a new house in the new residential section of Princeton near the Graduate School, and we approached it along a rainy new-laid pavement. The sitting room, where we waited a few moments, was comfortable but rather somber. With its walls densely lined with books, it was preeminently the room of a scholar—though there were a few carefully chosen articles of ornament: two small panes of Dutch stained glass, for example, which Mr. More had brought back from Europe and had had inlaid in the glass of a large window at the further end of the room.

But Mr. More did not make us wait long: he appeared almost at once, brisk enough, and greeted us with an alertness and an evident pleasure at having people come to see him, very attractive in a man of sixty-five. He was short and had picked up some of the plumpness that goes with a sedentary occupation. He had a Roman nose, a pale gray eye and an iron lock of hair on his forehead—in general, a peculiar iron-gray aspect. There was in his face much strength and some nobility, but a curious absence of color.

Affably he attended to the tea and began talking about T. S. Eliot, whom he had suggested inviting to Princeton to lecture. I was surprised to see how much he admired Eliot. He told us, in reply to our questions, that Eliot was 'tall and thin, quite strikingly good-looking,' and that he, More, had gone to Eliot's house in London and had met people there. He explained to us that Eliot's grandfather had been chancellor of Washington University in St. Louis at the time when he, More, had been a student there, so that he had already known the poet's family. And as he went on, I came to realize that it was for him a matter of deep gratification to have made the acquaintance of another writer of high intellectual distinction who had come like More himself out of that old Middle-Western world, who had the freedom of that literary life of Europe from which More's provincialism had largely shut him out, and who had been kind enough to bring More into contact with it—a man who, with all his brilliant reputation, his position as a god of the young, was yet a scholar and a serious critic, preoccupied with problems of morality, and striving, although by a different route, just as More himself was, to find his way back to the Christian religion.

We talked about Eliot's influence among the students, and More demurred over Eliot's poetry. I asked him whether he didn't admire *The Waste Land*. 'Well, one can see,' he conceded, 'that it's written by a man of parts.' But it seemed to be *The Hippopotamus* which presented the most serious difficulties. 'I must say that it reads aloud very well,' he confessed; but he couldn't understand what Eliot meant by it. I suggested that it was a satire on the Church. 'But,' Mr. More protested, 'I can't understand how Eliot reconciles that with his present position.' I reminded him that Eliot had written the poem a good many years before; but Mr. More only shook his head and repeated that he could not reconcile those two things. Nor could he follow Eliot's enthusiasm for Baudelaire: 'It seems to me that he finds in Baudelaire . . . things that aren't there.' I admitted that there might be something in that, but asked him why he could not admire Baudelaire. 'Why,' he replied—he had an abrupt hesitation, as over the difficulty of dealing urbanely with a subject about which he felt so strongly, with an author of whom he so greatly disapproved, and upon whom, if he had been writing an essay, he would certainly have visited his stinging indignation—'I'm old-

fashioned about Baudelaire. I recognize his power—and his significance in his time—but as a guide to life—!' He stopped, and neither
Gauss nor I tried to debate the matter further.

It was the moment of the great controversy over Humanism, and
we tried to draw him out on this subject. I had been hearing from a
friend at Harvard of the belief of the fanatical Babbitt that his doctrine was gradually but surely taking possession of all the ablest
minds of the time, and of the legend, circulated among his students,
that the old man had a great map in his study and stuck a thumb-
tack into it at every point where a Humanist center was supposed to
have sprung up. But Mr. More was much more sensible and less pretentious. When Gauss asked him whether he felt it was true that a
great tide of Humanism was rising: 'Well,' he replied, 'I'd rather say
that it was having a great splurge just now, but it's partly based on
misunderstanding.' Yet he spoke with evident satisfaction of an article on Stuart P. Sherman which Seward Collins had recently published in the *Bookman*. Sherman had been the favorite disciple who
had turned renegade to the Humanist band—the split had come
when Sherman praised Whitman—and Seward Collins had now re-
pudiated Sherman. 'It seems,' remarked Mr. More, 'as if something
like a conversion had taken place there.'

Gauss and More discussed their first acquaintance. The Dean in
those now remote days had been an eager young journalist and poet,
just back from the Paris of the nineties, with long yellow hair and a
flowing Latin Quarter tie, and he had written a furious letter of protest to More over a review of some French life of Sainte-Beuve
which the latter had published in the *Nation*. 'It wasn't a slating,
was it?' said More, almost chuckling at the memory of past ferocity.
'It was just a bit—contemptuous.' He had answered Gauss's letter
and received a second letter equally violent. Then he had invited
Gauss to lunch and had found him, he said, quite amiable and mild.
One of the great sources of More's strength, I realized, lay in the
fact that he always knew precisely what he thought and was always
ready to face anybody down, uncompromisingly and promptly. I
looked at Gauss: his golden locks were gone and had left a prodi-
giously high domed bald forehead. With his fine profile of a blond
South German Dante, in his Princetonian soft shirt and tweed golf
suit, he sat today, lying back in his chair, the great expounder of
French romanticism, hobnobbing with the great anti-romantic. So
much subtler a mind than More, with so much wider a range of im-

aginative sympathy, and correspondingly so much less fixed in his opinions, he looked out coolly through his eyeglasses without rims on those prejudices and principles of More's which years ago had aroused his indignation. The amenities and responsibilities of Princeton had dimmed the flamboyance of his romanticism. But Paul Elmer More, still just as positive, still nearly as narrow as then, sat attentively forward in his chair, still ready to face anybody down.

Dean Gauss now remembered Mithra and asked for light from Mr. More on the subject. Mr. More, who had the pride of learning, replied with immediate gusto: 'Why, I don't suppose I know any more about Mithraism than you do, Christian!'—At this moment there came into the room a sister of Mr. More's, who lived with him. She was a pleasant old lady, with none of her brother's asperity —dressed in black and very deaf. She had just been going through her bureau-drawers, she said—'And it's so hard to know what to throw away! It's really not worth the trouble trying to sort things!' Mr. More admitted rather perfunctorily and speaking loudly in order to make her hear, that this did constitute a perplexing problem, and quickly brought the conversation back to Mithra.

'Well,' he demanded in a brisk businesslike manner, pouring his sister a cup of tea, 'what d'ye want to know about Mithraism, Christian?' His voice, nasal, clear and Middle-Western, had a suggestion, not unattractive, of the homely plain-spoken manner of the old successful American merchant or banker. 'The Mithraic bee,' began Gauss, 'was a symbol of immortality—' 'I've never heard of that,' Mr. More caught him up. 'Where'd you find that?' 'I can't remember where,' replied Gauss. 'That's what I wanted to ask you. I read it years ago in some book and I can't remember now what it was. I thought you might know.' But Mr. More did not know: he mentioned all the books he had read that dealt with Mithraism and said that there was nothing in any of them about it. What he knew, it was plain, he knew: he needed to consult no index. 'I suppose,' Dean Gauss pursued, 'that the bee came to stand for immortality through the belief that bees were bred spontaneously in the carcasses of dead animals. It was really the carrion-fly. Virgil talks about it in the *Georgics*.' 'The "out of the strong came forth sweetness" of the Bible,' put in Mr. More. 'Yes,' said Gauss. 'Clovis was a Mithraist—' 'That I didn't know,' said Mr. More. 'Yes, Clovis was a Mithraist,' the Dean pursued, 'and his emblem before his conversion was the

bee.' 'Is that a guess?' demanded Mr. More. 'No,' said the Dean. 'I
read it all somewhere, but I can't remember where.' Clovis's bee,
which Mr. More had never heard of and as to which, failing definite
authority, he was not prepared to indulge in speculation, seemed to
have made him a shade impatient. He delivered, however, a short
lecture on what he did know about Mithraic myths; and it was
amazing how much he knew and how accurately he was able to re-
tail it. He traced Mithra, the God of Light, from the Vedic hymns
into Persian mythology, and from the Orient into Greece, indicat-
ing his various transformations with confidence, lucidity and logic,
but with a curious effect of his having retained them as ideas without their passing through the picture-making imagination. And yet
the Mithra he described was alive, devoid of mystery, form or color
though he was. It reminded me of a book called *Error's Chains*,
which I had used to look at in my grandfather's library and which
had had many illustrations of the heathen gods, old line drawings
done from paintings and statues.—Miss More was sitting beside me
on the couch and could not hear the general conversation, so we
talked separately from time to time while the discussion of Mithraism proceeded. 'You might just as well take it all out and burn it
up!' she declared, still thinking of her bureau-drawers. 'When it's
been accumulating as long as that, it's not worth the trouble to go
through it and pick things out to save!'

At this point Mr. Frank Jewett Mather arrived. He was a cheerful
little man in a checked vest and spats, with the cocky pointed mustache of an old beau and the rosiness of a child. And he turned out
to know a lot about Mithraism. He told us that it had had a great
success with the Roman soldiers because it had promised them a sure
immortality, and that it had developed in the third century into a
serious competitor to Christianity.—Mr. More's sister suddenly got
up: 'I'm going to burn up all that old stuff!' she announced, with the
air of one who has finally arrived at a thoroughly satisfactory
resolution—and she said good-by and went upstairs.—Mr. Mather
explained in detail the symbolism of Mithraic art. There was a Mithraic bull in the Museum, he said, which he had bought and brought
back from Europe and which was one of the best things the Museum had. 'I didn't know that,' said Gauss with interest. 'I must go
over and see it.' 'It's the best Mithraic bull on this side,' said Mather.
'The only really first-rate one.' It was a marble relief of the Sun-
God holding a bull by the horns; there was a dog which was leaping

at the throat of the bull and a snake which was attacking his testicles; the snake and the dog were Evil and Darkness. 'Let's go over and see it!' the Dean proposed to me.

Mr. More now reverted to the days of the *Nation*. He told us that Oswald Garrison Villard had sometimes disapproved of what he wrote but had always had somebody else speak to him about it. Mr. More seemed frankly delighted at this evidence that Villard had found him formidable. 'Afraid the "inner check" wouldn't work!' Frank Mather impishly put in. But Mr. More possessed no technique to deal with people who made jokes about Humanism and did not deign to reply to this. 'Who originated the term "inner check"? Was it you or Babbitt?' asked Mather. 'I was the first to use it,' said More. 'In the *Shelburne Essays*. But Babbitt has made much more of it than I have.' And he added, after a moment's pause: 'I think the phrase occurs once in Emerson.'

In the course of the conversation that followed, Mr. Mather ventured to remark that he didn't see how Humanism was going to get us very far by going back to the Council of Chalcedon. Mr. More was then nearing the completion of his series of volumes on Greek philosophy and Christianity. A man of true spiritual vocation, unable to remain a simple rationalist but prevented by a Protestant education and an obstinate hardheaded common sense from finding a basis in the mysticism of Rome, he had devoted long and diligent years to establishing an historical tradition which would justify his peculiar point of view. At that time he had just published the volume which brought the line of development to its climax with the promulgation at Chalcedon in the fifth century of the dogma of the Incarnation—a doctrine which, in laying down the dual nature of Christ, in representing him as both human and divine, had seemed to Mr. More to make it possible for him to preserve the philosophy of Plato, so attractive to his intellectual and esthetic side, and at the same time not to cut himself loose from the supernatural authority of religion. So he made no reply to this gibe—but presently, with a touch of severity, accused Mather of being 'a half-way Platonist like Santayana.' He seemed to me that day very clear-cut against the background of the college community. He was himself not really typical of the American academic world: he was an independent scholar, who had denounced in the most vigorous language the lack of sincerity and the incompetence of the colleges. He stood out, not merely through his distinction of learning, his Greek and Sanskrit and Hebrew and Persian and the rest, but by reason of his unremitting seriousness, his stubborn insistence on the importance of maintaining in one's relation to literature a position which should be realistic in the sense that it would never lose contact with moral problems as he himself understood them, his refusal to allow himself to be seduced by purely esthetic or intellectual satisfactions. Gauss told him about a student at one of the Sunday-night meetings who had put himself down as a 'synthetic hedonist'; More smiled, but said, 'I wonder what he meant.'

We discussed an exhibition of modern art then on view in New York. Gauss thought Seurat essentially classical, but Mather insisted that he was decadent: Seurat's figures, he said, seemed to be perfectly realized, but actually they were hanging in the air, like the characters of Proust or Henry James, with no real connection with anything. And this led us to contemporary writing. Mr. More, who in a recent essay had allowed his intolerance of his contemporaries to go to lengths of positive ill temper in characterizing as 'an explosion in a cesspool' Dos Passos's *Manhattan Transfer,* conceded now, with an evident desire to be fair, that he 'recognized the element of protest in Dos Passos and Joyce.' I said that, though there was protest in Dos Passos, I did not believe there was any in Joyce, and thus unfortunately deprived Mr. More of his only excuse for being polite about *Ulysses.* He was afterwards to give more serious consideration to such writers as Joyce and Proust. His last volume of *Shelburne Essays* contained papers on these two novelists, which, uncongenial to More though the subjects were, show more grasp of what is really at issue in their books than most of the stuff which has been written to exalt them. The moralist in Paul Elmer More, who had always been at war with the poet and who had scored over him so crushing a victory, could usually be counted upon to formulate clearly—though of course a clear formulation may misrepresent a poet—the case of any writer, however abhorrent, who had a serious moral basis, even though the provincial prig who inseparably accompanied the moralist might prevent him from appreciating the artist's achievement. But at that time I do not think he had read *Ulysses;* and I myself was a little touchy on the subject, as my attention had just been called by Gauss to an editorial in *The New York Times* that morning in which one of their anonymous writers had ridiculed an article of mine on Joyce. Now I was further dismayed, as it seemed to me that these three men, in their fields of literature and art certainly among the ablest in the country, were themselves disposed to outlaw from literature the greatest literary artist then alive. The same confounded old academic inertia! I thought; the same old proprietary interest in the classics, which made them unwilling to believe that anything new could have great value! I remembered how thirteen years before it had been the same thing about Bernard Shaw, then already practically a classic. Dean Gauss had read *Ulysses*, but had not liked it much; and, though it turned out that Mather, the old rascal, had investigated Mrs. Bloom's soliloquy, he would not commit himself on the subject. Paul Elmer More, who, as I say, had evidently not yet read Joyce, began by trying to handle the matter without heat, but when I talked about the Homeric parallel—at the suggestion of such a fellow as Joyce's having the effrontery to associate himself with one of the major Greek classics—his arrogance suddenly started up from behind his deliberate urbanity, and he sharply cut down on the discussion—(it had also been a question of whether the characters in *Ulysses* were 'purposive' or mere passive recorders of impressions): 'But Homer's Ulysses knew what he wanted. He didn't need special explanations!' It seemed to me that there were so many misconceptions lodged behind this remark of Mr. More's that I had difficulty in knowing how to deal with it. The conversation became rather confused and took on a slightly acrimonious accent. Somebody changed the subject and Mr. More proposed showing us his new house.

We went upstairs. On one side of the hallway which led to Mr. More's study was a bookcase entirely filled with detective stories, which I was told he systematically graded with A's, B's, C's, and D's. On the shelves of his study were Plato and Plotinus and the Fathers of the Church. Frank Mather mischievously inquired where the Acts of the Council of Chalcedon were kept, and More as usual made no reply. The study was a small unpretentious room at the very top of the house: it had one large Morris chair and a table and a desk. On the walls hung two framed photographs, yellowish-brownish: one of Perugino's *Crucifixion* and the other of two battered Greek torsos, with both arms and legs broken off, awkwardly reclining together. They faced one another across the room, the Christian world and the Greek, and seemed to neutralize one another.

Then we descended and took our leave. Still chafing at More's attitude toward Joyce, I asked him, just as we were going out the door, whether he had ever read Eliot on *Ulysses*. He replied that he had not, and I told him that Eliot considered *Ulysses* a work of the highest importance. His whole attitude toward Eliot, so friendly before seemed, as if by reflex action, to stiffen. 'I don't see,' he retorted, 'what *Ulysses* has to do with Royalism, Anglo-Catholicism and Classicism!'—and added, 'That young man has a screw loose somewhere!' 'Would you agree with Huneker,' said Mather, 'that it's impossible for the same person really to like both Raphael and Goya?' 'I don't think,' Mr. More replied, 'that that pair is particularly well chosen; but I should say that a capacity for enjoying certain authors made it impossible to enjoy Dante or Shakespeare or Milton—or rather, I should say that, if a man liked certain things and claimed to enjoy Shakespeare and Dante, it would be impossible that he should really appreciate them!'

On this implacable dictum we went.

The next day I took a walk on the campus. It was dreary, misty and damp. I remembered the Mithraic bull and decided to look it up in the Museum. There it was, sure enough, right opposite the front door as I went in, shining in the dim afternoon: the white marble relief of Mithra, a naked youth in a peaked Phrygian cap, clasping the sacred bull, which had the dog and the snake that were Darkness and Evil threatening its throat and its balls. But the Sun-God was to kill the bull, and thereby to conquer the darkness and to make himself the creator of life, all the multiform life of the earth, which was to spring from the bull's ebbing blood. There they hung—once the light of those pagan caves to which the soldiers from their doomed legions had crept, once the Apollonian rivals of the Crucified—there they hung in the Princeton Museum on a Sunday afternoon! I went on to the glass-cases inside, but—Roman busts, Egyptian gods, Greek marbles—almost everything was a reproduction and gave me the impression of being denatured and canned. The afternoon light was gray, the rooms were becoming chill. I turned back and stood before the Mithra, which—round and complete and glowing— seemed the only thing alive in the Museum. I remembered with what amazement, a wonder that became exaltation, I had come upon the Apollo Belvedere when I had first visited Rome as a child—how I had turned back to stare at its beauty.

I went over to the University Library and sat down and wrote the *Times* a caustic letter about their sneering editorial on Joyce.

Then I went to see if Gauss were free. He had been busy all the afternoon and had evidently had a great many people: Sunday visitors, college officials, protesting parents of students whom he had disciplined. He always gave his closest attention to anything that was submitted for his decision and dealt with it according to his most scrupulous judgment; and I thought his mind was tired. And now he had to prepare his talk for the evening religious meeting. But he revived when I told him that I had been to see the bull and was all for going to the Museum at once. He got his hat and coat and stick, and we set out.

'It's curious,' he mused on the way, 'how closely it paralleled Christianity. They had a sacrifice, a communion and an atonement. The bull was killed in a cave, and that symbolized the resurrection.' —He spoke of his affection for More and told me a curious story. When More had come back recently from Italy, he had announced with gratification and assurance that he had discovered the finest picture in Florence. Gauss had said to him: 'I'll bet I can guess what it is! Don't tell me—I'll bet I can guess what you think is the finest picture in Florence!'—and he guessed Perugino's *Crucifixion*. He was right; More had been quite taken aback. 'But how did you know?' I asked. 'Why should he have liked that picture particularly?' 'Why, you see Christ way up there—so far above the world.'

But when we got to the Museum, it was dark, and we found that the front door had been locked. We squinted at the marble through the glass, but it was scarcely visible now: we could make out only a whitish blur at the bottom of the cavernous entrance hall. We walked around the building and found a side-door unlocked and went in. Obstinately, we climbed stairs, explored galleries, invaded classrooms and studios for classes, with their chalky plaster casts of famous statues; but all the doors into the Museum proper turned out to be locked tight for the night. A late student in one of the classrooms suggested that we might try to find the curator; but the curator was not in his office, and all the other offices were dark.

We walked back across the campus and parted. The Dean had to go to the library to look up some more about Mithra, and I remained in his office to type out my letter on Joyce.

The visit long haunted my memory, and now the news of Mr. More's death has brought it back into my mind: the empty academic week end, the new suburban house, the meetings for the discussion of religion designed to bring the students back to town, the

Acts of the Council of Chalcedon, the nice old lady with her firm resolution to burn all that old stuff up, the argument over Joyce, More himself with his lifelong consecration to that great world of culture and thought which he had succeeded in making real to others but which he could never quite rejoin himself, and Gauss and I peering at Mithra through the glass.

"Take the Witness!"

ROBERT BENCHLEY

Newspaper accounts of trial cross-examinations always bring out the cleverest in me. They induce day dreams in which I am the witness on the stand, and if you don't know some of my imaginary comebacks to an imaginary cross-examiner (Doe vs. Benchley: 482–U.S.–367–398), you have missed some of the most stimulating reading in the history of American jurisprudence.

These little reveries usually take place shortly after I have read the transcript of a trial, while I am on a long taxi ride or seated at a desk with plenty of other work to do. I like them best when I have work to do, as they deplete me mentally so that I am forced to go and lie down after a particularly sharp verbal rally. The knowledge that I have completely floored my adversary, and the imaginary congratulations of my friends (also imaginary), seem more worth while than any amount of fiddling work done.

During these cross-questionings I am always very calm. Calm in a nice way, that is—never cocky. However frantic my inquisitor may wax (and you should see his face at times—it's purple!), I just sit there, burning him up with each answer, winning the admiration of the courtroom, and, at times, even a smile from the judge himself. At the end of my examination, the judge is crazy about me.

Just what the trial is about, I never get quite clear in my mind. Sometimes the subject changes in the middle of the questioning, to allow for the insertion of an especially good crack on my part. I

"TAKE THE WITNESS!" By Robert Benchley from *The Benchley Roundup* selected by Nathaniel Benchley. Copyright, 1936 by Robert C. Benchley. Reprinted by permission of Harper & Row, Publishers.

don't think that I am ever actually the defendant, although I don't know why I should feel that I am immune from trial by a jury of my peers—if such exist.

I am usually testifying in behalf of a friend, or perhaps as just an impersonal witness for some one whom I do not know, who, naturally, later becomes my friend for life. It is Justice that I am after—Justice and a few well-spotted laughs.

Let us whip right into the middle of my cross-examination, as I naturally wouldn't want to pull my stuff until I had been insulted by the lawyer, and you can't really get insulted simply by having your name and address asked. I am absolutely fair about these things. If the lawyer will treat me right, I'll treat him right. He has got to start it. For a decent cross-examiner, there is no more tractable witness in the world than I am.

Advancing toward me, with a sneer on his face, he points a finger at me. (I have sometimes thought of pointing my finger back at him, but have discarded that as being too fresh. I don't have to resort to clowning.)

Q: You think you're pretty funny, don't you? (*I have evidently just made some mildly humorous comeback, nothing smart-alecky, but good enough to make him look silly.*)

A: I have never given the matter much thought.

Q: Oh, you haven't given the matter much thought, eh? Well, you seem to be treating this examination as if it were a minstrel show.

A (*very quietly and nicely*): I have merely been taking my cue from your questions. (*You will notice that all this presupposes quite a barrage of silly questions on his part, and pat answers on mine, omitted here because I haven't thought them up. At any rate, it is evident that I have already got him on the run before this reverie begins.*)

Q: Perhaps you would rather that I conducted this inquiry in baby talk?

A: If it will make it any easier for you. (*Pandemonium, which the Court feels that it has to quell, although enjoying it obviously as much as the spectators.*)

Q (*furious*): I see. Well, here is a question that I think will be simple enough to elicit an honest answer: Just how did you happen to know that it was eleven-fifteen when you saw the defendant?

A: Because I looked at my watch.

Q: And just why did you look at your watch at this particular time?

A: To see what time it was.

Q: Are you accustomed to looking at your watch often?

A: That is one of the uses to which I often put my watch.

Q: I see. Now, it couldn't by any chance, have been ten-fifteen instead of eleven-fifteen when you looked at your watch this time, could it?

A: Yes, sir. It could.

Q: Oh, it *could* have been ten-fifteen?

A: Yes, sir—if I had been in Chicago. (*Not very good, really. I'll work up something better. I move to have that answer stricken from the record.*)

When I feel myself lowering my standards by answering like that, I usually give myself a rest, and, unless something else awfully good pops into my head, I adjourn the court until next day. I can always convene it again when I hit my stride.

If possible, however, I like to drag it out until I have really given my antagonist a big final wallop which practically curls him up on the floor (I may think of one before this goes to press), and, wiping his forehead, he mutters, "Take the witness!"

As I step down from the stand, fresh as a daisy, there is a round of applause which the Court makes no attempt to silence. In fact, I have known certain judges to wink pleasantly at me as I take my seat. Judges are only human, after all.

My only fear is that, if I ever really am called upon to testify in court, I won't be asked the right questions. That *would* be a pretty kettle of fish!

The Night the Old Nostalgia Burned Down

FRANK SULLIVAN

MY OWN NEW YORK CHILDHOOD

When I was a boy, Fourteenth Street was where Twenty-third Street is now, and Samuel J. Tilden and I used to play marbles on the lot where the Grand Opera House still stood. Governor Lovelace brought the first marble from England to this country on August 17, 1668, and gave it to my Great-Aunt Amelia van Santvoort, of whom he was enamored. She had several copies made, and Sam Tilden and I used to amuse ourselves with them.

I remember the Sunday afternoons when Governor Lovelace would come to tea at our house, although I could not have been much more than a tad at the time. I can hear the rich clanking of the silver harness as his magnificent equipage, with its twelve ebony outriders in cerise bombazine, rolled up to our house at No. 239 East 174th Street. I was the envy of all the kids on the block because I was allowed to sit in the carriage while the Governor went in to take tea with Great-Aunt Amelia. I always chose Ada Rehan to sit beside me. She was a little golden-haired thing at the time and none of us dreamed she would one day go out from East 174th Street and shoot President Garfield.

Great-Aunt Amelia was a dowager of the old school. You don't see many of her kind around New York today, probably because the old school was torn down a good many years ago; its site is now occupied by Central Park. People used to say that the Queen, as they called Great-Aunt Amelia, looked more like my Aunt Theodosia than my Aunt Theodosia did.

But Aunt Caroline was really the great lady of our family. I can still see her descending the staircase, dressed for the opera in silk hat, satin-lined cape, immaculate shirt, white tie, and that magnificent, purple-black beard.

"Well, boy!" she would boom at me. "Well!"

"Well, Aunt Caroline!" I would say, doing my best to boom back at her.

She would chuckle and say, "Boy, I like your spirit! Tell Grimson I said to add an extra tot of brandy to your bedtime milk."

Oh, those lollipops at Preem's, just around the corner from the corner! Mm-m-m, I can still taste them! After school, we kids would rush home and shout, "Ma, gimme a penny for a lollipop at Preem's, willya, Ma? Hey, Ma, willya?" Then we would go tease Jake Astor, the second-hand-fur dealer around the corner. I shall never forget the day Minnie Maddern Fiske swiped the mink pelt from Jake's cart and stuffed it under Bishop Potter's cope.

Miss Hattie Pumplebutt was our teacher at P.S. 67. She was a demure wisp of a woman, with white hair parted in the middle, pince-nez that were forever dropping off her nose, always some lacy collar high around her throat, and paper cuffs. We adored her. Every once in a while she would climb up on her desk, flap her arms, shout "Whee-e-e! I'm a bobolink!," and start crowing. Or she would take off suddenly and go skipping about the tops of our desks with a dexterity and sure-footedness truly marvellous in one of her age. When we grew old enough, we were told about Miss Pumplebutt. She took dope. Well, she made history and geography far more interesting than a lot of non-sniffing teachers I have known.

One day, Jim Fisk and I played hooky from school and went to the old Haymarket on Sixth Avenue, which was then between Fifth and Seventh. We had two beers apiece and thought we were quite men about town. I dared Jim to go over and shoot Stanford White, never dreaming the chump would do it. I didn't know he was loaded. I got Hail Columbia from Father for that escapade.

Father was very strict about the aristocratic old New York ritual of the Saturday-night bath. Every Saturday night at eight sharp we would line up: Father, Mother, Diamond Jim Brady; Mrs. Dalrymple, the housekeeper; Absentweather, the butler; Aggie, the second girl; Aggie, the third girl; Aggie, the fourth girl; and twelve of us youngsters, each one equipped with soap and a towel. At a command from Father, we would leave our mansion on East Thirtieth Street and proceed solemnly up Fifth Avenue in single file to the old reservoir, keeping a sharp eye out for Indians. Then, at a signal from Papa, in we'd go. Everyone who was anyone in New York in those days had his Saturday-night bath in the reservoir, and it was there that I first saw and fell in love with the little girl whom I later made Duchess of Marlborough.

My Grandmamma Satterthwaite was a remarkable old lady. At the age of eighty-seven she could skip rope four hundred and twenty-two consecutive times without stopping, and every boy on the block was madly in love with her. Then her father failed in the crash of '87 and in no time she was out of pigtails, had her hair up, and was quite the young lady. I never did hear what became of her.

It rather amuses me to hear the youngsters of today enthusing about the croissants, etc., at Spodetti's and the other fashionable Fifth Avenue patisseries. Why, they aren't a patch on Horan's!

Mike Horan's place was at Minetta Lane and Washington Mews, and I clearly remember my father telling a somewhat startled Walt Whitman that old Mike Horan could bend a banana in two—with his bare hands! But I never saw him do it. We kids used to stand in front of his shop for hours after school waiting for Mike to bend a banana, but he never did. I can still hear the cheerful clang of his hammer on the anvil and the acrid smell of burning hoofs from the Loveland Dance Palace, across the way on Delancey Street, which was then Grand. Then the Civil War came and the property of the Loyalists was confiscated. I still have some old Loyalist property I confiscated on that occasion. I use it for a paperweight. Old Gammer Wilberforce was a Loyalist. We used to chase her down the street, shouting "Tory!" at her. Then she would chase us up the street, shouting:

> *Blaine, Blaine, James G. Blaine!*
> *Continental liar from the State of Maine!*

or:

> *Ma! Ma! Where's my Pa?*
> *Gone to the White House, ha, ha, ha!*

Of course, very few white people ever went to Chinatown in those days. It was not until the Honorah Totweiler case that people became aware of Chinatown. I venture to say that few persons today would recall Honorah Totweiler, yet in 1832 the Honorah Totweiler case was the sensation of the country. In one day the circulation of the elder James Gordon Bennett jumped seventy-four thousand as a result of the Totweiler case.

One sunny afternoon in the autumn of September 23, 1832, a lovely and innocent girl, twelfth of eighteen daughters of Isaac Totweiler, a mercer, and Sapphira, his wife, set out from her home in Washington Mews to return a cup of sugar—but let the elder Bennett tell the story:

> It is high time [Bennett wrote] that the people of these United States were awakened to the menace in which the old liberties for which our forefathers fought and bled, in buff and blue, by day and night, at Lexington and Concord, in '75 and '76, have been placed as a result of the waste, the orgy of spending, the deliberate falsifications, the betrayal of public trust, and the attempt to set up a bureaucratic and unconstitutional dictatorship, of the current Administration in Washington. Murphy must go, and Tammany with him!

After dinner on Sundays, my Grandpa Bemis would take a nap, with the *Times*, or something, thrown over his face to keep out the glare. If he was in a good humor when he awoke, he would take us youngsters up to Dick Canfield's to play games, but as he was never in a good humor when he awoke, we never went to Dick Canfield's to play games.

Sometimes, when we kids came home from school, Mrs. Rossiter, the housekeeper, would meet us in the hall and place a warning finger on her lips. We knew what that meant. We must be on our good behavior. The wealthy Mrs. Murgatroyd was calling on Mother. We would be ushered into the Presence, Mother would tell us to stop using our sleeves as a handkerchief, and then Mrs. Murgatroyd would laugh and say, "Oh, Annie, let the poor children alone. Sure, you're only young once." Then she would lift up her skirt to the knee, fish out a huge wallet from under her stocking, and give us each $2,000,000. We loved her. Not only did she have a pair of d——d shapely stems for an old lady her age, but she was reputed to be able to carry six schooners of beer in each hand.

I shall never forget the night of the fire. It was about three o'clock in the morning when it started, in an old distaff factory on West Twelfth Street. I was awakened by the crackling. I shivered, for my brother, as usual, had all the bedclothes, and there I was, with fully three inches of snow (one inch powder, two inches crust) on my bare back. The next morning there were seven feet of snow on West Twenty-seventh Street alone. You don't get that sort of winter nowadays. That was the winter the elder John D. Rockefeller was frozen over solid from November to May.

On Saturdays we used to go with Great-Aunt Tib to the Eden Musee to see the wax figure of Lillian Russell. There was a woman! They don't build girls like her nowadays. You can't get the material, and even if you could, the contractors and the plumbers would gyp you and substitute shoddy.

I was six when the riots occurred. No, I was *thirty*-six. I remember because it was the year of the famous Horace Greeley hoax, and I used to hear my parents laughing about it. It was commonly believed that Mark Twain was the perpetrator of the hoax, although Charles A. Dana insisted to his dying day that it was Lawrence Godkin. At any rate, the hoax, or "sell," originated one night at the Union League Club when Horace chanced to remark to Boss Tweed that his (Horace's) wife was entertaining that night. The town was agog for days, no one having the faintest notion that the story was not on the level. Greeley even threatened Berry Wall with a libel suit.

Well, that was New York, the old New York, the New York of gaslit streets, and sparrows (and, of course, horses), and cobblestones. The newsboy rolled the *Youth's Companion* into a missile and threw it on your front stoop and the postmen wore uniforms of pink velvet and made a point of bringing everybody a letter every day.

Eheu, fugaces!—

The Lost Childhood

GRAHAM GREENE

Perhaps it is only in childhood that books have any deep influence on our lives. In later life we admire, we are entertained, we may modify some views we already hold, but we are more likely to find in books merely a confirmation of what is in our minds already: as in a love affair it is our own features that we see reflected flatteringly back.

But in childhood all books are books of divination, telling us about the future, and like the fortune teller who sees a long journey in the cards or death by water they influence the future. I suppose that is why books excited us so much. What do we ever get nowadays from reading to equal the excitement and the revelation in those first fourteen years? Of course I should be interested to hear that a new novel by Mr. E. M. Forster was going to appear this spring, but I could never compare that mild expectation of civilized pleasure with the missed heartbeat, the appalled glee I felt when I found on a library shelf a novel by Rider Haggard, Percy Westerman, Captain Brereton or Stanley Weyman which I had not read before. No, it is in those early years that I would look for the crisis, the moment when life took a new slant in its journey towards death.

I remember distinctly the suddenness with which a key turned in a lock and I found I could read—not just the sentences in a reading book with the syllables coupled like railway carriages, but a real book. It was paper-covered with the picture of a boy, bound and gagged, dangling at the end of a rope inside a well with the water rising above his waist—an adventure of Dixon Brett, detective. All a long summer holiday I kept my secret, as I believed: I did not want anybody to know that I could read. I suppose I half consciously realized even then that this was the dangerous moment. I was safe so long as I could not read—the wheels had not begun to turn, but now the future stood around on bookshelves everywhere waiting for the child to choose—the life of a chartered accountant perhaps, a colonial civil servant, a planter in China, a steady job in a bank, happiness and misery, eventually one particular form of death, for surely we choose our death much as we choose our job. It grows out of our acts and our evasions, out of our fears and out of our moments of courage. I suppose my mother must have discovered my secret, for on the journey home I was presented for the train with another real book, a copy of Ballantyne's *Coral Island* with only a single picture to look at, a coloured frontispiece. But I would admit nothing. All the long journey I stared at the one picture and never opened the book.

But there on the shelves at home (so many shelves for we were a large family) the books waited—one book in particular, but before I reach that one down let me take a few others at random from the shelf. Each was a crystal in which the child dreamed that he saw life moving. Here in a cover stamped dramatically in several colours was Captain Gilson's *The Pirate Aeroplane*. I must have read that book six times at least—the story of a lost civilization in the Sahara and of a villainous Yankee pirate with an aeroplane like a box kite and bombs the size of tennis balls who held the golden city to ransom. It was saved by the hero, a young subaltern who crept up to the pirate camp to put the aeroplane out of action. He was captured and watched his enemies dig his grave. He was to be shot at dawn, and to pass the time and keep his mind from uncomfortable thoughts the amiable Yankee pirate played cards with him—the mild nursery game of Kuhn Kan. The memory of that nocturnal game on the edge of life haunted me for years, until I set it to rest at last in one of my own novels with a game of poker played in remotely similar circumstances.

And here is *Sophy of Kravonia* by Anthony Hope—the story of a kitchen-maid who became a queen. One of the first films I ever saw, about 1911, was made from that book, and I can hear still the rumble of the Queen's guns crossing the high Kravonian pass beaten hollowly out on a single piano. Then there was Stanley Weyman's *The Story of Francis Cludde*, and above all other books at that time of my life *King Solomon's Mines*.

This book did not perhaps provide the crisis, but it certainly influenced the future. If it had not been for that romantic tale of Allan Quatermain, Sir Henry Curtis, Captain Good, and, above all, the ancient witch Gagool, would I at nineteen have studied the appointments list of the Colonial Office and very nearly picked on the Nigerian Navy for a career? And later, when surely I ought to have known better, the odd African fixation remained. In 1935 I found myself sick with fever on a camp bed in a Liberian native's hut with a candle going out in an empty whisky bottle and a rat moving in the shadows. Wasn't it the incurable fascination of Gagool with her bare yellow skull, the wrinkled scalp that moved and contracted like the hood of a cobra, that led me to work all through 1942 in a little stuffy office in Freetown, Sierra Leone? There is not much in common between the land of the Kukuanas, behind the desert and the mountain range of Sheba's Breast, and a tin-roofed house on a bit of swamp where the vultures moved like domestic turkeys and the pi-dogs kept me awake on moonlight nights with their wailing, and the white woman yellowed by atebrin drove by to the club; but the two belonged at any rate to the same continent, and, however distantly, to the same region of the imagination—the region of uncertainty, of not knowing the way about. Once I came a little nearer to Gagool and her witch-hunters, one night in Zigita on the Liberian side of the French Guinea border, when my servants sat in their shuttered hut with their hands over their eyes and someone beat a drum and a whole town stayed behind closed doors while the big bush devil—whom it would mean blindness to see—moved between the huts.

But *King Solomon's Mines* could not finally satisfy. It was not the right answer. The key did not quite fit. Gagool I could recognize —didn't she wait for me in dreams every night in the passage by the linen cupboard, near the nursery door? and she continues to wait, when the mind is sick or tired, though now she is dressed in the theological garments of Despair and speaks in Spenser's accents:

> The longer life, I wote the greater sin,
> The greater sin, the greater punishment.

Yes, Gagool has remained a permanent part of the imagination, but Quatermain and Curtis—weren't they, even when I was only ten years old, a little too good to be true? They were men of such unyielding integrity (they would only admit to a fault in order to show how it might be overcome) that the wavering personality of a child could not rest for long against those monumental shoulders. A child, after all, knows most of the game—it is only an attitude to it that he lacks. He is quite well aware of cowardice, shame, deception, disappointment. Sir Henry Curtis perched upon a rock bleeding from a dozen wounds but fighting on with the remnant of the Greys against the hordes of Twala was too heroic. These men were like Platonic ideas: they were not life as one had already begun to know it.

But when—perhaps I was fourteen by that time—I took Miss Marjorie Bowen's *The Viper of Milan* from the library shelf, the future for better or worse really struck. From that moment I began to write. All the other possible futures slid away: the potential civil servant, the don, the clerk had to look for other incarnations. Imitation after imitation of Miss Bowen's magnificent novel went into exercise books—stories of sixteenth-century Italy or twelfth-century England marked with enormous brutality and a despairing romanticism. It was as if I had been supplied once and for all with a subject.

Why? On the surface *The Viper of Milan* is only the story of a war between Gian Galeazzo Visconti, Duke of Milan, and Mastino della Scala, Duke of Verona, told with zest and cunning and an amazing pictorial sense. Why did it creep in and colour and explain the terrible living world of the stone stairs and the never quiet dormitory? It was no good in that real world to dream that one would ever be a Sir Henry Curtis, but della Scala who at last turned from an honesty that never paid and betrayed his friends and died dishonoured and a failure even at treachery—it was easier for a child to escape behind his mask. As for Visconti, with his beauty, his patience and his genius for evil, I had watched him pass by many a time in his black Sunday suit smelling of mothballs. His name was Carter. He exercised terror from a distance like a snowcloud over the young fields. Goodness has only once found a perfect incarnation in a human body and never will again, but evil can always find a home there. Human nature is not black and white but black and grey. I read all that in *The Viper of Milan* and I looked round and I saw that it was so.

There was another theme I found there. At the end of *The Viper of Milan*—you will remember if you have once read it—comes the great scene of complete success—della Scala is dead, Ferrara, Verona, Novara, Mantua have all fallen, the messengers pour in with news of fresh victories, the whole world outside is cracking up, and Visconti sits and jokes in the wine-light. I was not on the classical side or I would have discovered, I suppose, in Greek literature instead of in Miss Bowen's novel the sense of doom that lies over success—the feeling that the pendulum is about to swing. That too made sense; one looked around and saw the doomed everywhere—the champion runner who one day would sag over the tape; the head of the school who would atone, poor devil, during forty dreary undistinguished years; the scholar . . . and when success began to touch oneself too, however mildly, one could only pray that failure would not be held off for too long.

One had lived for fourteen years in a wild jungle country without a map, but now the paths had been traced and naturally one had to follow them. But I think it was Miss Bowen's apparent zest that made me want to write. One could not read her without believing that to write was to live and to enjoy, and before one had discovered one's mistake it was too late—the first book one does enjoy. Anyway she had given me my pattern—religion might later explain it to me in other terms, but the pattern was already there—perfect evil walking the world where perfect good can never walk again, and only the pendulum ensures that after all in the end justice is done. Man is never satisfied, and often I have wished that my hand had not moved further than *King Solomon's Mines,* and that the future I had taken down from the nursery shelf had been a district office in Sierra Leone and twelve tours of malarial duty and a finishing dose of blackwater fever when the danger of retirement approached. What is the good of wishing? The books are always there, the moment of crisis waits, and now our children in their turn are taking down the future and opening the pages. In his poem 'Germinal' A. E. wrote:

> In ancient shadows and twilights
>   Where childhood had strayed,
> The world's great sorrows were born
>   And its heroes were made.
> In the lost boyhood of Judas
>   Christ was betrayed.